THOMAS H. BEVERIDGE

Graphing Pitfalls by STEVEN C. PITTS

STUDY GUIDE

FOURTH EDITION

PRINCIPLES OF
MACROECONOMICS

CASE / FAIR

Prentice Hall, Upper Saddle River, N.J. 07458

Production editor: Deneise Smith
Acquisitions editor: Leah Jewell
Associate editor: Teresa Cohan
Manufacturing Buyer: Ken Clinton

© 1996 by Prentice Hall, Inc.
A Simon & Schuster Company
Upper Saddle River, New Jersey 07458

Printed in the United States of America

10 9 8 7 6 5 4 3 2 1

ISBN 0-13-440868-3

Prentice-Hall International (UK) Limited, *London*
Prentice-Hall of Australia Pty. Limited, *Sydney*
Prentice-Hall Canada Inc., *Toronto*
Prentice-Hall Hispanoamericana, S.A., *Mexico*
Prentice-Hall of India Private Limited, *New Delhi*
Prentice-Hall of Japan, Inc., *Tokyo*
Simon & Schuster Asia Pte. Ltd., *Singapore*
Editora Prentice-Hall do Brasil, Ltda., *Rio de Janeiro*

Contents

Preface / v

Part One   INTRODUCTION

CHAPTER 1: The Scope and Method of Economics / 1

    1A: Graphing Tutorial / 19

CHAPTER 2: The Economic Problem: Scarcity and Choice / 29

CHAPTER 3: The Structure of the U.S. Economy: The Private, Public, and International Sectors / 51

CHAPTER 4: Demand, Supply, and Market Equilibrium / 61

CHAPTER 5: Supply, Demand, and the Price System / 91

Part Two   MACROECONOMICS

(Chapter 21 in Combined Text)

CHAPTER 6: Introduction to Macroeconomics / 103

(Chapter 22 in Combined Text)

CHAPTER 7: Measuring National Output and National Income / 117

(Chapter 23 in Combined Text)

CHAPTER 8: Macroeconomic Problems: Unemployment and Inflation / 135

(Chapter 24 in Combined Text)

CHAPTER 9: Aggregate Expenditure and Equilibrium Output / 151

(Chapter 25 in Combined Text)

CHAPTER 10: The Government and Fiscal Policy / 177

(Chapter 26 in Combined Text)

CHAPTER 11: The Money Supply and the Federal Reserve System / 197

(Chapter 27 in Combined Text)

CHAPTER 12: The Demand for Money, the Equilibrium Interest Rate, and Monetary Policy / 215

(Chapter 28 in Combined Text)

CHAPTER 13: Money, the Interest Rate, and National Income: Analysis and Policy / 233

(Chapter 29 in Combined Text)

CHAPTER 14: Aggregate Demand, Aggregate Supply, and Inflation / 255

(Chapter 30 in Combined Text)

CHAPTER 15: The Labor Market, Unemployment, and Inflation / 279

(Chapter 31 in Combined Text)
CHAPTER 16: Deficit Reduction, Stabilization Policy, and Macro Issues Abroad / 297

(Chapter 32 in Combined Text)
CHAPTER 17: Household and Firm Behavior in the Macroeconomy / 311

(Chapter 33 in Combined Text)
CHAPTER 18: Further Topics in Macroeconomic Analysis / 327

(Chapter 34 in Combined Text)
CHAPTER 19: Debates in Macroeconomics: Monetarism, New Classical Theory, and Supply-Side Economics / 341

(Chapter 35 in Combined Text)
CHAPTER 20: Economic Growth and Productivity / 355

Part Three INTERNATIONAL ECONOMICS

(Chapter 36 in Combined Text)
CHAPTER 21: International Trade, Comparative Advantage, and Protectionism / 369

(Chapter 37 in Combined Text)
CHAPTER 22: Open-Economy Macroeconomics: The Balance of Payments and Exchange Rates / 389

(Chapter 38 in Combined Text)
CHAPTER 23: Economic Growth in Developing Nations / 411

(Chapter 39 in Combined Text)
CHAPTER 24: Economies in Transition and Alternative Economic Systems / 421

Preface

This Study Guide has been developed to accompany *Principles of Macroeconomics* by Karl Case and Ray Fair. For students using Case and Fair's *Principles of Economics* (Chapters 1–39), the corresponding chapter numbers appear in parentheses. When referring to specific pages, the *Macroeconomics* reference is given first. I have devised this Guide to help you as you learn the concepts that are presented in the text; if used consistently throughout your course, this Guide can enable you to master the material in what is likely to be your first or second economics course. In addition, you'll be given opportunities to learn how to apply these concepts in a variety of situations. Most economists stress the need to develop competence in three major areas—the application of economic concepts to real—world situations, the interpretation of graphs, and the analysis of numerical problems. This Guide gives you practice in developing these important skills.

I believe that learning how to apply concepts creates a better and more long-lasting understanding of the material than mere memorization does. A reasonable goal for a non-economics major is to have absorbed enough insight to understand the economic content of an article in a publication like *The Wall Street Journal* or *Newsweek*.

STUDY GUIDE CONTENTS

The Study Guide contains one chapter for each chapter in the text. In general, each chapter has two large sections and an Answers and Solutions section.

- The *Objectives: Point by Point* section tells you what you should be able to accomplish after you've studied the material. It gives a summary of the chapter's important ideas. Each point is followed by some multiple choice questions, so that you can monitor how well you're understanding the concepts. You'll find some applications and examples, along with specific learning tips, graphing pointers and "helpful hints". Concepts that may prove particularly troublesome are covered here. Many of these "tricks" and memory aids have been suggested to me by students.

- The *Practice Test* section contains *Multiple Choice Questions* and *Application Questions*. These questions provide opportunities to practice the skills—graphing, numerical analysis, application of concepts—presented in the text. Go through this section thoroughly. These exercises give you an opportunity to try your hand at using economic principles and practices—often in fairly complex situations. Do the problem sets in the textbook, too. The *Multiple Choice Questions* are quite tough. Think of each multiple choice question as four true-false statements; don't just decide on the one "right" answer—determine why the other three options are wrong.

- The *Answers and Solutions* feature numerical and graphical solutions. Be aware, though, that real-world analysis is much more difficult to condense into such a simple form.

STUDY RECOMMENDATIONS

I recommend the following procedure for using this Guide to improve your effective understanding and use of the key principles and practices from the text.

1. Read the textbook chapter. There is no substitute for this step! Ideally, you should do this *before* the material is presented in class; in any case, *don't wait* until the day before your prof has scheduled a test! Use the *Point by Point* section of the Guide to identify the key issues and to test your knowledge.

2. Attend class regularly. In study after study, researchers have shown that regularity of class attendance is the single best predictor of performance.

3. Now that you're acquainted with the material, use the *Tips* to polish your understanding.

4. Complete the practice sections to test your ability to utilize key concepts. If you fail to complete an exercise correctly, even after having seen the answers, reread the text. If you're still stuck, ask your prof for clarification.

5. Before a scheduled examination, read the *Point By Point* sections for review.

With a conscientious and consistent use of this Guide, you can improve your understanding of economics and your ability to use and apply the concepts contained in this field of study. Learning can be interesting, as well as enjoyable.

This Guide has been written with the hope that, after the final exam, it will have helped you to gain a better understanding of economic issues and analysis and of the exciting and challenging concerns that we must address in our contemporary world.

Best wishes to you with your study of economics. I hope that you will find it to be a rewarding and worthwhile experience, and that this Guide will stimulate you in your endeavors.

Please send any comments or suggestions about this study guide to me, care of Economics Editor, Prentice Hall, 1 Lake Street, Upper Saddle River, NJ 07458.

Thomas Beveridge
Hillsborough, North Carolina
September, 1995

ACKNOWLEDGMENTS

I am grateful to the many students whose questions, through the years, have given me a better insight into the difficulties that arise when microeconomics is approached for the first time. The practice material included in this Guide springs largely from such "after class" discussions.

My gratitude is due to Steven Pitts (Houston Community College) who reviewed the entire Guide and contributed the Graphing Tutorial in Chapter 1. Although the majority of the Graphing Pointers are from my pen, Steven provided the initial suggestion for this feature and created numerous fine examples. Dennis Placone (Clemson University) and Charles Michaelopoulos (Virginia Polytechnic Institute and State University) reviewed Chapter 5. Finally, Mark Suchon (Houston Community College) deserves credit for providing a detailed list of typos and errors that had eluded all other eyes. The efforts of these reviewers and other correspondents have added much to the quality of the final product. Needless to say, any remaining *lapsi calami* are my responsibility.

This book is dedicated to Pam, to our son Andrew, (who believes that the marginal propensity to consume exceeds 1 and who did much to disrupt this Guide's production), to my parents, and to the memory of Diana Fuerman Kongable, who would have enjoyed its attempts at humor.

THE SCOPE AND METHOD OF ECONOMICS

1

OBJECTIVES: POINT BY POINT

After completing this chapter, you should be able to accomplish the objectives listed below.

General Comment

Much of this chapter is devoted to setting out the framework of economics. Don't be overwhelmed and don't try to remember it all. Chapter 1 is simply a good place to gather together this information, which will be dealt with more fully as the chapters go by.

OBJECTIVE 1: Define economics.

Because of conditions imposed by nature and the choices previously made by society, resources are scarce. Economics studies how we choose to use these resources. In a sense, it is the "scientific study of choice." (page 1)

PRACTICE

1. Which one of the following best describes the study of economics? Economics studies
   A. how businesses can make profits.
   B. how the government controls the economy and how people earn a living.
   C. how society uses its scarce resources to satisfy its unlimited desires.
   D. the allocation of income among different sectors of the economy.
   Answer: C. All of the options represent aspects of the study of economics. However, the most general statement is given in C—economics is the study of choice.

OBJECTIVE 2: State four reasons for studying economics.

A study of economics helps us to learn a way of thinking, to understand society, to understand national and global affairs, and to be an informed voter. Essential to the economic way of thinking is the concept of "opportunity cost"—choices involve forgoing some options. Accordingly, the applicability of the economic way of thinking is very extensive. (page 2)

OBJECTIVE 3: Distinguish between the concepts of opportunity cost, marginal cost, and sunk costs.

"Marginal" is a frequently used term in economics and it's important to understand it right away. "Marginal" means "additional" or "extra." "Marginal cost," then, means "additional cost."

Suppose you've bought a non-returnable, non-transferable ticket to the zoo for $10. This is a *sunk cost*. You've paid whether or not you visit the zoo.

Let's change the example a little. Suppose you win a free admission to the zoo and decide to go this Saturday. The trip is not entirely free, however. You still have to bear some costs—travel, for example. There is certainly an additional cost (caused by the trip to the zoo). It is a *marginal cost*. Suppose you always buy lunch on Saturdays. The cost of lunch is not a marginal cost since you'd have had lunch whether or not you went to the zoo. In this sense, the cost of lunch is not contingent on the trip to the zoo—it's not an extra cost.

You choose to visit the zoo this Saturday. The *opportunity cost* is the value of the activity you would have undertaken instead—that is, the next most-preferred activity. Perhaps it might be playing a round of golf or studying for a big economics test. The opportunity cost of the trip to the zoo is the value you attach to that *one* activity you would otherwise have chosen.   (page 2)

> **Opportunity Cost and Marginalism:** The "big concept" in this chapter is *opportunity cost*, with *marginalism* and *efficiency* a close second and third. You'll see all three repeatedly throughout the textbook. For practice on the concept of opportunity cost, try Application question 5 below. For practice on marginal thinking, look at Application question 8.

> **TIP:** Any time you make a choice, remember that an opportunity cost is involved.

PRACTICE

2. Your opportunity cost of attending college does not include
   A. the money you spend on meals while at college.
   B. your tuition.
   C. the money you spend on traveling between home and college.
   D. the income you could have earned if you'd been employed full-time.
   Answer: A. You would have bought food whether or not you were at college. All the other expenses occur solely because of attending college.

3. _____ may be defined as the extra cost associated with an action.
   A. Marginal cost.
   B. Sunk cost.
   C. Opportunity cost.
   D. Action cost.
   Answer: A. See p. 3.

4. Jean owns a French restaurant—*La Crème*. Simply to operate this week, he must pay rent, taxes, wages, food costs, and so on. This amounts to $1,000 per week. This evening, a diner arrives and orders some Château Neuf du Pape wine to go with her meal. Jean has none and sends out to Wine World for a bottle. It costs $20, and Jean charges his guest $30. Which of the following is true for Jean?
   A. The marginal cost of the wine is $20.
   B. The marginal cost of the wine is $30.
   C. The sunk cost of the meal is $1,020.
   D. The sunk cost of the meal is $1,030.
   Answer: A. The sunk cost is the up-front expense of $1,000. The extra cost that Jean bears for buying the wine is $20.

OBJECTIVE 4: Define market efficiency in terms of profit opportunities.

The rapid elimination of profit opportunities is a signal that a market is operating efficiently. The stock market is a good example. If a stock is priced "too low," there will be increased bidding and the price will be driven higher, eliminating the excess profits. At a farmers' market, Farmer Brown may charge 60¢ for a dozen eggs although the going rate is 50¢. She might make excess profits for a while, but this will not persist in an efficient market.   (page 4)

OBJECTIVE 5: Make clear the difference between microeconomic and macroeconomic concerns.

Economics is split into two broad parts. *Microeconomics* focuses on the operation of individual markets and the choices of individual economic units (firms and households, for example). *Macroeconomics* deals with the broad economic variables such as national production, total consumer spending, and overall price movements. Economics also contains a number of subfields, such as international economics, labor economics, and industrial organization. (page 7)

PRACTICE

5. **Macroeconomics** approaches the study of economics from the viewpoint of
   A. individual consumers.
   B. the government.
   C. the entire economy.
   D. the operation of specific markets.
   Answer: C. Macroeconomics looks at the big picture—the entire economy.

6. **Microeconomics** approaches the study of economics from the viewpoint of
   A. the entire economy.
   B. the government.
   C. the operation of specific markets.
   D. the stock market.
   Answer: C. Microeconomics examines what is happening with individual economic units (households and firms) and how they interact in specific markets.

7. Which of the following is most appropriately a microeconomic issue?
   A. The study of the relationship between the unemployment rate and the inflation rate.
   B. The forces determining the price level in an individual market.
   C. The determination of total output in the economy.
   D. The aggregate behavior of all decision-making units in the economy.
   Answer: B. Microeconomics examines what is happening with individual economic units (households and firms) and how they interact in specific markets.

OBJECTIVE 6: Distinguish between positive and normative economics.

Economists classify issues as either positive or normative. Positive questions explore the behavior of the economy and its participants without judging whether the behavior is good or bad. *Positive economics* collects data that describe economic phenomena (descriptive economics) and constructs testable—cause-and-effect—theories to explain the phenomena (economic theory). *Normative economic questions* evaluate the results of behavior and explore whether the outcomes might be improved. (page 9)

PRACTICE

8. A difference between positive statements and normative statements is that
   A. positive statements are true by definition.
   B. only positive statements are subject to empirical verification.
   C. economists use positive statements and politicians use normative statements when discussing economic matters.
   D. positive statements require value judgments.
   Answer: B. A positive statement is not necessarily true by definition and can be disproved by empirical verification.

OBJECTIVE 7: Explain the value of the ceteris paribus assumption within the context of economic modeling.

Economists (and other scientists) construct models—formal statements of relationships between variables of interest—that simplify and abstract from reality. Graphs, words, or equations can be used to express a model. In testing the relationships between variables within a model it is convenient to assume *ceteris paribus*, that all other variables have been held constant. (page 12)

PRACTICE

9. "An increase in the price of shampoo will cause less shampoo to be demanded, *ceteris paribus*." *Ceteris paribus* means that
   A. there is a negative relationship between the price and quantity demanded of shampoo.
   B. the price of shampoo is the only factor that can affect the amount of shampoo demanded.
   C. other factors may affect the amount of shampoo demanded but that these are assumed not to change in this analysis.
   D. the price of shampoo is equal for all buyers.
   Answer: C. The price of shampoo is equal for all buyers and there may be a negative relationship between the price and quantity of shampoo demanded, but *ceteris paribus* means that any other factors that may affect the amount of shampoo demanded are assumed to be constant.

OBJECTIVE 8: State the fallacies discussed in the text, give examples, and explain *why* such statements are fallacious.

Beware of false logic! The *fallacy of composition* involves the claim that what is good for one individual remains good when it happens for many. The fact that one farmer gains by having a bumper harvest *doesn't* mean that all farmers will gain if each has a bumper crop. The *post hoc, ergo propter hoc* fallacy occurs when we assume that an event that happens after another is caused by it. (page 13)

Two examples of the fallacy of composition: One person who stands up to see a good play at a football game derives a benefit—therefore all will benefit similarly if the entire crowd stands up. Running to the exit when there is a fire in a theater will increase your chances of survival—therefore, in a fire, we should all run for the exit.

PRACTICE

10. Which of the following is **not** an example of the fallacy of composition?
    A. Jane leaves work at 4:00 each day and avoids the rush-hour traffic at 5:00. Therefore, if businesses regularly closed at 4:00, all commuters would avoid the rush-hour traffic
    B. John stands up so that he can see an exciting football play. Therefore, if the entire crowd stands up when there is an exciting play, all spectators will get a better view.
    C. Since society benefits from the operation of efficient markets, IBM will benefit if markets become more efficient.
    D. Since Mary on her own can escape from a burning building by running outside, individuals in a crowded movie theater are advised to run outside when there is a fire.
    Answer: C. This example is arguing from the general to the specific. The fallacy of composition argues from the specific to the general.

OBJECTIVE 9: State and explain the four criteria used to assess the outcomes of economic policy.

Economists construct and test models as an aid to policy-making. Policy-makers generally judge proposals in terms of efficiency, equity (fairness), growth, and stability.

(page 15)

PRACTICE

11. The nation of Arboc claims to have achieved an equitable distribution of income among its citizens. On visiting Arboc, we would expect to find that
    A. each citizen receives the same amount of income.
    B. Arbocali residents believe that the distribution of income is fair.
    C. Arbocali residents believe that the distribution of income is equal.
    D. each citizen receives the amount of income justified by the value of his or her contribution to production.
    Answer: B. Whether or not the distribution of income is equitable depends on what Arbocali citizens believe to be fair.

    Use the following information to answer the next two questions.

    Nicola and Alexander each have some dollars and some apples. Nicola values a pound of apples at $3 while Alexander values a pound of apples at $1.

12. In which of the following cases has an economically efficient trade taken place?
    A. The market price of apples is $3 per pound. Nicola sells apples to Alexander.
    B. The market price of apples is $1 per pound. Alexander sells apples to Nicola.
    C. The market price of apples is $2 per pound. Nicola sells apples to Alexander.
    D. The market price of apples is $2 per pound. Alexander sells apples to Nicola.
    Answer: D. When the market price of apples is $2 per pound and Alexander is the seller, he gains $1. Nicola also gains because she receives goods she values at $3 for a payment of only $2.

13. In which of the following cases has an economically efficient trade not taken place?
    A. The market price of apples is $3 per pound. Alexander sells apples to Nicola.
    B. The market price of apples is $1 per pound. Nicola sells apples to Alexander.
    C. The market price of apples is $4 per pound. Alexander sells apples to Nicola.
    D. The market price of apples is $2 per pound. Nicola sells apples to Alexander.
    Answer: C. An efficient trade can occur only when some participant is better off and no participant is worse off. In Option A, Alexander gains and Nicola does not lose. In Option B, Nicola gains and Alexander does not lose. In Option D, Alexander and Nicola both gain. In Option C, Alexander gains but Nicola loses.

OBJECTIVE 10: Construct and interpret graphs.

Economic graphs depict the relationship between variables. A curve with a "rising" (positive) slope indicates that as one variable increases, so does the other. A curve with a "falling" (negative) slope indicates that as one variable increases in value, the other decreases in value. Slope is easily measured by "rise over run"—the extent of vertical change divided by the extent of horizontal change. (page 19)

> **TIP:** Economists almost automatically begin to scribble diagrams when asked to explain ideas, and you'll need to learn how to use some of the tools of the trade. In economics, graphs often feature financial variables like "price," "the interest rate," or "income." Usually the dependent variable is placed on the vertical axis and the independent variable on the horizontal axis. In graphing economic variables, however, it's a pretty safe bet that the *financial* variable will go on the vertical axis every time. Application questions 9 and 10 and the Tutorial offer some graphing practice.

TIP: Make a point of examining the graphs you see accompanying economics-based articles in the daily newspaper or news magazines. It's quite common to find examples of deceptive graphs, especially when variables are being compared over time. A graph comparing, say, the difference between government spending and tax revenues can be quite misleading if the vertical axis does not start at zero.

Graphing Pointer: It is a natural tendency to shy away from graphs—they may seem threatening—but this is a mistake. To work with economic concepts, you must master all the tools in the economist's toolkit. Trying to avoid graphs is as unwise as trying to cut a piece of wood without a saw. See the Graphing Tutorial if you are uneasy.

PRACTICE

Use the diagram below to answer the next four questions.

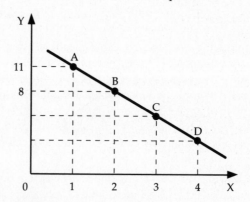

14. In the diagram above, the slope of the line is
    A. positive and variable.
    B. positive and constant.
    C. negative and variable.
    D. negative and constant.
    Answer: D. The diagram shows a straight line—straight lines have a constant slope. Visually, or by using the "rise over run" formula, the relationship is negative because, as one variable increases in value, the other decreases in value.

15. The slope of line between Point A and Point B is
    A. 3.
    B. ⅓.
    C. −3.
    D. −⅓.
    Answer: C. Use the "rise over run" formula. The rise is −3 (from 11 to 8) and the run is +1 (from 1 to 2).

16. At Point D, the value of Y is
    A. −3.
    B. 3.
    C. 5.
    D. 2.
    Answer: D. As X "steps up" in value by 1, Y "steps down" in value by 3. At Point B, X has a value of 2 and Y has a value of 8. Moving to Point D, X increases by 2 and Y decreases by 6, from 8 to 2.

17. In the diagram above, when the line reaches the vertical (Y) axis the value of Y will be
    A. 3.
    B. 8.
    C. 11.
    D. 14.
    Answer: D As X "steps down" in value by 1, Y "steps up" in value by 3. At Point A, X has a value of 1 and Y has a value of 11. X decreases by 1 and Y increases by 3, from 11 to 14.

PRACTICE TEST

I. MULTIPLE CHOICE QUESTIONS.

Select the option that provides the single best answer.

B 1. Local farmers reduce the price of their tomatoes at the farmers' market. The price of corn is 30¢ per ear. A passing economist notes that, *ceteris paribus* buyers will purchase more tomatoes. Which of the following is TRUE? The economist is
   A. implying that the price of tomatoes will fall even further.
   B. assuming that the price of corn remains at 30¢ per ear.
   C. assuming that tomatoes are of a better quality than before.
   D. implying that corn is of a poorer quality than before.

B 2. Which of the following is **not** given in the textbook as a criterion for judging the results of economic policy?
   A. Economic stability.
   B. Employment.
   C. Efficiency.
   D. Equity.

D 3. Economic growth may occur if
   A. more machines become available.
   B. more workers become available.
   C. workers become more efficient.
   D. all of the above.

A 4. Economics is the study of how
   A. scarce resources are used to satisfy unlimited wants.
   B. we choose to use unlimited resources.
   C. limitless resources are used to satisfy scarce wants.
   D. society has no choices.

B 5. The opportunity cost of Choice X can be defined as
   A. the cheapest alternative to Choice X.
   B. the most highly-valued alternative to Choice X.
   C. the price paid to obtain X.
   D. the most highly-priced alternative to Choice X.

D 6. In economics, efficiency means that
   A. income is distributed equally among all citizens.
   B. there is a low level of inflation and full unemployment of economic resources.
   C. total productivity is increasing at a constant and equal rate within each sector of the economy.
   D. the economy is producing those goods and services that citizens desire and is doing so at the least possible cost.

_C_ 7. Which of the following statements is true?
   A. Microeconomics studies consumer behavior, while macro-economics studies producer behavior.
   B. Microeconomics studies producer behavior, while macro-economics studies consumer behavior.
   C. Microeconomics studies behavior of individual households and firms, while macroeconomics studies national aggregates.
   D. Microeconomics studies inflation and opportunity costs, while macroeconomics studies unemployment and sunk costs.

_B_ 8. Which of the following statements is true?
   A. There is a positive relationship between the price of a product and the quantity demanded.
   B. There is a positive relationship between the number of umbrellas bought and the amount of rainfall.
   C. There is a negative relationship between height and weight.
   D. There is a negative relationship between sales of ice cream and noon temperature.

_A_ 9. Oliver Sudden discovers that if he cuts the price of his tomatoes at the farmers' market, his sales revenue increases. Expecting similar results, all the other tomato sellers follow his example. They are guilty of committing
   A. the fallacy of composition.
   B. the fallacy of *post hoc, ergo propter hoc.*
   C. the fallacy of correlation.
   D. *ceteris paribus.*

_D_ 10. The quantity of six-packs of Quite Lite beer demanded per week (Qd) in Hometown is described by the following equation:

$$Qd = 400 - 100P,$$

   where P (in dollars) is the price of a six-pack. This equation predicts that
   A. 300 six-packs will be bought this week.
   B. a $1 rise in price will cause 100 more six-packs to be bought this week.
   C. 300 six-packs will be bought per $100 this week.
   D. a 50¢ rise in price will cause 50 fewer six-packs to be bought this week.

_D_ 11. The *ceteris paribus* assumption is used
   A. to make economic theory more realistic.
   B. to make economic analysis more realistic.
   C. to avoid the fallacy of composition.
   D. to focus the analysis on the effect of a single factor.

Use the diagram below to answer the next four questions.

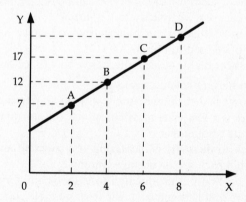

_B_ 12. In the diagram above, the slope of the line is
   A. positive and variable.
   B. positive and constant.
   C. negative and variable.
   D. negative and constant.

_A_ 13. The slope of line between Point A and Point B is
   A. ½.
   B. ⅖.
   C. –⅖.
   D. –½.

_D_ 14. At Point D, the value of Y is
   A. 5.
   B. 8.
   C. 19.5.
   D. 22.

_A_ 15. In the diagram above, when the line reaches the vertical (Y) axis the value of Y will be
   A. 2.
   B. ½.
   C. 7.
   D. 12.

Use the diagrams below to answer the next four questions.

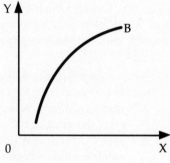

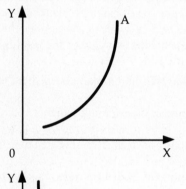

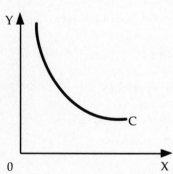

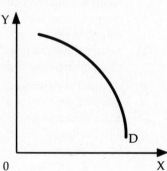

_C_ 16. Of the four diagrams, which curve has a slope that is negative and decreasing?
   A. A.
   B. B.
   C. C.
   D. D.

_A_ 17. Of the four diagrams, which curve has a slope that is positive and increasing?
   A. A.
   B. B.
   C. C.
   D. D.

_B_ 18. Of the four diagrams, which curve has a slope that is positive and decreasing?
   A. A.
   B. B.
   C. C.
   D. D.

_A_ 19. Of the four diagrams, which curve appears to be described by the equation $y = x^2$?
   A. A.
   B. B.
   C. C.
   D. D.

_D_ 20. During the debate about balancing the federal government's budget, it has been proposed that Medicaid benefits be reduced. This proposal has been criticized because low-income families (who receive Medicaid) would spend a higher percentage of their income on medical services than high-income families would spend. This argument is based on concerns about
   A. economic growth.
   B. efficiency.
   C. economic stability.
   D. equity.

Use the following information to answer the next two questions. The Channel Tunnel, linking the United Kingdom and France, was originally planned to cost $100 million. After work had begun and the two excavators were under the English Channel, with $70 million already spent, the estimate of the total bill was revised to $150 million.

_B_ 21. To an economist, the $70 million that had already been spent is best thought of as a
   A. sunk cost that was important in determining whether to complete the project.
   B. sunk cost that was not important in determining whether to complete the project.
   C. marginal cost that was important in determining whether to complete the project.
   D. marginal cost that was not important in determining whether to complete the project.

_D_ 22. At this point the marginal cost of completion was best estimated as
   A. $30 million.
   B. $50 million.
   C. $70 million.
   D. $80 million.

II. APPLICATION QUESTIONS.

1. The small nation of Smogland is unhappily situated in a valley surrounded by mountains. Smogland's Secretary of the Environment has determined that there are 4000 cars, each of which pollutes the air. In fact, Smogland's air is so unhealthy that it is rated as "hazardous." If emission controls, costing $50 per car, are introduced, the air quality will improve to a rating of "fair." A survey has revealed that, of the 40,000 inhabitants, 10,000 would value the air quality improvement at $5 each, and the other 30,000 would value it at $7 each. The Secretary of the Environment has asked you to analyze the issue and make a recommendation.

2. Refer to the following diagram.

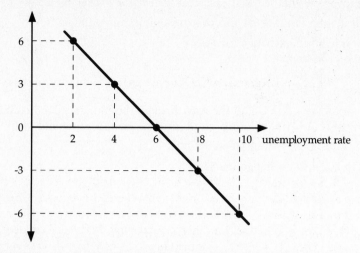

a. Construct a table from the data presented in the diagram.
b. Calculate the slope of the line.
c. Calculate the inflation rate when the unemployment rate is 9%.
d. Calculate the inflation rate when the unemployment rate is 5%.

3. What are some elements of the opportunity cost of "clean" air? In total, the "cost" of cleaner air increases as we remove more and more pollution. Do you think, however, that the extra (marginal) cost of cleaner air increases as we progressively remove pollution? Graph the behavior of "extra cost" (vertical axis) and "cleanness of air" (horizontal axis).

4. Suppose that the opportunity cost of attending today's economics class is study time for a math test. By not studying you will lose fifteen points on your test. Attending the econ. class will increase your future econ. test score by no more than three points. Was your choice—to attend the econ. class—rational?

5. Suppose you had a summer internship in a bank just before your senior year. You are "noticed" and are offered a full-time position in the bank, with a salary of $25,000 a year. A rival bank, also keen to attract you, offers you $27,000 for a similar position. After much thought, you decide to return to college to complete your economics degree. Based on the information given, what was the opportunity cost of your decision?

If you had chosen one of the banking jobs instead of resuming your studies, how could you have explained your decision to your parents, who would have pointed out that you would have "wasted" three years of college? How might "sunk costs" figure into your explanation?

6. Choose a local natural resource with which you are familiar, e.g., an acre of farmland or a nearby lake.
a. List three alternative uses for your chosen raw material.
b. Choose one of the three uses. What is the opportunity cost of this use? Should you include the cost of clean-up (if this is appropriate) following use?
c. Is the resource renewable or not? If not, should this be factored into your calculations?
d. Describe how your community has chosen to use the resource so far, if at all. Who and what have determined that choice?

7. Suppose you're asked to choose one job out of three. Job A pays $30,000; Job B, $20,000; and Job C, $15,000. In all other respects they are identical. Which would you choose? What is the opportunity cost of your choice? Is it rational to choose Job C? What is the opportunity cost of Job C?

8. Suppose you're offered three deals, each of which will give you $11 in return for $8. Your profit will be $3 in each case. *Deal A* is a straight swap—$11 for $8.

Deal B involves four steps and you can quit at any point.

Step 1. $5 in exchange for $2
Step 2. $3 for $2
Step 3. $2 for $2
Step 4. $1 for $2

What would you do? Go all the way through the four steps and collect a total of $3 profit? A better solution, stopping after two steps, would yield $4.

Deal C also involves four steps.

Step 1. $4 in exchange for $1
Step 2. $4 for $2
Step 3. $2 for $2
Step 4. $1 for $3

Would you collect your $3 profit or stop after two steps and gain $5?

Moral: If the effects of extra (marginal) steps are assessed, you can raise your profits above $3. Without examining each step, the chance of greater profits would have been missed.

9. Using your own intuition, graph each of the following relationships in the space on the following page.
   a. height and weight of males.
   b. (on the same graph) height and weight of females.

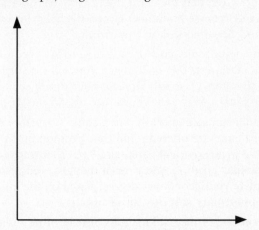

   c. Do these lines have a positive slope or negative slope?
   d. Have you drawn the relationships differently? If so, why? By referring to your own observations, you have constructed a model!
   e. Which factors have you "held constant"?
   f. i. Again using your own intuition, sketch in the space below the relationship between the price of California wine and the consumption of California wine.
      ii. According to your theory and your diagram, is there any point, even if wine is free, at which consumers will not wish to buy any more wine?
      iii. Will the total number of dollars spent on wine remain the same at every price level?

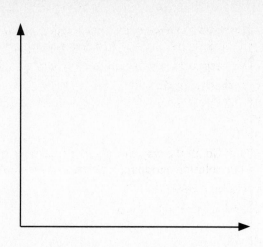

g.   i. Using your own intuition, sketch in the space below the relationship between the interest rate and house purchases.

    ii. According to your theory and your graph, is there any interest rate that will completely deter house purchases?

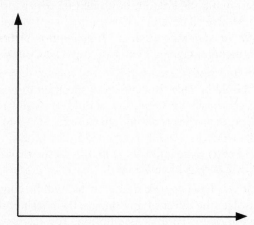

10. Suppose there is a relationship between two variables, X (on the horizontal axis) and Y (on the vertical axis), and that you have collected the following data.

X	2	4	6	8	10
Y	5	6	7	8	9

a. Do we have a positive or a negative relationship?
b. Describe (in words) what these data would look like graphically.
c. Calculate the slope (rise-over-run) of the line.

d. Graph the relationship below.

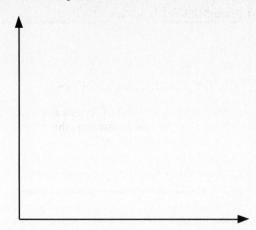

11. Suppose that you have a new brand of low alcohol, reduced-calorie beer, "Quite Lite," that you intend to market. What variables do you think will be important in determining the amount of Quite Lite that people will want to buy? You should be able to develop a fairly long list of variables. You have begun to construct an economic model of consumption behavior. Now prune down your list to include, say, the five most important variables.

Now work out in which way each variable will impact the consumption of Quite Lite. You should be able to work out a specific cause-and-effect pattern in each case. A higher price for Quite Lite should cause less to be bought. A price hike for competing beers should increase the demand for Quite Lite. Note that not all variables have been included in the model; an all-inclusive list would (1) be cumbersome and (2) distract from the major elements in the model. You have wielded Ockham's razor!

The variables that you have compiled in your list will be continually changing their values. To isolate the effect of any one on the consumption of Quite Lite you must invoke the *ceteris paribus* assumption. You might think of this as being the economic equivalent of the "standard temperature and pressure" conditions applied in the natural sciences.

Use the model that you developed for Quite Lite beer. Putting "quantity demanded" on the horizontal axis, graph each of the relationships in the model.

12. Which of the following statements are positive and which are normative?
    a. The moon is made of green cheese.
    b. States to the west of the Mississippi have lower state income tax rates than states to the east have.
    c. The federal government should be made to balance its budget.
    d. The most serious economic problem confronting the nation is unemployment.
    e. We should abolish the minimum wage.
    f. We should index-link the minimum wage to the rate of price inflation.
    g. If the federal budget deficit is reduced, then interest rates will decrease.

ANSWERS AND SOLUTIONS

PRACTICE TEST

I. SOLUTIONS TO MULTIPLE CHOICE QUESTIONS

1. B. If the price of corn fell, perhaps very sharply, buyers might buy more corn and fewer tomatoes. Therefore, the economist is assuming that the price of corn is not going to change. That's what *ceteris paribus* implies.

2. B. Unemployment is certainly an important economic variable, but it is not one of the criteria for evaluating the results of economic policy. See p. 15.

3. D. Growth will occur if resources become more plentiful or more productive.

4. A. Economics is about choice—how we ration scarce resources to meet limitless wants.

5. B. Price is not necessarily a reliable guide to value for a particular individual. Opportunity cost is the measure of the value placed on the next most-preferred item forgone as a result of Choice X.

6. D. Efficiency means that producers are using the least costly method of production to supply those goods that are desired by consumers.

7. C. To review the micro/macro distinction, see p. 8.

8. B. There is a *negative* relationship between price and quantity demanded, so A is incorrect. The greater the rainfall, the larger the number of umbrellas bought.

9. A. Just because an action done by one individual produces a given outcome, the same action done by many need not.

10. D. Put in numbers. If P = $2, then Qd will equal 400 − 100(2), or 200. If the price rises by 50¢, then Qd will equal 400 − 100(2.5), or 150—a fall of 50.

11. D. The *ceteris paribus* assumption freezes the effect of all but one change so that the effects of that change may be examined.

12. B. The diagram shows a straight line—straight lines have a constant slope. Visually, or by using the "rise over run" formula, the relationship is positive because, as one variable increases in value, the other also increases in value.

13. A. Use the "rise over run" formula. The rise is +5 (Y goes from 7 to 12) and the run is +2 (X goes from 2 to 4).

14. D. As X "steps up" in value by 2, Y "steps up" in value by 5. At Point C, X has a value of 6 and Y has a value of 17. Moving to Point D, X rises by 2 and Y rises by 5, from 17 to 22.

15. D. As X "steps down" in value by 2, Y "steps down" in value by 5. At Point A, X has a value of 2 and Y has a value of 7. X decreases by 2 and Y decreases by 5, from 7 to 2.

16. C. The relationship shows that as the X variable increases in value, the Y variable decreases in value—a negative relationship. The slope is decreasing because, as X increases in value, the decrease in the value of Y becomes smaller and smaller.

17. A. The relationship shows that as the X variable increases in value, the Y variable also increases in value—a positive relationship. The slope is increasing because, as X increases in value, the increase in the value of Y becomes larger and larger.

18. B. The relationship shows that as the X variable increases in value, the Y variable also increases in value—a positive relationship. The slope is decreasing because, as X increases in value, the increase in the value of Y becomes smaller and smaller.

19. A. As x assumes higher values, the values of y will increase more rapidly.

20. D. For equity, read "fairness". Critics of the proposal argue that it is unfair to make poor families spend a larger part of their lower income on medical services.

21. B. The $70 million had already been spent and was unrecoverable—a sunk cost. Sunk costs should have no impact on the decision to continue the project. See p. 3.

22. D. To complete the project would cost $80 million more than had already been spent.

II. SOLUTIONS TO APPLICATION QUESTIONS

1. The (marginal) cost of the air quality improvement is valued at $50 × 4000, or $200,000. The benefit derived from the improvement is valued at ($5 × 10,000) + ($7 × 30,000), or $260,000. Smogland should proceed with the implementation of emission controls.

2. a.

UNEMPLOYMENT RATE (%)	INFLATION RATE (%)
2.0	6.0
4.0	3.0
6.0	0.0
8.0	−3.0
10.0	−6.0

   b. Slope is −1.5.
   c. −4.5%.
   d. 1.5%.

3. In order to have cleaner (if not clean) air, we might wish to reduce emissions of cars, homes, and factories. The next most preferred use of the resources used to achieve this would be included in the opportunity cost. An initial 5% improvement in the quality of the air might be accomplished quite simply—perhaps by requiring more frequent car tune-ups—but, progressively, the "cost" of achieving more stringent air cleanliness standards will rise. The marginal cost will increase. This will graph as an upward-sloping line that rises progressively more steeply.

4. The answer cannot be determined given the information. This choice may well have been rational. Perhaps the three extra points save you from flunking the course while, in the math class, you are confident of making an easy "A."

5. The opportunity cost is the salary forgone—$27,000 if you had chosen the first bank. Presumably, the offer of the job at the bank was based on your abilities—some of which would have been developed while at college. That time, then, was not wasted. You could have taken the bank job and explained that the three years of college got you the internship and sufficient skills to be noticed in the first place. Also, the three college years cannot be relived—decisions should be based on the future, not the past.

6. This is an open question. The natural resource might be a river, a seam of coal, deer, a piece of waste land used as a dump, prime agricultural land, or downtown lots. The main point is that using the resource one way means that it is not available for other uses. The final part of the question may lead you into a consideration of private property rights, social pressure, and the role of the government.

7. Choose Job A! The opportunity cost is $20,000 (the value of the next best alternative forgone—Job B). The opportunity cost of both Job B and Job C is $30,000—the value of the surrendered Job A. Choosing either B or C is not rational since the reward is less than the cost.

9. a. and b. See the diagram below.

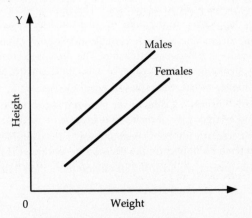

   c. Both positive—as height increases, so does weight.

d. Probably the lines will be different. Perhaps, at any given height, males may weigh more than females, for example.
e. Race, geographical location and age are factors that have been ignored.
f. i. See the diagram on the next page.
   ii. Even if wine is free, consumers are likely to reach a point of satiation. This is shown on the diagram as the quantity at which the line reaches the horizontal axis.
   iii. It depends on your demand for wine, of course, but probably not. In general, we'll find that total spending declines at high prices.

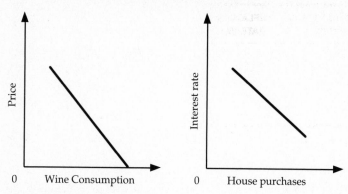

g. i. See the diagram above.
   ii. It depends on the demand for houses, of course, and is shown as the point at which the line reaches the vertical axis.

10. a. It's a positive relationship.
    b. The line would be "rising" to the right.
    c. Rise over run: Y rises by one unit every time X rises by two units, so the slope is +½.
    d. See the diagram below.

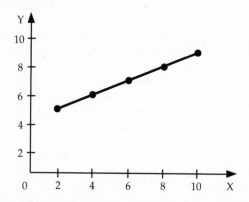

11. Your shortlist of variables probably will include the price of Quite Lite, the prices of its competitors, advertising, the time of year, health attitudes, the income of potential buyers (launching a new product during an economic downturn might be difficult, for instance), and so on.

    The negative relationship you will have modeled (if not, why not?) between price and quantity demanded is called the demand curve. A movement along this curve indicates that price has changed causing a change in the amount of beer demanded, with all other variables held constant (*ceteris paribus*). (Keep this conclusion in mind when you read Chapter 4.)

12. Positive statements are testable; normative statements are opinions.
    a. Positive. A statement need not be correct to be positive.
    b. Positive. Data can be gathered and analysis undertaken.
    c. Normative, as signaled by the use of "should".
    d. Normative. This is an opinion, even during the Great Depression.
    e. Normative. This is an opinion, as signaled by the use of "should".
    f. Normative. This is an opinion, as signaled by the use of "should".
    g. Positive. This statement can be tested.

APPENDIX TO CHAPTER 1

1A

Introduction: Why a Special Section on Graphs?

Many of you will be surprised by the amount of mathematics—geometry in particular—that you encounter in economics. Professors introduce a new concept and quickly draw a graph on the blackboard to illustrate the idea. Once past the initial chapter, the Case and Fair textbook reinforces the notion that economic theory and graphs are inseparable. This unexpected union of a social science course and mathematical methodology baffles some students. Often, you struggle so much with the techniques that you miss the powerful insights that economics has to offer. This section is designed to help you gain a working understanding of graphing techniques and to help you apply this knowledge to economics.

Why Are Graphs Important?

Graphs are important for several reasons. First, graphs represent a compact way to convey a large amount of information. An old adage says that "one picture is worth one thousand words". This is particularly true in economics as the movement of an economic variable over time or the relationship between two economic variables can be quickly grasped through the use of graphs. Second, as this textbook mentions in the appendix to Chapter 1, economics uses quantitative (mathematical) techniques more than any other social science. Every academic discipline possesses its own "tool kit" that must be mastered in order to truly appreciate the content of the course. In an economic principles class, the primary "tool" is graphs. Third, there is a clear correlation between student success in economics and graphing skills. Research on student performance indicates that of the skills that lead to success (verbal, quantitative reasoning, graphing), graphing ability is vital. Fourth, an important component of a vibrant democratic society *economic literacy*: a basic understanding of certain central economic concepts. Citizens who follow current events will constantly encounter graphs as print and television journalists use the visual medium to communicate with their audience.

Why Graphs Trouble Many Students

There are several factors that may cause you to have difficulty with graphs. Several years may have elapsed since you completed a high school geometry course. Consequently, many graphing skills that were developed have been forgotten. More fundamentally, you read everyday; however, you do not practice math everyday. Therefore, most students will enter an economic principles class with a stronger reading ability than a mathematical ability. Because of this, you must remember that the graphs in this textbook are not photographs worthy of only a glance; *graphs must be studied*.

General Tips for Studying Graphs

Here are some general tips that should assist you in developing your graphing skills:

1. *Relax*! Remember that math is simply another language; therefore, graphs are just a specific form of communication;
2. When studying a graph, first identify the labels that are on the graph axes and curves. These labels are like road signs that inform the reader;
3. Once the labels are recognized, try to understand what economic intuition lies behind the curve (e.g., the demand curve indicates that as the product price falls, the amount that consumers wish to buy increases);
4. Get into the habit of tracing the graphs that are in the text and copying the graphs as reading notes are taken; and
5. *Draw, draw, draw*!!! The process of learning economics must be an active process. Graphing skills can be enhanced only by repeated attempts to graph economic concepts.

What Are Graphs?

Graphs are a visual expression of quantitative information. Economic theory attempts to establish relationships between important concepts. If the value of a concept changes, the concept is considered a *variable*. Graphs illustrate the relationship between two variables. If two variables have a *direct* (positive) relationship, the value of one variable increases as the value of the other variable increases. If two variables have an *inverse* (negative) relationship, the value of one variable decreases as the value of the other variable increases.

Example 1: As children get older, they grow taller. Thus, there exists a direct relationship between a child's age and his or her height.

AGE	6	7	8	9	10
HEIGHT	48″	50″	52″	54″	56″

This relationship can be graphed:

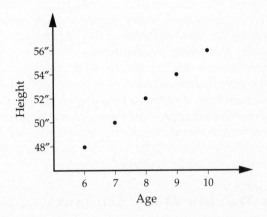

Example 2: After attending class, sleeping, eating, and working at a part-time job, a student has seven hours that can be used for studying or socializing. There exists an inverse relationship between time spent studying and time spent socializing.

STUDYING	7	5	3	1	0
SOCIALIZING	0	2	4	6	7

A graph of this relationship is shown below:

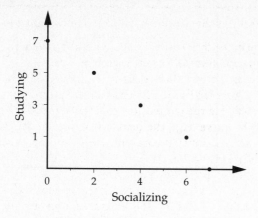

Types of Graphs

There are two types of graphs. *Descriptive* graphs relate the observed association of two variables. The graphs in Examples 1 and 2 are descriptive graphs. Newspapers often express monthly unemployment data in descriptive graphs. *Analytical* graphs convey the hypothetical relationship, or association, between two variables. The existence of association is derived from economic theory and its accuracy is the object of economic research.

Example 3: An understanding of a firm's goals and its constraints leads to the development of a hypothesis which states that as wages rise, a firm will hire fewer workers. Graphically, this relationship is expressed as:

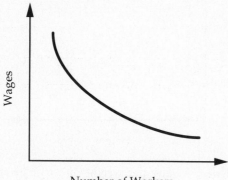

Often, the value of one of the variables determines the value of the other variable. In these cases, the former variable is called the *independent* variable; the latter variable is called the *dependent* variable. Normally (but not always), the independent variable is placed on the horizontal axis and the dependent variable is placed on the vertical axis.

Drawing Graphs

Earlier, we examined the direct relationship between a child's age and his or her height. One would expect another direct relationship between a child's age and his or her weight.

AGE	6	7	8	9	10
WEIGHT	70 lbs	75 lbs	80 lbs	85 lbs	90 lbs

Example 4: Graph this relationship on the axes below.

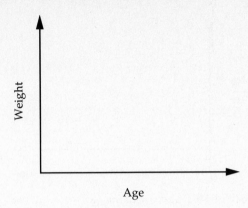

Combining the two series of data yields the table below:

AGE	6	7	8	9	10
HEIGHT	48″	50″	52″	54″	56″
WEIGHT	70 lbs	75 lbs	80 lbs	85 lbs	90 lbs

Example 5: Graph the height-weight combination for each age.

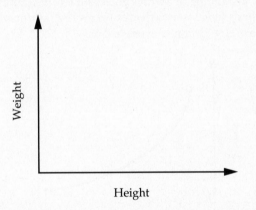

Is the relationship between height and weight direct or inverse? _____
Because the graph depicts the changes in two variables over time, it is called a *scatter diagram*.

Example 6: Graph the relationship between the annual U.S. unemployment rate (U%) and the years 1984–1993.

Y E A R	1984	1985	1986	1987	1988	1989	1990	1991	1992	1993
U%	7.5	7.2	7.0	6.2	5.5	5.3	5.5	6.7	7.4	6.8

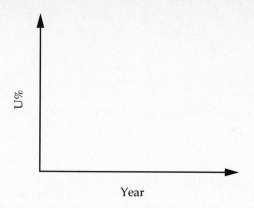

Because this graph depicts the movement of one variable over time, it is called a *time-series* graph.

Between what years is there a direct relationship? _____

Between what years is there an inverse relationship? _____

Reading Graphs

In addition to graphing economic relationships, students must develop the skill of reading graphs. Below are a time-series graph of the movement of the poverty rates for U.S. families between 1984 and 1993 and a scatter diagram indicating the association between poverty rates and unemployment rates. Study both graphs and answer the questions that follow.

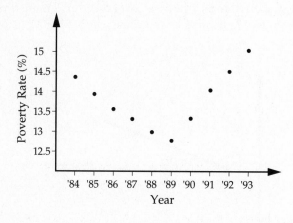

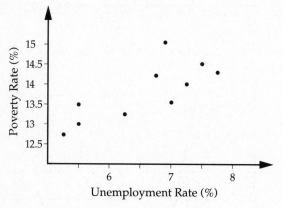

Example 7:

1. What are the poverty rates in:
   a. 1984 _____
   b. 1990 _____
   c. 1993 _____

2. What are the poverty rate/unemployment rate combinations in:
   a. 1986 _____ _____
   b. 1989 _____ _____
   c. 1992 _____ _____

3. When is there a direct relationship between poverty rates and time?

4. Is there ever an inverse relationship between poverty rates and unemployment rates?

Understanding and Calculating Slopes

The *slope* of a curve is one measure of the relationship between two variables. It indicates both the type of relationship (direct or inverse) and the rate of change of one variable as the other variable changes. For a straight line, the slope is constant. For a curve, the slope changes from one point along the curve to another. At any particular point, the slope of the curve is identical to the slope of the straight line that is tangent to that point. The slope of a line is calculated by identifying two points on the line and computing the ratio of the change in the variable on the vertical axis and the change in the variable on the horizontal axis. (In high school geometry, this was referred to as "the 'rise'; over the 'run'"; more formally, the slope was the "change in Y (ΔY) divided by the change in X (ΔX)".)

Example 8:

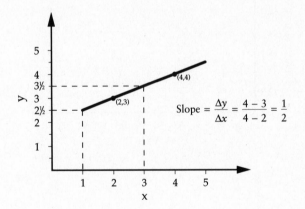

$$\text{Slope} = \frac{\Delta y}{\Delta x} = \frac{4 - 3}{4 - 2} = \frac{1}{2}$$

Example 9:

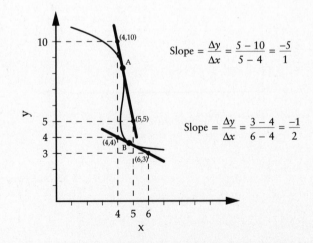

$$\text{Slope} = \frac{\Delta y}{\Delta x} = \frac{5 - 10}{5 - 4} = \frac{-5}{1}$$

$$\text{Slope} = \frac{\Delta y}{\Delta x} = \frac{3 - 4}{6 - 4} = \frac{-1}{2}$$

In Example 8, any two points along the line will show a slope of ½. In Example 9, the slope varies: at point A, the slope is −5; at point B the slope is −½. These slope numbers can be interpreted as indicating the unit change in the value of Y in response to a one unit change in X. For Example 8, Y will increase by ½ unit in response to a one unit change in X. At point A in Example 9, Y decreases by 5 units and, at point B, Y decreases by ½ unit in response to a one unit change in X. The fact that the slope is positive in Example 8 means that there is a direct relationship between X and Y (as X increases, Y increases). The negative slope in Example 9 illustrates an inverse relationship between X and Y (as X increases, Y decreases).

Solving Equations

Often, the economic relationship between two concepts can be expressed algebraically with an equation. The advantage of this approach is that we can calculate the specific impact that a change in one variable has upon another variable.

Example 10: It is a reasonable assumption that as the price of a good rises, more of that good will be supplied. This positive relationship can be expressed with an equation. Let P represent price and Qs represent quantity supplied. For our purposes, let Qs = −10 + 80P. Thus, if P = 1, then Qs = 70. The table below captures this relationship:

Price	1	2	3	4	5
Quantity supplied (Qs)	70	150	230	310	390

1. What is Qs if P = 7? _____

2. What is Qs if P = 10? _____

The table can be graphed. The line is a supply curve, as you will see in Chapter 4—it is usually labeled "S".

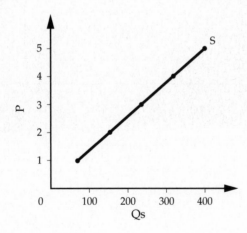

3. What is the slope of the line? _____

If the equation is Qs = −10 + 50P, the slope of the line will change. Below is a new table:

Price	1	2	3	4	5
Quantity supplied (Qs)	40	90	140	190	240

4. Draw this new line on the graph below. Label it S1.

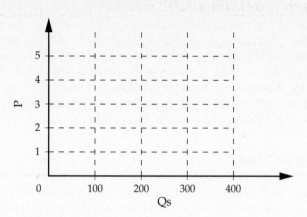

5. What is the slope of this line? _____

If the equation for the supply curve is Qs = –20 + 75P, answer the questions below.

6. Complete the following table:

Price	1	2	3	4	5
Quantity supplied (Qs)					

7. Graph the line represented in the table on the graph below. Label it S2.

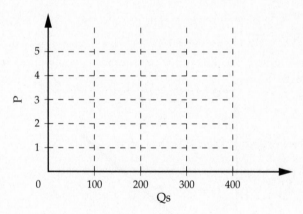

8. What is the slope of the line? _____

9. What is Qs if P = 8? _____

10. What is Qs if P = 20? _____

SOLUTIONS TO PROBLEMS IN APPENDIX 1

Example 4:
See the diagram below.

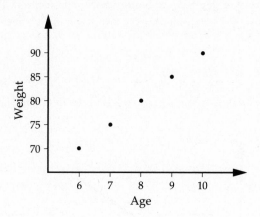

Example 5:
See the diagram below.

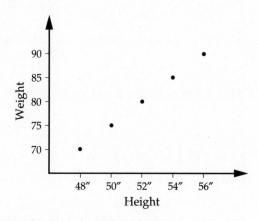

The relationship between height and weight is direct.

Example 6:
See the diagram below.

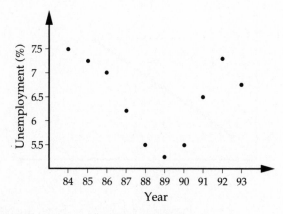

Between 1989 and 1992, there is a direct relationship.
Between 1984 and 1989, there is an inverse relationship.

Example 7:
1. a. 14.4%
    b. 13.5%
    c. 15.1%
2. a. 13.6% and 7.0%
    b. 12.8% and 5.3%
    c. 14.5% and 7.4%
3. There is a direct relationship between poverty rates and time from 1989 to 1993.
4. Yes, there is an inverse relationship between poverty rates and unemployment rates from 1992 to 1993.

Example 10:
1. $Qs = -10 + 80P = -10 + 80(7) = 550$.
2. $Qs = -10 + 80P = -10 + 80(10) = 790$.
3. Slope = rise/run = 1/80. A 1 unit increase in P leads to an 80 unit increase in Qs.
4. See the diagram below.

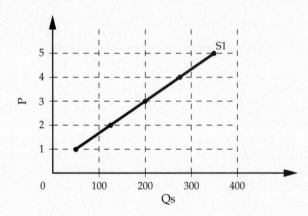

5. Slope = rise/run = 1/50. A 1 unit increase in P leads to a 50 unit increase in Qs.
6.

Price	1	2	3	4	5
Quantity supplied (Qs)	55	130	205	280	355

7. See the diagram below.

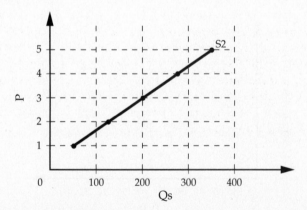

8. Slope = rise/run = 1/75. A 1 unit increase in P leads to a 75 unit increase in Qs.
9. $Qs = -20 + 75P = -20 + 75(8) = 580$.
10. $Qs = -20 + 75P = -20 + 75(20) = 1480$.

THE ECONOMIC PROBLEM: SCARCITY AND CHOICE

2

OBJECTIVES: POINT BY POINT

After completing this chapter, you should be able to accomplish the objectives listed below.

OBJECTIVE 1: Identify the three basic economic questions.

Economics studies the production and consumption choices that are made by society and the outcomes that occur. Solutions must be found to three "basic questions": *what* goods should be produced?; *how* should the goods be produced?; and *for whom* should the goods be produced? Every economy (consisting of firms, households, and the government sector) must transform its scarce natural, capital, and human resources into usable production. In a complex society the opportunity to cooperate and specialize offers great scope for increased production—but decisions must be made regarding the extent of cooperation, who specializes in what, and how goods are distributed. (page 28)

Opportunity Cost: Economics has to do with making choices when constraints (scarcity) are present. Constrained choice occurs, for example, when you go to the grocery store with only a $5 bill in your pocket—you have to make choices based on this limitation. Unconstrained choice would be if you were allowed to take as many groceries home as you wanted, free of charge. Sadly, though, we know there's "no such thing as a free lunch."

Practical examples of the consequences of choice and the costs of such choices include: present vs. future benefits (for example, do you study hard now so that, at exam time, reviewing is easier, or do you take it easy now and sweat it before the exam?), and capital vs. consumer production (for example, should we produce taxicabs or sports cars?).

> **TIP:** Everyone has been confronted with some version of the following scene: A favorite grandmother gives you a free choice from two or more items (ice cream sundaes, for example). From your viewpoint, is your chosen ice cream sundae free? Or is there an opportunity cost? If you have a range of sundaes from which to choose, what is the cost? The dollar amount of the chosen sundae? All the other sundaes you could have had? The opportunity cost is the next most favorite sundae.

PRACTICE

1. Which of the following statements about the operation of an economy is false? Each economy has a mechanism to determine
   A. what is produced.
   B. how to satisfy all of the desires of its citizens.
   C. how much is produced.
   D. how goods and services are distributed among its citizens.
   Answer: B. Because resources are limited, the economy cannot satisfy all the desires of its citizens.

OBJECTIVE 2: Explain what is meant by "comparative advantage" and relate this concept to the theory that individuals can gain from specialization and exchange.

A producer has a *comparative advantage* in the production of Good A if, compared with another producer, she can produce Good A at a lower opportunity cost.

The *theory of comparative advantage* provides the rationale for free trade. Given a two-country, two-good world, Ricardo showed that trading partners can benefit from specialization in the production of the good in which they have the comparative advantage. The increased production could be traded. In terms of the *production possibility frontier* (ppf) diagram, trade will be advantageous if the ppfs have differing slopes because differing slopes indicate differing costs.   (page 30)

> **TIP:** If you're like most individuals, you'll need several numerical examples to strengthen your grasp of comparative advantage. The Applications take you through all the steps included in the text.

Comparative advantage hinges on the concept of opportunity cost. The producer (person, firm, or country) with the lowest opportunity cost will hold the comparative advantage in that product. Don't be misled—it is irrelevant whether or not the producer can produce *more* of the good. The issue revolves around the relative opportunity costs.

PRACTICE

Use the following information to answer the next five questions. Arboc and Arbez are two economies that produce computer chips and VCRs. In Arboc, a one-unit increase in computer chips requires a four-unit decrease in VCR production. In Arbez, a one-unit increase in computer chips requires a three-unit decrease in VCR production. In each economy, costs remain constant.

2. Which of the following statements is false?
   A. In Arboc, the opportunity cost of 1 computer chip is 4 VCRs.
   B. In Arbez, the opportunity cost of 1 computer chip is 3 VCRs.
   C. The opportunity cost of 1 computer chip is greater in Arboc than in Arbez.
   D. An increase in the Arbocali production of computer chips requires a decrease in the Arbezani production of VCRs.
   Answer: D. An increase in the Arbocali production of computer chips requires a decrease in the *Arbocali* production of VCRs. In fact, both independent economies might choose to increase computer chip production.

3. Which of the following statements is true?
   A. In Arboc, the opportunity cost of 1 VCR is 4 computer chips.
   B. In Arbez, the opportunity cost of 1 VCR is 3 computer chips.
   C. The opportunity cost of 1 VCR is greater in Arbez than in Arboc.
   D. Arbez can produce more VCRs than Arboc can produce.
   Answer: C. We don't know whether Arbez has an absolute advantage in VCRs (Option D). The information tells us only about relative performance. Arbez, in fact, may be a very small country capable of producing only a few VCRs. In Arboc, the opportunity cost of a VCR is ¼ of a computer chip, and in Arbez, the opportunity cost of a VCR is ⅓ of a computer chip.

4. In _____, the opportunity cost of 1 computer chip is _____ VCRs, which is less than the opportunity cost of 1 computer chip in _____.
   A. Arboc, ¼, Arbez.
   B. Arboc, 4, Arbez.
   C. Arbez, 3, Arboc.
   D. Arbez, ⅓, Arboc.
   Answer: C. In Arboc, each computer chip "costs" 4 VCRs. In Arbez, each computer chip "costs" 3 VCRs. VCRs cost less in Arbez.

5. In _____, the opportunity cost of 1 VCR is _____ computer chips, which is less than the opportunity cost of 1 VCR in _____.
   A. Arboc, ¼, Arbez.
   B. Arboc, 4, Arbez.
   C. Arbez, 3, Arboc.
   D. Arbez, ⅓, Arboc.
   Answer: A. In Arboc, each VCR "costs" ¼ of a computer chip. In Arbez, each VCR "costs" ⅓ of a computer chip. VCRs cost less in Arbez.

6. According to the information above,
   A. Arboc has a comparative advantage in the production of both goods.
   B. Arboc has a comparative advantage in producing computer chips, and Arbez has a comparative advantage in producing VCRs.
   C. Arboc has a comparative advantage in producing VCRs, and Arbez has a comparative advantage in producing computer chips.
   D. Arbez has a comparative advantage in the production of both goods.
   Answer: C. Arboc has a comparative advantage in the production of VCRs (1 VCR costs ¼ of a computer chip), and Arbez has a comparative advantage in the production of computer chips (1 computer chip costs 3 VCRs). Note: No country can be relatively better at producing both goods!

OBJECTIVE 3: Explain why a production possibility frontier has a negative slope and why the slope depicts the concept of opportunity cost.

Choosing to employ resources for one use prevents them from being employed for other uses—there is an *opportunity cost* involved in the choice. The *production possibility frontier* portrays graphically the opportunity cost of transferring resources from one activity to another in a two-good environment. Assuming that all resources are fully employed, as more of Good A is produced, fewer resources are available to produce Good B.   (page 33)

> **Why Does the ppf Slope Downward?:** The production possibility frontier is the key piece of economic analysis in this chapter. It's always presented as having only two goods or bundles of goods. It slopes downward because "the more you get of one thing the less you get of the other." The more you study economics, the less time you have for other activities. The opportunity cost of an extra hour of studying economics is the value of an hour of other activities.

Graphing Pointer: When drawing a ppf, remember that the frontier extends from the vertical axis to the horizontal axis. It is a mistake to leave the frontier unconnected to the axes. If the frontier is not connected, it implies that an infinitely large quantity of either good could be produced, which is exactly the opposite message that the ppf is intended to give.

Graphing Pointer: Don't be concerned with which goods should be placed on the vertical axis and which goods should be placed on the horizontal axis. Regardless of the placement, scarce resources dictate that the slope of the ppf is negative. This is a case (one of many) where the geometry (a negative slope) is directly linked to economic theory (scarce resources). Recognizing these linkages helps graphical understanding.

Graphing Pointer: The slope of the ppf is the geometric representation of the opportunity costs of transferring resources from one activity to another activity. Due to scarcity, additional time spent studying results in less time for other activities. If you place study time on the horizontal (X) axis and "all other activities" time on the vertical (Y) axis, the graphical analysis of the cost of one hour of studying (the loss of other activities due to extra studying) is the change in Y divided by the change in X. The slope of a curve can be measured by the "rise" over the "run".

PRACTICE

7. Along the production possibility frontier, trade-offs exist because
    A. buyers will want to buy less when price goes up, but producers will want to sell more.
    B. not all production levels are efficient.
    C. at some levels, unemployment or inefficiency exists.
    D. the economy has only a limited quantity of resources to allocate between competing uses.

    Answer: D. Along the ppf, resources are fully and efficiently employed. However, since resources are scarce, an increase in the production of Good A requires that resources be taken from the production of Good B.

OBJECTIVE 4: Interpret what is depicted by a production possibility frontier.

The ppf shows all the combinations of Good A and Good B that can be produced when all resources are employed efficiently. Points inside the ppf represent unemployment and/or inefficiency while points outside are currently unattainable. An outward movement of the ppf represents growth. Growth occurs if more resources become available or if existing resources become more productive (e.g., through better education, more efficient techniques of production, or technological innovations).   (page 34)

Production and Economic Efficiency: The thought of a great volume of production, with all resources employed, is an attractive one. For this reason, it's often difficult to understand that, in serving the needs of consumers, producing the right goods is more important than mere quantity. This distinction lies at the heart of most confusion about productive and economic efficiency. Having the Eskimo economy fully employed and producing refrigerators may help you see the point. It would be "better" (more efficient) for the Eskimos to have some unemployment but be producing warm clothing. Turning out the refrigerators is productively efficient, while making the warm clothing is economically efficient. Ideally, you'd want to be on the ppf (being productively efficient) and producing the economically efficient mix of output.

> **TIP:** Think of the ppf as a way to depict opportunity cost and constrained choice. In general, you want to be somewhere on the curve because any production combination inside the curve means that you're losing production, which is inefficient. Production on the curve means that resources are being used to the maximum (no unemployment). The inefficiency of a mismatch between an "efficient" production mix and society's needs is easily explained-just because we're producing "on the line" doesn't mean we're meeting society's needs as effectively as possible. Employing all our resources to produce taxicabs, for example, is unlikely to be desirable!

> **Graphing Pointer:** Suppose we are on the ppf and, at one point, can produce 16 cars and 5 pickups while, at another point, we can produce 12 cars and 7 pickups. Note that the opportunity cost is calculated by looking at the *change* in production levels—2 extra trucks cost 4 cars.

> **Graphing Pointer:** Reducing unemployment does not shift the ppf. Remember the underlying assumptions! The ppf is drawn *given* a set of resources (whether or not the resources are being used). Unemployment represents a situation where the resources are not fully utilized. If unemployment is reduced, the economy moves closer to the ppf.

PRACTICE

8. Which of the following is not an assumption underlying the ppf?
   A. Technological knowledge is fixed.
   B. Resources are fully employed.
   C. Resources are efficiently employed.
   D. The quantity of labor resources is variable.
   Answer: D. When drawing a ppf, the quantity of all resources is assumed to be fixed.

9. The production possibility frontier represents
   A. the maximum amount of goods and services that can be produced with a given quantity of resources and technology.
   B. those combinations of goods and services that will be demanded as price changes.
   C. the maximum amount of resources that are available as the wage level changes.
   D. those combinations of goods and services that will be produced as the price level changes.
   Answer: A. The production possibility frontier represents what it is "possible to produce" given the available resources and technology.

10. The Arbezani economy is operating at a point inside its ppf. This may be because:
   A. the economy has very poor technological know-how.
   B. Arbez is a very small nation and can't produce much.
   C. poor management practices have led to an inefficient use of resources.
   D. Arbez has only a small resource base.
   Answer: C. Very poor technological know-how or a small resource base will result in a ppf that is close to the origin. Fully and efficiently employed resources would still be on the ppf.

OBJECTIVE 5: Explain why increasing opportunity costs occur and how this relates to the production possibility frontier diagram.

Increasing opportunity costs are present when the production possibility frontier bulges outwards from the origin. Increasing costs occur if resources are not equally well suited to the production of Good A and Good B.   (page 36)

> **TIP:** Why is the ppf bowed-out? The geometry of the ppf flows from its economics. A bowed-out production possibility frontier indicates that the opportunity cost is increasing as resources become more heavily allocated to the production of one good. The ppf has that bowed-out shape because of the lack of adaptability of resources to different uses. A farmer wishing to produce dairy products, for example, will select the most suited resources first, and production will increase sharply. Further increases will be less easy to achieve and more expensive in terms of lost production of other goods as resources more suited to other endeavors are pressed into dairy service.

> **Graphing Pointer:** Productive resources have different abilities, so the opportunity cost of re-allocating the resources are different and the ppf is bowed outward (concave with respect to the origin). If resources are identical in their productive abilities, the opportunity cost of re-allocation would be constant and the ppf would be a straight line (a constant slope).

PRACTICE

11. There are increasing costs in the economy of Arbez. To portray this fact in a production possibility diagram we should
    A. move the ppf outwards (up and to the right).
    B. draw the ppf bulging outwards.
    C. shift the ppf's endpoint on the horizontal axis to the right.
    D. shift the ppf's endpoint on the vertical axis upwards.
    Answer: B. The slope of the ppf represents the behavior of opportunity cost as production level changes. A straight ppf represents constant costs. To show increasing costs the ppf is bowed outwards from the origin.

OBJECTIVE 6: Identify ways in which economic growth may occur.

Economic growth may occur if an economy increases the quantity or quality of its resources-the production possibility frontier shifts outward. Additionally, technological change and innovation can increase productivity.   (page 37)

Investment and Capital: "Investment" and "capital" are two terms that have very specific meanings in economics. Beware! Investing doesn't just mean buying something. To an economist, investing means only the creation of capital. What, then, is capital? Capital refers to man-made resources usable in production. A hammer is capital; a share of GM stock is not. A nail is capital; a dollar bill is not. Buying a hammer or nail is capital investment; buying GM stock is not!

If this capital/non-capital distinction is giving you problems, ask yourself if the purchase of the item in question increases the economy's ability to produce. If it does, it's an investment in capital.

OBJECTIVE 7: Identify and distinguish how the two "pure" types of economic system differ in their solutions to the three basic questions. State the "mistakes" to which an unregulated market system is prone.

The two "pure" types of economic system are the command economy and the *laissez-faire* economy. A *command (planned) economy* has a central agency that coordinates production and finds answers for the three basic questions. In a *laissez-faire (market) economy*, the three basic questions are answered through the operation of individual buyers and sellers following their own self-interest in markets.

All economies, in fact, are driven by a mixture of market forces and government intervention and regulation. Government intervention is felt to be necessary to correct *laissez-faire* "mistakes" such as an excessive inequality in the distribution of income, inadequate provision of public goods, and periodic spells of unemployment or inflation.   (page 41)

PRACTICE

12. Advocates comparing the performance of a pure *laissez-faire* system with that of a command economy would claim that a pure *laissez-faire* system would do all of the following except
    A. promote efficiency.
    B. stimulate innovation.
    C. achieve an equal income distribution.
    D. be directed by the decisions of individual buyers and sellers.
    Answer: C. A pure *laissez-faire* system, which rewards those who contribute most, would have an unequal income distribution.

PRACTICE TEST

I. MULTIPLE CHOICE QUESTIONS.

Select the option that provides the single best answer.

_____ 1. Since the nation of Arboc is operating at a point inside its ppf, it
    A. has full employment.
    B. has unemployed or inefficiently employed resources.
    C. must cut output of one good to increase production of another.
    D. will be unable to experience economic growth.

_____ 2. Arboc commits more of its resources to capital production than does Arbez. _____ should experience a(n) _____ rapid rate of economic growth.
    A. Arboc, more.
    B. Arbez, more.
    C. Arboc, less.
    D. Both, equally.

_____ 3. Which of the following does not count as a productive resource?
    A. Capital resources, such as a tractor.
    B. Natural resources, such as a piece of farmland.
    C. Financial resources, such as a twenty-dollar bill.
    D. Human resources, such as a hairdresser.

Use the following diagram to answer the next four questions.

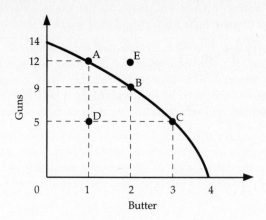

4. Point E might become attainable if this economy
   A. becomes more efficient.
   B. reduces wages.
   C. improves the quality of its workforce.
   D. encourages emigration.

5. A movement from A to B and then to C indicates that
   A. the cost of additional butter is decreasing.
   B. the cost of additional guns is increasing.
   C. the economy is becoming more efficient.
   D. the cost of additional butter is increasing.

6. To move from D to A indicates that
   A. the opportunity cost would be zero.
   B. some butter would have to be given up.
   C. there would have to be an increase in the quantity of resources.
   D. the opportunity cost would be 7.

7. The opportunity cost of producing another unit of butter is
   A. higher at B than at C.
   B. lower at D than at C.
   C. higher at A than at B.
   D. equal at D and at C.

8. A production possibility frontier illustrates all of the following concepts except
   A. scarcity.
   B. unlimited wants.
   C. opportunity cost.
   D. constrained choice.

9. Of the following, the least serious problem for *laissez-faire* economies is
   A. unemployment.
   B. income inequality.
   C. provision of public goods.
   D. satisfaction of consumer sovereignty.

Use the following production possibility table to answer the next three questions. Suppose that wheat is on the Y-axis.

Alternative	A	B	C	D	E	F
Wheat	0	1	2	3	4	5
Tobacco	15	14	12	9	5	0

_____ 10. The opportunity cost of a unit of wheat as the economy moves from C to D is
   A. −3 units of tobacco.
   B. 3 units of tobacco.
   C. −⅓ unit of tobacco.
   D. ⅓ unit of tobacco.

_____ 11. The opportunity cost of a unit of tobacco as the economy moves from C to B is
   A. 2 units of wheat.
   B. −2 units of wheat.
   C. ½ unit of wheat.
   D. −½ unit of wheat.

_____ 12. An output of 3 units of wheat and 7 units of tobacco indicates that
   A. this economy has poor technology.
   B. resources are being used inefficiently.
   C. tobacco is preferred to wheat.
   D. it is not possible for this economy to produce at a point on the production possibility frontier.

_____ 13. Which of the following is most likely to shift the production possibility frontier outward?
   A. A sudden expansion in the labor force.
   B. An increase in stock prices.
   C. A shift of productive resources from capital goods to consumer goods.
   D. A general increase in the public's demand for goods.

_____ 14. Which of the following is _least_ likely to be a public good?
   A. Medical treatment for cancer patients.
   B. The National Park system.
   C. The police force.
   D. National defense.

_____ 15. Private markets work best when
   A. they are competitive.
   B. they are regulated by a government agency.
   C. a monopolist is present.
   D. public goods are demanded.

_____ 16. The opportunity cost along an increasing-cost ppf must be
   A. positive and increasing.
   B. positive and decreasing.
   C. negative and increasing.
   D. negative and decreasing.

_____ 17. For Jill to have a comparative advantage in the production of pins means that, relative to Jack, with the same resources
   A. Jill is relatively better at producing pins than at producing needles.
   B. Jill is relatively better at producing both pins and needles.
   C. Jill can produce fewer needles than Jack can produce.
   D. Jill can produce more pins than Jack can produce.

_____ 18. Each of the following is a basic concern of any economic system except
   A. the allocation of scarce resources among producers.
   B. the mix of different types of output.
   C. the distribution of output among consumers.
   D. the quality of resources allocated among consumers.

The table below shows the maximum output of each good in each country, e.g. maximum Arbezani production of goat milk is 3 units.

	Arboc	Arbez
Goat Milk	3	6
Bananas	5	2

_____ 19. According to the table above,
A. Arbez has a comparative advantage in producing both goods.
B. Arbez has a comparative advantage in the production of bananas, and Arboc has a comparative advantage in the production of goat milk.
C. Arbez has a comparative advantage in the production of goat milk, and Arboc has a comparative advantage in the production of bananas.
D. Arboc has a comparative advantage in the production of both goods.

_____ 20. The nation of Regit has a bowed-out production possibility frontier with potatoes on the vertical axis and steel on the horizontal axis. A movement down along the ppf will incur _____ costs; a movement up along the ppf will incur _____ costs.
A. increasing, increasing.
B. increasing, decreasing.
C. decreasing, increasing.
D. decreasing, decreasing.

II. APPLICATION QUESTIONS.

1. Farmer Brown has four fields that can produce corn or tobacco. Assume that the trade-off between corn and tobacco within each field is constant. The maximum yields are given in this table:

Field	A	B	C	D
Corn	40	30	20	10
Tobacco	10	20	30	40

a. Draw Farmer Brown's ppf.
b. To be on the ppf, what conditions must hold true?
c. Brown is currently producing only corn: If he wants to produce some tobacco, in what order would he switch his fields from corn to tobacco production?
d. Explain your answer to c.

2. Two countries, Arboc and Arbez, produce wine and cheese, and each has constant costs of production. The maximum amounts of the two goods for each country is given in the table below.

Arboc	Arbez	Goods
40	120	wine
20	30	cheese

a. Draw the production possibility frontier for each country.

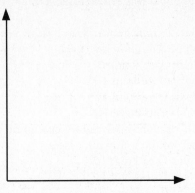

b. Calculate the opportunity cost of wine in Arboc and in Arbez.
c. In which country, then, is wine production cheaper?
d. Answer questions b. and c. for cheese production—remember that the opportunity costs are reciprocals of one another.

Note that Arbez has an advantage in both goods in terms of total production, but a comparative advantage only in wine production.

Now assume that Arboc becomes more efficient and can double its output of both wine and cheese.

e. Graph the new ppf on the diagram above.
f. Which good should Arboc now produce?

Suppose, instead, that Arbez has a specific technological advance that permits it to increase cheese production to a maximum of 90.

g. Now which nation should produce wine?

3. In a national contest, the first prize is a town. The winner receives a furnished house, a general store and gasoline station, a pick-up truck, and 100 acres of land. The store comes fully stocked with everything you might find in a country general store. The town is located 100 miles from a small city. It is the shopping center for about a thousand families who live in the countryside. In addition, the road through the town is fairly well traveled. Suppose you win the contest and decide to try running the town as a business for at least a year.
a. Describe the resources available to the economy of your town. What is the potential labor force? What are the natural resources?
b. Describe the capital stock of your town.
c. List some of the factors that are beyond your control that will affect your income.
d. List some of the decisions you must make that could affect your income, and explain what their effects might be.
e. At the end of the year, you must decide whether to stay or go back to college. How will you decide? What factors will you weigh in making your decision? What role do your expectations play?

4. The following data give the production possibilities of an economy that produces two types of goods, guns (horizontal axis) and butter (vertical axis).

PRODUCTION POSSIBILITIES	GUNS	BUTTER
A	0	105
B	10	100
C	20	90
D	30	75
E	40	55
F	50	30
G	60	0

a. Graph the production possibilities frontier.
b. Explain why Point D is efficient while Point H (30 guns and 45 units of butter) is not.
c. Calculate the per-unit opportunity cost of an increase in the production of guns in each of the following cases.
   i. From Point A to Point B?
   ii. From Point B to Point C?
   iii. From Point E to Point F?
   iv. From Point F to Point G?
d. Calculate the per-unit opportunity cost of an increase in the production of butter in each of the following cases.
   i. From Point G to Point F?
   ii. From Point D to Point C?
   iii. From Point C to Point B?
   iv. From Point B to Point A?
e. Using the production possibility frontier concept, explain what will happen if this nation declares war on one of its neighbors.

5. Draw a production possibilities frontier with farm goods (x-axis) and manufacturing goods (y-axis) on the axes. In each of the following cases, explain what will happen to the production possibilities frontier.

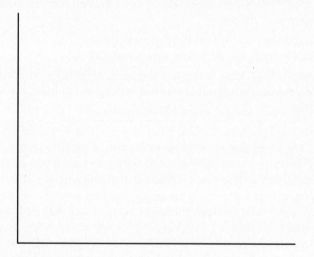

a. There is an increase in the unemployment rate.
b. There is an improvement in farming techniques.
c. There is a decrease in quantity of physical capital.
d. The productivity of workers doubles.
e. The government requires farmers to slaughter a portion of their dairy herds.

6. Consider the following ppf diagram.

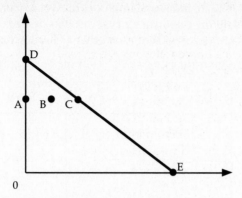

a. Which point is "best?" and which is "worst?"
b. Now suppose that you're told that the axes measure food (horizontal) and moonshine whisky (vertical). Would your answer be different?
c. Point B may be preferable to Point D, although Point B in terms of production Point B is less efficient. Why might it be preferable?

7. The nation of Arbez can produce two goods, corn and steel. The table shows some points on the Arbezani ppf.

Alternative	A	B	C	D	E	F
Corn	0	1	2	3	4	5
Steel	20	16	12	8	4	0

a. Draw the ppf in the space below.

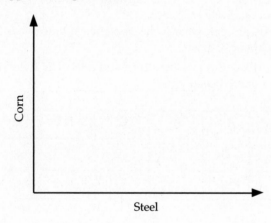

b. Moving from Alternative A to B, B to C, and so on, calculate the opportunity cost of each additional unit of corn. Going from F to E, E to D, and so on, calculate the opportunity cost *per unit* of steel. Confirm that the pairs of values are reciprocals of each other. (This must always be true.)

Opportunity Cost of 1 Unit of:

Alternative	Corn	Steel
A–B		
B–C		
C–D		
D–E		
E–F		

c. Consider each of the following situations.

Situation X: Arbez is producing 4 units of corn and no steel. What is the opportunity cost of 1 extra unit of corn and 1 extra unit of steel?

Situation Y: Arbez is producing 4 units of corn and 4 units of steel. What is the opportunity cost of 1 extra unit of corn and 1 extra unit of steel?

d. Why do you find a different set of answers in Situation X and Situation Y?

e. Now consider a new situation, Situation Z: Arbez is producing 3 units of corn and 5 units of steel. What is the opportunity cost of 1 extra unit of corn and 1 extra unit of steel?

f. Which Situation (X, Y, or Z) is the most productively efficient and which the least productively efficient?

g. On the Arbezani ppf, what is the cost of each unit of corn and what is the cost of each unit of steel?

The nation of Arboc also produces corn and steel. The following table shows some points on the Arbocali ppf.

Alternative	A	B	C	D	E	F
Corn	0	1	2	3	4	5
Steel	20	16	12	8	4	0

h. On the Arbocali ppf, what is the cost of each unit of corn and what is the cost of each unit of steel?

i. Point to ponder: Because steel is relatively cheaper to produce in Arboc/Arbez and corn is relatively cheaper to produce in Arboc/Arbez, might mutually beneficial trade be possible?

8. Refer to the following diagram.

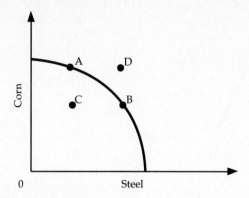

a. Which point is unattainable?
b. To achieve this currently unattainable production combination, what must happen (two possible answers)?
c. Which point represents unemployment or inefficiency?
d. Will a movement from B to A will increase corn production or steel production?
e. What is the opportunity cost of moving from C to B?

9. Draw the axes of a ppf. Use corn (on the vertical axis) and steel (on the horizontal axis) as the two goods.

Choose a point, A, that represents some corn and some steel production. Suppose that this point is on the ppf—it's a maximum point. Split the diagram up into quarters, with Point A in the center.

a. Is a production mix to the south-west possible?
b. Would such a mix be productively efficient?
c. Would such a mix be economically efficient?
d. Is a move to the north-east quadrant possible? What do you know about it?

Only the north-west and south-east quadrants are possible locations in which productively efficient output alternatives can occur.

e. What would happen if the present level of corn production (at Point A) was reduced?

If steel production does not change, unemployment occurs. The unemployed resources can be absorbed by the steel industry and more steel can be produced. A parallel case can be made given cutbacks in steel production. Can you see how the ppf *must* have a negative slope and that it portrays the concept of opportunity cost?

10. Use the diagrams below to answer this question.

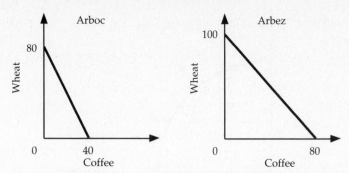

a. What is the opportunity cost of one unit of coffee in Arboc?
b. What is the opportunity cost of one unit of coffee in Arbez?
c. Which country has a comparative advantage in the production of coffee?
d. What is the opportunity cost of one unit of wheat in Arboc?
e. What is the opportunity cost of one unit of wheat in Arbez?
f. Which country has a comparative advantage in the production of wheat?
g. *Ceteris paribus*, ignoring other issues, which good should Arboc produce and which good should Arbez produce?

11. Draw a production possibility curve. Put guns on the vertical axis and butter on the horizontal axis. Suppose that the technology for producing butter improves but the technology for producing guns does not. Describe how your diagram would change. In general, how will this technological advance affect the opportunity cost of producing guns?

12. Jennie has set 10 hours this weekend to study for an Economics test and a Physics test. She believes that, with no studying at all, she would score 40 points on each test. Suppose that for each hour studying Econ. she can raise her Econ. score by 10 points, and that for each hour studying Physics she can raise her Physics score by 5 points.

a. Draw a production possibility frontier graph and show all the points that are feasible if Jennie has 10 hours to divide between Econ. and Physics. Put "hours of study for Econ." on the vertical axis and "hours of study for Physics" on the horizontal axis.

b. Show Point A, where Jennie studies Econ. for 5 hours and Physics for 5 hours.

c. Show Point B, where Jennie studies Econ. for 0 hours and Physics for 10 hours.

d. True or false? Jennie can score 60 on the Econ. test and 80 on the Physics test.

e. True or false? Jennie is lying when tells us that, in fact, she scored 80 on both tests.

f. Jennie decides to spend 4 hours studying for the Econ. test. What's the highest score she can expect to get on the Physics test?

g. If Jennie was satisfied with 60 on both tests, how many hours would she have had to study?

h. True or false? If Jennie scored 70 on both tests we know that she did not study for the full 10 hours.

i. Draw a line (labeled EE) showing all the points which have exactly 2 hours of study time for the Econ. test.

ANSWERS AND SOLUTIONS

PRACTICE TEST

I. SOLUTIONS TO MULTIPLE CHOICE QUESTIONS

1. B. To be on the ppf, Arboc must have all of its resources fully and efficiently employed. Since it is operating inside the ppf, at least one of these conditions must have been violated.

2. A. If Arboc produces relatively more capital, then it is expanding its resource base more rapidly and, *ceteris paribus*, it will grow more rapidly.

3. C. Financial resources may be used to purchase real productive resources but are not themselves productive. Note that, to an economist, "investment" is the creation of real productive capacity, not merely the purchase of stock in a company.

4. C. To reach Point E the economy must grow, shifting out its ppf. This could occur if the labor force became more efficient.

5. D. This is an increasing cost ppf. As we increase the production of one good (butter), the cost in terms of the other good increases. In this case, a one-unit increase in butter (A to B) costs 3 guns; the move from B to C costs more (4 guns).

6. A. Opportunity cost is defined (loosely) as the quantity of Good B given up to increase production of Good A. The quantity of butter remains at 1 unit while gun production is increased.

7. B. See the answer to Question 6. Opportunity cost of one unit of butter is zero at Point D. The opportunity cost of one unit of butter at Point C is 5 guns.

8. B. The ppf depicts what it is possible to produce but nothing about what is wanted.

9. D. *Laissez-faire* economies respond well to the needs of private consumers, in general. One exception worth noting is the provision of public goods.

10. B. The opportunity cost is positive. A one-unit increase in wheat results in a three-unit decrease in tobacco production.

11. C. A two-unit increase in tobacco results in a one-unit decrease in wheat.

12. B. This point is inside the ppf. (We could be producing two more units of tobacco with the same amount of wheat production, for example.) This indicates that our resources are unemployed and/or inefficiently employed.

13. A. The labor-force expansion represents an increase in productive resources. Note that the ppf depicts what can be supplied—demand is not reflected in the diagram.

14. A. Parks, police, and defense, which become available to all once they become available, do not lend themselves to private sale and purchase as readily as cancer treatment. The benefits of treatment can be retained exclusively by the purchaser.

15. A. A general theme in economics is that private competition is highly efficient in providing most goods.

16. A. Opportunity cost is *always* negative. With a curving ppf, the cost of producing one good in terms of the other accelerates as production level increases.

17. A. Comparative advantage is a relative concept. If, relative to Jack, Jill is better at producing pins, then she has a comparative advantage in this.

18. D. The first three answers are statements of the three "basic" questions. In any case, resources are allocated among producers, not consumers.

19. B. The cost of one unit of goat milk in Arbez is 1 and ⅔ unit of bananas while the cost of one unit of goat milk in Arboc is ⅓ unit of bananas. Arboc has the advantage here. One unit of bananas in Arbez costs ⅗ unit of goat milk while one unit of bananas in Arboc costs 3 units of goat milk. Arbez has the advantage in bananas.

20. A. A bowed-out ppf indicates increasing costs; the costs increase whether the movement is down along the ppf or up along the ppf.

II. SOLUTIONS TO APPLICATION QUESTIONS

1. a. Your ppf should include the following points:

| Corn | 100 | 90 | 70 | 40 | 0 |
| Tobacco | 0 | 40 | 70 | 90 | 100 |

There will be a straight line between each of the points.

b. Resources fully employed, and employed in the more efficient activity. For example, Field A may be producing its maximum output of tobacco, but (since the opportunity cost of tobacco production in that field is high) it should be used to produce tobacco only after the other fields have been switched over to tobacco production. If it is switched before Field B, for instance, Brown will be producing inefficiently and inside his ppf.

c. D, C, B, A.

d. See the explanation for b.

2. a, e. See the diagrams below.

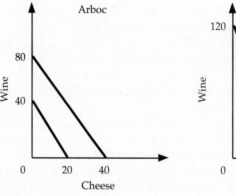
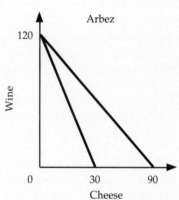

b. 1 wine = ½ cheese, 1 wine = ¼ cheese.

c. Arbez.

d. 1 cheese = 2 wine (Arboc), 1 cheese = 4 wine (Arbez). Arboc can produce cheese more cheaply than Arbez can.

f. Arboc should still produce cheese since the comparative costs have not changed.

g. Arboc. Recompute the opportunity costs. Note that the relative steepness of the ppfs has changed.

3. a–b. This question is intended to get you to think about all of the decisions that must be made in an economic system. The owner has land, labor, and capital at his/her disposal. The capital stock includes the store, the gas station, inventories, trucks, the house, and so forth. The road is also capital even though it was produced by the government. We are not told much about the natural resources of the town. These would include the fertility of the land. The potential labor force includes some fraction of those who live nearby.

    c. The people who travel the road, the general economic circumstances of the people who live nearby, the weather, gasoline prices, the potential for competition from other stores, and so forth.

    d. What to sell, whether to advertise, what prices to change, whether to fix up the town, how many people to hire, and so forth.

    e. I will add up all the future income I will earn, net of costs. I must consider all the alternatives and my expectations about them. How much will I earn here? How much will college cost? What am I likely to earn when I have graduated from college? I also need to consider carefully the personal pleasure I will derive from the two situations.

4. a. See the diagram below.

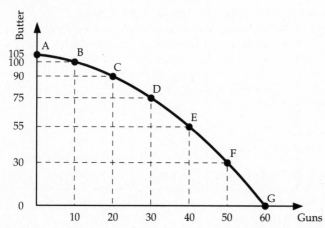

    b. Point D is on the ppf, indicating full employment of resources while Point H is inside the curve, indicating underproduction and an underutilization of scarce resources.

    c. i.   ½ unit of butter.
        ii. 1 unit of butter.
        iii. 2½ units of butter.
        iv. 3 units of butter.

    d. i.   ⅓ of a gun.
        ii. ⅔ of a gun.
        iii. 1 gun.
        iv. 2 guns.

    e. The ppf will not shift position! We would expect the balance of production to shift in favor of guns. If unemployment exists, indicated by a bundle of goods inside the ppf, war production will shift the economy towards the ppf.

5. a. No change in the position of the ppf.
    b. The end of the ppf on the x-axis will shift out. The end on the y-axis will not move.
    c. The ppf would shift inwards.
    d. The ppf would shift outwards.
    e. The end of the ppf on the x-axis will shift in. The end on the y-axis will not move.

6. a. You might think C and A are "best" and "worst," respectively—but the question is a trap! What do we mean by "best"? Perhaps a particular point inside the ppf is better than a particular point on it. There's not enough information to give a complete answer.

    b. Clearly, all points on the ppf are not created equal, and Point E might be the "best" choice of those depicted.

    c. The "best" output mix depends on what best meets society's wants. If you think about it, what society *wants* isn't shown on a ppf diagram—only what can be *produced*.

7. a. See the diagram below.

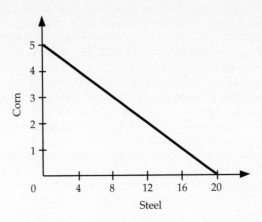

b.

	Production	Opportunity Cost of 1 Unit of:	
Alternative	*Corn*	*Steel*	
A–B	4 steel	¼ corn	
B–C	4 steel	¼ corn	
C–D	4 steel	¼ corn	
D–E	4 steel	¼ corn	
E–F	4 steel	¼ corn	

c. Situation X: 0 steel; 0 corn.
    Situation Y: 4 steel; ¼ corn.
d. In Situation X there are still some unemployed (inefficiently used) resources.
    In Situation Y, Arbez is already utilizing all of its resources, and a trade-off
    is necessary. (Plot the points on the diagram to see the difference.)
e. Situation Z: 1 steel; 0 corn.
f. Situation Y is the most productively efficient. Either X or Z is the least
    productively efficient—we don't have enough information.
g. Each unit of corn costs 4 units of steel; each unit of steel costs ¼ unit of corn.
h. Each unit of corn costs 2 units of steel. Each unit of steel costs ½ unit of corn.
i. Arbez; Arboc. Yes, trade can be mutually beneficial.

8. a. D.
    b. The economy must either grow (more resources) or experience a technological
        improvement.
    c. C.
    d. Corn.
    e. There is no opportunity cost; more steel is produced without any reduction in
        corn production. Note that there are "free lunches" if the economy is operating
        at an inefficient point.

9. a. Yes.
    b. No, because it is possible to produce more of each good. Also some resources are
        unemployed.
    c. No, not relative to Point A, where consumers would have more of each good
        available to them.
    d. It is beyond the maximum level of production, given current resources and
        technology.
    e. Resources would be released and transferred to steel production.

10. a. 2 units of wheat.
    b. 1¼ units of wheat.
    c. Arbez.
    d. ½ unit of coffee.
    e. ⁹⁄₁₀ unit of coffee.
    f. Arboc.
    g. Arboc should specialize in wheat production and Arboc should specialize in coffee production.

11. The ppf would pivot at its "guns" endpoint and become flatter, which indicates that it is possible to produce a greater maximum quantity of butter than before, while still producing the same maximum quantity of guns. The slope of the ppf represents opportunity cost. Producing only guns means that we surrender a larger quantity of butter than before—the opportunity cost of guns has increased (and the opportunity cost of butter has decreased).

12. a. See the diagram below.

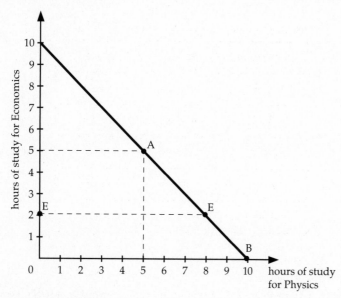

    b. See the diagram above.
    c. See the diagram above.
    d. True. Economics: 40 + (10 × 2) = 60. Physics: 40 + (5 × 8) = 80.
    e. True. Economics: 40 + (10 × 2) = 60. Physics: 40 + (5 × 8) = 80. If she gets 80 on the Physics test, 60 is the maximum she can get on the Economics test.
    f. She has 6 hours for Physics. Physics: 40 + (5 × 6) = 70.
    g. Economics: 40 + (10 × 2) = 60. Physics: 40 + (5 × 4) = 60. This totals 6 hours.
    h. True. Economics: 40 + (10 × 3) = 70. Physics: 40 + (5 × 6) = 70. This totals 9 hours.
    i. See the diagram above.

THE STRUCTURE OF THE U.S. ECONOMY: THE PRIVATE, PUBLIC, AND INTERNATIONAL

3

OBJECTIVES: POINT BY POINT

After completing this chapter, you should be able to accomplish the objectives listed below.

General Comment

This chapter contains a lot of facts and numbers. Try to look past these to the broader issues. The topics that carry over most powerfully to later chapters are those dealing with the organization of industry—the four different "types"—and the major elements of government spending and tax collections. It will help if you split the chapter into its two main parts (pp. 53–57, pp. 59–66) and read each separately.

OBJECTIVE 1: Outline the private/public sector distinction in the U.S. economy. Indicate the elements each sector contains.

The *private sector* contains all decision-making units not owned by the government. These decision-making units in the private sector include households, nonprofit organizations, and firms. The *public sector* is comprised of federal, state, and local government.

The key private/public sector distinction is that decisions in the private sector are subject to independent choice and that resources are owned privately.   (page 49)

PRACTICE

1. The private sector would include each of the following except
    A. Lockheed.
    B. Boy Scouts.
    C. NASA.
    D. Nationsbank.
    Answer: C. Although it supplies military hardware to the government, Lockheed is a private corporation. NASA, on the other hand, is funded and run by the government.

2. The public sector would include each of the following organizations except
    A. the United Way, a charitable organization.
    B. the U.S. Air Force.
    C. the office staff of your local Senator.
    D. the District Court in your county.
    Answer: A. The United Way is a private nonprofit organization.

OBJECTIVE 2: List, and distinguish among, the three different legal categories of profit-making firms.

Sole proprietors have the disadvantage of unlimited liability—their personal assets, outside the firm, might be taken if their company runs up sufficiently high debts. Advantage: The sole proprietor is his or her own boss and free to follow his or her business instincts. Also, s/he keeps all of the profits s/he makes. Usually, *partnerships* have the same unlimited liability drawback. Indeed, perhaps it's worse—partners may be held responsible not only for their debts, but also those of their partners! Advantage: greater expertise and financial resources. *Corporations* have the advantage of limited liability because they exist as separate legal entities—XYZ, Inc. can be taken to court. If the firm runs up debts, the owners' maximum liability is the value of their stock investment. After-tax profits may be distributed as dividends or held by the company as retained earnings. A major disadvantage is that the corporation's management structure may become cumbersome. Also, owners of corporations are subject to double taxation. (page 50)

PRACTICE

3. The most common form of business organization is
   A. the proprietorship.
   B. the partnership.
   C. perfect competition.
   D. the corporation.
   Answer: A. Perfect competition is not a form of business organization—it is a market structure. Check the textbook for the distinction. In 1990, 73.7% of firms were proprietorships. See Table 3.1.

4. In terms of total sales, the most important form of business organization is
   A. the proprietorship.
   B. the partnership.
   C. monopoly.
   D. the corporation.
   Answer: D. Monopoly is not a form of business organization—it is a market structure. Check the textbook for the distinction. In 1990, 89.6% of total sales were accounted for by corporations. See Table 3.1.

5. The Cumfy Chair Corporation has a net income of $300,000 in 1996. Of this income, $160,000 is paid in taxes and $40,000 is retained to buy capital. The Cumfy Chair Corporation will pay dividends of
   A. $140,000.
   B. $120,000.
   C. $100,000.
   D. more than $100,000 but less than $140,000.
   Answer: C. Net income—the profits of a corporation—may be split up into corporate income tax payments, dividends, and retained earnings.

OBJECTIVE 3: Identify and distinguish among the four forms of market organization (structure).

Firms are organized along industry lines. Industries, which can be defined broadly or more narrowly, produce similar products. They can be classified as:
   a. perfectly competitive
   b. monopolistically competitive
   c. oligopolistic, or
   d. monopolistic.

In perfect competition, firms sell identical products and each is an insignificant player in the market. As a result no perfectly competitive firm can control the price it receives. However, the monopoly can—it is the industry supplier. The monopolistically competitive firm can, too—to the extent that it sells a differentiated product. The oligopolist can—the firm is a major market player, and its product may be differentiated, too. (page 53)

TIP: Bring to mind a clear example of each of the four forms of market organization.

Perfect competition—the usual example is agricultural products, but the stock market and the large numbers of typists and word processors around your college campus who produce resumes and term papers are good examples, too.

Monopolistic competition—local radio stations, restaurants, shoe stores, and hairdressers are all "classic" examples of this category.

Oligopoly—the oil industry, the car industry.

Monopoly—the local electric company or water utility. If you don't buy electricity or water from them, you pretty much do without. (Most full-blown monopolies are closely controlled by the government and may be run by the state.) Cable TV is a private-sector example but, again, note that it is supervised by the government. Note, too, the definition of an "industry" (cable TV) is quite narrow.

TIP: Note that a "firm" is any unit engaged in production; it doesn't have to be a formal organization with special premises. A street entertainer (who produces "entertainment") is a firm.

TIP: Study carefully Figure 3.1, which compares the characteristics of the four types of industry organization—Case and Fair devote seven chapters in the microeconomics section of the textbook to the distinctions summarized in this table! The concepts of perfect competition and monopoly frequently crop up in macroeconomics courses, too.

TIP: The concept of an industry is a little fuzzy. We can talk about the electronics industry and the entertainment industry in general but we may wish to be more specific. Is there a Michael Jordan "industry," for example? Is there an alcohol "industry," or is it more sensible to split this up into the hard liquor, wine, and beer industries? You might be able to make a case for the view that the "light" beers represent a special market of their own and that nonalcoholic beers are another separate entity. Clearly, the concept of an industry (or market) is flexible.

PRACTICE

6. Each of the following is true for perfect competition except that
   A. there are many firms.
   B. new firms are excluded.
   C. firms market virtually identical products.
   D. individually, firms have no control over the market price.
   Answer: B. In perfect competition there are no *barriers to entry* into the industry, so new firms cannot be excluded.

7. Each of the firms in Industry A sells a slightly differentiated product. A seller wishing to enter this industry would find it easy to do so. This industry is
   A. perfectly competitive.
   B. monopolistically competitive.
   C. oligopolistic.
   D. monopolistic.
   Answer: B. This industry is not a monopoly since there is more than one firm. It is not an oligopoly since entry is easy. It is not perfectly competitive since there is some product differentiation.

8. Each of the following is true for monopoly except that
   A. there is one firm in the industry.
   B. barriers to entry exist that prevent new firms from entering the industry.
   C. only one close substitute exists for the monopolist's product.
   D. the monopolist has some control over the price of his product.
   Answer: C. In a monopoly, there are no close substitutes for the firm's product.

9. Each of the following is a characteristic of an oligopoly except that
   A. there are a few large firms.
   B. firms sell a standardized product.
   C. new entry of firms is difficult but not impossible.
   D. each firm typically behaves "strategically" with respect to other firms.
   Answer: B. In some oligopolistic industries, e.g., oil, the product is standardized, but this is not a requirement.

OBJECTIVE 4: Identify the major types of expenditure for the federal and state/local levels of government.

The government is a major employer of resources and purchaser of goods. The federal government is the largest and most rapidly growing branch of government. National defense and Social Security payments represent over 40% of federal spending while education, public welfare, health and hospitals, and highways are the main expenditure categories for state and local government.   (page 59)

TIP: Note the important distinction between government purchases and transfer payments—the former is a payment for goods and services received by the government; the latter is not. A welfare check is given precisely because the recipient is *not* providing a service.

PRACTICE

10. The salary of your local Senator is classified as
    A. a government transfer payment.
    B. a government interest payment.
    C. government spending.
    D. a government subsidy payment.
    Answer: C. Your local Senator's salary (which he or she has earned for work performed) is government spending. A transfer payment is a payment that requires no good or service in return. Your Senator would strongly resent the implication if you answered Option A!

OBJECTIVE 5: Identify the major sources of revenue for the federal and state/local levels of government.

The main sources of federal revenue are social insurance taxes and income taxes—individual income taxes and corporate income taxes. At the state and local levels, sales and property taxes are the main sources of revenue.   (page 64)

PRACTICE

11. The largest single source of federal revenue is
    A. sales taxes.
    B. property taxes.
    C. social insurance taxes.
    D. individual income tax.
    Answer: D. See Table 3.9 and p. 65.

12. The largest single source of state and local revenue is
    A. sales taxes.
    B. property taxes.
    C. social insurance taxes.
    D. personal income taxes.
    Answer: A. See Table 3.10 and p. 66.

13. In 1991, taxes as a percentage of GDP were _____ in the United States than in Germany, and _____ in the United States than in Japan.
    A. higher, higher.
    B. higher, lower.
    C. lower, higher.
    D. lower, lower.
    Answer: D. See Figure 3.3 on p. 63.

OBJECTIVE 6: Describe and give reasons for the changing expenditure patterns within the federal government budget over the past decade.

The end of the Cold War signaled a decrease in defense spending. The "graying" of the population has resulted in increased expenditures on medical care. In the early 1990s, falling interest rates slowed the rate of increase in interest payments, but persistent deficits and interest rate hikes have meant that federal government interest payments have risen over the past decade. (page 63)

OBJECTIVE 7: Outline the trends that have occurred in international trade over the past three decades.

The *international sector* of the U.S. economy is growing in importance. The U.S. exports over 10% of its production and buys a similar amount of imports from foreigners. (page 66)

PRACTICE

14. By 1994, exports were _____ of GDP and imports were _____ of GDP.
    A. 10.7%, 12.1%.
    B. 10.7%, 21.2%.
    C. 11.2%, 10.7%.
    D. 21.1%, 10.7%.
    Answer: A. See p. 67.

15. In 1994, the most important component of U.S. exports was
    A. industrial supplies and materials.
    B. capital goods (except automotive).
    C. consumer goods (except automotive).
    D. food, feeds, and beverages.
    Answer: B. See p. 67.

I. MULTIPLE CHOICE QUESTIONS.

Select the option that provides the single best answer.

_C_ 1. Which of the following would not be included in the private sector?
A. AT&T.
B. Matthew Mark University, a Baptist seminary.
C. North Virginia State University.
D. The World Wildlife Fund, a nonprofit organization.

_A_ 2. The type of business organization with limited liability from debt for its owner(s) is a
A. proprietorship.
B. partnership.
C. corporation.
D. company.

_B_ 3. The restaurant industry in Hometown has many small establishments, each with its own "specialties" and atmosphere. This restaurant market is
A. perfectly competitive.
B. monopolistically competitive.
C. a monopoly.
D. an oligopoly.

_C_ 4. Statement 1: "After all the corporation's expenses have been paid, the retained earnings are distributed to the stockholders."
Statement 2: "Welfare checks are a part of transfer payments."
Statement 1 is _____; Statement 2 is _____.
A. false, false.
B. true, true.
C. false, true.
D. true, false.

_B_ 5. A(n) _____ industry is the most likely industry to have substantial barriers to entry.
A. perfectly competitive.
B. monopolistic.
C. monopolistically competitive.
D. oligopolistic.

_A_ 6. Government expenditures are made up of
A. government purchases, transfer payments, and interest payments.
B. government purchases, welfare payments, and national defense.
C. transfer payments, national defense, and social security payments.
D. transfer payments, tax payments, and interest payments.

_A_ 7. For firms in perfect competition,
A. output is homogeneous.
B. each firm controls a relatively large portion of the market.
C. each firm is free to select its own price level.
D. advertising is essential to remain competitive.

_D_ 8. In perfect competition, each firm
A. advertises aggressively to stay competitive.
B. controls a substantial share of its local market.
C. places importance on customers who have brand loyalty.
D. has to make do with the price arrived at by market forces.

_A_ 9. The biggest single revenue-earner for the federal government is the
   A. individual income tax.
   B. corporate income tax.
   C. sales tax.
   D. payroll tax.

_A_ 10. The best example of an oligopoly is
   A. the U.S. automobile industry.
   B. your local electricity supplier.
   C. the shoe industry.
   D. clothing stores.

_B_ 11. As a percentage of GDP, total government expenditures
   _____ and government employment _____
   between 1980 and 1994.
   A. increased, increased.
   B. increased, decreased.
   C. decreased, increased.
   D. decreased, decreased.

_D_ 12. Which of the following is not a government transfer payment?
   A. Social Security payments to the elderly.
   B. Unemployment compensation.
   C. Payments to the widow of a war veteran.
   D. Social insurance tax payment by an employee.

II. APPLICATION QUESTIONS.

1. Are your local radio broadcasts a public good? Is a Broadway musical a public good? Of the two goods, why is the market system more likely to underproduce radio broadcasts. In practice, how has radio reduced the problem of non-payers?

2. Suppose that you're the Chair of the President's Council of Economic Advisers. The President is committed to balancing the budget before the next election and asks you how this can be achieved. (Remember, if the President isn't re-elected, you lose your job too!)

   Come up with three distinct policy recommendations. If the President cuts expenditures, where should the cuts fall? Be specific! Who would be hurt by such a proposal? Would it affect particular social or regional groups? Does the political power of a state, such as Texas or California, have any bearing on the political decision process? If taxes are to be raised, which ones? Again, who might be hurt by a specific tax hike? Should producers be taxed, or should consumers? Wage earners or investors? Are there any parts of the budget that are "not negotiable" (veterans' benefits or Medicare, for example)?

3. Give the advantages and disadvantages of organizing a firm as a
   a. proprietorship
   b. partnership
   c. corporation
   d. Give an example of each form of business organization.

4. You are considering setting up a small business. Which factors would you take into account when deciding whether to establish a single proprietorship or a partnership?

5. Think up a simple business enterprise—such as doing yard work, typing term papers, opening a hot dog stand, or selling vitamins—and decide which would be the most appropriate form of legal organization for your firm. Why is this form of organization the best choice? List the drawbacks that might occur. How might you solve the problems? What advantages do the other forms of organization offer, for example? If you have a proprietorship, how would you feel about giving up control/ownership of "your" business to a group of unknown shareholders and about making decisions by committee?

Major point: No single legal organization is always "best"—it depends upon the particular circumstances of the business and the objectives of the owner(s).

6. In a sense, the three levels of government specialize. For the federal government, defense and the postal service are major sources of employment. Why? Because there's a need for a "national" organization. At the state level, education and highways are the main sources of employment. At the local level, fire, police, and sanitation (all "local" issues) are prominent.

   Now do a thought experiment: Try to imagine what would happen if Washington tried to control fire, police, and sanitation, while turning national defense over to local government. Not very efficient! Also, observe that the public sector can *complement* private endeavors through the provision of public goods (roads and education, for example) and through the enforcement of compliance with a legal system designed to protect the rights of private consumers and firms.

7. Make up a list of industries. Now categorize each of the industries you've named into one of the four market organizations (perfect competition, etc.). Do you see a pattern in the list? Most of the examples you've listed will be oligopolistic or monopolistically competitive industries and most will be heavily committed to TV advertising.

   Are all of your classifications unambiguous? How did you arrive at a decision in each case?

   Starting again, come up with your own examples for the "perfect competition" and "monopoly" categories. To get you started, I suggest the stock market, the local farmers' market, and typing services (perfect competition) and a local utility (monopoly).

8. What are the three kinds of legal organization for the firm? List them and give your own example of the sort of firm you'd expect to find in each category.

9. List the four categories of market organization. Into which market structure is entry easiest?

10. Which form of legal organization is most likely for each of the following businesses?
    a. Coca Cola   _____
    b. a medical practice   _____
    c. a legal firm   _____
    d. a plumbing firm   _____
    e. a car manufacturer   _____
    f. a small tobacco grower   _____
    g. a small country store   _____
    h. MTV   _____
    i. a law firm   _____
    j. McDonald's   _____

    In each case, which factors lead you to your answer and what do you think is the main advantage that each firm derives from this form of organization?

PRACTICE TEST

I. SOLUTIONS TO MULTIPLE CHOICE QUESTIONS

1. C. A state university is financed by the government.

2. C. Corporations have limited liability. See p. 52. Note that a partnership may have limited liability, but only in some cases.

3. B. The "many firms" condition excludes monopoly and oligopoly. The presence of "differentiation" excludes perfect competition.

4. C. Retained earnings are just that—retained (by the corporation). Welfare checks are payments that do not require a service in return—i.e., transfers.

5. B. To maintain exclusive control, monopolies typically construct high barriers to entry from would-be competitors.

6. A. National defense is an element in government purchases, and welfare payments are included in the more general category of "transfer payments."

7. A. Because there is no product differentiation in perfect competition-output is homogeneous-there is no reason to advertise. Each firm is "small."

8. D. Each firm in perfect competition is a price taker, accepting the price established by market forces. Also see the answer to Question 7.

9. A. Individual income taxes are now the largest component of federal revenues. See Table 3.9.

10. A. Electricity is generated by a monopolist. Shoe production and retail clothing stores are monopolistically competitive. The auto industry has a few "big" firms.

11. B. See Table 3.5.

12. D. This is a tax payment by an individual to the government.

II. SOLUTIONS TO APPLICATION QUESTIONS

1. Local radio broadcasts are a public good—my consumption does not diminish your consumption. The musical is not a public good—if I buy a seat, fewer seats are available for others. The market system is likely to underproduce local radio because it is impossible to exclude non-payers. In practice, commercial radio does not sell programming to listeners; it sells listeners to advertisers who pay for advertising time.

2. The answer to this question is open to opinion. Most economists would claim that, to cut the deficit, the government must increase taxes or reduce transfer payments and expenditures.

3. a. proprietorship: advantages—the proprietor is his own boss, keeps all the profits, the firm is flexible, possible tax breaks

   disadvantages—unlimited liability, no pool of specialized experience at the top

   b. partnership: advantages—pool of expertise

   disadvantages—unlimited liability, less flexibility, greater need for consultation between partners

   c. corporation: advantages—limited liability, market power, political power

   disadvantages—possible lack of communication and coordination

   d. proprietorship: corner grocery store; partnership—law firm; corporation—Exxon.

4. The most important consideration is likely to be financial-can the business be started without outside help. Additionally, can the business be run effectively with only one individual in control—can a manager be hired?

5–7. The answer to each question is open to opinion.

8. Proprietorship, a family grocery store; partnership, a legal firm; corporation, a manufacturing firm.

9. Perfect competition; monopolistic competition; monopoly; oligopoly. Perfect competition is easiest for a firm to enter.

10. a. corporation.
    b. partnership.
    c. partnership.
    d. proprietorship.
    e. corporation.
    f. proprietorship.
    g. proprietorship.
    h. corporation.
    i. partnership.
    j. corporation.

DEMAND, SUPPLY, AND MARKET EQUILIBRIUM

OBJECTIVES: POINT BY POINT

After completing this chapter, you should be able to accomplish the objectives listed below.

General Comment

The single best piece of advice, particularly for this essential chapter, is "practice, practice, practice." A second piece of advice must be "draw, draw, draw." Don't be put off by the graphs—try to develop a solid intuitive feel for demand and supply by talking your way through how the market should behave.

In most of the multiple-choice questions in this chapter, the *first* thing to do is to start to sketch a demand and supply picture.

Get into the habit of asking "What should happen to demand?" and "Will this make supply increase or decrease?". Predict whether price should rise or fall in a given circumstance (common sense should carry you a long way here). Don't try to avoid graphs—they'll make your course a lot easier *and* more rewarding. If you have some initial problems, check the Appendix to Chapter 1 and the "Graphing Pointers" sections in this Guide.

OBJECTIVE 1: Define and apply quantity demanded and quantity supplied, and state the law of demand and the law of supply.

Quantity demanded is the amount of a product that a household would buy, in a given period, if it could buy all it wanted at the current price. *Quantity supplied* is the amount of a product that a firm would be willing and able to offer for sale at a particular price during a given time period. The *law of demand* states that there is a negative relationship between the price and the quantity demanded of a product. When the price of McDonald's fries increases, we buy less. The *law of supply* states that there is a positive relationship between the price and the quantity supplied of a product. When McDonald's raises its hourly wage, we want to work more hours there. (page 76/84)

OBJECTIVE 2: Draw and interpret demand and supply graphs.

A *demand schedule* is a table showing how much of a given product households would be willing and able to buy at different prices in a given time period; a *demand curve* shows this relationship graphically. Demand curves slope downward.

(page 77)

A *supply schedule* is a table listing how much of a product a firm will supply at alternative prices in a given time period; a *supply curve*, shows this relationship graphically. Supply curves slope upward. (page 87)

> **Graphing Pointer:** These graphs *always* have price on the vertical axis and quantity (demanded or supplied, as appropriate) on the horizontal axis. It is a bad, though common, mistake to reverse the variables.

PRACTICE

1. At each price shown, estimate how many apples per month you might demand.

PRICE PER APPLE	QUANTITY DEMANDED
60¢	
50¢	
40¢	
30¢	
20¢	
10¢	

You have constructed a demand schedule. Now, in the blank space to the right of the demand schedule, draw vertical (price) and horizontal (quantity) axes. Plot your monthly demand curve for apples. Label the curve D_1.

Answer: This line is unlikely to be smooth like those in the textbook, but it should have a general downward slope—the lower the price, the more you're likely to buy. You should have the horizontal axis labeled "quantity demanded" and the vertical axis labeled "price."

2. In the diagrams below, match each of the numbers with the appropriate term below to produce a correct demand or supply diagram for apples.
    A. Price of apples.
    B. Price of apples.
    C. Quantity of apples supplied.
    D. Quantity of apples demanded.
    E. Demand curve.
    F. Supply curve.

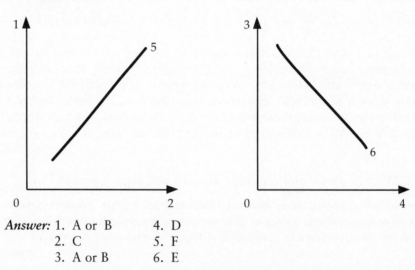

Answer: 1. A or B   4. D
          2. C   5. F
          3. A or B   6. E

OBJECTIVE 3: Identify the determinants of demand and supply and indicate how each must change for demand and supply to increase or decrease.

The willingness and ability of a household to buy units of a good (quantity demanded) are likely to depend principally on the price of the good itself. Other factors—including the household's income and wealth, the prices of other products, tastes and preferences, and expectations about price, income, and wealth—will influence demand.

Comment: This section of the textbook will probably be your most frustrating section. Be patient—time spent understanding demand/supply analysis will serve you well in future chapters.

When you constructed your demand schedule and demand curve with varying price levels in Practice Question 1, you made assumptions about your income level, wealth, prices of other goods, and so on. Change the assumptions and you will change the diagram. The curve shifts position—a *change in demand*.

Factors that can cause a change in demand are:
a. income
b. wealth
c. prices of related products
d. tastes or preferences of the household
e. expectations. (page 79)

Increases in income and wealth, improved preferences, or expectations of a higher price, income, or wealth will increase demand for normal goods. An increase in the price of a substitute product or a decrease in the price of a complementary product will also increase demand, i.e., the entire demand curve shifts to the right. Graphically, an increase in demand (D_1 to D_2) appears as shown below:

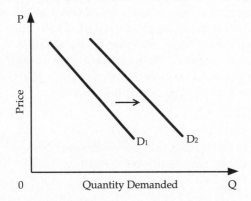

> **TIP:** When shifting the demand or supply curve, think in terms of the curve sliding *left* for a decrease (demand less or supply less) and *right* for an increase (demand more or supply more), not up and down.

> **Graphing Pointer:** You might naturally associate "rise" and "fall" with a vertical shift. This causes no problems in the case of demand, and you'd expect to be correct in using the same approach in the case of supply—but you'd be wrong!

The decision to supply is affected by the ability to earn profits (that is, the difference between revenues and costs). The willingness and ability of a firm to offer units of a good for sale (quantity supplied) are likely to depend principally on the price of the good itself. If other factors important to producers change, then the supply curve diagram will change. The supply curve shifts position—a *change in supply.*

Factors that can cause a change in supply are:
a. changes in costs of production (input prices)
b. new costs and market opportunities
c. changes in prices of related products. (page 87)

Improvements in technology, decreases in the costs of inputs and other costs of production, or increases in the price of complementary products will increase supply. Decreases in the price of substitute products will also increase supply, i.e., the entire supply curve will shift to the right. Graphically, an increase in supply (S_1 to S_2) appears as shown below:

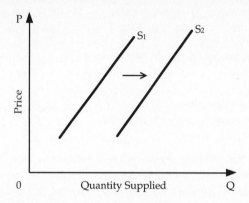

Graphing Pointer: At first glance, a leftward shift of a supply curve looks like the supply curve has moved up, but it's still a *decrease* in supply—at each price level, less is being supplied. Second, when considering if a given factor will cause supply to increase or decrease, ask "Will this change increase or decrease profits?". Producers will want to supply more if their profits are rising—so, if the answer to the question is "increase profits," you should predict an increase (rightward shift) in supply.

TIP: These lists of factors that can change demand or supply should be kept in a place very close to your heart! Write them on an index card and review them frequently.

Demand: Pick a good that you buy frequently (preferably a name brand), such as Exxon gasoline. Do "thought experiments." What would your demand do if Exxon hiked the price of its gas? If your income fell? If the price of engine oil (a complement) increased? If the price of Mobil gas (a substitute) decreased?

Supply: Perhaps you have a part-time job—that is, you supply labor. Think of factors that would affect how many hours you would work per week. The wage (price) you earn would affect the quantity of labor you supply. What other factors would make you more or less willing and able to work?

Note the reference to the *short run* and the *long run* on page 87. These are important economic concepts that you'll meet later on. Essentially, suppliers will be more responsive to demand-side changes in a longer time period than they will be in a shorter time period.

Graphing Pointer: The "change in demand" and "change in supply" concepts are tough; ask yourself, what would you do if the price of a good (say, steak) remains constant and your income rises substantially? If you would buy more steak, this is an increase in demand. To graph this change, draw a hypothetical (negatively sloped!) demand curve for steak (D1). Choose a point (A1) on the curve and identify the associated quantity demanded. Choose another price and repeat the operation with point B1. To construct the new demand curve which results from the higher income, pick a point immediately to the right of A1 and label it A2. This point represents the additional purchases due to the additional income. Draw a point directly to the right of B1 which will indicate the effects of higher income. Label this point B2. Draw a line through B1 and B2 and label this line D2—your new demand curve! Repeat this graphing exercise for each of your "thought experiments" mentioned above. As you practice this for all of the factors which change demand and supply, your mastery of graphical analysis will develop.

(These "thought experiments" will be easier for demand factors than for supply factors because you buy things everyday while most of you are not producers. Once again, be patient and ask yourself: if you were a business owner committed to maximizing profits, how would you respond if your product's price remained the same but one of the supply factors changed?)

Graphing Pointer: Many students feel that a "curve" must be curved. Our demand and supply curves are models, however. Keep it simple—draw straight lines.

TIP: When you are told to imagine that income or some other variable has changed, imagine an *enormous* change—this will help you work out the effects. If a can of Pepsi has risen in price, suppose that it has tripled in price—it's easier to see what will happen to the quantity demanded or supplied of Pepsi and to the demand for Coke.

PRACTICE

3. A decrease in the supply of American cars might be caused by
   A. an increase in the price of imported Japanese cars.
   B. an increase in the wages of U.S. car workers.
   C. an increase in demand that causes car prices to rise.
   D. a reduction in the cost of steel.
   Answer: B. The supply of American cars will decrease if input prices, such as the wages of U.S. car workers, increase. See p. 87.

4. Energizer and Duracell's Coppertop batteries are substitutes. The Energizer Bunny increases the price of its batteries. Equilibrium price will _____ and quantity exchanged will _____ in the market for Duracell.
   A. rise, rise.
   B. fall, rise.
   C. fall, fall.
   D. rise, fall.
   Answer: A. If Energizer increases the price of its batteries, consumers will switch over to substitutes such as Duracell, increasing the demand for Duracell. This will raise both equilibrium price and quantity. See p. 80.

5. Barney's Bowling Balls and Fred's Bowling Shoes are complements. Fred notices a decrease in the quantity demanded of bowling shoes (a movement along his demand curve). This could have been caused by
   A. a decrease in the income of Fred's customers.
   B. an increase in the price of Fred's Bowling Shoes.
   C. an increase in the price of Barney's Bowling Balls.
   D. an increased expectation that Fred will reduce the price of his bowling balls in the near future.
   Answer: B. This is a change in quantity demanded, not a change in demand! The only thing that can cause a change in quantity demanded is a change in price. See p. 78.

6. As the price of oranges increases, orange growers will
   A. use more expensive methods of growing oranges.
   B. use less expensive methods of growing oranges.
   C. increase the supply of oranges.
   D. decrease the supply of oranges.
   Answer: A. An increase in price results in an increase in quantity supplied. Suppliers are able to produce more because, at the higher price, they can afford to hire more expensive resources. See p. 87.

7. The supply of oranges will shift to the right if
   A. very bad weather afflicts the Florida orange groves.
   B. oranges are rumored to have been treated with an insecticide that causes heart disease.
   C. the Florida government requires that all orange workers are given more substantial health benefits by employers.
   D. citrus growers see the price of grapefruits decreasing permanently.
   Answer: D. As the price of grapefruits falls, citrus farmers will switch over to another production option—oranges. See p. 89.

OBJECTIVE 4: Derive market demand and market supply curves from individual demand and supply schedules.

Market demand is the sum of all the quantities of a good or service demanded per period by all the households buying in the market for that good or service. The *market demand curve* is a summing of all the individual demand curves. At a given price level, the quantity demanded by each household is determined and the total quantity demanded is calculated. (page 84/91)

The *market supply curve* is a horizontal summing of all the supply curves for a given product.

PRACTICE

8. If the firms producing fuzzy dice for cars must obtain a higher price than they did previously to produce the same level of output as before, then we can say that there has been
   A. an increase in quantity supplied.
   B. an increase in supply.
   C. a decrease in supply.
   D. a decrease in quantity supplied.
   Answer: C. Draw the supply curve. At the same output level and at a higher price, the supply curve has shifted to the left—a decrease in supply. See p. 87.

9. The market supply curve for wheat depends on each of the following except
   A. the price of wheat-producing land.
   B. the price of production alternatives for wheat.
   C. the tastes and preferences of wheat consumers.
   D. the number of wheat farmers in the market.
   Answer: C. Tastes and preferences are determinants of demand, not supply. See p. 87.

OBJECTIVE 5: Differentiate between a shift of a demand curve or supply curve and a movement along a curve, and depict these cases correctly on a graph.

When important factors other than the price of the product change, such as tastes or income, the entire demand curve shifts position. This is called a *change in demand* to distinguish it from a movement along the demand curve, which represents a *change in quantity demanded* and which can be caused *only* by a change in the price of the commodity. (page 82)

Similarly, when important factors other than price change for a producer, the amount of a given product offered for sale will change even if the price level is unchanged. This is a *change in supply*. If *only* the price of the product itself changes, there will be a movement along the original supply curve—a *change in quantity supplied*. (page 89)

> **Graphing Pointer: Changes in Quantity Demanded (Supplied) vs. Changes in Demand (Supply).** Some students experience confusion regarding the distinction between a "change in quantity demanded" and a "change in demand." Perhaps the distinction is rather artificial; the six factors (listed on page 76) that affect demand do include price of the product. However, we regard the price–quantity demanded relationship as the most important and draw the demand curve with these two variables on the axes, assuming that all other factors are fixed at a "given" level. This is the *ceteris paribus* assumption.
>
> Look at a demand curve; price and quantity demanded can have a range of values while all other variables (income, other prices, etc.) are fixed at a particular level. If price changes, we move along the curve; if another factor changes, our *ceteris paribus* assumption is broken and we must redraw the price-quantity demanded relationship.
>
> The *only* thing that can cause a "change in the quantity demanded" of Pepsi is a change in the price of Pepsi—a movement from one point on the demand curve to another point on the same demand curve.
>
> If any other factor on the list changes we will have to redraw the entire diagram—a "change in demand"—because the "all else being equal" assumption has been broken.
>
> Similarly, a "change in the quantity supplied" of chicken can only be caused by a change in the price of chicken. A change in any other factor on the list on page 87 of the text causes a "change in supply."

> **Graphing Pointer:** Remember—if you would do more of the activity (buying more, producing more) because of the change in a factor (demand, supply), draw a new curve to the right of the original curve. If you reduce the activity, draw the new curve to the left of the original curve.

> **TIP:** Here is an example that points up the difference between a "change in quantity demanded" and a "change in demand". In the diagram below, we have a demand curve for Ford Rangers on the left and a demand curve for Dodge Rams on the right.
>
> Initially, the price of the Ranger is $17,000 and 2,000 are demanded per week. The Ram sells for $16,000 and has 2,500 demanders at that price. (Note: It's irrelevant whether the Ram's price is above, below, or equal to that of the Ranger—at any realistic prices, each truck will have some enthusiasts.)

TIP, *continued:*

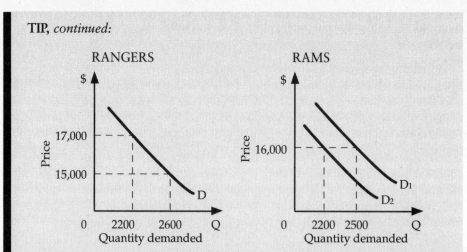

RANGERS

RAMS

Suppose that the price of Rangers decreases to $15,000. More truck-buyers will order Rangers—an increase in quantity demanded as there is a movement along the demand curve from A to B. Some of those new Ford customers would have bought the Dodge Ram but now will not. At the same price ($16,000) as before, demand for Rams has decreased, perhaps to 2,200. The entire demand curve for Rams has shifted.

PRACTICE

10. Return to Practice Question 1. Suppose that the prices of other fruits you might buy increase. What would happen to the number of apples you demand per month? Sketch this change on your diagram. Label the demand curve D_2. What is likely to happen to the price of apples?

 Answer: See your diagram for Practice Question 1. Presumably you'd demand more apples at each price. The demand curve shifts right, to D_2. Because apples are more popular now, the price of apples will likely rise.

11. A "change in demand" means
 A. the quantity demanded changes as price changes.
 B. a movement along a given demand curve or schedule.
 C. a shift in the position of the demand curve.
 D. a change in the shape of a demand curve.

 Answer: C. A "change in demand" means that, at every price level, more or less is being demanded. This is represented as a shift in the position of the demand curve. See p. 83.

12. Which of the following will cause a decrease in the demand for tennis racquets?
 A. A rise in the price of squash racquets.
 B. A rise in the price of tennis racquets.
 C. A rise in the price of tennis balls.
 D. A fall in the price of tennis shoes.

 Answer: C. A decrease in the demand for tennis racquets will occur if a complement (tennis balls) increases in price because fewer tennis balls will be bought. See p. 81.

OBJECTIVE 6: Provide explanations for the slope of a typical demand curve.

Demand curves slope down—as price rises, quantity demanded falls. We know this intuitively, but economists have explored this important relationship ("social law") more analytically. The higher the price of a good, lowfat milk for instance, the higher the opportunity cost of buying it, (i.e., the more of other goods we will give up, and the less willing we will be to buy lowfat milk).

Utility is a conceptual measure of satisfaction. Successive units of a good bestow satisfaction, but typically at a decreasing rate—the second cup of coffee may be less enjoyable than the first. Accordingly, the price we will be willing to pay will decrease.

As the price of steak rises, you become poorer because your food dollar can't stretch as far as it did before (this is called the *income effect*), and you seek cheaper substitutes such as chicken (this is called the *substitution effect*). Both effects result in a decrease in the quantity demanded of steak as its price increases.   (page 78)

PRACTICE

13. The demand curve has
    A. "price" on the vertical axis, "quantity demanded per time period" on the horizontal axis, and an upward sloping demand curve.
    B. "price" on the horizontal axis, "quantity demanded per time period" on the vertical axis, and an upward sloping demand curve.
    C. "price" on the vertical axis, "quantity demanded per time period" on the horizontal axis, and a downward sloping demand curve.
    D. "price" on the horizontal axis, "quantity demanded per time period" on the vertical axis, and a downward sloping demand curve.
    Answer: C. See p. 77.

14. We are trying to explain the law of demand. When the price of pretzels rises,
    A. the opportunity cost of pretzels increases along the demand curve.
    B. sellers switch production and increase the quantity supplied of pretzels.
    C. income rises for producers of pretzels.
    D. the opportunity cost of other goods increases.
    Answer: A. See p. 78.

OBJECTIVE 7: Distinguish the relationship that exists between two goods that are substitutes and the relationship that exists between two goods that are complements.

If, when the price of Good A rises, the demand for Good B also rises, then A and B are *substitutes*; however, if the demand for B falls when the price of A rises, then A and B are *complements*.   (page 80)

> **TIP:** Think of several ready-made examples of substitute goods and complementary goods from your own life. Working with your own examples (e.g., during an exam) makes it easier to work through the analysis correctly. Here are a few examples:
>
> **Substitutes:** Coke and Pepsi, prerecorded audio tapes and CDs.
>
> **Complements:** peanut butter and jelly, CDs and CD players, cars and gasoline, cameras and film, left and right shoes.

15. The demand for JIF peanut butter will decrease if there is
    A. an increase in the price of JIF peanut butter.
    B. an increase in the price of Peter Pan peanut butter.
    C. a decrease in the demand for jelly.
    D. an increase in the price of bread.
    Answer: D. Bread and peanut butter are complements. An increase in the price of bread will result in less bread being bought and a lower demand for JIF to spread on it. See p. 81.

16. Good A and Good B are substitutes for one another. An increase in the price of A will
    A. increase the demand for B.
    B. reduce the quantity demanded of B.
    C. increase the quantity demanded of B.
    D. reduce the demand for B.
    Answer: A. Suppose A is Coke and B is Pepsi. If Coke rises in price, we would buy less Coke (a fall in quantity demanded of Coke) and more of Pepsi (an increase in the demand for Pepsi). See p. 80.

OBJECTIVE 8: Distinguish between a good that is normal and a good that is inferior.

When income increases, demand increases for *normal* goods. If demand for a good decreases when income increases, then the good is *inferior*. (page 80)

> **TIP:** Think of several ready-made examples of both normal goods and inferior goods from your own life. Working with your own examples (during an exam, for instance) makes it easier to work through the analysis correctly. Here are a few examples:
>
> **Normal goods:** movie tickets, steak, and more expensive imported beers.
>
> **Inferior goods:** second-hand clothes, store-brand (versus name-brand) foods, generic medicines, rice, beans, bus rides.

PRACTICE

17. You expect your income to rise. For a normal good, this would result in
    A. an increase in quantity demanded and a fall in price.
    B. an increase in demand and a fall in price.
    C. an increase in quantity demanded and a rise in price.
    D. an increase in demand and a rise in price.
    Answer: D. If you expect your income to rise, you will demand more of a normal good. This will cause the price to increase. See p. 80.

18. The demand for Good A has been increasing over the past year. Having examined the following facts, you conclude that Good A is an inferior good. Which fact led you to that conclusion?
    A. The price of Good A has been increasing over the past year.
    B. An economic slowdown has reduced the income of the traditional buyers of Good A.
    C. Good B, a substitute for Good A, has cut its price over the last twelve months.
    D. Household wealth has increased among the traditional buyers of Good A.
    Answer: B. Inferior goods experience increasing popularity as income levels fall. See p. 80.

19. Turnips are available in both the United States and in Mexico. During the past year, incomes have grown by 10% in each country. The demand for turnips has grown by 12% in the United States and grown by 3% in Mexico. We can conclude that turnips are
   A. normal goods in the United States and normal goods in Mexico.
   B. normal goods in the United States and inferior goods in Mexico.
   C. inferior goods in the United States and normal goods in Mexico.
   D. inferior goods in the United States and inferior goods in Mexico.
   Answer: A. In each case, demand has increased as income has increased. See p. 80.

OBJECTIVE 9: Determine equilibrium price and quantity and detail the process by which the market moves from one equilibrium situation to another when demand or supply shifts.

In the market for a particular good or service, quantity demanded may be greater than, less than, or equal to quantity supplied. *Equilibrium* occurs when quantity demanded equals quantity supplied. There is no tendency for the price to change because, at that price, there is a perfect match between the quantity of the good demanded and the quantity supplied. (page 92)

TIP: **Equilibrium.** The notion of equilibrium is important throughout the remainder of the course. The simple, less analytical, way to think about this concept is as "the point where the lines cross." It will help your understanding if you remember that equilibrium is the "balance" situation in which there is no tendency for change—unless some outside factor intervenes.

Graphing Pointer: Sometimes demand and supply will change position simultaneously. If the magnitudes of the shifts are unknown, then either the effect on equilibrium price or on equilibrium quantity *must* be uncertain. It's easy to forget this important fact, particularly when demand and supply are still new concepts to you. See the following Tip for assistance.

TIP: **Changes in Equilibrium Price and Quantity.** If demand and supply change position simultaneously, break down each situation into two separate graphs, one for the "demand shift" and the other for the "supply shift." In each case, decide the direction of change in price and quantity, and then add them together.

Example: Demand decreases and supply increases.

	PRICE CHANGE	QUANTITY CHANGE
Demand-side effect	decrease	decrease
Supply-side effect	decrease	increase
Total effect	decrease	uncertain

In this case, where demand decreases and supply increases, we predict a certain decrease in price and an uncertain change in equilibrium quantity.

> **Graphing Pointer:** A change in price does not cause the demand curve or the supply curve to shift position. Analyze the following sequence of events for errors. "Demand goes up. That makes price go up, which encourages sellers to supply more. But, when more is supplied, price goes down. When price goes down, demand goes up again, and so on."
>
> *Answer:* A. demand increase from D_1 to D_2 will make price rise from P_1 to P_2. Sellers will supply more from Q_1 to Q_2—an increase in *quantity supplied*, not an increase in supply, as the statement claims. Price, therefore, will *not* go back down. The remainder of the statement is incorrect. Draw this example.

PRACTICE

20. Equilibrium quantity will certainly decrease if
    A. demand and supply both increase.
    B. demand and supply both decrease.
    C. demand decreases and supply increases.
    D. demand increases and supply decreases.
    Answer: B. A decrease in demand will decrease equilibrium quantity. Similarly, a decrease in supply will decrease equilibrium quantity.

21. The market for canned dog food is in equilibrium when
    A. the quantity demanded is less than the quantity supplied.
    B. the demand curve is downsloping and the supply curve is upsloping.
    C. the quantity demanded and the quantity supplied are equal.
    D. all inputs producing canned dog food are employed.
    Answer: C. A market is in equilibrium when price has adjusted to make the quantity demanded and the quantity supplied equal. See p. 92.

22. Equilibrium price will certainly increase if
    A. demand and supply both increase.
    B. demand and supply both decrease.
    C. demand decreases and supply increases.
    D. demand increases and supply decreases.
    Answer: D. An increase in demand will increase equilibrium price. Similarly, a decrease in supply will increase equilibrium price.

23. In the market for mushrooms, the price of mushrooms will certainly increase if
    A. the supply curve shifts right and the demand curve shifts right.
    B. the supply curve shifts right and the demand curve shifts left.
    C. the supply curve shifts left and the demand curve shifts right.
    D. the supply curve shifts left and the demand curve shifts left.
    Answer: C. When demand increases and supply decreases, both shifts are prompting a price increase.

24. In the market for broccoli, the equilibrium quantity of broccoli will certainly increase if the supply of broccoli _____ and the demand for broccoli _____
    A. increases, increases.
    B. increases, decreases.
    C. decreases, increases.
    D. decreases, increases.
    Answer: A. An increase in supply will increase the quantity traded; similarly, an increase in demand will increase the quantity traded.

OBJECTIVE 10: Define excess demand and excess supply and predict their effects on the existing price level.

If the quantity demanded is greater than the quantity supplied of a good, there is *excess demand*, and we would expect the price of that good to rise. If quantity supplied is greater than the quantity demanded of a good, there is an *excess supply*, and we would expect the price of that good to fall. (page 93/94)

25. When there is an excess supply, quantity supplied _____ quantity demanded. Price will _____
    A. exceeds, rise.
    B. is less than, fall.
    C. is less than, rise.
    D. exceeds, fall.
    Answer: D. An excess supply occurs when quantity supplied exceeds quantity demanded. This excess supply will force price down. See p. 94.

26. The equilibrium price of a gallon of unleaded gas is $1.10. At a price of 84¢
    A. quantity supplied will be less than quantity demanded, causing an excess demand for unleaded gas.
    B. quantity supplied will be greater than quantity demanded, causing an excess supply of unleaded gas.
    C. quantity supplied will be greater than quantity demanded, causing an excess demand for unleaded gas.
    D. quantity supplied will be less than quantity demanded, causing an excess supply of unleaded gas.
    Answer: A. If the current price is less than the equilibrium price, an excess demand will occur (quantity supplied will be less than quantity demanded). This excess demand will force price to increase.

OBJECTIVE 11: Understand the role of the *ceteris paribus* and time held constant assumptions in demand and supply analysis.

When dealing with changes in demand and/or supply determinants, it is crucial to treat each change in isolation—that is, to assume that no other change has occurred. It is also crucial to conduct supply and demand analysis in a given time period.

(page 83)

PRACTICE TEST

I. MULTIPLE CHOICE QUESTIONS.

Select the option that provides the single best answer.

_____ 1. Households are
    A. suppliers in the input market.
    B. demanders in the labor market.
    C. suppliers in the product market.
    D. demanders in the input market.

_____ 2. Good C increases its price. The demand for Good D increases. The goods are
    A. complements.
    B. substitutes.
    C. normal.
    D. inferior.

_____ 3. The demand for prerecorded tapes is downsloping. Suddenly the price of tapes rises from $8 to $10. This will cause
    A. demand to shift to the left.
    B. demand to shift to the right.
    C. quantity demanded to increase.
    D. quantity demanded to decrease.

_____ 4. All of the following will shift the supply curve of frisbees to the right except
   A. an increase in price of frisbees.
   B. an improvement in the production processes used to manufacture frisbees.
   C. a reduction in the price of plastic from which frisbees are made.
   D. an improvement in storage resulting in fewer defective frisbees.

_____ 5. Along a given supply curve for eggs
   A. supply increases as price increases.
   B. supply increases as technology improves.
   C. quantity supplied increases as price increases.
   D. quantity supplied increases as technology improves.

_____ 6. Price is currently below equilibrium. There is a situation of excess _____. We would expect price to _____
   A. demand, rise.
   B. demand, fall.
   C. supply, rise.
   D. supply, fall.

_____ 7. You expect your income to rise. For a normal good, this would result in
   A. an increase in quantity demanded and a fall in price.
   B. an increase in demand and a fall in price.
   C. an increase in quantity demanded and a rise in price.
   D. an increase in demand and a rise in price.

_____ 8. The price of frisbees (a normal good) will definitely increase if
   A. there is an improvement in the technology of making frisbees and frisbees become more popular.
   B. the cost of plastic used to produce frisbees increases and people have more leisure time to throw frisbees.
   C. frisbee workers negotiate a wage increase and boomerangs (a frisbee-substitute) decrease in price.
   D. a sales tax is imposed on frisbees and (because of widespread unemployment) incomes fall.

_____ 9. A rightward shift in the supply of U.S. cars might be due to
   A. an increase in the price of steel.
   B. a reduction in foreign competition.
   C. the introduction of cost-saving robots.
   D. increased popularity of foreign cars.

_____ 10. If the market is initially in equilibrium, a technological improvement will cause price to _____ and quantity demanded to _____
   A. fall, fall.
   B. rise, rise.
   C. fall, rise.
   D. rise, fall.

_____ 11. The price of beans rises sharply. Which of the following cannot be true?
   A. The supply of beans may have decreased with no change in the demand for beans.
   B. The demand for beans may have increased with no change in the supply of beans.
   C. The demand for beans may have increased with an increase in the quantity supplied of beans.
   D. The supply of beans may have increased with an increase in the quantity demanded of beans.

_____ 12. The market for peas is experiencing an excess supply. You should predict that
   A. price will increase, quantity demanded will fall, and the quantity supplied will rise.
   B. price will increase, quantity demanded will rise, and the quantity supplied will fall.
   C. price will decrease, quantity demanded will rise, and the quantity supplied will fall.
   D. price will decrease, quantity demanded will fall, and the quantity supplied will rise.

_____ 13. Equilibrium price will certainly decrease if
   A. demand and supply both increase.
   B. demand and supply both decrease.
   C. demand decreases and supply increases.
   D. demand increases and supply decreases.

_____ 14. If a demander demands less of a product at each possible price, there has been
   A. a decrease in the quantity demanded.
   B. a decrease in demand.
   C. an increase in demand.
   D. an increase in the quantity demanded.

_____ 15. Chuck's Chips and Debi's Dip are complements. Costs of chip production fall. At the same time a government health report alleges that dip consumption causes bone cancer. For Debi's Dip, the equilibrium price will _____ and the equilibrium quantity will _____
   A. fall, be indeterminate.
   B. be indeterminate, rise.
   C. be indeterminate, fall.
   D. be indeterminate, be indeterminate.

_____ 16. Suppose there is a simultaneous increase in the demand for legal secretaries and a decrease in the supply of legal secretaries. If there is no change in the wage paid to legal secretaries
   A. there will be an excess demand for legal secretaries.
   B. there will be an excess supply of legal secretaries.
   C. law firms will have no difficulty in hiring the desired number of legal secretaries at the current wage.
   D. the supply of legal secretaries will decrease even more.

Use the diagram below to answer the next six questions. The diagram refers to the demand for and supply of hot dogs. The hot dog market is initially in equilibrium at Point A. Assume that hot dogs are a normal good.

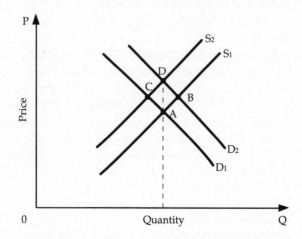

_____ 17. The hot dog market moves from Point A to a new equilibrium at Point B. There has been
   A. an increase in demand and an increase in supply.
   B. an increase in demand and an increase in quantity supplied.
   C. an increase in quantity demanded and an increase in quantity supplied.
   D. an increase in quantity demanded and an increase in supply.

_____ 18. The movement from Point A to Point B might have been caused by
   A. an increase in the price of hamburgers (a substitute for hot dogs).
   B. an increase in the price of fries (a complement for hot dogs).
   C. a new widespread belief that meat products are bad for the heart.
   D. a decrease in the price of ketchup (an ingredient used in making hot dogs).

_____ 19. The hot dog market moves from Point A to a new equilibrium at Point C. There has been
   A. a decrease in demand and a decrease in supply.
   B. a decrease in demand and a decrease in quantity supplied.
   C. a decrease in quantity demanded and a decrease in quantity supplied.
   D. a decrease in quantity demanded and a decrease in supply.

_____ 20. The movement from Point A to Point C might have been caused by a
   A. decrease in the price of hamburgers (a substitute for hot dogs).
   B. tightening of sanitary regulations required for the preparation of hot dogs.
   C. decrease in the wages of workers in the hot dog industry.
   D. decrease in the price of hot dog buns.

_____ 21. The hot dog market moves from Point A to a new equilibrium at Point D. There has been
   A. an increase in demand and an increase in supply.
   B. an increase in demand and a decrease in supply.
   C. a decrease in demand and an increase in supply.
   D. a decrease in demand and a decrease in supply.

_____ 22. The movement from Point A to Point D might have been caused by
   A. an increase in the price of hot dogs and no change in the equilibrium quantity of hot dogs.
   B. an expected increase in the income of hot dog consumers and a hike in the wages of hot dog preparers.
   C. an expected decrease in the price of hot dogs and an increase in the cost of making hot dogs.
   D. a decrease in the income of hot dog consumers and a reduction in the cost of making hot dogs.

_____ 23. Generic aspirin is an inferior good. As Jorge's income decreases we would expect
   A. a decrease in Jorge's demand for generic aspirin.
   B. an increase in Jorge's quantity demanded of generic aspirin.
   C. an increase in Jorge's demand for generic aspirin.
   D. a decrease in Jorge's quantity demanded of generic aspirin.

_____ 24. The supply of computer software packages increases. As a result, the demand for personal computers rises. These two goods are _____. The price of microchips, used to produce personal computers, will _____
   A. substitutes, increase.
   B. substitutes, decrease.
   C. complements, increase.
   D. complements, decrease.

_____ 25. Along a given demand curve for corn, which of the following is not held constant?
A. The price of corn.
B. The income of corn farmers.
C. The income of corn demanders.
D. The price of wheat.

_____ 26. The law of demand is best illustrated by
A. the price of Pepsi rising, leading consumers buy more Coke.
B. increased purchases of Coke as the price of Coke decreases.
C. an increase in income which results in reduced purchases of store-brand soft drinks.
D. an increase in income which results in increased purchases of Coke.

Use the table below to answer the next three questions. The table refers to the demand for and supply of tuna.

PRICE OF TUNA	QUANTITY DEMANDED	QUANTITY SUPPLIED
90¢	30	80
80¢	45	70
70¢	60	60
60¢	75	50
50¢	90	40
40¢	105	30

_____ 27. The equilibrium price is _____ and the equilibrium quantity is _____
A. 70¢, 60.
B. 60¢, 75.
C. 60¢, 50.
D. 70¢, 70.

_____ 28. There would be an excess demand for tuna if the price were at
A. 90¢.
B. 80¢.
C. 70¢.
D. 60¢.

_____ 29. If the price were 80¢, there would be
A. an excess demand of 70.
B. an excess demand of 25.
C. an excess supply of 25.
D. an excess supply of 70.

_____ 30. New costly regulations to protect workers are introduced in the production of tuna. We would expect the equilibrium price of tuna to _____ and the equilibrium quantity of tuna to
_____
A. increase, increase.
B. increase, decrease.
C. decrease, increase.
D. decrease, decrease.

II. APPLICATION QUESTIONS.

1. Consider the following information regarding the quantity of corn demanded and supplied per month at a number of prices.

Price per bushel	Quantity demanded	Quantity supplied
40¢	39,000	83,000
35¢	48,000	78,000
30¢	58,000	74,000
25¢	67,000	67,000
20¢	75,000	62,000
15¢	81,000	59,000

   a. What is the equilibrium price? What is the equilibrium quantity?
   b. Describe the situation when the price is at 40¢ per bushel and predict what will happen.
   c. Describe the situation when the price is at 15¢ per bushel and predict what will happen.
   d. Explain what would happen if a serious transport strike reduced corn output (at each price) by 30,000 bushels.

2. DoughCrust Bread is a normal good produced by the DoughCrust Bakery. What will happen to the equilibrium price and quantity of DoughCrust Bread in each of the following situations?
   a. Due to a recession, households which buy DoughCrust experience a decrease in income.
   b. The cost of wheat used in DoughCrust increases significantly.
   c. DoughCrust buys improved ovens that reduce the costs of DoughCrust bread.
   d. Luvly Loaf, a rival, cuts the price of its bread.
   e. Consumers become health-conscious and switch to low-calorie breads.

3. How will each of the following changes affect the supply of hamburgers?
   a. There is an increase in the price of hamburger buns (used in the production of burgers).
   b. There is an increase in the price of hamburgers.
   c. Producers discover that the price of cheeseburgers is increasing.

4. Pietro Cavalini sells ice cream at the beach. He is in competition with numerous other vendors. How will each of the following changes affect the demand for Pietro's ice cream?
   a. Hot dog vendors reduce the price of hot dogs. Hot dogs are substitutes for ice cream.
   b. The cost of refrigeration decreases.
   c. Fine weather attracts record crowds to the beach.

5. The market for videocassettes has supply and demand curves given by
   $Qs = 3P$ and $Qd = 60 - 2P$, respectively.
   a. Complete the following table.

Price	Quantity Demanded	Quantity Supplied
$30	_____	_____
$25	_____	_____
$20	_____	_____
$15	_____	_____
$10	_____	_____
$ 5	_____	_____
$ 0	_____	_____

   b. Calculate the equilibrium price and quantity. You can do this either by graphing the curves or algebraically.
   c. Suppose that the current market price is $20. Calculate the number of units that will be traded.
   d. Suppose that the demand equation changed to $Qd = 80 - 2P$. Is this an increase or a decrease in demand? Suggest what might have caused such a change.
   e. Calculate the new equilibrium price and quantity.

6. Here is a demand and supply schedule for bread in East Yeastville, Colorado.

PRICE ($)	QUANTITY DEMANDED	QUANTITY SUPPLIED
5.00	1,000	6,000
4.50	1,300	4,500
4.00	1,600	4,000
3.50	2,000	3,500
3.00	3,000	3,000
2.50	3,200	2,700
2.00	4,000	2,200
1.50	4,500	1,800
1.00	5,400	1,400
.50	7,000	1,200

   a. Find equilibrium price and equilibrium quantity.
   b. Graph the demand (D_1) and supply (S_1) schedules in the space below and confirm the equilibrium values.

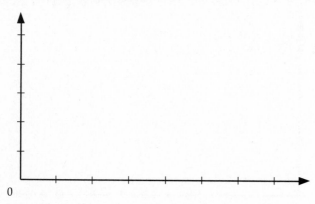

   c. At a price of $1, is there an excess demand or supply? How great is the excess?

Suppose supply increases by 1,800 units at each price level.

   d. Draw the new supply curve (S$_2$) on the graph in b. above.

   e. At the original equilibrium price level, is there an excess demand or an excess supply?

   f. What will now happen to price, quantity demanded and quantity supplied?

7. The diagram below shows the labor market. D is the demand for labor and S is the supply. The minimum wage is $4.55 and unemployment is 150 workers.

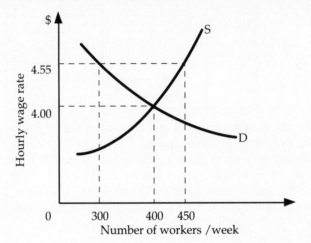

If the minimum wage law was revoked, the wage would fall to an equilibrium level of $4.00, and there would be no unemployment because quantity demanded would be equal to quantity supplied. However, the number of workers demanded would rise by only 100, not 150. Reconcile this apparent contradiction.

8. Here are the demand schedules for orange juice for 3 buyers in the orange juice market and the supply schedules for 3 sellers in the orange juice market.

Price/ gallon	Quantity demanded by:			Quantity supplied by:		
	Brown	Black	White	Gray	Green	Scarlett
$5	1	0	0	5	10	14
$4	3	2	0	4	7	9
$3	7	5	4	3	6	7
$2	9	9	5	0	4	5
$1	11	12	7	0	0	1

   a. Graph market demand (D$_1$) and market supply (S$_1$).

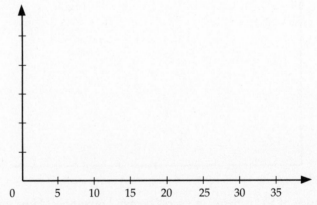

   b. Show equilibrium price (P*) and quantity (Q*).

c.   Now suppose the farm workers who pick oranges are given a higher wage rate. Show on your graph the changes that will occur in the orange juice market. Label any new demand curve D₂ and supply curve S2. Discuss why curves shift, why price changes, and the significance of excess demand or excess supply. Note that you don't have the data to draw precise curves.

d.   Suppose now that, in addition to the orange pickers' higher wage rate, All-Cola, a substitute for orange juice, reduces its price. Sketch in the new demand curve for orange juice (D₃), and explain the reason why you moved the curve as you did.

9. a.   Draw a demand and supply graph for milk, and establish the equilibrium price (P*).

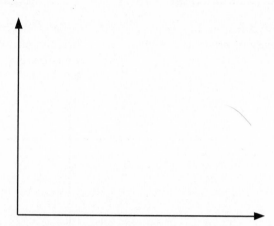

b.   There is an increase in demand for milk (from D₁ to D₂). How will this change affect the equilibrium price?

c.   In terms of the diagram you just sketched, what is the only way that the equilibrium price can increase, if the supply curve doesn't shift?

d.   Draw in the new demand curve. Now trace through the process by which a new equilibrium is established.

On one diagram you can display the distinction between a change in demand and a change in quantity demanded.

10. Mooville is a small town in Texas. Assume that beef is a normal good. What happens to the amount of beef demanded or supplied in each of the following cases? Draw a separate demand and supply graph for each part of this question, label the axes, and show how the change will shift the demand and/or the supply curve. Explain any curve shifts in each case. Show initial and final equilibrium price (P* and P**) and initial and final equilibrium quantity (Q* and Q**) for beef.

a.   A subsidy that reduces production costs for beef producers.

b.   A reduced supply of fish (consumers view beef and fish as substitutes).

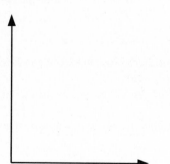

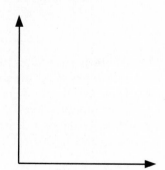

c. A rise in the wage rate in the beef industry.

d. A rise in income.

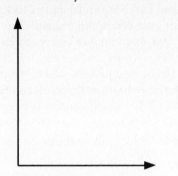
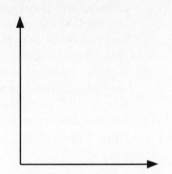

e. An improvement in the productivity of producing beef.

f. A bad tomato crop (beef and ketchup are complements and tomatoes are used to produce ketchup).

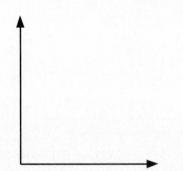
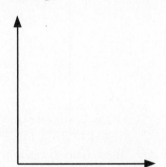

11. Think of some commodity that you like. Try to avoid "lumpy" things, like cars or houses, and pick something like coffee, movies, CDs, or long-distance phone calls.
    a. Roughly sketch your demand curve for this good. Does it intersect the price axis? Where? How much of this commodity would you buy at a zero price?

    b. Are there substitutes for this commodity? How does the availability of substitutes affect the shape of your curve?
    c. How would your demand curve change in response to an increase in the price of a substitute?
    d. How would your demand curve change if you won the lottery and were to receive $2,000 per week for life?

12. Assume that the Boston Red Sox baseball team charges $5 per ticket for all seats at all regular season games. Assume also that the capacity of their stadium, Fenway Park, is 35,000. In August, the Red Sox played games against the New York Yankees (a great rival) and the Cleveland Indians (a team in last place) on consecutive Sundays. All tickets to the Yankees game were sold out a month in advance, and many people who wanted tickets could not get them. At the Cleveland game, there were many vacant seats.
   a. Draw an imaginary demand and supply graph for the Yankees' game and another for the Indians' game.
   b. Is there a pricing strategy that would fill the stadium for the Cleveland game? Would such a policy bring the Red Sox higher, or lower, revenue?

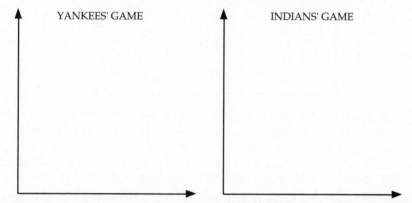

13. During the 1980s, home prices in the northeastern United States doubled. The result was a significant increase in new home construction and a large increase in the demand for labor in the region. At the same time, though, high home prices caused a drop in the supply of labor as people found it too expensive to live in the region. Draw a diagram of the labor market and discuss the impact of these events on wages and thus on the costs of doing business in the Northeast.

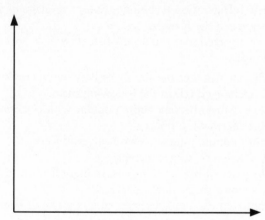

14. In London, cabbies must be able to demonstrate a knowledge of at least 400 streets in order to obtain a license. This is quite difficult, so the number of cabbies is rather limited.

    a. Draw a demand and supply diagram for taxi service in London. How has this diagram been affected by the presence of the test?

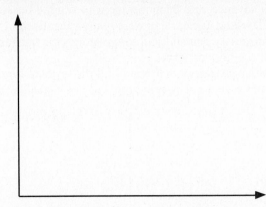

    b. How has the presence of the test affected usage of other forms of public transport—for example, the red double-decker buses and the "tube" (subway)? How have these prices responded?

    c. If the effect of restricting the numbers of cabbies is to reduce the number of customers, why might cabdrivers favor the restriction?

15. Indicate in each case whether demand for steak (a normal good) will increase (I), decrease (D), or remain unchanged (U) in the following cases.

    a. _____ Pork, a substitute for steak, decreases in price.

    b. _____ High levels of unemployment sweep the nation.

    c. _____ The price of steak falls.

    d. _____ The price of steak sauce increases dramatically.

    e. _____ A government report establishes a conclusive link between the consumption of steak and cancer.

    f. _____ New refrigeration techniques reduce spoilage of steaks before they reach the market.

    g. _____ It is expected that the price of steak will skyrocket within two months.

16. Indicate in each case whether the supply of beer will increase (I), decrease (D), or remain unchanged (U) in the following cases.

    a. _____ Wine coolers become more popular with consumers.

    b. _____ Beer decreases in price.

    c. _____ States impose a new tax on beer producers.

    d. _____ Beer workers' wages increase.

    e. _____ The price of hops, an important ingredient in brewing, decreases.

    f. _____ Costs of transportation decrease.

    g. _____ Improved technology results in less waste of beer.

    h. _____ The economy enters a downturn and many beer-drinkers become unemployed.

    i. _____ Fuel costs rise at the brewery.

17. Indicate in each case whether the market price and quantity of popcorn will increase (I), decrease (D), or be uncertain (U) in the following cases. Assume that popcorn and lemonade are normal goods.

   Price   Quantity

   a. _____ _____ The price of lemonade, a complement of popcorn, rises while the harvest of popping corn is unusually poor this year.

   b. _____ _____ Consumers' income falls; low-cost migrant workers cause the cost of popping corn to decline.

   c. _____ _____ Oil, used in popcorn production, falls in price; consumers expect an imminent rise in the price of popcorn.

   d. _____ _____ Eating popcorn is shown to be healthy; new hybrid corn is less expensive to produce and provides higher yields.

18. Kornville is a small town in rural Virginia. Work out what will happen to the amount of corn supplied in each of the following cases and explain your answer.

   Result A = increase in the supply of corn.
   Result B = decrease in the supply of corn.
   Result C = increase in the quantity supplied of corn.
   Result D = decrease in the quantity supplied of corn.

   a. _____ A new government tax is imposed on corn.

   b. _____ Landlords raise the rent on land used for growing corn.

   c. _____ A new spray, effective in controlling insects harmful to corn plants, is made available.

   d. _____ The local senator campaigns effectively for an increase in the price of corn, which can be grown in Kornville.

   e. _____ The local senator campaigns effectively for a rise in the price of tobacco.

   f. _____ Many corn-growing farmers suffer bankruptcy.

   g. _____ The cost of diesel fuel, used in farm machinery, falls.

   h. _____ Red McPinkie unionizes agricultural workers and raises their wages.

   i. _____ Tougher laws stop foreign workers from working at harvest time.

   j. _____ Cornflakes (which are made from corn) become much more popular. (Careful!)

ANSWERS AND SOLUTIONS

PRACTICE TEST

I. SOLUTIONS TO MULTIPLE CHOICE QUESTIONS

1. A. In the input market, firms demand inputs and household supply inputs.

2. B. To check your answer, put in a pair of substitutes, such as Pepsi and Coke. If Pepsi increases in price, we will buy less Pepsi and the demand for Coke will increase.

3. D. A change in price leads to a movement along the demand curve. This is a "change in quantity demanded." An increase in price causes a decrease in quantity demanded.

4. A. A change in price leads to a movement along the supply curve. See p. 87.

5. C. A movement along a supply curve (a change in quantity supplied) can only be caused by a change in the price of the good itself. See p. 87.

6. A. Draw the demand and supply diagram. In equilibrium, quantity demanded equals quantity supplied. At lower prices, quantity demanded exceeds quantity supplied.

7. D. For a normal good, higher income will stimulate additional demand. Higher demand will cause the equilibrium price to rise. See p. 80.

8. B. If the cost of plastic increases, supply will decrease. If buyers have more leisure time, demand for leisure goods (like frisbees) will increase. A decrease in supply, coupled with an increase in demand, will push up the price.

9.   C. A rightward shift—an increase in supply—will occur if costs are reduced.

10. C. A technological improvement will increase supply. This will drive down the equilibrium price. As the price decreases, quantity demanded will increase.

11. D. If the price of beans rises, then it cannot have been caused by an increase in the supply of beans.

12. C. An excess supply means that quantity supplied is greater than the quantity demanded. To reduce the excess supply, sellers will accept lower prices. As price falls, quantity demanded will increase and quantity supplied will decrease.

13. C. A decrease in demand will drive down price; an increase in supply will drive down the price. Draw the diagram to confirm the result.

14. B. Try drawing this. At each price level the demand curve will be further to the left.

15. D. Chip supply increases because costs have fallen. This will increase chip (and dip) demand. The health report will reduce demand for dip. Because we don't know which has the stronger effect on the demand for dip, the change in both equilibrium price and quantity is indeterminate.

16. A. Higher demand and less supply will lead to an excess demand if the wage level doesn't increase.

17. B. The demand curve has shifted right from D_1 to D_2. As the price increased, quantity supplied increased.

18. A. There has been an increase in demand. This could have been due to an increase in the price of hamburgers because consumers would wish to buy fewer hamburgers and would switch over to demanding hot dogs.

19. D. The supply curve has shifted left, from S_1 to S_2. As the price increased, quantity demanded decreased.

20. B. There has been a decrease in supply. This could have been due to a tightening of the sanitary regulations required for the preparation of hot dogs (which would have increased costs and/or reduced the number of sellers).

21. B. The demand curve has shifted right, from D_1 to D_2, and the supply curve has shifted left, from S_1 to S_2.

22. B. An expected increase in the income of hot dog consumers will increase demand for a normal good, and a hike in the wages of hot dog preparers will increase costs and reduce supply. Option A is incorrect—it describes the effect rather than the cause.

23. C. As income changes, it changes the *demand* for a good. A decrease in income results in a decrease in the demand for a normal good. A decrease in income results in an increase in the demand for an inferior good. See p. 80.

24. C. If the supply of software increases, the price will fall. As one might expect, software and computers are complements—the evidence in the question bears this out. As the quantity of computers traded increases, the demand for microchips will increase, which pushes up their price. See p. 81.

25. A. A movement along a demand curve is a change in quantity demanded. The only factor that can cause such a change is a change in the price of the good. See p. 77.

26. B. The law of demand relates the relationship between the price of a good and the quantity demanded. See p. 77.

27. A. Equilibrium occurs where quantity demanded equals quantity supplied. See p. 92.

28. D. At 60¢, quantity demanded is 25 units greater than quantity supplied.

29. C. At 80¢, quantity supplied is 25 units greater than quantity demanded.

30. B. The new regulations will decrease the supply of tuna which, in turn, will increase the equilibrium price and decrease the equilibrium quantity.

II. SOLUTIONS TO APPLICATION QUESTIONS

1.   a.   25¢. 67,000 bushels.
     b.   There is an excess supply of 44,000 bushels at a price of 40¢ per bushel. Pressure is present to force price down.
     c.   There is an excess demand of 22,000 bushels at a price of 15¢ per bushel. Pressure is present to force price up.
     d.   Supply would shift to the left by 30,000 bushels. Equilibrium price would increase to 35¢ per bushel and the equilibrium quantity would be 48,000 bushels.

2. a. A decrease in income will reduce demand. Equilibrium price will fall and equilibrium quantity will fall.
    b. An increase in the cost of wheat will decrease supply. Equilibrium price will rise and equilibrium quantity will fall.
    c. A decrease in the cost of wheat will increase supply. Equilibrium price will fall and equilibrium quantity will rise.
    d. A fall in the price of a substitute will reduce the demand for DoughCrust. Equilibrium price will fall and equilibrium quantity will fall.
    e. There will be a decrease in demand. Equilibrium price will fall and equilibrium quantity will fall.

3. a. Supply will decrease—cost of inputs has increased.
    b. Supply will not change. A change in the price of a good results in a change in quantity supplied.
    c. Supply of hamburgers will decrease—producers will switch resources to cheeseburger production.

4. a. Hot dogs are substitutes for ice cream. Demand for ice cream will decrease.
    b. No effect on demand. Changes in the cost of refrigeration will affect supply.
    c. Demand will increase as the number of buyers increases.

5. a.

QUANTITY PRICE	QUANTITY DEMANDED	SUPPLIED
$30	0	90
$25	10	75
$20	20	60
$15	30	45
$10	40	30
$ 5	50	15
$ 0	60	0

    b. Equilibrium price is $12 and equilibrium quantity is 36.
        In equilibrium, Qd = Qs, therefore,
        $$60 - 2P = 3P$$
        $$60 = 5P \text{ and } P = 12.$$
        If P = 12, then Q = 60 − 2(12) = 36.
    c. At $20, there is an excess supply of 40 units. It's a buyers market—only 20 units will be traded.
    d. This is an increase in demand. Tastes might have changed, consumer incomes may have risen (if videocassettes are a normal good), and so on.
    e. Equilibrium price is $16 and equilibrium quantity is 48.
        In equilibrium, Qd = Qs, therefore,
        $$80 - 2P = 3P$$
        $$80 = 5P \text{ and } P = 16.$$
        If P = 16, then Q = 80 − 2(16) = 48.

6. a. $3; 3,000.
    b. See the diagram below.

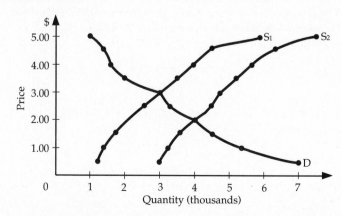

c. There is an excess demand equal to 4,000 units (5,400 − 1,400).
d. See the diagram above ($2, 4,000).
e. There will be an excess supply of 1,800 units.
f. Price will fall to $2; quantity demanded and supplied will move to 4,000 units.

7. The unemployment was removed because 100 extra jobs were created (increase in quantity demanded) and, because the wage had become too low, 50 workers decided to cease offering themselves for employment (decrease in quantity supplied).

8. a. See the diagram below.

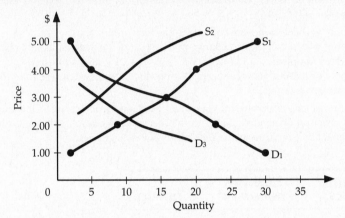

b. P* = $3; Q* = 16.
c. See the diagram above. There will be no change in demand! Costs have risen, reducing profits, so supply will shift to the left (although we can't say how far). At $3, an excess demand now exists, which will push prices higher.
d. See the diagram above. Demand for orange juice will fall (although we can't say by how much). Consumption of All-Cola will rise and some consumers of orange juice will substitute the relatively cheap All-Cola.

9. a. See the diagram below.

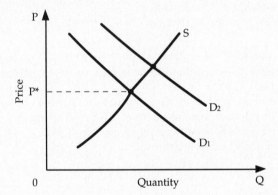

b. Increase.
c. The demand curve must shift to the right.
d. Excess demand, leading to pressure for price to rise, will cause a reduction in the quantity demanded and an increase in the quantity supplied. This will continue until a new equilibrium is established.

10.

a. The subsidy will increase supply. Price will fall and output will rise.

b. The price of fish will increase and consumers will switch to beef. The demand for beef will increase. Price will rise and output will rise.

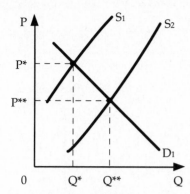

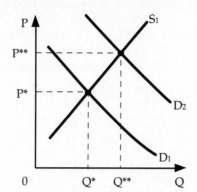

c. Costs of production have risen. This will decrease supply. Price will rise and output will fall.

d. Beef is a normal good. Higher incomes will cause the demand curve to shift right. Price will rise and output will rise.

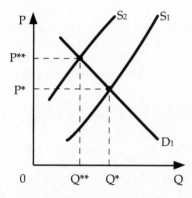

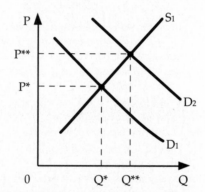

e. Costs of production will fall. Supply will shift to the right. Price will fall and output will rise.

f. A poor tomato crop will drive up the price of tomatoes (and ketchup). Less ketchup will be used so less beef will be demanded. Price and output will fall.

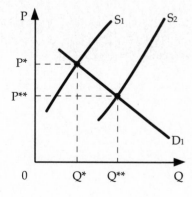

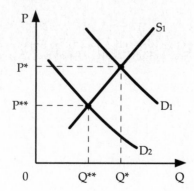

11. a. Presumably, your demand curve is downsloping and intersects the price axis at some point.
    b. With a greater number of substitutes, you will be more sensitive to changes in the price of your good. The curve will tend to be flatter.
    c. Presumably, the demand curve would shift to the right.
    d. If this is a normal good, demand would increase. If it is an inferior good, demand would decrease.

12. a. The supply curves are the same (vertical at 35,000). In the Yankees' case, at a price of $5 per ticket, there is an excess demand. In the Indians' case, at a price of $5 per ticket, because demand is so low, there is an excess supply. See the diagram below.

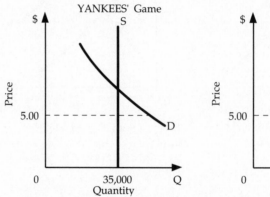
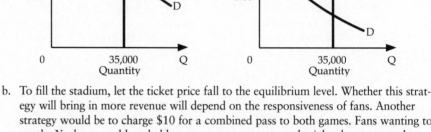

    b. To fill the stadium, let the ticket price fall to the equilibrium level. Whether this strategy will bring in more revenue will depend on the responsiveness of fans. Another strategy would be to charge $10 for a combined pass to both games. Fans wanting to see the Yankees would probably pay out more money and might also come to the second game.

13. Demand for labor would increase and, as workers moved away from the region, supply of labor would decrease. Wages, then, would increase and the costs of doing business in the Northeast would rise.

14. a. The test has reduced the supply of cabbies. This has forced up the price of taxi rides in London.
    b. Given the raised price of cab rides, the demand for substitutes will have increased. Other forms of public transportation will have been able to increase their prices.
    c. Cabbies who have passed the test and earned their license like the scheme because it reduces competition. This is especially true if the degree of substitutability with other types of public transportation is slight.

15. a. D   b. D   c. U   d. D
    e. D   f. I or U   g. I

16. a. U   b. U   c. D   d. D
    e. I   f. I   g. I   h. U
    i. D

17. a. U and D   b. D and U   c. I and U   d. U and I

18. a. B   b. B   c. A   d. C
    e. B   f. B   g. A   h. B
    i. B   j. C

SUPPLY, DEMAND, AND THE PRICE SYSTEM 5

OBJECTIVE 1: Explain and demonstrate how the market uses the price-rationing mechanism to allocate resources and distribute output.

The price system has two important functions—it rations scarce output and determines how productive resources are allocated. Because of scarcity, rationing always occurs. Price rationing operates to distinguish those who are "willing and able" to buy from those who are only able but no longer willing, i.e., it allocates according to the willingness and ability of consumers to pay—those who are willing and able to pay as the price increases will get the good.

Demand is constrained by income and wealth but within those limits, individual preferences will prevail. If demand increases, price rises, signaling producers that profits may be made. More of the good will be produced with resources being switched from other lines of production. (page 104)

> **TIP:** Note the lobster example in the text, which describes the rationing and allocative roles that prices play in the marketplace.
>
> Note, too, that the profit motive is highly durable. Limitations (such as price ceilings or rationing) placed on the operation of the market can lead to black markets so that demand can be serviced.

PRACTICE

1. In a free market, nonprice rationing must occur when _____ exists.
   A. an excess demand.
   B. an excess supply.
   C. a perfectly vertical demand curve.
   D. a perfectly horizontal demand curve.
   Answer: A. Given an excess demand, either price will increase (price rationing) or nonprice rationing must be enforced.

2. In a free market, the rationing mechanism is
   A. price.
   B. quantity.
   C. demand.
   D. supply.
   Answer: A. Given an imbalance between quantity demanded and quantity supplied, a free market will adjust price to achieve equilibrium.

Use the following diagram to answer the next five questions. Assume that the demand curve and the supply curve each must be in one the three possible positions shown. The initial market demand and market supply curves for Sam's Supreme Submarine Sandwiches are D_1 and S_1.

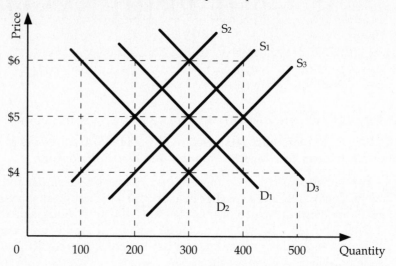

3. There is an increase in the cost of ingredients. If the price is held at the initial equilibrium level, there will be an excess
   A. demand of 100 units.
   B. demand of 200 units.
   C. supply of 100 units.
   D. supply of 200 units.
   Answer: A. Supply has fallen to S_2. Demand is unchanged. At a price of $5, quantity demanded is 300 units and quantity supplied is 200 units.

4. There is a simultaneous increase in demand and decrease in supply. At the initial equilibrium price, there will be an excess
   A. demand of 200 units.
   B. demand of 400 units.
   C. supply of 200 units.
   D. supply of 400 units.
   Answer: A. Supply has decreased to S_2. Demand has increased to D_3. At a price of $5, quantity demanded is 400 units and quantity supplied is 200 units.

5. There is a simultaneous decrease in demand and decrease in supply. At the initial equilibrium price there will be
   A. an excess demand of 200 units.
   B. an excess demand of 100 units.
   C. an excess supply of 200 units.
   D. equilibrium.
   Answer: D. Supply has decreased to S_2. Demand has decreased to D_2. At a price of $5, quantity demanded is 300 units and quantity supplied is 300 units. Equilibrium prevails.

6. Herman reduces the price of his Humongous Hoagie (a substitute for the Supreme Submarine). At the Supreme Submarine's initial equilibrium price, there will be an excess
   A. demand of 100 units.
   B. demand of 200 units.
   C. supply of 100 units.
   D. supply of 200 units.
   Answer: C. Demand has decreased to D_2. Supply has not changed. At a price of $5, quantity demanded is 200 units and quantity supplied is 300 units.

7. Herman reduces the price of his Humongous Hoagie (a substitute for the Supreme Submarine). *Following* any shifts in the curves, we would expect a(n) _____ in the Supreme Submarine market.
A. increase in quantity demanded and an increase in quantity supplied.
B. increase in quantity demanded and a decrease in quantity supplied.
C. decrease in quantity demanded and an increase in quantity supplied.
D. decrease in quantity demanded and a decrease in quantity supplied.
Answer: B. Demand has decreased to D_2. Supply has not changed. There is an excess supply which will cause Sam's price to fall. A fall in price will increase quantity demanded and decrease quantity supplied.

OBJECTIVE 2: List nonprice rationing policies designed to supplant the price-rationing mechanism, identify the rationale behind these, and analyze their effects.

Price rationing may be thought "unfair"—poor people might be priced out of the market for some essentials—so other nonprice rationing methods, including queuing, ration coupons, favored customers, and lotteries, are applied. Such schemes usually involve hidden costs (queuing costs time, for example) that may make them inefficient. Note that different types of rationing benefit different groups of people.

(page 106)

At many colleges, basketball tickets are distributed on a first-come first-served basis—meaning that students must queue, perhaps for days, to get tickets to the big game. Not-so-hidden costs include the inconvenience, loss of study time, and possible health effects. As an example of a lottery, colleges may allocate dorm rooms, not by price or need, but by random number selection.

> **Graphing Pointer:** Remember that a price ceiling stops the price going higher (just like a ceiling in a room), while a price floor is a lower limit. To have an effect on equilibrium price, a ceiling must be set *below* the equilibrium price and a floor *above* the equilibrium price.
>
> **Comment:** The conceptual companion of a price ceiling is a price floor. A price ceiling sets a maximum price; a price floor sets a minimum price. The minimum wage is a price floor. An effective price ceiling creates an excess demand; an effective price floor creates an excess supply. This may be confusing—to have a ceiling below the equilibrium price.

PRACTICE

8. A price ceiling is established below the equilibrium price. We can predict that
A. quantity demanded will decrease.
B. quantity supplied will be greater than quantity demanded.
C. demand will be less than supply.
D. quantity supplied will decrease.
Answer: D. Price will be reduced by the price ceiling. A decrease in price causes quantity supplied to decrease (not a shift in the supply curve).

9. A price ceiling is set below the equilibrium price. We can predict that
A. there will be a leftward shift in the demand curve.
B. there will be a leftward shift in the supply curve.
C. quantity demanded will be greater than quantity supplied.
D. quantity supplied will be reduced to equal quantity demanded.
Answer: C. A change in price does not cause the demand and/or supply curve to shift position! If price is "too low," an excess demand (quantity demanded greater than quantity supplied) will occur.

10. Ticket scalping will be successful if
    A. demand is relatively steep.
    B. demand is relatively flat.
    C. the official price is below the equilibrium price.
    D. the official price is above the equilibrium price.
    Answer: C. The steepness of the demand curve is irrelevant in this case. The important issue is that an excess demand for tickets exists because the official price has been set too low.

OBJECTIVE 3: Explain, using words and/or diagrams, how an oil import fee would affect the domestic production and total consumption of oil.

The text offers the imposition of a tax on imported oil (an oil import fee) as an example of the usefulness of demand and supply analysis. The analysis shows that a new tax will raise the domestic price of oil, cutting quantity demanded and encouraging domestic production. The size of these changes depends on the slopes of the demand and supply curves or, more accurately, the responsiveness of demand and supply to price changes. Although the imposition of this tax would raise government revenues, reduce dependence on foreign oil, and stimulate domestic production of oil, inefficient domestic producers may be sheltered from lower-priced foreign competition.
(page 113)

Which consumers are most likely to be penalized by an oil import fee? Within the market, some buyers will have a demand that is relatively unresponsive to price changes, while others will be more able to trim demand if price rises. Would a price hike discriminate more against the poor (who may have little choice in their fuel consumption) than against those who are better off (who can afford to buy other kinds of heating)?

PRACTICE

Refer to the following diagram for the next three questions. The world price of oil is $20 per barrel.

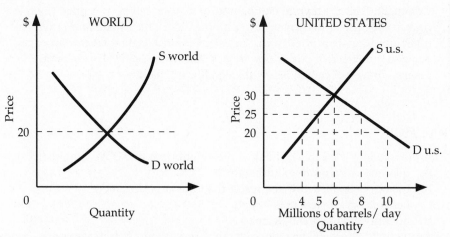

11. If the world price is the market price in the United States, then there will be an
    _____ of _____ million barrels per day.
    A. excess supply, 10.
    B. excess supply, 6.
    C. excess demand, 10.
    D. excess demand, 6.
    Answer: D. At $20 per barrel, quantity supplied is 4 million and quantity demanded is 10 million.

12. Suppose that the United States imposes a $5 per barrel import fee. This will result in each of the following except
   A. a decrease in imports to 3 million barrels per day.
   B. an increase in the quantity supplied of oil in the U.S. to 5 million barrels per day.
   C. a decrease in the quantity demanded of oil in the U.S. to 8 million barrels per day.
   D. a decrease in U.S. imports of oil by 3 million barrels per day.
   Answer: D. Oil imports had been 6 million barrels per day. After the imposition of the fee, oil imports are 3 million barrels per day. Imports decreased by 3 million barrels per day.

13. An import fee of $5 per imported barrel of oil will generate a tax revenue of
   A. $3 million per day.
   B. $5 million per day.
   C. $8 million per day.
   D. $15 million per day.
   Answer: D. Imports are 3 million barrels per day. Each barrel yields a tax revenue of $5.

14. Suppose that the United States wishes to become self-sufficient in oil. This could be done by
   A. establishing a price ceiling (maximum price) of $15 per barrel of oil.
   B. establishing a price ceiling (maximum price) of $30 per barrel of oil.
   C. imposing a fee of $10 per barrel on foreign oil.
   D. imposing a fee of $30 per barrel on foreign oil.
   Answer: C. A fee of $10 per barrel on foreign oil will result in equilibrium in the U.S. market.

PRACTICE TEST

I. MULTIPLE CHOICE QUESTIONS.

Select the option that provides the single best answer.

_____ 1. A ticket to a concert by the Screeming Habdabs costs $35. Just before the concert, however, tickets are being exchanged for $100. To a ticket-holder, the opportunity cost of actually attending the concert is
   A. $35.
   B. $65.
   C. $100.
   D. $135.

_____ 2. In a free market, 2000 patients each purchase an operation to receive an artificial heart at a price of $500,000 per operation. Without the artificial heart, each patient would die. The government decides that this price is too high and imposes a maximum price of $200,000. Everything else equal,
   A. more patients will now die.
   B. fewer patients will now die.
   C. more patients will now die only if the demand curve is vertical.
   D. more patients will now die only if the demand curve is horizontal.

Use the diagram below to answer the next two questions. The world price for gasoline is 50¢ per gallon. The equilibrium price in the U.S. market is $1.50.

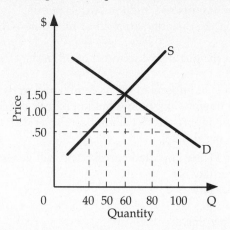

3. Assume that the U.S. neither imports nor exports gasoline. At the world price for gasoline, there is an _____ of gas in the U.S. market of _____ units.
   A. excess supply, 60.
   B. excess supply, 100.
   C. excess demand, 60.
   D. excess demand, 100.

4. The government imposes an import tax that raises the price of gas to $1.00 per gallon. If the domestic supply of gas increased by 30 million gallons per day,
   A. the excess demand of gas would be eliminated.
   B. government tax revenues would be 30 million times 50¢.
   C. quantity demanded would increase.
   D. the equilibrium price would remain at $1.50.

5. The supply curve of bottled water on an island is completely vertical. The market for bottled water is in equilibrium. A ferryload of thirsty holidaymakers arrives and the demand for bottled water increases. Which of the following statements is true?
   A. Price will serve as a rationing device.
   B. Price will not serve as a rationing device because the quantity supplied cannot change.
   C. Price will not serve as a rationing device because the equilibrium quantity demanded cannot change.
   D. Price will not serve as a rationing device because neither the equilibrium quantity demanded nor the equilibrium quantity supplied can change.

6. A price ceiling is set above current equilibrium price. If supply decreases, price would
   A. increase.
   B. decrease.
   C. not change.
   D. be indeterminate.

7. The government has decided that the free market price for baby formula is "too high." Which of the following rationing proposals will result in the least misallocation of baby formula resources?
   A. Proposal A: establish an official price ceiling, then let sellers decide how to allocate baby formula among customers.
   B. Proposal B: issue coupons for baby formula that cannot be resold.
   C. Proposal C: issue coupons for baby formula that can be resold.
   D. Proposal D: establish a price ceiling and require purchasers to queue.

Use the graph below to answer the next two questions. Suppose a price ceiling of $1 is set.

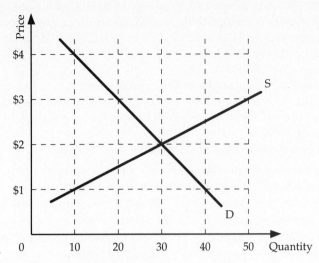

_____ 8. The price ceiling will cause an
   A. excess supply of 40 units.
   B. excess demand of 40 units.
   C. excess demand of 30 units.
   D. excess supply of 30 units.

_____ 9. If the price ceiling is left in place, we would predict that, eventually,
   A. demand would decrease until quantity demanded and quantity supplied were equal at a price of $1.
   B. supply would increase until quantity demanded and quantity supplied were equal at a price of $1.
   C. the market participants will be convinced that $1 is the equilibrium price.
   D. a persistent excess demand would lead to the emergence of non-price rationing practices such as queuing.

_____ 10. A government imposed ceiling on apartment rents, if set above the equilibrium rent level, would
   A. have no effect on the housing market.
   B. lead to a persistent shortage of apartments.
   C. lead to a persistent surplus of apartments.
   D. shift the supply curve for apartments to the right.

II. APPLICATION QUESTIONS.

1. Consider the following diagram which shows the market for fluid milk. Quantity is in thousands of gallons.

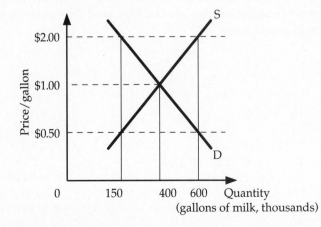

a. Calculate total income for dairy farmers.
b. Suppose that this income level is felt to be inadequate, and that a political decision is made to boost farm income to $1,200,000. Suppose the government establishes a price floor at $2.00, with the government buying the excess supply. How much milk will be supplied? What has happened to the size of the dairy industry?
c. Who gets the milk?
d. What has happened to the price for consumers?
e. The plan achieves the income objective, but what else has it done? There are costs involved with tampering with the price mechanism. What are they?
f. What can the Government do with the surplus milk?

Now suppose the government establishes a price ceiling of 50¢ per gallon.
g. How much milk would consumers actually receive?
h. Which plan is better for a milk consumer who pays no state tax? Why?

Now suppose the government tells the farmers that they are responsible for selling the milk they produce at a price the market can bear but that the government will give a supplement of $1.50 per gallon.
i. How much milk will farmers provide?
j. How much milk would consumers actually receive?
k. At which price would 600,000 gallons be demanded?
l. How much will this income-support scheme cost the government?
m. Compare the side effects of this proposal with those of the price floor.

2. In the *Applications* section of Chapter 4, we examined the market for video-cassettes where the supply and demand curves are given by Qs = 3P and Qd = 60 − 2P, respectively.

Now the government imposes a price ceiling of $5 in this market.
a. What will happen to the positions of the demand and supply curves?
b. Given the price ceiling, determine the extent of the excess demand or supply that is present.
c. Suppose that the government increases the price ceiling to $15. Determine the extent of the excess demand or supply that is present.

3. The freeze that destroyed a good portion of the South American coffee crop in the mid–1970s increased the price of tea. Demonstrate why, using supply and demand diagrams.

4. Illustrate each of the following with demand and/or supply curves.
a. A situation where the quantity supplied is completely unresponsive to changes in price.
b. A labor demand curve, with wage on the vertical axis, where, as the wage decreases the increase in the number of workers demanded progressively decreases.
c. A situation of excess demand created by a price ceiling.
d. The effect of an increase in income on the price of an inferior good.
e. The effect of a sharp increase in electricity rates on the demand for and price of air conditioners.

5. In many Eastern European cities, there is a thriving market in farm produce.
   a. Draw a demand and supply diagram below for the Warsaw egg market. Label the curves D_1 and S_1 respectively. Show the equilibrium price (P_1) and quantity (Q_1).

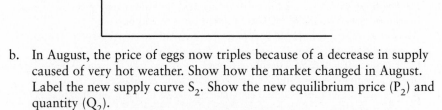

   b. In August, the price of eggs now triples because of a decrease in supply caused of very hot weather. Show how the market changed in August. Label the new supply curve S_2. Show the new equilibrium price (P_2) and quantity (Q_2).
   c. Is the Warsaw egg market operating efficiently?
   d. Suppose the government decided to maintain the initial price (P_1). Should it impose a price ceiling or a price floor? Explain whether an excess demand or an excess supply will result.
   e. Is the Warsaw egg market now operating efficiently?
   f. How do you think suppliers might react to the price ceiling?
   g. Suggest what nonprice methods might develop to circumvent the imbalance in this market.

6. Use the following demand and supply schedule to answer the questions.

Price	Quantity Demanded	Quantity Supplied
$6	10	70
$5	20	60
$4	30	50
$3	40	40
$2	50	30
$1	60	20

   a. Determine the equilibrium price.
   b. Determine the equilibrium quantity.
   c. Now the government establishes a price ceiling of $2. Will there be an excess demand or an excess supply? Of how many units?
   d. What will happen to the quantity supplied?
   e. Given this change, will there be an overallocation or an underallocation of resources to the production of this good?
   f. Such a price ceiling interferes with which function of the price system?

7. Several members of a college faculty were standing in a rather long line at the student cafeteria. One was heard to remark that she wished the cafeteria would increase prices. Can you explain why?

8. Who gained and who lost from government intervention in the market in each of the following cases?
   a. In the fall of 1993, Congress scrapped subsidies for honey producers. Until 1988, a price floor was in place, with the government purchasing surpluses. From 1980 to 1988, $525 million was spent.
   b. In 1991, the minimum wage was raised to $4.25 per hour. Who gained and who lost from this wage floor? How do teenagers fit into your answer?

ANSWERS AND SOLUTIONS

PRACTICE TEST

I. SOLUTIONS TO MULTIPLE CHOICE QUESTIONS

1. C. The opportunity cost is the value of the next best alternative given up, i.e., in monetary terms, whatever the $100 offered price would buy.
2. A. A price ceiling is in effect and an excess demand exists. Assuming an upward sloping supply curve, fewer operations will be offered.
3. C. The price is below the equilibrium price, with quantity demanded being 100 and quantity supplied being only 40. An excess demand of 60 exists.
4. A. The increase in supply would eliminate the excess demand and eliminate government tax revenues.
5. A. Demand has increased causing an excess demand. Price will rise to remove the imbalance.
6. A. A price ceiling above the equilibrium price will have no effect. A decrease in supply, therefore, will result in a higher price.
7. C. Issuing coupons that can be resold will lead to a market for coupons with those willing and able to pay the most receiving the right to buy baby formula.
8. C. An effective price ceiling (set below the equilibrium price) will create an excess demand. Quantity demanded is 40, but quantity supplied is only 10, so an excess demand of 30 exists.
9. D. Demand and supply curves do not shift in response to changes in price!
10. A. To be effective, a price ceiling must be set below the equilibrium price.

II. SOLUTIONS TO APPLICATION QUESTIONS

1. a. $400,000.
   b. 600,000 gallons. The dairy industry has expanded.
   c. 150,000 gallons for the consumer, and the rest is taken by the government.
   d. The price for consumers of milk has risen to $2.00. It is more expensive for the poor to buy milk.
   e. Many things—milk is now more expensive and less plentiful for consumers. Taxpayers—who needn't be milk consumers—will have to pick up the subsidy tab. There will be storage and administrative costs, too. Also, there is an overallocation of resources toward milk production.
   f. The surplus milk can't be sold in the open market: it might be destroyed, stored, or processed into powdered milk for distribution to less developed countries In general, there is an income-redistribution not just towards the farmers but also *away from* taxpayers. The distorting side effects of this proposal are legion.
   g. Consumers will receive 150,000 gallons. In this case there will be an excess demand.
   h. The second plan is better in that the price of milk is lower.
   i. 600,000 gallons, as before. Including the $1.50 per gallon government payment,

farmers will supply 600,000 gallons and receive $2.00 per gallon.

j.   600,000 gallons are produced and all will be sold to consumers.

k.   50¢ per gallon.

l. $900,000, as before, i.e., $1.50 per gallon × 600,000 gallons.

m.   Although the administrative costs may be greater, as well as the incentive for farmers to cheat, the new proposal may be better than the first because there are no storage costs, and prices to consumers fall.

2. a.   Nothing! A change in price leads to movements along the given demand and supply curves.

   b.   Equilibrium price is $12, therefore the price ceiling is effective and will cause an excess demand of 35.

   c.   The price ceiling is set above the equilibrium price—it will have no effect on the original market conditions.

3.   Higher coffee prices increased the demand for tea (a substitute). See the diagrams below.

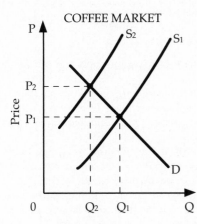

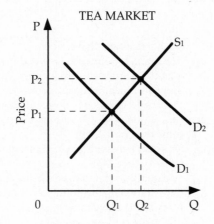

4. See the diagrams below.

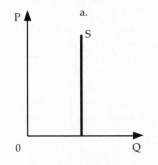

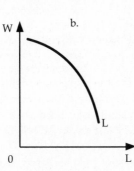

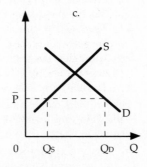

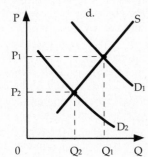

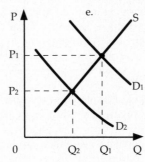

5. a. See the diagram below.

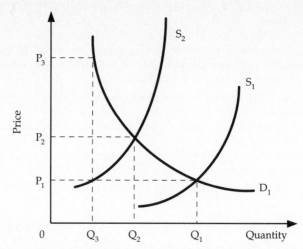

b. See the diagram above.
c. The market is efficient, in that it is reflecting the change in supply and equalizing quantity demanded and quantity supplied.
d. The government should impose a price ceiling to place an upper limit on price. Quantity demanded will exceed quantity supplied—there will be an excess demand.
e. This is now a seller's market. Output is restricted to Q_3. At that output, an excess demand exists.
f. Suppliers may withdraw eggs from the controlled Warsaw market—selling them either outside Warsaw or on the black market within the city. Sub-standard (small or damaged) eggs may be offered for sale. Egg quality may be sacrificed.
g. Other rationing methods, such as queuing or preferred customers, might be used. Black markets with higher prices are likely to develop. Eggs may be sold as part of a "package" of commodities.

6. a. Equilibrium price is $3.
b. Equilibrium quantity is 40.
c. There will be an excess demand of 20 units.
d. Supply will decrease.
e. Given demand and the reduction in supply, fewer resources than society would desire are being allocated to the production of this good.
f. The allocative function is constrained.

7. Higher prices would reduce quantity demanded and cut down on waiting time. If you value your time highly, you would probably be willing to pay higher prices to avoid waiting in line.

8. a. There was a transfer of wealth from taxpayers in general to the nation's 2,000 commercial beekeepers. Honey consumers also lost because the market price was kept higher than it should have been. There was an overallocation of resources to honey production. Note that honey consumption was less than its most efficient level despite the excess supply.
b. There was a transfer of wealth from employers to minimum-wage employees with jobs. There was a reduction in the quantity of labor demanded—fewer workers were hired. Workers who could not find jobs lost as a result of the wage floor. The level of unemployment increased amongst the poor and unskilled—those least able to afford a reduction in job opportunities. Teenagers are amongst the least experienced workers, and evidence suggests that they suffered as a result of the minimum wage. Indeed, to redress the balance, a sub-minimum wage was introduced from 1991–93 for teenagers.

INTRODUCTION TO MACROECONOMICS

6

COMBINED TEXT

21

OBJECTIVES: POINT BY POINT

After completing this chapter, you should be able to accomplish the objectives listed below.

General Comment

This chapter is an "introduction." The material skimmed over here will be explored more completely in subsequent chapters. Think of this chapter as a road map showing major points of interest.

> **TIP:** Different economists support different interpretations of how the economy fits together. If you're grade-oriented (or even if you're not) , it might be a good idea to identify the preferences of your own instructor, even if it's for no other reason than that it will help you to identify the areas of controversy.

OBJECTIVE 1: Briefly describe the development of Keynesian macroeconomic theory and place it within the context of then-current economic events.

Macroeconomics was born out of the dark days of the Great Depression in the 1930s when the labor market didn't clear in the way that the classical model predicted it should—wages were "sticky" and unemployment persisted for years. A theoretical re-think was performed by John Maynard Keynes, who argued that the level of employment is not determined by prices and wages but by the level of aggregate demand for goods and services. Macroeconomics remains a controversial area of study. (page 120/546)

> **TIP:** Refer to Chapter 1 to refresh your memory on the distinction between micro- and macroeconomics.

Evolution: Macroeconomics evolves in light of new information and phenomena. Keynes's economic theory was a product of, and response to, his own (unemployment-ridden) era. Existing theory couldn't analyze the conditions that he observed. Later developments have followed the same pattern—an orthodox view; some fresh, "awkward" real-world facts; a revision of the theory.

The sixties had high levels of demand, a booming war-time economy, and a quest for the Great Society. Employment levels and job opportunities were high but so was the inflation rate. This environment differed from the one that prompted Keynes to rethink economic analysis—inflation hadn't been a critical factor for him. A new controversy arose—between Keynesians and "monetarists." More on this in Chapter 19 (34).

Next came the soaring oil prices in the seventies and the phenomenon of stagflation—supply-side economics was born. See Chapter 19 (34).

PRACTICE

1. The classical economists assumed that wages were _____ upward and _____ downward.
   A. flexible, flexible.
   B. flexible, not flexible.
   C. not flexible, flexible.
   D. not flexible, not flexible.
   Answer: A. The classical economists believed that the wage would respond to shifts in the demand for, and supply of, labor. See p. 121/547.

2. Aggregation refers to
   A. the behavior of all individuals in a group taken together.
   B. the calculation of average values by adding together and dividing.
   C. forecasting future values, based on past data.
   D. the development of the microeconomic foundations of macroeconomics.
   Answer: A. See p. 120/546.

3. The classical economists predicted that, if the demand for labor fell, then
   A. the wage would increase, the supply of labor would increase, and unemployment would occur.
   B. the wage would decrease, the supply of labor would decrease, and unemployment would occur.
   C. the wage rate would fall to clear the market, resulting in higher unemployment.
   D. the wage rate would fall to clear the market, reducing the quantity of labor supplied and eliminating unemployment.
   Answer: D. Try drawing the labor market using demand and supply curves. The classical economists used microeconomic tools. Unfortunately, they failed to take into account contracts, minimum wages, and the possibility that the wage level could become stuck.

4. Keynes believed that the level of employment is determined by
   A. the wage level.
   B. the aggregate (overall) price level.
   C. aggregate demand.
   D. stock prices.
   Answer: C. Keynes's macroeconomic model is driven by aggregate demand. When there is an increase in the demand for goods and services, there is an increase in employment.

5. At the beginning of 1996, the Lifeguards' Union negotiates a wage contract of $6 per hour for lifeguards. The summer of 1996 is especially bleak, with little bathing. Although the demand for lifeguards decreases, their hourly wage rate does not. This is an example of a
   A. macroeconomic price.
   B. price control.
   C. sticky price.
   D. price ceiling.
   Answer: C. If the price of lifeguard services were influenced by changes in market conditions, the price (wage) should have fallen. The contractual agreement made the price "sticky."

OBJECTIVE 2: Describe the four main concerns of macroeconomics and provide simple definitions of inflation and unemployment.

Major topics of concern in macroeconomics are: inflation (a general increase in the aggregate price level); aggregate output of the economy and the business cycle; the level of employment (and the rate of unemployment, which is the proportion of labor force that is unemployed); and the economy's relationship with the rest of the world. (page 123/550)

PRACTICE

6. _____ is when there are extremely rapid increases in the overall price level.
   A. Inflation.
   B. Stagflation.
   C. Hyperinflation.
   D. Superflation.
   Answer: C. See p. 124/551.

7. A recession occurs when aggregate output declines for _____ consecutive _____.
   A. two, months.
   B. two, quarters.
   C. three, months.
   D. three, quarters.
   Answer: B. See p. 125/552.

8. In a recession we expect to see unemployment _____ and output _____.
   A. increasing, increasing.
   B. increasing, decreasing.
   C. decreasing, increasing.
   D. decreasing, decreasing.
   Answer: B. In question 6 we defined a recession as a period of decreasing output. As output decreases (usually because of falling aggregate demand), the unemployment lines lengthen.

OBJECTIVE 3: Explain how macroeconomic issues relate to the government's policy decisions. List four policies that the government may use to influence the economy. Indicate the principal tools of each policy.

Macro problems may be attacked through the use of fiscal, monetary, incomes, and supply-side policy actions. *Fiscal policy* involves manipulating the amount of taxation and government spending; *monetary policy* involves adjusting the quantity of money available; *incomes policy* involves imposing controls on wages and prices; and *supply-side policy* is intended to manipulate aggregate supply. (page 126/553)

9. The notion that the government can stabilize the economy is known as
    A. classical macroeconomics.
    B. supply-side economics.
    C. proactive business cycle management.
    D. fine-tuning.
    Answer: D. "Fine tuning" suggests that the government can adjust macro-economic variables (inflation and unemployment) very precisely through carefully selected policy actions.

10. The economy is in a recession. Using fiscal policy tools, the government might _____ government spending and _____ taxes.
    A. increase, increase.
    B. increase, decrease.
    C. decrease, increase.
    D. decrease, decrease.
    Answer: B. Raising government spending will increase aggregate demand. Cutting taxes will also increase aggregate demand.

11. In 1971, President Nixon banned wage and price increases. This is an example of a(n)
    A. fiscal policy.
    B. monetary policy.
    C. incomes policy.
    D. supply-side policy.
    Answer: C. See p. 127/554.

12. Policies designed to control the amount of money in circulation are known as
    A. fiscal policies.
    B. monetary policies.
    C. incomes policies.
    D. supply-side policies.
    Answer: B. See p. 126/553.

13. The President initiates a new policy designed to stimulate production directly rather than to operate on aggregate demand. Such a policy is a(n)
    A. incomes policy.
    B. supply-side policy.
    C. fiscal policy.
    D. monetary policy.
    Answer: B. Rather than affect demand, the President's policy is intended to influence the economy's ability to supply. See p. 127/554.

OBJECTIVE 4: List the four economic sectors and describe how they interact through markets.

The circular flow model represents the linkages among the four different sectors of the economy—households, firms, the government, and the rest of the world. There are three major markets—goods-and-services, labor, and money—and the four sectors interact in each of these. (page 128/554)

> **TIP:** Note that the circularity makes an important point—each dollar spent is also a dollar earned as income by producers. You will see this concept again.

Note that there are numerous markets within each "market"—the goods-and-services market contains the market for cars, coffee, corn flakes, and cotton swabs, for example. Each "market" is a macroeconomic aggregation. (page 129/556)

TIP: Learn the model! The macro model begun in this chapter will be built upon through successive chapters, but the logic within it will remain the same. You'll find the going easier if you master each step as it is presented, rather than waiting and trying to make sense of it all at once in its completed form or before a test. The circular flow diagram (p. 128/555) is a great place to start. Throughout the remainder of your macro course the fourfold division—consumers/businesses/government/international—will be present, and the three markets will be at, or close to, center stage.

TIP: As Case and Fair advise, you'll find macroeconomics easier if you think in terms of the "typical" consumer or firm. Macroeconomists don't claim that all individuals respond in the same way in each circumstance, but they do try to draw out the general tendency, and you should strive to do the same. Macroeconomics is interested in the forest, not the trees.

TIP: Ignore exceptions! Inflation, for example, occurs when the general (aggregate) price level is rising. Some prices (VCRs, CDs, calculators) may be falling—but the general price trend is upward. Similarly, although you have a friend who has just found a job, the general unemployment rate can still be rising.

PRACTICE

14. Households are
    A. only demanders in the money market.
    B. only suppliers in the money market.
    C. both demanders and suppliers in the money market.
    D. neither demanders nor suppliers in the money market—banks are.
    Answer: C. Households deposit (supply) funds and borrow (demand) funds. See p. 130/557.

15. The main point to draw from the circular flow diagram is that
    A. saving will always equal investment.
    B. every dollar of expenditure is also a dollar of income.
    C. exports equal imports.
    D. wages equal income.
    Answer: B. Option D is incorrect—other payments (rent and dividends, for example) are part of income. Because we typically run a trade deficit in the United States, we know that exports and imports are not necessarily equal. Saving and investment are not mentioned explicitly in the diagram—more about them later.

16. In our model of the macroeconomy, each of the following is a market arena in which households, firms, the government, and the rest of the world interact except
    A. the goods-and-services market.
    B. the foreign trade market.
    C. the labor market.
    D. the money market.
    Answer: B. Modeling in economics, as in other sciences, involves selection. Our model chooses to exclude the foreign trade market as a separate arena. See p. 129/556.

OBJECTIVE 5: Use aggregate demand and aggregate supply curves to provide a description of the macroeconomy.

Aggregate demand (AD) and aggregate supply (AS) can be depicted in a diagram.

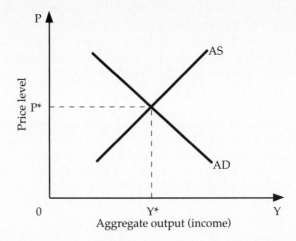

The overall price level (P) is on the vertical axis and aggregate output (Y) is on the horizontal axis. At the price level (P*) where AD and AS are equal, the economy is in equilibrium—equilibrium output is Y*. Keynes claimed that we can shift the aggregate demand curve; the supply-siders claimed that we can shift the aggregate supply curve. If we can shift one or both of these curves, output (and employment) and the price level (inflation) can be adjusted.   (page 132/558)

> **Graphing Pointer:** Note that P and Y are aggregate values—the AS/AD diagram is not the same as, say, a graph showing the demand and supply of a single good like coffee.

PRACTICE

17. The aggregate demand curve has a downward slope because of changes in
     A. the goods-and-services market.
     B. the money market.
     C. the labor market.
     D. the global market.
     Answer: B. The textbook cautions that, although the aggregate demand curve *looks* like an "ordinary" demand curve, it is not. The slope is *not* determined by the income and substitution effects of Chapter 4 but by actions occurring in the money market. See p. 133/559.

18. Aggregate demand is the demand for goods and services by
     A. households.
     B. the private sector (households and firms).
     C. the public (government) sector.
     D. all sectors in the economy.
     Answer: D. Aggregate demand is the *total* demand by all sectors.

Use the following diagram and your intuition to answer the next four questions. Note: These questions extend further than the material covered in the text, but you should be able to see your way to the correct answer.

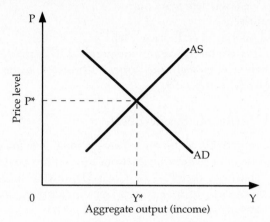

19. A(n) _____ in government spending is an expansionary fiscal policy; a(n) _____ in taxes is an expansionary fiscal policy.
    A. increase, increase.
    B. increase, decrease.
    C. decrease, increase.
    D. decrease, decrease.
    Answer: B. The adjective "expansionary" refers to the impact on aggregate demand—not whether government spending or taxes are expanding or not.

20. There is an increase in government spending. Given the diagram above, we predict that aggregate output will _____ and that the overall price level will _____.
    A. increase, increase.
    B. increase, decrease.
    C. decrease, increase.
    D. decrease, decrease.
    Answer: A. An increase in government spending increases aggregate demand. As demand shifts right, equilibrium output and price level will increase.

21. There is an increase in government spending. Given the diagram above, we predict that unemployment will _____ and that inflation will _____.
    A. increase, increase.
    B. increase, decrease.
    C. decrease, increase.
    D. decrease, decrease.
    Answer: C. As aggregate output increases, job opportunities will open up. As the overall price level rises, inflation occurs.

22. Refer to the diagram. Which of the following situations would permit stagflation to occur?
    A. An increase in aggregate demand.
    B. A decrease in aggregate demand.
    C. An increase in aggregate supply.
    D. A decrease in aggregate supply.
    Answer: D. If aggregate supply decreases (shifts left), aggregate output level will fall, causing unemployment to increase and the overall price level to increase, stimulating inflation.

23. In an aggregate demand/aggregate supply diagram, _____ is plotted on the vertical axis and _____ is plotted on the horizontal axis.
    A. price, quantity.
    B. overall price level, aggregate output.
    C. quantity, price.
    D. aggregate output, overall price level.
    Answer: B. This is an "aggregate" diagram—aggregate measures are called for. As in Chapter 4, though, the "price" variable goes on the vertical axis. See the diagram on p. 132/559.

OBJECTIVE 6: Describe the business cycle.

The U.S. economic record this century has shown a long-term underlying expansion (growth trend), but there have been fluctuations around this trend. Economists call these fluctuations "business cycles"—the Great Depression being the most grave example. Each cycle consists of four phases—peak, recession, trough, and expansion. One goal of government economic policy has been to smooth out business cycles and have the economy stay on a more even keel.   (page 134/560)

> **TIP:** Do a little simple macroeconomic research. Find out the current position of the economy in the business cycle. Is the economy in the expansion phase, for example? Also, listen for reports on unemployment rates (nationally and for your state) and the inflation rate. These numbers are reported each month. Why might your state's unemployment rate differ from the national value?

PRACTICE

Use the following diagram of a business cycle to answer the next two questions.

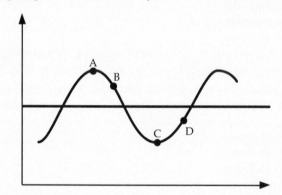

24. In the diagram of a business cycle, _____ is on the vertical axis; _____ is on the horizontal axis.
    A. inflation, unemployment.
    B. unemployment, inflation.
    C. gross domestic product, time.
    D. time, gross domestic product.
    Answer: C. The diagram plots output level over time. Add this information to the diagram above. See the diagram on p. 134/561.

25. In the diagram above, the expansion of the business cycle occurs at point _____ and the recession occurs at point _____.
    A. A, B.
    B. A, C.
    C. B, C.
    D. D, B.
    Answer: D. The peak is at point A, the recession at point B, the trough at point C, and the expansion at point D.

26. A measure of the overall rate of inflation is provided by
    A. the level of the GDP price deflator.
    B. the percentage change in the level of the GDP price deflator.
    C. the level of the GDP price deflator divided by 12.
    D. the level of the GDP price deflator multiplied by 12.
    Answer: B. The rate of inflation is the rate of change in the overall price level.
    See p. 137/563.

PRACTICE TEST

I. MULTIPLE CHOICE QUESTIONS.

Select the option that provides the single best answer.

C   1. Which of the following is not a macroeconomic variable?
        A. the interest rate.
        B. the general price level.
        C. the price of beer.
        D. gross domestic product.

B   2. Keynes argued that the primary determinant of the level of economic activity is
        A. the amount of money there is to spend.
        B. the aggregate demand for goods and services.
        C. the aggregate price level.
        D. the demand for labor.

C   3. In the money market, each of the following is traded except
        A. Treasury notes.
        B. corporate bonds.
        C. capital gains.
        D. shares of stock.

A   4. A Keynesian fiscal policy intended to pull the economy out of a slump might include cutting
        A. taxes to increase aggregate demand.
        B. government spending to increase aggregate supply.
        C. government spending to increase aggregate demand.
        D. taxes to increase aggregate supply.

A   5. Each of the following represents a policy available to the government except
        A. transfer policy.
        B. incomes policy.
        C. fiscal policy.
        D. monetary policy.

D   6. Which of the following is not a phase of a typical business cycle?
        A. Recession.
        B. Trough.
        C. Peak.
        D. Inflation.

D   7. One objective of supply-side policies was to increase aggregate _____ by _____ personal tax rates.
        A. demand, increasing.
        B. demand, decreasing.
        C. supply, increasing.
        D. supply, decreasing.

_B_ 8. Employment typically rises during
  A. a period of stagflation.
  B. a period of inflation.
  C. a recession.
  D. the period from the peak to a trough in a business cycle.

_C_ 9. Each of the following is an example of a transfer payment except
  A. a welfare check.
  B. social security benefits.
  C. interest on a Treasury bond.
  D. veterans' benefits.

_A_ 10. In the labor market, suppliers are
  A. households.
  B. households and firms.
  C. firms and government.
  D. firms.

_B_ 11. In the circular flow model
  A. households purchase resources.
  B. firms and the government purchase resources.
  C. government sells resources.
  D. households produce goods and services.

_C_ 12. As the economy moves into a recession, we typically see inflation _____ and unemployment _____.
  A. increasing, increasing.
  B. increasing, decreasing.
  C. decreasing, increasing.
  D. decreasing, decreasing.

_D_ 13. In 1981, President Reagan cut tax rates for individuals and for businesses. This was an example of a(n)
  A. fiscal policy.
  B. monetary policy.
  C. incomes policy.
  D. supply-side policy.

_A_ 14. Stagflation is characterized by _____ unemployment and a _____ price level.
  A. high, rising.
  B. high, falling.
  C. low, rising.
  D. low, falling.

_B_ 15. To know where the economy is in the business cycle, one must know
  A. the unemployment rate.
  B. the rate of change in the level of economic activity.
  C. the rate of change in the price level.
  D. the rate of change in the unemployment rate.

_C_ 16. Consider the aggregate demand and aggregate supply diagram on p. 132/559 of the textbook. If aggregate supply shifted to the left, the economic result is best described as
  A. inflation.
  B. hyperinflation.
  C. stagflation.
  D. recession.

_B_ 17. Regulations on pollution and health and safety concerns are eased by the government. Such a policy is a(n)
  A. incomes policy.
  B. supply-side policy.
  C. fiscal policy.
  D. monetary policy.

_A_   18. "Sticky" prices in a given market suggest that excess demand
_____ be sustained and excess supply _____
be sustained.
A. can, can.
B. can, cannot.
C. cannot, can.
D. cannot, cannot.

_D_   19. Which of the following statements is true?
A. During a period of hyperinflation, we would expect an increase
in the value of savings, because everyone needs to have more
money.
B. During a period of high inflation, fine-tuning would call for
an increase in the money supply.
C. Stagflation is defined as a rapid increase in the overall price level.
D. The percentage change in the GDP price deflator is a good
measure of inflation.

_A_   20. In sequence, the four phases of a business cycle are
A. the trough, the expansion, the peak, and the recession.
B. the recession, the peak, the expansion, and the trough.
C. the trough, the expansion, the recession, and the peak.
D. the trough, the recession, the expansion, and the peak.

II.   APPLICATION QUESTIONS.

1. Devise a hypothesis about the link between household income and household
spending. As one increases, does the other increase or decrease? Which variable
is the "cause" and which the "effect"? Why is your theory an abstraction?
Is your theory invalidated if one household behaves differently?

2. How do you personally participate in the markets for goods and services,
labor and finance?

3. Our aggregate demand and supply analysis is not yet theoretically rigorous,
but a decent knowledge of demand and supply can help us interpret current
affairs with this model.

Below is an aggregate demand and aggregate supply diagram, with equilibrium
at Y*. Suppose that, at this output level, there are large quantities of unemployed
resources in the economy.

Assume that the more production there is, the higher employment will be.
The aggregate demand (AD) curve represents total demand in the economy,
and the aggregate supply (AS) curve total supply.

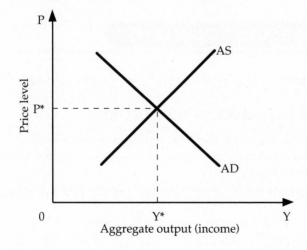

a. What comprises total demand for goods in the U.S. economy?
b. Given the income level, what will happen to the level of consumption spending by households if saving increases?
c. How will aggregate demand be affected by an increase in saving?
d. How could you represent this change in aggregate demand on the diagram?
e. In terms of output (and employment), what would be the impact of the change in aggregate demand?
f. Ignoring the foreign sector of the economy, how could such a shift in aggregate demand be prevented?
g. Suppose the government reduced income taxes on households. What effect is this likely to have on consumption, aggregate demand, output level, employment, unemployment, and the aggregate price level?

4. Draw an aggregate demand and aggregate supply graph for the economy. Suppose aggregate demand increases. What happens to quantity traded? What should happen to employment? If the government managed to increase aggregate demand (and cut unemployment), what other problems might it face?

5. Identify the following topics as either predominantly macroeconomic (MAC) or microeconomic (MIC).
a. _____ gross domestic product
b. _____ the demand for beer
c. _____ inflation
d. _____ the price of gold relative to the price of silver
e. _____ unemployment among economics professors
f. _____ wages in regulated public utilities
g. _____ economic growth
h. _____ stagflation
i. _____ price of medical care
j. _____ job discrimination
k. _____ recession
l. _____ apartment rents
m. _____ total employment
n. _____ household income
o. _____ national income
p. _____ business cycles
q. _____ the budget deficit
r. _____ the money supply

6. Two flow diagrams are presented in the text. After going over the section in the text, draw each of them from your memory and understanding. For the "market" diagram, label the arrows between the sectors and markets.

ANSWERS AND SOLUTIONS

PRACTICE TEST

I. SOLUTIONS TO MULTIPLE CHOICE QUESTIONS

1. C. The price of a single good (like beer) is microeconomic in nature.
2. B. Keynes believed that aggregate demand is the driving force in determining macro-economic activity. See p. 121/547.
3. C. Capital gains occur when an asset is sold at a higher price than its purchase price. See p. 131/557.
4. A. Keynesian fiscal policy focuses on aggregate demand. To move the economy out of a slump, the government could cut taxes. This would give taxpayers more income to spend. See p. 126/553.
5. A. It is true that transfer payments, e.g., welfare, may be increased or decreased, but this is as a part of fiscal policy. See p. 126/553 for a discussion of the types of policy.

6. D. A business cycle reflects changes in production level. The missing phase is the expansion. See p. 134/561.

7. D. Supply-side policies affected aggregate supply. A cut in tax rates was intended to increase production. See p. 127/554.

8. B. See the discussion of U.S. business cycles since 1970 beginning on p. 136/562. Note that if aggregate supply decreases, the economy can experience inflation and increasing unemployment—i.e., stagflation.

9. C. Transfers are payments that require no good or service in return. Interest on a bond is a fee (reward) for lending the government money. See p. 131/558.

10. A. See the circular flow diagram on p. 128/555.

11. B. See the circular flow diagram on p. 128/555.

12. C. When the economy is slowing down, it is harder to sell goods (harder to raise prices) and harder to find a job. Note that if a decrease in aggregate supply has caused the recession, inflation will increase—i.e., stagflation.

13. D. This could have been classified as a fiscal policy, but fiscal policies, in fact, focus on adjusting aggregate demand. The tax rate changes, as noted in the text, were designed to stimulate aggregate supply by increasing worker and business effort.

14. A. Stagflation combines stagnation (high unemployment) with inflation (rising aggregate price level). See p. 123/550.

15. B. If the rate of change is positive, the economy is expanding; at the peak and at the trough, the rate of change is zero; in a recession, the rate of change is negative. See p. 134/561.

16. C. As aggregate supply shifts left, aggregate output decreases and economic growth falters. Also, the aggregate price level will increase (inflation). It is true that inflation occurs (Option A) and that a recession occurs (Option D) but, for a description of the complete situation, stagflation is more comprehensive. See p. 123/550 for the definition of stagflation.

17. B. This policy, which makes production less regulated, cheaper, and more attractive, is intended to influence the economy's ability to supply. See p. 127/554.

18. A. When prices are sticky (not very responsive to demand or supply changes), a situation of excess demand or excess supply can persist because, in either case, price does not move to eliminate the market imbalance. See p. 120/546.

19. D. See p. 137/563. Inflation, we shall see, has more than one cause, but increasing the money supply will aggravate the problem. Fine-tuning refers to the supposed ability of the government to make quite precise adjustments in inflation and unemployment. During hyperinflation, the value of currency is decreasing rapidly. The worst thing to do is hold money—it is better to spend it before it falls further in value. Stagflation is more than just inflation.

20. A. See p. 134/561.

II. SOLUTIONS TO APPLICATION QUESTIONS

1. There is a positive relationship between household income (independent variable) and household spending (dependent variable). The theory is an abstraction because it excludes all other factors that might affect household spending. If, in general, households behave as predicted by the theory, it is supported, exceptions notwithstanding.

2. In the market for goods and services, you are probably a buyer (e.g., groceries), in the market for labor you are probably a seller, and, in the money market, you are a seller if you save and a buyer if you borrow (e.g., student loans).

3. a. Consumption, investment, government spending, and net exports.
   b. Consumption will decrease.
   c. Aggregate demand will fall because consumption has fallen.
   d. The AD curve would shift to the left.
   e. Equilibrium output would decrease. Because fewer goods are being produced, we can predict increased unemployment.
   f. Such a decrease in aggregate demand may be prevented by increasing investment spending or increasing government spending. Another possibility is that another factor could make consumption increase again.
   g. If the government reduced income taxes on households, after-tax income would increase, and consumption would increase (making AD shift right). Output level and employment would increase, unemployment would decrease, and the aggregate price level would increase.

Note: One way, perhaps, to alleviate unemployment is through fiscal policy actions—changing the levels of government spending and/or taxes.

4. Refer to the diagram on p. 132/559 of the textbook. An increase in aggregate demand would cause the equilibrium output level to increase. As more is being produced, more workers will be hired. An increase in demand, though, will cause the overall price level to increase (inflation). A government fiscal policy to increase aggregate demand might involve cutting taxes and/or increasing government spending—these measures would increase the federal budget deficit.

5.
a.	MAC	f.	MIC	k.	MAC	p.	MAC
b.	MIC	g.	MAC	l.	MIC	q.	MAC
c.	MAC	h.	MAC	m.	MAC	r.	MAC
d.	MIC	i.	MIC	n.	MIC		
e.	MIC	j.	MIC	o.	MAC		

6. Refer to the text for the solutions to this exercise.

MEASURING NATIONAL OUTPUT AND NATIONAL INCOME

7

COMBINED TEXT

22

OBJECTIVES: POINT BY POINT

After completing this chapter, you should be able to accomplish the objectives listed below.

General Comment

Most students find this chapter a bit of a chore. Memorize the important definitions: GDP, the components of the expenditure approach, depreciation, saving (non-consumption), and disposable income.

OBJECTIVE 1: Define gross domestic product (GDP) and its components. Detail those transactions that are excluded from GDP calculations. Distinguish between GDP and GNP.

There is a family of national income accounts, but the key measure of current domestic economic activity is *gross domestic product*. GDP is the market value of all final goods and services produced within the economy. Second-hand sales, sales of intermediate goods, public and private transfers payments, and the value of financial transactions are all excluded. (page 143/569)

> **TIP:** There's no substitute for learning the rationale behind the concept of GDP. Productive economic activity within the economy results in new final goods and services. Sales of final goods plus (or minus) change in inventories will capture this. Compare this idea of new productive activity with the items that are excluded from GDP.

> **TIP:** Consider the logic behind the exclusion of some items from GDP calculations, such as transfer payments (public and private), intermediate goods, second-hand sales, and financial transactions. We're measuring *current* production of goods and services. Why are these categories excluded?
>
> Moonlighting, "do it yourself" activities, barter, and illegal activities don't show up either, although current goods and services are provided through these activities. How much would GDP change if, for example, the sale of drugs were decriminalized?

The distinguishing feature between GDP and GNP, which is location of production, can be seen in the case of Georgia peaches harvested by Mexican migrant workers. The value of these services adds to U.S. production and, therefore, is counted in U.S. GDP. U.S. GNP focuses on ownership of resources and ignores location. U.S. GNP would exclude the services of the migrant farm workers because they are not performed by U.S. citizens.

PRACTICE

1. U.S. gross domestic product for 1996 is defined as the total market value of all
   A. final goods and services sold in 1996.
   B. goods and services produced in 1996 by productive resources owned by U.S. citizens.
   C. final goods and services produced in 1996 within U.S. boundaries by productive resources owned by U.S. citizens.
   D. final goods and services produced in 1996 within U.S. boundaries.

   Answer: D. Ownership of resources is irrelevant in GDP calculations; the location of production is—it must be within U.S. boundaries. See p. 143/569.

2. _____ goods are goods that are not resold to someone else.
   A. Intermediate.
   B. Final.
   C. Transfer.
   D. Consumer durable.

   Answer: B. Consumer durables may not be resold (except as second-hand goods)—they are final goods. Goods that are resold are intermediate goods or second-hand goods. See p. 143/569.

3. Jean, an avid gardener, buys a packet of carrot seeds. The packet of seeds _____ counted in GDP as a final product; the carrots Jean grows and consumes _____ counted in GDP as a final product.
   A. is; are.
   B. is; are not.
   C. is not, are.
   D. is not, are not.

   Answer: B. The seeds are sold to the final user. Because Jean grows and eats the carrots, they never reach a market and will not be counted (although they do represent a part of production). This is one of the limitations of the GDP concept.

4. Many Arbezani workers cross the border to work in Arboc although few Arbocalis work in Arbez. We should expect that Arbezani GDP will be _____ than its GNP and that Arbocali GDP will be _____ than its GNP.
   A. greater, greater.
   B. greater, smaller.
   C. smaller, greater.
   D. smaller, smaller.

   Answer: C. GDP measures production by location. More resources are producing in Arboc. GNP measures production by ownership. See p. 144/570.

5. Wheat is used in the production of bread. Wheat is a(n) _____ good; bread is a(n) _____ good.
   A. final, final.
   B. final, intermediate.
   C. intermediate, final.
   D. intermediate, intermediate.

   Answer: C. The wheat is used in producing the bread. To count both it and the bread as final products would be double counting. See p. 143/569.

OBJECTIVE 2: Use the expenditure approach to calculate GDP. Distinguish between gross investment and net investment. Discuss the meaning of depreciation and the problems of measuring it. Define the three categories of personal consumption expenditures.

Two methods, the *expenditure approach* and the *income approach*, are used to calculate GDP. The two methods produce the same result, because a dollar spent is also a dollar received as income. The expenditure approach is summed up by:

$$GDP = C + I + G + (EX - IM)$$

where   C = personal consumption expenditures
         I = gross private domestic investment
         G = government purchases
         (EX − IM) = net exports   (page 145/571)

> **TIP:** To organize your thoughts, refer to the aggregate demand/aggregate supply diagram in Chapter 6 (21) of the textbook. The market value of production is the equivalent of price times quantity and can be visualized in two ways. We can measure the market value by focusing on the demand side (expenditure) or by focusing on the supply side (income of producers). We'll see later (in Chapter 14 (29)) that aggregate demand is made up of C + I + G + (EX − IM).

Gross private investment includes residential investment, non-residential investment, and *changes* in the level of business inventories—not financial transactions, or putting money in your savings account. Depreciation is the allowance made by businesses for the deterioration of capital as time passes. This is certainly a cost of production. Net investment is gross investment minus depreciation.   (page 147/573)

> **TIP:** "Change in inventories" is an important part of the analysis. What would happen to (total) inventories if (total) demand in the economy was bigger than (total) supply? Inventories would fall. Unexpected inventory change is an important part of the economy's signaling mechanism. Falling inventories tell producers to increase production; unpleasantly high inventory levels tell producers to cut back production. Watch for this point in Chapter 9 (24).

Consumption expenditures are divided among spending on durable goods (e.g., a car), nondurable goods (e.g., gasoline), and services (e.g., an oil change).

PRACTICE

6. The expenditure approach equation is
   A. C + I + G + (EX + IM).
   B. C + I + G − (EX + IM).
   C. C + I + G + (EX − IM).
   D. C + I + G − (EX − IM).
   Answer: C. Net exports (EX − IM) are added to the total. See p. 146/572.

7. Peter Rachman builds some apartment buildings. This expenditure is best described as
   A. residential consumption.
   B. residential investment.
   C. durable consumption.
   D. inventory investment.
   Answer: B. All new construction is classified as investment. See p. 147/573.

8. Gross private investment has three components:
   A. Business investment in plant and equipment, residential construction, and inventory investment.
   B. Business investment in plant and equipment, residential construction, and net exports of machinery.
   C. Stocks, bonds, and real estate.
   D. Purchases of new firms, purchases of existing firms, and purchases of residential housing stock.
   Answer: A. See p. 147/573.

9. Having totaled the other components of GDP, Arbez finds that (i) business inventories have fallen during the last year while (ii) imports have exceeded exports. (i) will _____ GDP; (ii) will _____ GDP.
   A. increase, increase.
   B. increase, decrease.
   C. decrease, increase.
   D. decrease, decrease.
   Answer: D. A decrease in inventories means that, on balance, sales have exceeded production. If imports have exceeded exports, net exports are negative.

10. GDP is 1,200, consumption is 900, gross private domestic investment is 150, exports are 50, and imports are 125. Depreciation is 40. Government spending is
    A. 15.
    B. 75.
    C. 225.
    D. 265.
    Answer: C. $GDP = C + I + G + (EX - IM)$. $1,200 = 900 + 150 + G + (50 - 125)$. Depreciation is not relevant in this calculation.

11. The capital stock at the end of 1996 is equal to the capital stock at the beginning of 1996
    A. plus depreciation.
    B. minus depreciation.
    C. plus net investment.
    D. plus gross investment.
    Answer: C. The change in the capital stock is net investment. See p. 148/575.

OBJECTIVE 3: Outline the procedure and rationale for determining GDP through the income approach. Distinguish among the various national income accounts.

The *income approach* totals the income payments of the productive resources (employee compensation [wages and salaries, mostly], rental income, net interest, proprietors' income, corporate profits, and net factor payments to the rest of the world) plus two other non-income charges (depreciation and indirect taxes minus subsidies) that affect the market value of production. Income payments of productive resources are called *national income*. (page 149/576)

Note that GDP adds in payments to foreign factors and subtracts payments earned abroad by U.S. citizens. GNP does not count either of these factor payments and, to get to GNP from GDP, we must *subtract* payments to foreign factors and *add* payments earned abroad by U.S. citizens.

> **TIP:** Think of saving as non-consumption. You don't have to put money into the bank for an economist to consider as "saved" the income left over after you've bought what you want.

PRACTICE

12. The best measure of the total income of households is
    A. GDP.
    B. GNP.
    C. national income.
    D. personal income.
    Answer: D. National income measures the income earned by productive resources. Some income though, doesn't reach households—retained earnings, social insurance payments. Some income received by households is unearned—transfer payments such as welfare. Personal income records the income received by all households after these adjustments have been made.

13. Using the income approach, GDP is equal to
    A. National income + Depreciation + (Indirect Taxes + Subsidies).
    B. National income + Depreciation + (Indirect Taxes − Subsidies).
    C. National income − Depreciation − (Indirect Taxes + Subsidies).
    D. National income − Depreciation + (Indirect Taxes − Subsidies).
    Answer: B. The value of production equals the costs of resources plus other production costs (depreciation and indirect taxes) minus offsetting subsidies. See p. 150/576.

14. GDP minus _____ the rest of the world and minus _____ equals NNP.
    A. net factor payments to, depreciation.
    B. net factor payments to, indirect taxes minus subsidies.
    C. net factor receipts from, depreciation.
    D. net factor receipts from, indirect taxes minus subsidies.
    Answer: A. GDP includes net factor payments to the rest of the world. GNP subtracts these payments. NNP subtracts depreciation from GNP.

15. Personal disposable income can be used for each of the following purposes except
    A. personal consumption expenditures.
    B. personal income tax payments.
    C. personal transfer payments to foreigners.
    D. personal saving.
    Answer: B. Personal income tax payments have been taken into account before personal disposable income is calculated. Note that another use of personal disposable income is as interest paid by consumers to businesses.

OBJECTIVE 4: Distinguish between real GDP and nominal GDP and explain why real GDP is the preferred measure of production. Discuss why a chain-type quantity index is used to measure real GDP. Discuss how the GDP price index is constructed.

Nominal GDP measures production in current dollars, while *real GDP*, a measure of output that controls for price changes, is calculated by constructing a chain-type quantity index. The Bureau of Economic Analysis (BEA) used to use fixed price weights when determining real GDP. That method is flawed—prices may be inaccurate or nonexistent for some goods. The current BEA method of estimating real GDP uses a sequence of pairs of base years.

The GDP price index, which measures how the overall price level is changing, previously was calculated by the fixed-weights method but, in 1995, the BEA adopted the chain-type annual weights GDP price index. One drawback of the new system is that GDP can no longer be expressed in "constant" dollars, however, by dividing a given year's nominal GDP and its components by that year's GDP price index, a reasonable estimate of real GDP and its components can be made. (page 155/580)

> **TIP:** In a previous tip, nominal GDP was likened to price times quantity. If price changes, so does the value of nominal GDP. To derive the real quantity produced, we can divide $(P \times Q)$ by P—at the macro level, this is the GDP price index.

> **TIP:** A common mistake in macroeconomics is failing to distinguish between real and nominal values, as in the case of GDP. *Real* values correct for the effect of price changes, *nominal* values don't. Example: Your nominal wage is simply the number of dollars in your pay check; your real wage (spending power) also depends on prices in the grocery store. When your grandmother tells you how wonderfully cheap things were back in the good old days, she's comparing nominal values that shouldn't be compared. Ask her about hourly wage levels back in those same good old days.

> **TIP:** Note that the formula
> GDP price index = (Nominal GDP ÷ real GDP) × 100
> can be rearranged to get
> Real GDP = (Nominal GDP ÷ GDP price index) × 100.

PRACTICE

16. If real GDP decreases from 1996 to 1997, we can conclude that
    A. production levels are lower in 1997.
    B. price levels are lower in 1997.
    C. there is less unemployment in 1997.
    D. we need more information before commenting.
    Answer: A. Real GDP measures the level of real production.

Use the fixed-weights method and following information about prices of goods in Arboc to calculate the economy's production for the next three questions.

	PRODUCTION			PRICES		
Good	Year 1	Year 2	Year 3	Year 1	Year 2	Year 3
Goat Milk	200	180	160	2.00	2.40	2.50
Bananas	80	90	100	3.00	3.20	3.10

17. Nominal GDP in Year 1 is _____ and nominal GDP in Year 2 is _____
    A. 640, 720.
    B. 640, 736.
    C. 630, 720.
    D. 630, 736.
    Answer: A. Nominal GDP for Year 1 = (200 × 2.00) + (80 × 3.00) = 640.
    Nominal GDP for Year 2 = (180 × 2.40) + (90 × 3.20) = 720.

18. In Year 1 prices, real GDP in Year 2 is _____ and real GDP in Year 3 is _____
    A. 640, 620.
    B. 640, 630.
    C. 630, 640.
    D. 630, 620.
    Answer: D. Real GDP for Year 2 = (180 × 2.00) + (90 × 3.00) = 630. Real GDP for Year 3 = (160 × 2.00) + (100 × 3.00) = 620.

19. The GDP fixed-weight price index for Year 3, using Year 1's prices to get real GDP, is
    A. 82.8877.
    B. 87.3239.
    C. 114.5161.
    D. 120.6452.
    Answer: C. Nominal GDP for Year 3 = (160 × 2.50) + (100 × 3.10) = 710. Real GDP for Year 3 = (160 × 2.00) + (100 × 3.00) = 620. GDP price index = (nominal GDP/real GDP) × 100 = (710/620) × 100 = 114.5161.

20. In Arbez, between 1995 and 1996, nominal GDP rose by 3.9% while real GDP fell by 1.3%. We can conclude that the overall price level
    A. rose by about 5.2% between 1995 and 1996.
    B. rose by about 2.6% between 1995 and 1996.
    C. fell by about 2.6% between 1995 and 1996.
    D. fell by about 5.2% between 1995 and 1996.
    Answer: A. If real GDP had been unchanged, the increase in nominal GDP would tell us that prices had risen by 3.9%. Because real GDP did fall, the increase in price level must have been even greater.

21. In Arboc, nominal GDP is 4,000 opeks and real GDP is 3,000 opeks. The GDP price index is
    A. 25.
    B. 33.33.
    C. 75.
    D. 133.33.
    Answer: D. To find the GDP price index, divide nominal GDP by real GDP and then multiply by 100.

Use the chain-type annual weights method and following information about prices of goods in Arboc to calculate the economy's production for the next two questions.

	PRODUCTION		PRICES	
Good	Year 1	Year 2	Year 1	Year 2
Goat Milk	200	180	2.00	2.40
Bananas	80	90	100	3.00

22. The bundle quantity in Year 1 is _____ The bundle quantity in Year 2 is _____. Use Year 1 as the base year.
    A. 600, 720.
    B. 600, 630.
    C. 640, 720.
    D. 640, 630.
    Answer: D. The bundle quantity for Year 1 = (200 × 2.00) + (80 × 3.00) = 640. The bundle quantity for Year 2 = (180 × 2.00) + (90 × 3.00) = 630.

23. The bundle quantity in Year 1 is _____. The bundle quantity in Year 2 is _____. Use Year 2 as the base year.
    A. 736, 780.
    B. 736, 720.
    C. 640, 780.
    D. 640, 720.
    Answer: B. The bundle quantity for Year 1 = $(200 \times 2.40) + (80 \times 3.20)$ = 736. The bundle quantity for Year 2 = $(180 \times 2.40) + (90 \times 3.20)$ = 720.

OBJECTIVE 5: Outline the shortcomings of GDP and per capita GDP as a measure of social well-being.

It's tempting to equate a rising GDP, or even a rising per capita GDP, with greater well-being, but the limitations of the national income measure disallow this. GDP measures the "market value" of production; but not all goods and services affecting our well-being reach a market—the "underground economy" is a significant example. GDP doesn't count "bads" such as pollution, and changes in GDP simply might be due to activities, such as child care or house work, being recorded in the market when they previously weren't. GDP ignores pollution, the distribution of spending power, and what kinds of goods are being produced—all of these factors can affect the well-being of individuals in society.   (page 157/583)

PRACTICE

24. GDP includes
    A. the market value of goods and services produced in the underground economy.
    B. the value of satisfaction derived from amusement parks.
    C. the expenditures involved in changing aerosol production away from the use of CFCs (chlorofluorocarbons).
    D. purchases of illegal substances that are produced in the United States.
    Answer: C. The expenditures needed to change production of aerosols would be represented in investment expenditures.

The Family of Accounts

Collected below is the entire family of national income and production accounts, showing how to move from one account to another. Applications 4 and 6, below, give you practice in calculating the different values.

Gross Domestic Product	$C + I + G + (EX - IM)$ OR National income + depreciation + (indirect taxes – subsidies) + net factor payments to the rest of the world
Gross National Product	GDP – net factor payments to the rest of the world
Net National Product	GNP – depreciation
National Income	NNP – (indirect taxes – subsidies)
Personal Income	National income + personal interest income and transfer payments – retained earnings and social insurance payments
Personal Disposable Income	Personal income – personal taxes

I. MULTIPLE CHOICE QUESTIONS.

Select the option that provides the single best answer.

___A___ 1. The value of GDP can be found by adding together
   A. government spending, consumption, net exports, and gross private investment.
   B. wages, consumption, gross private investment, and imports.
   C. consumption, government spending, transfer payments, and net exports.
   D. wages, investment, government spending, and depreciation.

___A___ 2. For national accounting purposes, which of the following is not considered to be investment?
   A. Accumulation of inventories on a grocery shelf.
   B. Construction of a residential housing scheme.
   C. Purchase of 100 shares of Exxon stock by Prof. Fair from Prof. Case.
   D. Purchase of a new machine by the Case and Fair Manufacturing Corp.

___C___ 3. Which of the following would be included in 1996 GDP?
   A. The purchase in 1996 of a 1995 model car.
   B. The purchase in 1996 of a share of GM common stock.
   C. The purchase in 1997 of a car produced in 1996.
   D. Two of the above would be counted.

___D___ 4. Nominal GDP is higher this year than last. We can conclude that
   A. production levels are higher this year.
   B. price levels are higher this year.
   C. there is less unemployment this year.
   D. we need more information before commenting.

___A___ 5. GNP minus _____ and minus _____ equals national income.
   A. investment, depreciation.
   B. indirect taxes and plus subsidies, depreciation.
   C. indirect taxes and plus subsidies, net investment.
   D. depreciation, net investment.

___C___ 6. Which one of the following most accurately reflects the amount of income actually received by households after taxes?
   A. gross domestic product.
   B. net national product.
   C. personal disposable income.
   D. personal income.

___D___ 7. Real gross domestic product
   A. refers only to manufacturing production.
   B. includes government transfers.
   C. excludes services.
   D. eliminates the effect of price changes on GDP.

___B___ 8. Which of the following items would be included in gross domestic product?
   A. The value of a German camera brought back to the United States by a G.I.
   B. The output of a U.S.-owned family farm in Kansas.
   C. The value of clean air.
   D. The value of imports into the United States.

_B_ 9. One problem of incorporating the government sector into GDP is that
   A. we must include transfer payments, so double counting occurs.
   B. some government production, such as national defense, is not sold.
   C. taxes reduce consumption and investment expenditures.
   D. the government adds nothing to the value of production.

_A_ 10. The value of imports is subtracted in the expenditure approach, because
   A. imports are included when the value of consumption and the other components of expenditure are calculated.
   B. imports take away from domestic production.
   C. imports are bought by foreigners.
   D. imports must be bought with foreign currency.

_C_ 11. The most likely immediate response to an unforeseen surge in demand for a firm's product would be to
   A. cut the price of the final product.
   B. reduce inventory levels.
   C. build up inventory levels.
   D. reduce depreciation.

_D_ 12. Cambium and Xylem Timber Company of Ontario, Canada, produce and sell wooden furniture in the United States. The profits of this foreign-owned company are included in
   A. U.S. GDP and U.S. GNP.
   B. U.S. GDP but not U.S. GNP.
   C. U.S. GNP but not in U.S. GDP.
   D. neither U.S. GDP nor U.S. GNP.

_D_ 13. Net investment is
   A. depreciation plus inventory levels.
   B. depreciation minus inventory levels.
   C. gross investment plus depreciation.
   D. gross investment minus depreciation.

_B_ 14. The personal saving rate is the percentage of _____ that is saved.
   A. GDP.
   B. personal income.
   C. national income.
   D. personal disposable income.

_C_ 15. Transfer payments are _____ in national income and _____ in personal income.
   A. included, included.
   B. included, not included.
   C. not included, included.
   D. not included, not included.

_D_ 16. In Arboc, nominal GDP is 12,000 opeks and the GDP price index is 80. Real GDP is
   A. 150 opeks.
   B. 1,500 opeks.
   C. 9,600 opeks.
   D. 15,000 opeks.

_D_ 17. Which of the following would not be counted in GDP?
   A. $10 million worth of newly produced IBM PCs that IBM can't sell.
   B. A $1,000 fee charged by a lawyer to plead a court case which she does not win.
   C. The salary of a foreign basketball player playing in the NBA.
   D. The purchase of IBM stock just before its price increases.

_C_ 18. Which of the following would be included in U.S. GNP but not in U.S. GDP?
   A. Profit earned in the United States by Honda Corporation, a Japanese-owned company.
   B. Wages paid to Mexican migrant workers harvesting peaches for a U.S.-owned company.
   C. Rent paid to Sean Thornton, the American owner of a piece of land in Ireland.
   D. Dividends paid to U.S. citizens on stock in Honda Corporation, a Japanese-owned company.

_C_ 19. Which of the following statements about net investment is true?
   A. Net investment equals gross investment plus depreciation.
   B. When net investment is negative, the stock of capital has decreased.
   C. When net investment is negative, inventory levels are decreasing.
   D. When net investment is negative, inventory levels are increasing.

_D_ 20. In Arbez, nominal GDP is one billion opeks in both 1991 and 1996. The GDP price index is 50 in 1991 and 120 in 1996. We can conclude that
   A. prices and real GDP have both risen from 1991 to 1996.
   B. prices have risen and real GDP has fallen from 1991 to 1996.
   C. prices have fallen and real GDP has risen from 1991 to 1996.
   D. prices and real GDP have both fallen from 1991 to 1996.

II. APPLICATION QUESTIONS.

1. Examine the following list of goods and services. Which goods and services should be included in Freedonian GDP in 1995, which should be excluded, and why?

   2500 quarter-pounder hamburgers produced in 1995
   100 tons of coal from the mines in the Freedonian mountains
   2 Freedonian Drof automobiles, sold in 1995, produced in 1994
   3 Freedonian Drof automobiles, sold in 1996, produced in 1995
   3 American-built Fords produced in 1995 and sold in 1995
   Welfare benefits for Freedonian citizens
   625 pounds of beef used in hamburgers
   Wages of hamburger employees

2. Below are some nominal GDP figures for the nation of Regit.

YEAR	NOMINAL GDP	PERCENTAGE CHANGE	GDP PRICE INDEX	REAL GDP	PERCENTAGE CHANGE
1991	4268.6		0.9700	____	____
1992	4539.9	____	1.0000	____	____
1993	4900.4	____	1.0390	____	____
1994	5244.0	____	1.0840	____	____
1995	5513.8	____	1.1310	____	____
1996	5672.6	____	1.1760	____	____

   a. Calculate the percentage change in nominal GDP from one year to the next, i.e., divide the difference in GDP by the GDP in the first year.
   b. Calculate real GDP.
   c. Use the real GDP figures to calculate the percentage change in real GDP from one year to the next.
   d. Write a brief report on the similarities and differences between the "percentage change" columns.

3. In Macrovia, the only two goods produced are bread and wine. In 1985, bread cost 90¢ a loaf and wine cost $4.00 a bottle. 800 loaves of bread and 180 bottles of wine were produced. In 1990, bread cost $1.00 a loaf and wine cost $5.00 a bottle. 1000 loaves and 200 bottles of wine were produced. In 1995, bread cost $1.20 a loaf and wine cost $5.50 a bottle. 1200 loaves and 220 bottles of wine were produced.

   a. Calculate the nominal GDP for each of the three years.
   b. Calculate the real GDP for each of the three years. Use 1990 as the base year and the fixed-weight method.
   c. Calculate the GDP fixed-weight price index for each of the three years. Use 1990 as the base year.
   d. Calculate the bundle quantities for 1985 and 1990 using 1985 as the base year.
   e. Determine quantity indexes using 1985 as the base year.
   f. Determine the percentage change in the quantity index from 1985 to 1990.
   g. Calculate the bundle quantities for 1985 and 1990 using 1990 as the base year.
   h. Determine quantity indexes using 1990 as the base year.
   i. Determine the percentage change in the quantity index from 1985 to 1990.
   j. Complete the following table.

	QUANTITY INDEX IN BASE YEAR 1985	QUANTITY INDEX IN BASE YEAR 1990	SQUARE ROOT OF PRODUCT
1985	_____	_____	_____
1990	_____	_____	_____

   k. How much has real GDP changed from 1985 to 1990?

4. You are given the following information by a colleague who is doing research on the Freedonian economy. Since she has never taken an economics course, she has turned to you for help using the information she has found.

Compensation of Employees	1175.2
Corporate Taxes	53.9
Macrovian Exports of Goods and Services	94.4
Consumption of Fixed Capital	160.8
Personal Taxes	150.5
Personal Consumption Expenditures	878.2
Government Purchases of Goods and Services	400.4
Indirect Business Taxes (and other miscellaneous items)	122.4
Business Retained Earnings	10.7
Gross Private Domestic Investment	322.7
Government Transfer Payments and Interest	83.9
Macrovian Imports of Goods and Services	70.5
Payroll Taxes	110.1

   Use the information above to calculate
   a. GDP _____
   b. National Income _____
   c. Personal Income _____
   d. Personal Disposable Income _____
   e. The government deficit _____
   f. Net exports _____

5. a. A Macrovian farmer produces 2000 bushels of wheat which he sells to a miller for 20¢ a bushel. The farmer receives a payment of $_____ from the miller. The value added by the farmer is $_____.

   b. The miller grinds the wheat into flour. She makes 1200 pounds of flour which she sells to a baker for 40¢ per pound. The miller receives a payment of $_____ from the baker. The value added by the miller is $_____.

   c. The baker bakes the flour into 1000 loaves which he sells for 50¢ apiece to a food distributor. The baker receives a payment of $_____ from the distributor. The value added by the baker is $_____.

   d. The distributor sells 200 loaves to a local restaurant (Loafers) for $1.00 each. The remainder are sold to grocery stores at 80¢ each. The distributor receives payments totaling $_____. The value added by the distributor is $_____.

   e. At the retail level, Loafers sells 180 loaves at $1.50 each. 20 loaves are unsold and must be discarded. The grocery stores sell all of their consignment for $1.00 each. Retailers receive payments totaling $_____. The value added by the retailers is $_____.

   f. The total value added by all participants in the production process is $_____.

6. Given the following national income and product accounts data, compute:
   a. Gross private investment   _____
   b. Net exports   _____
   c. Gross domestic product   _____
   d. Gross national product   _____
   d. Net national product   _____
   e. National income   _____
   f. Personal income   _____
   g. Disposable income   _____

Depreciation	105
Compensation of employees	1, 407
Corporate profits	161
Dividends	49
Exports	133
Government purchases	448
Imports	147
Indirect taxes	371
Net interest income	182
Net private domestic investment	490
Personal consumption expenditures	1,377
Personal interest income	70
Receipts of factor income from the rest of the world	22
Personal taxes	392
Proprietors' income	168
Payments of factor income to the rest of the world	43
Rental income	21
Social insurance payments	238
Subsidies	28
Transfer payments	315

7. Arboc and Arbez are two neighboring nations. Each produces only corn. In each case, net factor income from the rest of the world is zero. Last year, sales of corn in each country were 500 units. Inventory rose by 50 in Arboc and fell by 25 in Arbez. Calculate GDP for:
   a. Arboc _____
   b. Arbez _____

   Suppose depreciation runs at 10% of GDP in each country. Calculate NNP for:
   c. Arboc _____
   d. Arbez _____

   Indirect taxes and subsidies are a greater percentage of GDP in Arboc (12%) than in Arbez (5%). Calculate national income for:
   e. Arboc _____
   f. Arbez _____

8. Use the table below to answer the following questions.

Year	Nominal GDP	Nominal GDP (% increase)	GDP Price Index	Real GDP	Real GDP (% increase)
1981	1,212.8	—	46.5		
1986	1,990.5		67.3		
1991	3,166.0		100.0		
1996	4,486.2		117.3		

   a. Calculate the percentage increase in nominal GDP from one year to the next.
   b. Use the GDP price index to derive real GDP.
   c. Calculate the percentage increase in real GDP from one year to the next.

9. The nation of Arboc produces pencils and notepads. Using the following information, calculate:

	Pencils	Notepads
Year 1	2,000 at 10¢ each	75 at $1.00 each
Year 2	2,400 at 15¢ each	60 at $1.10 each

   a. Nominal GDP for Year 1 _____
   b. Nominal GDP for Year 2 _____
   c. Real GDP for Year 1 (Year 1 as base) _____
   d. Real GDP for Year 2 (Year 1 as base) _____

10. Should each of the following enter into a measure of "the market value of all currently produced final goods and services"? Write Y for "yes" and N for "no."
    1. _____ the purchase of a new camera by Joe Blow
    2. _____ the gift of the same camera from Joe to Flo Blow
    3. _____ the purchase of the same camera by F. Stop Fitzgerald at a yard sale
    4. _____ the purchase of a new camera by the CIA
    5. _____ the services of a photographer hired by the CIA
    6. _____ the services of a photographer hired by Joe and Flo Blow on the occasion of their wedding
    7. _____ the services of Cousin Bo Blow (amateur photographer extraordinaire) to photograph the wedding
    8. _____ the production of a camera that remains unsold at the factory
    9. _____ the purchase of a Japanese camera by Joe Blow

10. _____ the use of welfare money by Moe Blow to buy a new camera
11. _____ the provision of welfare money to Moe Blow
12. _____ the use of welfare money to buy a second-hand camera
13. _____ the use of welfare money to open a bank account
14. _____ the use of welfare money to buy Kodak stock on the stock exchange
15. _____ the purchase of in-store surveillance equipment for "The Camera Cabin"
16. _____ the purchase of a camera for display in "The Camera Cabin"
17. _____ the purchase of film by Joe Blow
18. _____ the purchase of a U.S. camera by Josef von Blau (a German tourist)
19. _____ the purchase, in Germany, of a U.S. camera, by Josef von Blau
20. _____ the payment for the services of a camera repairman hired by Joe Blow who fails to repair the broken camera
21. _____ the payment for the services of the trashman who takes the broken camera to the city dump

ANSWERS AND SOLUTIONS

PRACTICE TEST

I. SOLUTIONS TO MULTIPLE CHOICE QUESTIONS

1. A. This is the expenditure approach. See the equation on p. 146/572.

2. C. The stock transfer does not represent the production of any additional goods or services.

3. C. We are interested in measuring how much has been produced in 1996 (whether or not it is sold in that year). The stock purchase adds no production, so it is not counted.

4. D. Nominal GDP measures the current value of production. This value might have increased because more goods and services were produced this year than last (with correspondingly lower unemployment), or because prices are higher this year than last. In short, we must be wary of reading too much into the change in this single figure . See p. 154/580.

5. B. See Table 7.4 (22.4).

6. C. This is the after-tax income of all households. See p. 153/580.

7. D. Real GDP certainly includes manufacturing production, but it includes other forms of production too, including services. "Real" variables are variables that have had the effects of price changes removed. See p. 155/581.

8. B. The German camera is not U.S. production. The value of clean air is intangible. Imports are included in the value of consumption purchases, etc., and then subtracted from GDP.

9. B. GDP measures the market value of production—this is difficult when there is not an explicit market. Note that transfer payments are not included in GDP.

10. A. See p. 149/576.

11. B. If the demand for orange juice surges at the Food Tiger grocery store, the shelves begin to empty even before the management decides to raise the price.

12. B. The profits of a foreign-owned company are included in U.S. GDP (which is concerned with the location of production) but not in U.S. GNP (which is concerned with ownership of resources).

13. D. See p. 148/575.

14. D. See p. 154/580.

15. C. National income records payments to productive resources. Because a transfer is not a payment to a productive resource, it is excluded. Personal income measures income to households from all sources.

16. D. Real GDP = (nominal GDP divided by the GDP price index) × 100 = (12,000 / 80)100 = 15,000.

17. D. The purchase of stock is a financial transaction that does not reflect productive activity. Note that goods that are produced but not sold are included in inventory.

18. C. GNP measures production by resources owned by U.S. citizens, regardless of where output is produced.

19. B. Net investment will be negative if gross investment is less than depreciation. In that case, the addition to the capital stock is less than the reduction due to wear and tear. Note that net investment is gross investment *minus* depreciation. See the equation on p. 148/575.

20. B. Rising prices are indicated by the higher GDP price index in 1996. Real GDP = nominal GDP/GDP price index, therefore the real GDP is lower in 1996, (833,333,333 opeks instead of 2 billion opeks).

II. SOLUTIONS TO APPLICATION QUESTIONS

1. 2500 quarter-pounder hamburgers produced in 1995, 100 tons of coal from the mines in the Freedonian mountains, and 3 Freedonian Drof automobiles sold in 1996 but produced in 1995 are final items that would qualify for inclusion in 1995's GDP.

   The 2 Freedonian Drof automobiles produced in 1994 were not produced in 1995. The 3 American-built Fords were not produced in Freedonia. Welfare benefits for Freedonian citizens are transfer payments. The beef used in hamburgers and the wages of hamburger employees are costs of intermediate goods and services that are captured in the price of the hamburgers.

2. a.

NOMINAL YEAR	PERCENTAGE GDP	GDP CHANGE	REAL PRICE INDEX	PERCENTAGE GDP	CHANGE
1991	4268.6		0.9700	4400.6	
1992	4539.9	6.36	1.0000	4539.9	3.17
1993	4900.4	7.94	1.0390	4716.5	3.89
1994	5244.0	7.02	1.0840	4837.6	2.57
1995	5513.8	5.14	1.1310	4875.2	0.77
1996	5672.6	2.88	1.1760	4823.6	−1.06

   b–c. See the table above.

   d. The "percentage change" figures display similarities, e.g. 1993 is the best year and 1996 the worst in each case. Notably, the real values are consistently lower than the nominal values because of rising prices. The nominal result for 1996 is the most misleading—recording 2.8% growth while the economy in fact shrank in size.

3. a.

	1985	1990	1995
bread	800 × .9 = $720	1000 × $1.00 = $1000	1200 × $1.20 = $1440
wine	180 × $4.00 = $720	200 × $5.00 = $1000	220 × $5.50 = $1210
Nominal GDP	$1440	$2000	$2650
bread	800 × $1.00 = $800	1000 × $1.00 = $1000	1200 × $1.00 = $1200
wine	180 × $5.00 = $900	200 × $5.00 = $1000	220 × $5.00 = $1100
Real GDP	$1700	$2000	$2300
GDP price index	.8471	1.0000	1.1522

   b–c. See the table above.

d.

	1985	1990
bread	800 × .90 = $720	1000 × .90 = $900
wine	180 × $4.00 = $720	200 × $4.00 = $800
Bundle Quantity	(1985) $1440	$1700

e. Quantity index (1985): (1440 × 100) / 1440 = 100
    Quantity index (1990): (1700 × 100) / 1440 = 118.0556
f. Percentage change from 1985 to 1990 = [(118.0556 − 100) / 100] × 100 = 18.0556
g.

	1985	1990
bread	800 × $1.00 = $800	1000 × $1.00 = $1000
wine	180 × $5.00 = $900	200 × $5.00 = $1000
Bundle Quantity	(1990) $1700	$2000

h. Quantity index (1985): (1700 × 100) / 1700 = 100
    Quantity index (1990): (2000 × 100) / 1700 = 117.6471
i. Percentage change from 1985 to 1990 = [(117.6471 − 100) / 100] × 100 = 17.6471
j.

	QUANTITY INDEX IN BASE YEAR 1985	QUANTITY INDEX IN BASE YEAR 1990	SQUARE ROOT OF PRODUCT
1985	100.00	100.00	100.00
1990	118.0556	117.6471	117.8512

k.   Real GDP has grown by 17.85% from 1985 to 1990.

4. a. GDP = C + I + G + × = 878.2 + 322.7 + 400.4 + (94.4 − 70.5) = 1625.2.
    b. National Income = GDP − (Consumption of Fixed Capital + Indirect Business Taxes) = 1342.0.
    c. Personal Income = National Income + Government Transfer Payments and Interest − (Payroll Taxes + Corporate Taxes + Business Retained Earnings) = 1251.2.
    d. Personal Disposable Income = Personal Income − Personal Taxes = 1100.7.
    e. The government deficit = government spending (400.4) − taxes (53.9 + 150.5 + 122.4 + 110.1) + transfers (83.9) = 47.4.
    f. Net exports = 94.4 − 70.5 = 23.9.

5. a. $400. $400.
    b. $480. $80.
    c. $500. $20.
    d. $840. $340.
    e. $1,070. $230.
    f. $1,070.

6. a. Gross private investment = net private investment + depreciation = 490 + 105 = 595.
    b. Net exports = exports − imports = 133 − 147 = −14.
    c. Gross domestic product = personal consumption expenditures + gross private investment + government purchases + net exports = 1,377 + (490 + 105) + 448 + (133 − 147) = 2,406.
    d. Gross national product = GDP + receipts of factor income − payments of factor income = 2,406 + 22 − 43 = 2,385.
    e. Net national product = GNP − depreciation = 2,385 − 105 = 2,280.
    f. National income = NNP − (indirect taxes − subsidies) = 2,280 − (371 − 28) = 1,937.
    g. Personal income = NI − (corporate profits − dividends) − social insurance payments + personal interest income + transfer payments = 1,937 − (161 − 49) − 238 + 70 + 315 = 1,972.
    h. Disposable income = PI − personal taxes = 1,972 − 392 = 1,580.

7. a. GDP = GNP (because net factor payments are zero) = sales + inventory change = 500 + 50 = 550 units.
    b. GDP = GNP (because net factor payments are zero) = sales + inventory change = 500 − 25 = 475 units.
    c. Depreciation = 10% of GDP = 55. NNP = GNP − depreciation = 550 − 55 = 495 units.
    d. Depreciation = 10% of GDP = 47.5. NNP = GNP − depreciation = 475 − 47.5 = 427.5 units.
    e. National income = GDP − depreciation − (indirect taxes − subsidies) − net factor payments = 550 − 55 − 550(.12) − 0 = 429 units.
    f. National income = GDP − depreciation − (indirect taxes − subsidies) − net factor payments = 475 − 47.5 − 475(.05) − 0 = 403.75 units.

8. See the table below.

Year	Nominal GDP	Nominal GDP (% increase)	GDP Price Index	Real GDP	Real GDP (% increase)
1981	1,212.8	—	46.5	2,608.2	—
1986	1,990.5	64.1	67.3	2,957.7	13.4
1991	3,166.0	59.1	100.0	3,166.0	7.0
1996	4,486.2	41.7	117.3	3,824.6	20.8

Note: Rearrange the formula
   GDP price index = (Nominal GDP ÷ real GDP) × 100 to get:
   Real GDP = (Nominal GDP ÷ GDP price index) × 100

9. a. Nominal GDP for Year 1 $275
    b. Nominal GDP for Year 2 $426
    c. Real GDP for Year 1 (Year 1 as base) $275
    d. Real GDP for Year 2 (Year 1 as base) $300

10.

1. Y	7. N	12. N	17. Y
2. N	8. Y	13. N	18. Y
3. N	9. N	14. N	19. Y
4. Y	10. Y	15. Y	20. Y
5. Y	11. N	16. Y	21. Y
6. Y			

MACROECONOMIC PROBLEMS: UNEMPLOYMENT AND INFLATION

8

COMBINED TEXT

23

OBJECTIVES: POINT BY POINT

After completing this chapter, you should be able to accomplish the objectives listed below.

OBJECTIVE 1: Define labor force and unemployment rate and give the official definition of employed. Describe the limitations of the unemployment rate statistic, outlining the effects of "discouraged workers" on official unemployment statistics.

The *labor force* totals the employed and unemployed. The *employed* include any person 16 years of age or older who:
   a.   works one hour or more per week for pay, or
   b.   works fifteen or more hours a week without pay in a family enterprise, or
   c.   has a job but is temporarily absent from work.

The *unemployed* must be available and looking for work. Otherwise, they are considered to be out of the labor force. Some workers, *discouraged* by their inability to find jobs, stop looking for work and drop out of the labor force.   (page 165/591)

The *unemployment rate* is the ratio of unemployed persons (who have no job and are actively seeking employment) to the labor force. An analysis of unemployment reveals large ethnic, gender, and regional differences in unemployment rates.
(page 166/592)

> **TIP:** Remember that, to be officially "unemployed," a member of the labor force must not have a job, or recently have had a job, and must be looking actively for work. Behind this distinction is the concept of the "discouraged" worker. Memorize the definitions of unemployment rate, participation rate, inflation, and the three types of unemployment and their causes.

PRACTICE

The population of Arbez is 150,000, of which 100,000 are aged 16 or older. Of this 100,000, 60,000 have jobs, and 40,000 do not. 20,000 are unemployed but actively seeking jobs, and there are 20,000 who have given up the job search in frustration.

1.   What is the unemployment rate? _____

2. What is the labor-force participation rate? _____
   Answers: The unemployment rate is 25%; the labor-force participation rate is 53.33%.

   Of the 150,000 Arbezanis, only 100,000 are of an age that qualifies them to be in the labor force. Of the 100,000, 60,000 are employed, and an additional 20,000 are unemployed (without jobs, seeking work). The remaining 20,000 discouraged workers have dropped out of the labor force. There are, then, 80,000 workers in the labor force.

   Unemployment rate = unemployed / labor force = 20,000/80,000 = 25%.

   Labor-force participation rate = labor force / population = 80,000 / 150,000 = 53.33%.

3. During a recession, we expect to see output _____ and unemployment _____.
   A. increasing, increasing.
   B. increasing, decreasing.
   C. decreasing, increasing.
   D. decreasing, decreasing.
   Answer: C. By definition, a recession occurs when real GDP falls for two or more quarters. As output falls, more workers are laid off. See p. 164/590.

4. Typically, workers in a fishing-gutting factory have a high rate of absenteeism. Phyllis the Filleter has been "off sick" this week. She is correctly classified as
   A. employed.
   B. unemployed.
   C. a discouraged worker.
   D. not in the labor force.
   Answer: A. If Phyllis is temporarily absent, with or without pay, she is considered employed. See p. 166/592.

5. The labor force is comprised of
   A. the employed plus the unemployed.
   B. the employed minus the unemployed.
   C. the employed, the unemployed, and discouraged workers who could work.
   D. the employed plus the unemployed minus discouraged workers who could work.
   Answer: A. Discouraged workers are not counted as part of the labor force.

6. In Arbez, there are 80,000 persons in the labor force and the unemployment rate is 25%. As the economy moves out of a long recession and job openings increase, 5,000 discouraged workers become "encouraged" and begin searching for a job. The unemployment rate will become
   A. 18.75%.
   B. 23.5294%.
   C. 29.4118%.
   D. 31.25%.
   Answer: C. Initial unemployment rate = 25% = unemployed / 80,000. The number unemployed is 20,000. When 5,000 new (unemployed) workers enter the labor force, the unemployment rate = 25,000 / 85,000 = 29.4118%.

7. The nation of Regit has a population of 1 million citizens. The labor-force participation rate is 80%. The number of Arbocalis with jobs is 728,000. The unemployment rate is
   A. 7.20%.
   B. 8.00%.
   C. 9.00%.
   D. 9.89%.
   Answer: C. The unemployment rate = unemployed ÷ labor-force = 72,000 / 800,000 = .09. Labor force = participation rate × population = .8 × 1,000,000 = 800,000. Unemployed = 800,000 − 728,000 = 72,000.

8. The nation of Noil has a population of 1 million citizens. The labor-force participation rate is 80%. 50,000 persons are unemployed in March. By June, 10,000 persons have given up seeking employment. This is the only change over the quarter. We can conclude that the unemployment rate was
   A. 6.25% in March and 7.50% in June.
   B. 6.25% in March and 6.25% in June.
   C. 6.25% in March and 5.06% in June.
   D. 5.00% in March and 6.25% in June.
   Answer: C. In March, the unemployment rate = unemployed ÷ labor-force = 50,000 / 800,000 = .0625. In June, the unemployment rate = unemployed ÷ labor-force = 40,000 / 790,000 = .05063.

OBJECTIVE 2: Distinguish among, and give examples of, frictional, structural, and cyclical unemployment. Define the natural rate of unemployment and describe the economic and social costs of unemployment.

The three types of unemployment are:

frictional—short-run unemployment due to the movement of individuals between jobs, while seeking a better match for their skills.

structural—longer-term unemployment, caused by changing tastes or changing technology that make some job skills less desirable. Automation or change in public preferences (foreign cars instead of U.S. cars) might cause structural unemployment.

cyclical—caused by recessions and depressions.   (page 170/596)

The first two types of unemployment are inevitable in a healthy, dynamic economy. Together, they comprise the rather imprecise concept of the *natural rate of unemployment*—the rate of unemployment that occurs during the normal operation of the economy. Full employment doesn't imply zero percent unemployment.
                                                              (page 171/597)

Recessions and cyclical unemployment result in lost output and adverse social consequences (broken homes, alcoholism, and suicide), and lower investment and economic growth. However, such downturns may weed out inefficient firms, cut imports, and reduce inflation.   (page 173/599)

> **TIP:** Think of **full employment** as 100% employment minus the natural rate of unemployment. The economy may have a lower or higher rate of employment than 93 to 96%, but such a divergence will be *temporary*. Note that, even when unemployment is greater than zero, society can still be at a point on (not inside) its production possibilities frontier.

PRACTICE

9. Unemployment caused by short-run job/skill matching problems is
   A. frictional unemployment.
   B. structural unemployment.
   C. cyclical unemployment.
   D. natural unemployment.
   Answer: A. See p. 170/596.

10. Recessions have all of the following beneficial effects except
    A. inflation is reduced.
    B. efficiency is improved.
    C. investment is increased.
    D. the balance of payments improves because imports decrease.
    Answer: C. Typically, investment falls during a recession. See p. 173/599.

11. During the Great Depression of the 1930s, many laborers found great difficulty finding a job. They were
    A. frictionally unemployed.
    B. structurally unemployed.
    C. cyclically unemployed.
    D. discouraged workers.
    Answer: C. In the 1930s, aggregate demand was low throughout the economy. See p. 171/597.

12. The unemployment rate that occurs as a normal consequence of the efficient functioning of the economy is
    A. frictional rate of unemployment.
    B. structural rate of unemployment.
    C. cyclical rate of unemployment.
    D. natural rate of unemployment.
    Answer: D. See p. 171/597. This rate includes both frictional and structural unemployment.

13. For many years, Noil was a traditional agrarian economy, specializing in rice production. In the past few years, however, due to loans from the World Bank, Noil has developed a thriving industrial sector, and farming (although increasingly mechanized) has declined. We would conclude that, over the past few years, frictional unemployment has _____ and structural unemployment has _____.
    A. increased, increased.
    B. increased, decreased.
    C. decreased, increased.
    D. decreased, decreased.
    Answer: A. As the economy's structure is changing, new skills are being required and old skills are becoming obsolete—structural unemployment is increasing. As skills become more specific and more complex, the search time to find a suitable job increases—frictional unemployment increases.

OBJECTIVE 3: Define inflation. Outline the problems of price indexes such as the Consumer Price Index.

Inflation is a rise in the overall price level. It can be measured by a price index (such as the Consumer Price Index). The CPI and most other price indexes are based on a typical "basket" of commodities and measure how the price of the basket changes over time. Clearly, the effectiveness of a price index depends on how well its basket of commodities reflects the economy as time passes and prices change.

(page 173/599)

TIP: Each price index has a *base year* that is assigned an index value of 100. Use the following formula to calculate the price index for a given year:

$$\frac{\text{price of bundle in given year}}{\text{price of bundle in base year}} \times 100 = \text{given year's index}$$

In the base year itself, this becomes 1.00×100. An index of more than (less than) 100 in a given year indicates that prices are more than (less than) those in the base year.

TIP: Be careful! If the CPI rises from 120 to 132, the rate of inflation is *not* 12%, but 10% $[(132 - 120) \div 120]$. Don't just subtract one value from the other—be sure to divide by the value of the first year's price index.

PRACTICE

14. If the CPI is 135 in Year 2 and 120 in Year 1, what is the percentage change in the price level between the years?
   A. 12.5%.
   B. 15%.
   C. 20%.
   D. 35%.
   Answer: A. The price index changes by 15 relative to the initial price level of 120. (15 / 120) × 100 = 12.5%.

OBJECTIVE 4: Indicate who gains and who loses from inflation. Distinguish between anticipated and unanticipated inflation and indicate how their impacts on the economy differ. Describe the concept of the real interest rate and outline the effect of anticipated inflation on it.

The costs of inflation are difficult to measure. Some inefficiencies occur, and administrative costs may increase. Also, the amount of capital investment may decrease, affecting the long-term growth rate of the economy. Unanticipated inflation is more troublesome than anticipated inflation. Losers include those on fixed incomes and lenders (creditors), while winners include borrowers (debtors). Indexation can reduce the impact of inflation. (page 178/604)

> **TIP:** Despite some "menu costs" (the costs of changing price tags, printing new catalogs, etc.), **fully anticipated** inflation is not much of a problem. Rational economic behavior can continue. However, when the rate of inflation is variable and unpredictable, persons run the risk of making "bad" deals and try to compensate by overestimating wage claims and price increases. Adding this safety margin fuels the fires of inflation.

> **TIP:** Common sense should help you work out who wins and who loses during inflation; if it doesn't, memorize this part of the chapter!

Note that the difference between the market interest rate and the real interest rate is defined in the textbook as the inflation rate, but the associated example refers to the *anticipated* inflation rate. The market interest rate is determined by the anticipated inflation rate.

PRACTICE

15. Inflation is expected to run at 10% during 1996. Instead, it slows to 3%. This change will hurt
   A. creditors.
   B. debtors.
   C. creditors and debtors equally, because it's the same for both parties.
   D. neither, because inflation is lower.
   Answer: B. If inflation is higher than expected, creditors lose because they will fail to compensate themselves through a higher interest rate. When inflation is lower than expected, debtors lose because they are paying an interest rate that is "too high."

16. Inflation is expected to run at 10% during 1996. Instead, it slows to 3%. During 1996, there has been
    A. an anticipated deflation.
    B. an unanticipated deflation.
    C. an anticipated reduction in inflation.
    D. an unanticipated reduction in inflation.
    Answer: D. The change was not expected. This is not a deflation—the price level is still rising at 3% a year. A deflation occurs when the price level (not the rate of increase in the price level) falls.

17. The real interest rate is 4%. Inflation is expected to run at 10% during 1996. During 1996, the market interest rate is _____. If, during 1996, the actual inflation rate is 4%, _____ lose.
    A. 6%, lenders.
    B. 6%, borrowers.
    C. 14%, lenders.
    D. 14%, borrowers.
    Answer: D. The interest rate = expected inflation rate + real interest rate = 10% + 4% = 14%. Unanticipated deflation hurts borrowers.

18. Which of the following statements is false?
    A. When interest rates are high, the opportunity cost of holding cash is high.
    B. The more difficult it becomes to predict the rate of inflation, the more the level of investment decreases.
    C. Individuals on fixed incomes gain during periods of deflation.
    D. In the mid-1970s, prices were lower than in the early 1990s, and, therefore, inflation was lower too.
    Answer: D. Historically, Option D is false; inflation rates were higher in the mid-1970s than in the early 1990s. See Table 8 (23).9 in the textbook. Option D is false theoretically, too. The fact that the price level is low doesn't imply that the rate of increase will also be low.

19. The difference between the interest rate on a loan and the inflation rate is
    A. the profit margin.
    B. the real interest rate.
    C. the anticipation markup.
    D. the nominal interest rate.
    Answer: B. See p. 180/606.

PRACTICE TEST

I.   MULTIPLE CHOICE QUESTIONS.

Select the option that provides the single best answer.

_____ A _____ 1. A newly-qualified dental school graduate, Phil McCafferty, is looking for a place to set up practice. He is _____ unemployed.
    A. frictionally.
    B. structurally.
    C. cyclically.
    D. residually.

_____ A _____ 2. The unemployment rate will fall if
    A. there is an increase in the number of discouraged workers.
    B. there is a recession.
    C. the number in the labor force decreases.
    D. there is a decrease in the population.

_D_ 3. Francine loses her job because of the introduction of labor-saving machinery. Because she has few marketable skills, she stops looking for work. We would consider her to be _____ unemployed.
   A. cyclically.
   B. frictionally.
   C. structurally.
   D. none of the above.

_B_ 4. Labor-saving robots are introduced into a car assembly line. The resulting unemployment is
   A. frictional.
   B. structural.
   C. mechanical.
   D. cyclical.

_B_ 5. Arbez is producing at the full-employment level of production. There is
   A. no unemployment.
   B. some frictional and structural unemployment.
   C. some cyclical unemployment.
   D. a maximum participation rate.

_B_ 6. Recently, a flood of cheap computer chips has poured over the border from Arboc to Arbez. Thousands of workers in the Arbezani computer chip industry have lost their jobs. This unemployment is best described as
   A. frictional.
   B. structural.
   C. competitive.
   D. cyclical.

_A_ 7. Oliver Sudden has been jobless for the last six months and he is still looking for the right job. He has turned down several jobs that are appropriate for his skills and that pay well. He is
   A. frictionally unemployed.
   B. structurally unemployed.
   C. voluntarily unemployed.
   D. a discouraged worker.

_C_ 8. A fully anticipated increase in the inflation rate can lead to
   A. increased efficiency.
   B. greater speculative activity.
   C. higher market interest rates.
   D. a decrease in barter.

_B_ 9. Unanticipated inflation erodes the purchasing power of money. _____ is hurt least by unanticipated inflation.
   A. A person on a fixed income.
   B. A lender.
   C. A creditor.
   D. A borrower.

_B_ 10. The Consumer Price Index has risen from 110 to 121 during the last year. We should estimate the annual inflation rate for the last year at about
   A. 9.1%.
   B. 10%.
   C. 11%.
   D. 12%.

C 11. With unanticipated inflation, there will be all of the following except
A. greater risks involved in long-term contracts.
B. less investment.
C. more rapid growth in the economy.
D. falling real rewards for lenders.

B 12. Your real wage has risen by 3% while the inflation rate has risen by 7%. Your nominal wage must have $R + I = N$
A. risen by 4%.
B. risen by 10%.
C. fallen by 4%.
D. fallen by 10%.

A 13. As the economy moves out of a recession, the discouraged-worker effect will tend to _____ the unemployment rate.
A. increase.
B. decrease.
C. leave unaffected.
D. have no influence on.

D 14. Which of the following statements about the labor market is true?
A. Discouraged workers are those workers who have voluntarily chosen to become unemployed.
B. The labor force includes everyone over the age of 16, including those who are unemployed.
C. The labor-force participation rate is the ratio of employed persons to the total labor force.
D. The natural rate of unemployment is usually taken to be the sum of frictional and structural unemployment.

A 15. Which of the following statements about inflation is false?
A. The real interest rate is equal to the nominal interest rate plus the anticipated inflation rate. $R = N + I$.
B. Changes in the CPI tend to overstate changes in the cost of living.
C. During periods of unanticipated inflation, debtors benefit at the expense of creditors.
D. "Inflation" is an increase in the overall level of prices; when the overall level of prices decreases, it's called "deflation."

B 16. As a result of access to the Internet, there is an increase in the speed with which unemployed workers are matched with suitable jobs. This will
A. increase the natural rate of unemployment.
B. decrease the natural rate of unemployment.
C. not affect the natural rate of unemployment but reduce structural unemployment.
D. not affect the natural rate of unemployment but reduce frictional unemployment.

Use the following information to answer the next two questions. The Arbocali Bureau of Labor Statistics provides you with the following information.

Employed	360,000
Unemployed	40,000
Not in the labor force	100,000
Population (aged 16–65)	500,000

B 17. The Arbocali unemployment rate is
A. 8%.
B. 10%.
C. 11.11%.
D. 40%.

D 18. The labor-force participation rate is
A. 36%.
B. 40%.
C. 72%.
D. 80%.

D 19. We would expect to see each of the following during a recession except
A. decreased production.
B. a worsening balance of payments.
C. an increased incidence of psychological disorder and stress.
D. decreased capacity utilization rates.

A 20. In an economy where inflation is usually unpredictable, the degree of risk associated with investment
A. increases.
B. decreases.
C. depends on the nominal interest rate.
D. is not affected.

C 21. Hester Investor wishes to earn a 6% real return on a $500 loan that she is planning to make to Buck Poor. Last year the inflation rate was 2%, but Hester expects the inflation rate to rise to 4%. She should charge an interest rate of
A. 3%.
B. 4%.
C. 10%.
D. 12%.

D 22. The nation of Arboc has recently been at the trough of a business cycle and is moving through the next phase. The unemployment rate is rising. Which of the following is a plausible explanation?
A. After the trough, Arboc will move into the recession phase, and unemployment rises during recessions.
B. After the trough, different sectors of the Arbocali economy will recover at different rates, so the average unemployment rate may increase.
C. Firms will not hire extra workers until the recovery is assured, therefore the numbers of workers employed will be artificially reduced.
D. The expansion phase will encourage previously discouraged workers to re-enter the labor force, leading to an initial increase in the number without jobs.

II. APPLICATION QUESTIONS.

1. Can you think of any adaptations that have been made in our economy to alleviate the redistributional effects of inflation?

2. a. The market interest rate on a savings account is 5%. The inflation rate is 2%. Calculate the real interest rate that savings account depositors will earn.

   b. Suppose that the nominal interest rate that banks charge on loans is subject to a price ceiling of 7%. To be worthwhile, banks require a real interest rate of 4% or more. The inflation rate is currently 5%. Describe what will happen in this market.

3. The following table provides information on inflation rates and unemployment rates for Arboc over a seven-year period.

YEAR	INFLATION RATE	UNEMPLOYMENT RATE
1990	0.0	7.5
1991	–2.0	9.0
1992	4.0	5.0
1993	6.0	4.0
1994	10.0	2.5
1995	2.0	6.0
1996	–4.0	10.5

Arboc has a population of 1,000,000. The labor-force participation rate is 90%.

   a. Calculate the number of workers unemployed in 1990.

   b. Calculate the number of workers employed in 1996.

   Assume that the citizens of Arboc, when trying to determine the inflation rate for the next twelve months, base their calculations solely on the current inflation rate.

   c. During the period from 1991 to 1994, will borrowers be gaining or losing?

   d. In 1994, the market interest rate was 12%. Calculate the real interest rate.

   e. Use the aggregate demand-aggregate supply analysis to suggest how the economy has adjusted from 1994 to 1996.

4. Gilligan is a small island economy containing six individuals. In each of the following cases, determine if the individual is employed, unemployed, or not in the labor force.

   a. Krystal Krazy Ph. D., 32, works 20 hours per week and is looking for a full-time job.

   b. Lisa Looney, 20, is a student who is not working.

   c. Maggie Madd, 74, works 10 hours a week doing accounting services for her son, Norman Neurotic.

   d. Norman Neurotic, 50, works full-time but hates his job and really wants a new job.

   e. Olivia Opprest, a housewife, does not work outside the home and isn't looking for other employment.

   f. Pete Paranoid, 40, used to work as a fisherman but believed that everyone hated him and has given up in disgust.

   g. Calculate the labor-force participation rate.

   h. Calculate the unemployment rate.

5. Using the figures below, calculate the economic quantities for each year.

	1992	1997
Total population	200 million	210 million
Labor force	130 million	144 million
Employed	120 million	125 million

	1992	1997
a. the labor-force participation rate	_____	_____
b. the number unemployed	_____	_____
c. the unemployment rate	_____	_____

d. There is more likely to have been a recession in which year?
e. The President, denying that unemployment is growing, claims that:
   i. "We've created more jobs" and
   ii. "Some of the unemployed in the statistics have stopped seeking work."
   How would you respond to these points?

6. Answer the questions, based on the following information.

Year	Nominal GDP (Bill.)	Price Index	Real GDP (bill.)	Nominal Wage ($)	Real Wage
1996	4486.0	108		40,000	
1997	4710.3	112		40,800	

a. Between 1996 and 1997, nominal GDP has _____ by _____ %.
b. Between 1996 and 1997, inflation has _____ by _____ %.
c. Frank loaned Freda $500 in 1996 to be paid back in 1997. He guessed inflation would run at 5% and increased accordingly the interest rate on the loan. In the circumstances, who won?
d. Calculate the real GDP figures.
e. Now calculate the real wage of the typical worker in each year.
f. To have maintained her/his 1996 standard of living, the typical worker would need to have received a nominal wage of _____ in 1997.

7. Calculate the annual rates of inflation and complete the table below.

Year	Price Index	Rate of Inflation
1993	100.00	—
1994	113.00	
1995	121.50	
1996	126.70	
1997	125.10	

8. The following table shows the market value of a given basket of goods in a number of selected years. The hourly nominal wage is also given.

Year	Value of Market Basket	Price Index	Rate of Increase	Nominal Wage/Hour	Rate of Increase	Real Wage/Hour
1992	$887.00		—	$4.55	—	
1993	$993.44			$5.01		
1994	$1,132.52			$5.61		
1995	$1,245.78			$6.40		
1996	$1,320.52			$6.98		

a. Use the table above to calculate the price index values, with 1994 as the base year.

b. Using the price index values, calculate the real hourly wage.

c. Work out the rate of increase in the price index (what does it measure?) _____ , and the rate of increase in nominal wage/hour _____.

d. Compare the two "rates of increase" and the behavior of real wage/hour. Make up a rule of thumb linking these variables.

9. a. Distinguish between frictional, structural, and cyclical unemployment. Give an example of each. Suggest ways in which each of these types of unemployment might be reduced.

b. Suppose you've just become unemployed because of company cutbacks. Are you frictionally unemployed? Is it a good idea to accept the first job offer that comes along? Can you see any disadvantages to doing so?

ANSWERS AND SOLUTIONS

PRACTICE TEST

I. SOLUTIONS TO MULTIPLE CHOICE QUESTIONS

1. A. Job openings exist for Phil. It's merely a case of tracking down a position. See p. 170/596 for a discussion of the types of unemployment.

2. A. If there are more discouraged workers, the numbers on the unemployment rolls will decrease because workers who have ceased looking for a job (discouraged workers) no longer meet the definition of being "unemployed." See p. 169/595.

3. D. Francine has stopped seeking work—she is not classified as unemployed. See p. 169/595 on discouraged workers.

4. B. The skills of a group of workers have become obsolete, either through a change in demand or, as in this case, through a technological change. See p. 170/596.

5. B. The concept of full employment assumes that some (frictional and structural) unemployment will be present. See p. 170/596.

6. B. The new Arbocali computer chip industry represents a structural change. U.S. car- and steel-workers have experienced similar unemployment.

7. C. We don't know why Oliver became unemployed in the first place, but we do know that he could have accepted several suitable jobs but hasn't. He is best described as voluntarily unemployed.

8. C. The nominal interest rate is the real interest rate plus the anticipated inflation rate. See p. 180/606.

9. D. A borrower pays a lower rate of interest than s/he should have if inflation had been fully anticipated. In fact, if inflation is very high, the cost of a loan may be zero or negative. See p. 180/606.

10. B. The inflation rate = (change in CPI / initial CPI) × 100 = (11 / 110) × 100 = 10%.

11. C. If investment falls (as it will because unanticipated inflation hurts lenders), the economy will grow less rapidly because fewer capital resources are being created.

12. B. If the nominal wage rose by 7% and the inflation rate rose by 7%, the real wage would not have changed. For the real wage to have risen by 3%, the nominal wage must have risen by more than 7%—10%, in fact.

13. A. Discouraged workers, seeing an improving economy, will begin to look for jobs—and will be counted as unemployed whereas, previously, they were not.

14. D. See p. 169/595. Discouraged workers aren't classified as unemployed.

15. A. The real interest rate is equal to the nominal interest rate minus the anticipated inflation rate.

16. B. Structural and frictional unemployment should both be reduced, as will the natural rate (the sum of structural and frictional unemployment).

17. B. The labor force is the population minus those not in the labor force (500,000 – 100,000). The unemployment rate equals the number unemployed divided by the labor force. In this case, the unemployment rate equals 40,000 / 400,000, or 10%.

18. D. The labor-force participation rate equals the number in the labor force (400,000) divided by the population (500,000). See p. 166/592.

19. B. As the economy slows down, fewer imports are bought. See p. 173/599.

20. A. The more unpredictable a situation is, the riskier it is. See p. 181/607.

21. C. The nominal interest rate is the real interest rate (6%) plus the expected inflation rate (4%).

22. D. See p. 169/595.

II. SOLUTIONS TO APPLICATION QUESTIONS

1. Adjustable-rate mortgages, indexation of the tax system, and indexation of pension benefits are a few of the changes.

2. a. The real interest rate (3%) equals the market interest rate (5%) minus the inflation rate (2%).
   b. There will be an excess demand for loans. In fact, loans will dry up. The maximum nominal interest rate is 7%; with inflation, the maximum real interest rate is 2%, which is insufficient to induce banks to lend.

3. a. 900,000 × .075 = 67,500.
   b. 900,000 × .895 = 805,500.
   c. Inflation is increasing—borrowers gain and creditors lose.
   d. The market interest rate is based on the real interest rate plus the expected inflation rate. In 1994, the market interest rate was 12% and the expected inflation rate was 6%. The real interest rate was 6%.
   e. Inflation has decreased while unemployment has risen. The simplest explanation is that aggregate demand has declined from 1994 to 1996.

4. a. Employed.
   b. Not in labor force.
   c. Employed.
   d. Employed.
   e. Not in labor force.
   f. Not in labor force.
   g. 2 / 6 = .333.
   h. No one is unemployed in this economy.

5. a. The labor-force participation rate is labor force / population. In 1992, 130 / 200 = 65%; in 1997, 144 / 210 = 68.57%.
   b. Labor force equals the number employed plus the number unemployed. In 1992, the number unemployed = 130 million – 120 million = 10 million; in 1997, the number unemployed = 144 million – 125 million = 19 million.
   c. The unemployment rate = number unemployed / labor force. In 1992, number unemployed / labor force = 10 / 130 = 7.69%; in 1997, number unemployed / labor force = 19 / 144 = 13.19%.
   d. 1997, because the unemployment rate is higher in 1997.

e. i. It is possible for a growing economy to experience rising employment and rising unemployment but, if the increase in the participation rate outstrips the increase in job openings, the unemployment rate will rise.

ii. If, indeed, some individuals have stopped seeking work, then they would have dropped off the unemployment rolls. Admitting the presence of discouraged workers, on top of the listed unemployed, actually makes the President's performance worse!

6. a. risen; 5%. Percentage change = (change in nominal GDP / initial GDP) × 100 = (224.3 / 4,486) × 100 = 5%.

b. risen; 3.7%. Percentage change = (change in price index / initial price index) × 100 = (4 / 108) × 100 = 3.7%.

c. Frank as creditor, because anticipated inflation was greater than the actual inflation rate.

d. See the table below. Real GDP = (nominal GDP / price index) × 100.
Example: Real GDP for 1996 = (4,486 / 108) × 100 = 4,153.7.

Year	Nominal GDP (Bill.)	Price Index	Real GDP (bill.)	Nominal Wage ($)	Real Wage
1996	4,486.0	108	4,153.7	40,000	37,037.04
1997	4,710.3	112	4,205.6	40,800	36,428.57

e. See the table above. Real wage = (nominal wage / price index) × 100.
Example: Real wage for 1996 = (40,000 / 108) × 100 = 37,037.04.

f. Real wage in 1996 was $37,037.04 ($40,000 / 1.08). To maintain the same value in 1997, (x /1.12) = $37,037.04. Therefore, x = $37,037.04 (1.12) = $41,481.48.

7. See the table below.
Example: rate of inflation for 1995 = [(121.5 − 113) / 113] × 100 = 7.52%.

Year	Price Index	Rate of Inflation
1993	100.00	—
1994	113.00	13.00%
1995	121.50	7.52%
1996	126.70	4.28%
1997	125.10	−1.26%

8. a. See the table below.
Example: price index for 1993 = (nominal value 1993/nominal value in base year) × 100 = (993.44 / 1,132.52) × 100 = 87.72.

Year	Value of Market Basket	Price Index	Rate of Increase	Nominal Wage/Hour	Rate of Increase	Real Wage/Hour
1992	$887.00	78.32	—	$4.55	—	$5.81
1993	$993.44	87.72	12.0%	$5.01	10.1%	$5.71
1994	$1,132.52	100.00	14.0%	$5.61	12.0%	$5.61
1995	$1,245.78	110.00	10.0%	$6.40	14.1%	$5.82
1996	$1,320.52	116.60	6.0%	$6.98	9.1%	$5.98

b. See the table above. Example: real hourly wage for 1993 = (nominal wage 1993 / price index) × 100 = ($5.01 / .8772) × 100 = $5.71.

c. Inflation. See the table above. Example: rate of increase in nominal wage for 1993 = [(nominal wage 1993 - nominal wage 1992) / nominal wage 1992] × 100 = (.46 / 4.55) × 100 = 10.1%.

d. When inflation is rising faster than the rate of increase in the nominal wage, the real wage will fall.

9. a. See the definitions on pp. 171–172 (596–597). A graduate in economics or business entering the job market is frictionally unemployed. The graduate has desirable qualifications; it's only a matter of tracking down an acceptable job. Defense industry workers and military personnel are becoming structurally unemployed as a result of the end of the Cold War. "Restructuring" at IBM is another example. Cyclical unemployment occurred during the recession of 1991 as consumer confidence plummeted and demand declined.

    b. If the company cutbacks are due to a fall in demand that is being felt nationwide, you are cyclically unemployed. If this one industry is affected, perhaps due to aggressive foreign competition, you are structurally unemployed. Whether you should accept the first job that is offered depends on the costs and benefits of staying unemployed. If you think it unlikely that a sufficiently better job offer will materialize that will cover the costs of a continued search, you should accept.

AGGREGATE EXPENDITURE AND EQUILIBRIUM OUTPUT

9

COMBINED TEXT

24

OBJECTIVES: POINT BY POINT

After completing this chapter, you should be able to accomplish the objectives listed below.

General Comment

Give yourself plenty of time to understand the model developed in this chapter—it's the basis for what comes later. Can you prove that aggregate output does equal aggregate income? Can you confirm that income must equal consumption plus saving? Given the consumption function diagram, can you draw the related saving function diagram? Can you derive the consumption and saving equations? Can you see how unplanned inventory changes "balance" expenditures and output? Can you see why a $100 increase in investment is "multiplied"? If not, go back and work through this chapter again.

OBJECTIVE 1: Describe the relationship between consumption and income. Define the marginal propensity to consume (MPC) and the marginal propensity to save (MPS).

In the complete model of the economy, aggregate expenditure (AE) could be found by adding: $C + I + G + (EX - IM)$. That formula now simplifies to $AE = C + I$ because the model in this chapter has only two sectors (household and business) and only one market (goods). (page 190/616)

For households, income (Y) is split between consumption (C) and saving (S). Determinants of aggregate *consumption* include

   i.   household income,
  ii.   household wealth,
 iii.   interest rates, and
 iv.   household expectations about the future.

In the recession of the early 1990s, the Index of Consumer Confidence was a closely watched variable. As confidence sagged, so did consumer spending, especially on durable goods. (page 191/617)

If your wage increases by $100 each month, your consumption will rise too, but by something less than $100. The rest will be saved. How much of the extra $100 you choose to spend depends on your *marginal propensity to consume* (MPC). If you spend $80, MPC is 80 / 100 = .8. *Marginal propensity to save* (MPS) is 20 / 800 = .2 because any income not spent is saved ($20 out of $100). Clearly, MPC + MPS must sum to one (100% of any extra income must be spent or saved). (page 193/619)

> **TIP:** In Chapter 10 (25), we introduce taxes. This affects the calculation of MPC and MPS. You'll find the transition easier if you read the denominator term, "change in income," as "change in disposable income." In this chapter, the former term is identical with the latter (with no taxes, all income is disposable income); in Chapter 10 (25), MPC and MPS will be derived using the change in disposable income.

The consumption function shows the relationship between consumption spending and income; its slope ("rise" over "run") is the value of MPC ("change in consumption" over "change in income"). Algebraically, the consumption function is:

$$C = a + bY \qquad \text{(page 193/619)}$$

A similar function, the saving function, can be developed because the consumption and saving are related activities.

> **Graphing Pointer:** You can calculate MPS (and, therefore, MPC) quickly if you have the intercept value (a) and the income value (Y) where the consumption function intersects the 45° line. MPS = a / Y. Use this "trick" in Practice Question 6 below to confirm your result.

> **Graphing Pointer:** Use the same trick to find the slope of the AE curve (examined below).

PRACTICE

1. Aggregate consumption will certainly increase if
   A. income increases and wealth decreases.
   B. income increases and interest rates decrease.
   C. interest rates increase and household wealth increases.
   D. interest rates increase and consumer confidence about the future strengthens.
   Answer: B. Lower interest rates reduce the cost of borrowing. See p. 192/618.

2. Given the income level, saving is directly (positively) related to
   A. interest rates and wealth, and inversely (negatively) related to households' expectations about the future.
   B. interest rates, and inversely (negatively) related to wealth and households' expectations about the future.
   C. households' expectations about the future, and inversely (negatively) related to interest rates and wealth.
   D. wealth, and inversely (negatively) related to interest rates and households' expectations about the future.
   Answer: B. Higher interest rates encourage saving. As wealth increases and households become richer, and/or as households' expectations about the future improve, consumption increases. Given the income level, though, saving must decrease if consumption increases. See p. 192/618.

3. When MPC is .75, MPS is
   A. .25.
   B. .75.
   C. 3.00.
   D. 4.00.
   Answer: A. MPC + MPS = 1. See p. 194/620.

4. The consumption function is C = 200 + .9Y. The saving function is
   A. S = 200 − .1Y.
   B. S = −200 − .1Y.
   C. S = 200 − .9Y.
   D. S = −200 + .1Y.
   Answer: D. Recall that Y = C + S. The equations must sum to Y. The first term must be negative because consumption is positive. Also, recall that saving increases as income increases—the second term must be positive.

Use the following diagram to answer the next three questions.

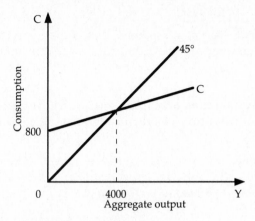

5. When income equals 4,000, consumption equals _____ and saving equals _____.
   A. 4,000, 0.
   B. 3,200, 800.
   C. 4,000, 4,000.
   D. 2,000, 2,000.
   Answer: A. The 45° line shows all the points at which the variable on the vertical axis equals the variable on the horizontal axis, in this case, where C = Y. If Y = 4,000, C = 4,000. If all income is being spent, saving must be zero.

Graphing Pointer: Pay particular attention to the answer of Practice Question 5. The 45° line contains no economic content. It is a reference line which aids reading the graph. The 45° line is very useful in determining when saving is zero (or positive or negative) when the consumption function is drawn. In this chapter and in future chapters, the 45° line will facilitate the determination of equilibrium aggregate output.

6. The equation for this consumption function is
   A. C = 800 + .75Y.
   B. C = 800 + .8Y.
   C. C = 4,000 + .75Y.
   D. C = 4,000 + .8Y.
   Answer: B. The intercept term (a) is 800. As income increases from 0 to 4,000, consumption increases from 800 to 4,000, an increase of 3,200. MPC = change in consumption/change in income = 3,200 / 4,000 = .8.

Graphing Pointer: Note the answer to Practice Question 6. When the consumption (saving) function intercepts the vertical axis, the associated value indicates the level of consumption (saving) which is independent of income. (If income = 0, this spending (saving) would still exist.)

7. If income is 6,000, consumption is _____ and saving is
   _____.
   A. 4,800, 1,200.
   B. 5,600, 400.
   C. 5,200, 1,000.
   D. 6,000, 0.
   Answer: B. When Y = 4,000, C = 4,000 and S = 0. MPC = .8. As income
   increases by 2,000 (from 4,000 to 6,000), consumption will increase by 2,000
   x .8, or 1,600. Consumption will total 5,600 (4,000 + 1,600). We know that
   Y = C + S, therefore S = Y − C. S = 6,000 − 5,600 = 400.

> **Graphing Pointer:** Note that Option C cannot be correct because C + S
> must equal income, and 5,200 + 1,000 does not equal 6,000.

**OBJECTIVE 2: Explain how actual and intended investment differ.
Describe the role of inventory change in establishing equilibrium in
the economy.**

The amount of planned investment is assumed to remain constant as output level
changes—investment will graph as a horizontal line. *Actual investment* can differ
from *planned investment* because of unplanned changes in the level of inventories.
(page 197/623)

> **TIP:** Investment is one of the most difficult concepts to learn. Economists
> use the word differently from others. Investment does *not* mean saving, not
> even financial investment. Investment is the purchase of new machinery and
> buildings (productive capacity) and changes in inventory levels.

Note that firms buy more than investment goods. They hire workers, for example.
To count this expenditure would be double counting—the wages are used by households for consumption and saving.

> **TIP:** Keep in mind that, in this model, actual investment will *always* equal
> saving. In equilibrium, planned investment will equal saving and unplanned
> inventory investment will be zero.

If production exceeds (is less than) planned sales and planned change in inventory,
there will be an unplanned increase (decrease) in inventory. (For an example of this,
see Application 3 below.) (page 198/624)

> **Unplanned Inventory Change and Equilibrium:** Unplanned changes in
> inventory draw the economy into equilibrium. Call expenditures "demand"
> and output "supply" for the moment. When "demand" is more than cur-
> rent "supply," firms are forced to reduce their previously accumulated
> inventory. Emptying shelves are the signal to increase production.
>
> When "demand" is less than "supply," unsold production is piling up—the
> signal to cut output.
>
> Firms feel no pressure to adjust production levels (i.e., there will be equi-
> librium), only when "demand" equals "supply."
>
> Also, when unplanned inventory change is not zero (either positive or
> negative), the actual level of investment differs from the level managers
> planned to have. If, for example, actual investment is "too low," managers
> will boost production to compensate.

> **TIP:** An economic system requires some mechanism to drive it towards equilibrium. In the market for coffee, the equilibrating mechanism is price. In our model, price is fixed and the equilibrating mechanism is unplanned inventory change. When unplanned inventory change occurs, it is a signal to adjust output.

PRACTICE

8. Investment refers to
   A. the purchase of new stock in a company.
   B. the purchase of new or existing stock in a company.
   C. the creation of capital stock.
   D. the stock of accumulated saving.
   Answer: C. Investment is addition to the capital stock. Financial transactions are excluded from GDP—review Chapter 7 (22).

9. The change in inventories is
   A. production minus sales.
   B. sales minus production.
   C. a value equal to or greater than zero, but cannot be negative.
   D. consumption minus saving.
   Answer: A. See p. 197/623.

OBJECTIVE 3: Derive and graph the planned aggregate expenditure (AE) function. State why its slope has a value of less than one. Describe the adjustment process when planned aggregate expenditure differs from aggregate output. Use the expenditure and output approach and the leakages/injections approach to specify the meaning of equilibrium in the model.

Planned aggregate expenditure is the sum of consumption and investment at each income level. Because investment is constant at each income level, the AE function is an upward sloping line whose slope equals MPC.   (page 198/624)

> **TIP:** Sometimes you'll find understanding easier if you talk about "output," and sometimes about "income." For example, "When unplanned inventory reductions occur, output level will rise" is more obvious than "When unplanned inventory reductions occur, income level will rise." However, "Output is split between consumption and saving" is much less intuitive than "Income is split between consumption and saving."

Equilibrium occurs when planned aggregate expenditure equals aggregate output (income)—i.e., when C + I = C + S. Only in this case will planned investment equal actual investment—there will be no unplanned inventory change. If expenditures exceed output, inventory levels are unexpectedly depleted. Firms respond by increasing production. Higher production results in higher income and, given MPC, more consumption spending. Spending rises, but at a slower rate than output rises. Eventually, the two will be equal. How big an increase in output level is needed to achieve equilibrium depends on the value of the multiplier.   page 203/629)

The conditions necessary for equilibrium can be stated in different ways.

   a. If there is a difference between actual and planned investment, the economy is not in equilibrium. Equilibrium condition: planned investment equals actual investment.
   b. Aggregate planned expenditure must equal aggregate output (income). Therefore, C + I = C + S. Equilibrium condition: planned investment must equal planned saving.

Note that there's no requirement that the equilibrium level of production will be enough to provide full employment to the economy's workers.

> **Graphing Pointer:** Planned investment is assumed constant regardless at all output levels—the graph linking planned investment and aggregate income is a line parallel to the horizontal axis. Consequently, the curve representing aggregate expenditures (the sum of consumption and planned investment in this model) is a line which is parallel to the consumption curve. (See the graph for Questions 18–22.)

> **Graphing Pointer:** Unlike most other curves you have seen, the consumption, investment, saving, and AE functions are all shown to increase by moving vertically upward (not to the right).

PRACTICE

Use the following table to answer the next six questions.

OUTPUT	CONSUMPTION	INVESTMENT	PLANNED AGGREGATE EXPENDITURE	UNPLANNED CHANGE IN INVENTORY
2,000	2,100	400	_____	_____
3,000	2,850	400	_____	_____
4,000	3,600	400	_____	_____
5,000	4,350	400	_____	_____
6,000	5,100	400	_____	_____
7,000	5,850	400	_____	_____

10. Complete the planned aggregate expenditure column in the table above.
    Answer: See the *Answers and Solutions* section.

11. Equilibrium output level is
    A. 3,000.
    B. 4,000.
    C. 5,000.
    D. 6,000.
    Answer: B. Equilibrium occurs where output equals planned aggregate expenditure.

12. Complete the unplanned change in inventory column in the table above.
    Answer: See the *Answers and Solutions* section. Unplanned change in inventory is the difference between output and planned aggregate expenditure.

13. In the table above, MPC is
    A. .6.
    B. .75.
    C. .8.
    D. .9.
    Answer: B. Every time income rises by 1,000, consumption rises by 750.

14. When income level is 0, consumption is
    A. 0.
    B. 250.
    C. 600.
    D. 1,000.
    Answer: C. When income is 2,000, consumption is 2,100. If income decreases by 2,000 and MPC is .75, consumption will decrease by 1,500.

15. When output is 6,000, firms will
    A. increase production.
    B. decrease production.
    C. increase planned investment.
    D. decrease planned investment.
    Answer: B. Output exceeds planned aggregate expenditure and inventories are too high. Firms would cut production.

OBJECTIVE 4: Analyze the effects on the macroeconomy of a change in planned investment or consumption. Describe the role of the multiplier in the inventory-adjustment process and, given MPC, derive the numerical value of the multiplier.

The *multiplier* measures the extent to which the output level will change given a particular initial change in the level of spending. It is calculated by the formula: $1 / (1 - MPC)$ or $1 / MPS$.   (page 204/630)

> **TIP:** You might find subsequent material easier if you focus more on the $1/MPS$ formula. The strength of the multiplier depends on how rapidly spending power leaks out of the circular flow diagram. This is even more obvious when leakages other than saving (taxes, imports) make their appearance.

> **TIP:** One quick way to visualize the multiplier is to use the following circular flow diagram.
>
>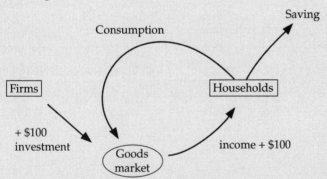
>
> You know that households split their income into consumption expenditures and saving. Some investment also takes place. Suppose MPC is .9 and MPS is .1. Suppose that an extra $100 of investment spending occurs and income rises by $100. Trace through the circular flow—consumption rises by $90, $81, $72.90, and so on. Where is the rest going? It's leaking away into saving (non-spending).
>
> The same $100 increase in investment, with a lower MPC, such as .5, gives a *less* substantial expansion in spending because the extra income drains away more quickly. The multiplier is smaller, right?
>
> The force of the expansion is lessened if spending power drains away more rapidly—as MPS increases. The multiplier value, then, is linked negatively to MPS and positively to MPC.

An increase in investment (or consumption) generates extra income. Extra income, however, stimulates consumption and saving—MPC and MPS determine how much consumption and saving will rise. Extra consumption generates more new income. The process of "spend-earn income-spend" runs out of steam as progressively more of the extra dollars leak away into saving.   (page 204/630)

> **TIP:** As shown in the textbook, the multiplier model works given a change in investment, but it is more general than that. The analysis works for any component of planned aggregate expenditure—in this chapter, consumption and investment and, in Chapter 10 (25), government spending.

> **Graphing Pointer:** Note that, graphically, equilibrium must occur where the AE function crosses the 45° line. The 45° line plots all the points where spending equals output—i.e., all the points where equilibrium might occur.

Example: If planned investment increases, the AE line shifts upwards. At the current output level, inventories unexpectedly fall. As firms raise production to restore desired inventory levels, income and consumption will rise, and the economy will move to the point where the new (higher) AE function crosses the 45° line. This same story can be told in terms of the saving-investment diagram which contains similar information.

> **TIP:** Memorize the two multiplier formulas given on p. 208/634. Also, memorize the likely values for the multiplier that might show up on a test. These are:

MPC	MPS	MULTIPLIER
.50	___	2.0
.60	___	2.5
.75	___	4.0
.80	___	5.0
.90	___	10.0

> For practice, fill in the MPS values and confirm the multiplier values using both formulas.

PRACTICE

By comparing the two cases that follow, you should get a good idea about how the multiplier operates.

CASE 1: ARBOC. In Arboc, MPC is .9. The economy is in equilibrium. Suddenly, there is a 100 opek increase in investment spending. This creates 100 opeks of extra income. The income is split 90:10 between new consumption and new saving. The new consumption generates additional income.

NEW EXPENDITURE	NEW INCOME	=	NEW SAVING	+	NEW CONSUMPTION
100.00	100.00	=	10.00	+	90.00
90.00	90.00	=	9.00	+	81.00
81.00	81.00	=	8.10	+	72.90
72.90	72.90	=	7.29	+	65.61
65.61	65.61	=	6.56	+	59.05
.	.		.		.
.	.		.		.
.	.		.		.
_____	_____		_____		_____
1,000.00	1,000.00	=	100.00	+	900.00

This process goes through many "rounds," only the first five of which are given. The final row gives the total results.

Notes

A. The initial "injection" of spending is 100; ultimately this will all become new saving. Indeed, the opeks will continue to circulate (generating more income and expenditure) until all of the "extra" 100 opeks have leaked away. *The leakage must equal the injection.* The multiplier's strength depends on how rapidly the injection of extra spending leaks away.

B. We know that income equals consumption plus investment. Income increased by 1,000, consumption increased by 900, and investment increased by 100.

CASE 2: ARBEZ. In Arbez, MPC is .8. The economy is in equilibrium. Suddenly, there is a 100 bandu increase in investment spending. This creates 100 bandu of extra income. Income is split 80:20 between new consumption and new saving.

16. Complete the table below.

   Answer: See the *Answers and Solutions* section.

NEW EXPENDITURE	NEW INCOME	=	NEW SAVING	+	NEW CONSUMPTION
100.00	_____	=	_____	+	_____
_____	_____	=	_____	+	_____
_____	_____	=	_____	+	_____
_____	_____	=	_____	+	_____
_____	_____	=	_____	+	_____
.	.		.		.
.	.		.		.
.	.		.		.
_____	_____	=	_____	+	_____
500.00	500.00	=	100.00	+	400.00

Notes

A. As in Case 1, the initial "injection" of spending leaks away to saving; ultimately all of this ends up as new saving.

B. Income increased by 500, consumption increased by 400, and investment increased by 100.

C. The expansion in income is less in Case 2 (the multiplier is smaller) because MPC is smaller (MPS is greater). The extra 100 units of spending leak away more slowly in Case 1 and are recycled more frequently.

> **Graphing Pointer:** Remember: The steeper the AE curve, the higher the value of the multiplier.

17. The formula for the multiplier is
   A. 1 / MPC.
   B. 1 / MPS.
   C. 1 / (1 − MPS).
   D. 1 / (1 + MPC).
   Answer: B. See p. 208/634.

Use the following diagram, which builds on the previous diagram, to answer the next five questions.

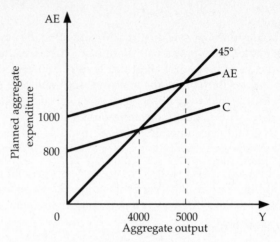

18. The level of investment in this economy is
    A. 200.
    B. 800.
    C. 1,000.
    D. 5,000
    Answer: A. AE = C + I. When Y = 0, AE = 1,000 and C = 800.

19. The slope of the AE function is
    A. .6.
    B. .75.
    C. .8.
    D. .9.
    Answer: C. The slope of the AE function depends on MPC. Question 6 above determined that MPC is .8. If we refer to the AE function by itself, we get the same result. Spending increases by 4,000 (from 1,000 to 5,000) as income increases from 0 to 5,000.

20. The multiplier has a value of
    A. 4.
    B. 5.
    C. 8.
    D. 10.
    Answer: B. The multiplier formula is 1 / (1 − MPC). MPC is .8.

21. If planned investment increases by 100, equilibrium output level will increase by _____. In equilibrium, saving will equal _____.
    A. 100, 200.
    B. 100, 300.
    C. 500, 200.
    D. 500, 300.
    Answer: D. The multiplier is 5. Equilibrium output will increase by 500 (100 × 5). In equilibrium, saving will equal investment. Recall that investment was 200 and rose further by a 100.

22. When the output level is 4,000, unplanned inventories will _____ by _____.
    A. increase, 1,000.
    B. increase, 200.
    C. decrease, 1,000.
    D. decrease, 200.
    Answer: D. At an output level of 5,000, planned aggregate expenditure is 5,000. When income falls by 1,000, consumption falls by 800 because MPC is .8. Therefore, we know that, at an output level of 4,000, planned aggregate expenditure is 4,200. Planned aggregate expenditure is 200 more than output and inventories will decrease accordingly.

23. If the slope of the AE function became steeper, MPC would become
_____ and the multiplier would become _____.
   A. larger, larger.
   B. larger, smaller.
   C. smaller, larger.
   D. smaller, smaller.
   Answer: A. See Case A and Case B above.

OBJECTIVE 5: Describe the reasoning behind the paradox of thrift and explain what is paradoxical.

The *paradox of thrift* shows that attempts to increase saving (an upward shift in the saving function and a downward shift in the consumption function) will be fruitless. There will be no change in total saving, but the economy will suffer a decrease in output (income) level. (page 207/633)

> **TIP:** The paradox of thrift is inevitable, given our model. Investment is constant and, when equilibrium is achieved, saving *must* equal that value. As long as investment behavior does not change, saving can neither increase nor decrease.

PRACTICE

25. Refer to the table used in Practice Question 10. The economy is in equilibrium. If saving increases by 100, equilibrium output will decrease by _____ and consumption will decrease by _____.
   A. 100, 100.
   B. 100, 400.
   C. 400, 100.
   D. 400, 400.
   Answer: D. MPC is .75 (Question 13); the multiplier is 4. If saving increases by 100, consumption decreases by 100 and output decreases by 400 (100 × 4). When output (income) decreases by 400, consumption is reduced by an additional 300. The total decrease in consumption is 400.

24. If households increase saving, the paradox of thrift indicates that, in equilibrium, consumption will _____ and output will _____.
   A. decrease, increase.
   B. decrease, decrease.
   C. not increase, increase.
   D. not increase, decrease.
   Answer: B. The increase in saving causes consumption to decrease. The decrease in consumption spending will make equilibrium output decrease. As income falls, consumption falls even more.

SUMMARY: EQUILIBRIUM CONDITIONS

Equilibrium can be described in several ways. Learn them all!

$$\text{Planned aggregate expenditure} = \text{aggregate output (income)}$$
$$C + S = C + I$$
$$S = I$$
$$\text{planned investment} = \text{actual investment}$$
$$\text{unplanned inventory change} = 0$$

Note: As the model is extended in later chapters, all but the first of these conditions will be modified.

I. MULTIPLE CHOICE QUESTIONS.

Select the option that provides the single best answer.

___A___ 1. MPC is _____ divided by _____
- A. consumption, income.
- B. change in consumption, income.
- C. change in consumption, change in income.
- D. consumption, change in income.

___A___ 2. The larger the MPC, the
- A. larger the value of the multiplier.
- B. steeper the slope of the saving function.
- C. smaller the value of the multiplier.
- D. flatter the slope of the consumption function.

Use the following table to answer the next three questions.

Income	Consumption	Investment
2,000	1,800	1,000
3,000	2,600	1,000
4,000	3,400	1,000
5,000	4,200	1,000
6,000	5,000	1,000
7,000	5,800	1,000

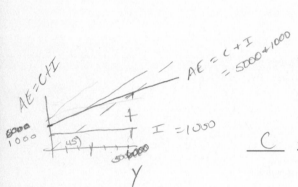

___C___ 3. The equilibrium income level is _____ and the equilibrium saving level is _____
- A. 7,000, 200.
- B. greater than 7,000, 1,000.
- C. 6,000, 1,000.
- D. 1,000, 100.

___B___ 4. The MPS is _____ and the multiplier is _____
- A. .1, 10.
- B. .2, 5.
- C. .2, 10.
- D. .1, 5.

___B___ 5. If planned saving suddenly rises by 100, then, at the new equilibrium, income will _____. Eventually, saving will _____
- A. fall by 100, fall by 100.
- B. fall by 500, not change.
- C. fall by 500, fall by 100.
- D. fall by 100, not change.

Use the following table to answer the next three questions.

Income	Consumption
0	100
100	180
200	260
300	340
1,000	900
2,000	1,700

6. Referring to the equation C = a + bY, the value of "a" is
   _____
   A. 0.
   B. 20.
   C. 80.
   D. 100.

7. Marginal propensity to consume is _____
   A. 80.
   B. .2.
   C. .8.
   D. .9.

8. An increase in investment of $100 would _____ income by _____
   A. raise, 500.
   B. raise, 100.
   C. lower, 500.
   D. lower, 100.

9. The economy is in equilibrium at an output level of 2,000. Now planned investment increases. At the initial output level, all of the following are true except
   A. aggregate expenditure is greater than aggregate output.
   B. saving is less than planned investment.
   C. inventory levels are rising unexpectedly.
   D. consumption level has remained unchanged.

10. A decrease in MPS would
    A. cause the consumption function to shift upwards, all along its length.
    B. cause the consumption function to shift downwards, all along its length.
    C. cause the consumption function to shift upwards, pivoting where it meets the vertical axis.
    D. have no effect on the consumption function.

11. In our model, MPC must be less than _____ and MPS must exceed _____
    A. one, one.
    B. one, zero.
    C. zero, one.
    D. zero, zero.

12. If planned investment suddenly decreases, the AE line will shift _____ and equilibrium saving will _____.
    A. upward, increase.
    B. upward, decrease.
    C. downward, increase.
    D. downward, decrease.

_B_ 13. Equilibrium occurs when aggregate output is equal to planned
_____ plus planned _____.
A. consumption, saving.
B. consumption, investment.
C. investment, saving.
D. inventories, investment.

_D_ 14. Aggregate output is currently less than planned aggregate expenditure.
We can predict that inventory levels are unexpectedly _____
and saving is _____ than planned investment.
A. increasing, greater.
B. increasing, less.
C. decreasing, greater.
D. decreasing, less.

_____ 15. Which of the following statements is true?
A. Savings is the difference between current income and current
consumption.
B. When expenditures are high, saving is less than actual investment.
C. Saving is a flow variable: savings is a stock variable.
D. When the interest rate falls, saving increases and consumption
decreases.

_____ 16. If income is zero, consumption will be
A. positive.
B. zero, because you can't spend what you don't have.
C. zero, because consumption and saving must sum to equal
income.
D. unknown—it depends on the slope of the consumption function.

_____ 17. As consumer uncertainty in the future increases, consumption will
_____ and saving will _____.
A. increase, increase.
B. increase, decrease.
C. decrease, increase.
D. decrease, decrease.

_____ 18. Firms have the least control over
A. inventory levels.
B. production levels.
C. planned investment.
D. purchases of new equipment.

_____ 19. MPC equals .9. Consumers receive an extra $100 of income. We can
say that
A. the consumption function has moved upwards.
B. the consumption function has moved downwards.
C. consumption spending increases by $100.
D. saving increases by $10.

_____ 20. MPC = .9. Planned investment = 100 and equilibrium income level
is 1,000. If income were at 800, what would be the level of saving?
A. 100.
B. 90.
C. 80.
D. 70.

Use the following diagram to answer the next five questions.

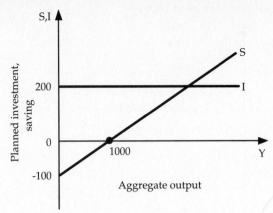

Aggregate output

_____ 21. The equation for this consumption function is
   A.   C = 100 + .8Y.
   B.   C = 100 + .9Y.
   C.   C = 200 + .8Y.
   D.   C = 200 + .9Y.

_____ 22. The multiplier value is
   A.   .9.
   B.   8.
   C.   9.
   D.   10.

_____ 23. The equilibrium output level is
   A.   200.
   B.   1,000.
   C.   3,000.
   D.   4,000.

_____ 24. If investment decreases by 50, equilibrium output will decrease
   by _____ and consumption will decrease by
   _____.
   A.   200, 450.
   B.   200, 500.
   C.   500, 450.
   D.   500, 500.

_____ 25. The equation for this saving function is
   A.   S = 100 + .1Y.
   B.   S = 100 + .9Y.
   C.   S = −100 + .1Y.
   D.   S = −100 + .9Y.

II. APPLICATION QUESTIONS.

1. The Arbezani Minister of Macroeconomics gives you the following data about
    Arbez.
    (1)   C = 300 + .75Y
    (2)   I = 200
    (3)   AE = C + I
    (4)   AE = Y
    a. Calculate the marginal propensity to consume and the marginal propen-
        sity to save.
    b. Derive the algebraic formula for the saving function.
    c. What are the four conditions necessary for the economy to be in
        equilibrium?
    d. Using your knowledge of the model, confirm that each equilibrium con-
        dition is consistent with the others.

e. Solve for equilibrium income. Calculate equilibrium income.
f. Graph equations (3) and (4) below.

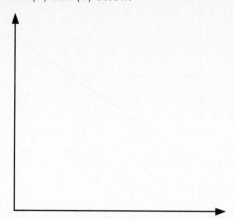

g. If GDP were 1,200, unplanned inventory accumulation would be how much?
h. If GDP were 2,200, unplanned inventory accumulation would be how much?
i. Based on these results, make up a rule relating the direction of unplanned inventory change, the 45° line, and the expenditure function.
j. How much saving will occur if GDP is 1,200?
k. How much saving will occur if GDP is 2,200?
l. Calculate the value of the multiplier.

When the economy is at the natural rate of unemployment, the output level is 2,800.
m. How much would investment have to change to create full employment?

The economy is at its original equilibrium income level. Now, because of a surge in consumer optimism, consumption increases by 100 at each income level.
n. Inventories are changing by how much? Are they rising or falling?
o. Calculate the new equilibrium income level.
p. Calculate the new equilibrium consumption level.
q. Calculate the new equilibrium saving level.
r. Calculate the new equilibrium investment level.
s. Explain the result that has emerged regarding the net amount of change in the level of saving.

2. Most of the ideas associated with the consumption function are quite intuitive. Try to prove to yourself that the theory reflects common sense. The following questions cover many of the main points about consumption and saving that are dealt with in this chapter.
   a. Suppose you have received a $100 per week wage increase (after tax). Would you spend:
      i. all of the extra $100?
      ii. some of the extra $100?
      iii. none of the extra $100?
   b. Would you save:
      i. all of the extra $100?
      ii. some of the extra $100?
      iii. none of the extra $100?
   c. The level of disposable income affects the amount spent and saved. Do you agree or disagree with the following statements?
      i. Other things, as well as income, affect how much I spend and save.
      ii. If I increase my personal consumption expenditures, I will have less available to save.
      iii. If I had no current income, I'd still try to buy food and other necessities.
      iv. Poor households spend a bigger proportion of their income than rich households do.

d. Given my income level, if I increase my personal spending by $1, my saving will _____ (increase/decrease) by _____ (more than/less than/exactly) a dollar.

In most other cases you should find yourself agreeing with the textbook's theory of consumption and saving.

3. Ask (or pretend to ask) five persons the following question:

"You are a typical consumer with an income of $100 per week. How much of your income will you set aside as saving?"

Now ask yourself (the owner of a small business):

How much of your expected value of production (which you forecast to be $500 per week) will you plan to plow back into the firm? (Remember you have employees and other bills to pay!)

Enter the results of the two questions in the table.

Saving	Investment

There's no single "right" answer—it depends on preferences, income level, wealth, and so on. It's unlikely saving and planned investment will be equal. Suppose saving totals $15 and planned investment equals $20.

a. Which is greater: C + I or C + S?
b. Which is greater: planned aggregate expenditure or aggregate output?
c. Will firms be able to meet the planned demand for output, given their current level of production?
d. What will happen?
e. Write the formula for actual investment.
f. Calculate actual investment.

So actual investment is forced to the saving level!

4. "Investment is equal to 100. Consumption is equal to income. MPC equals .9."
a. Saving is equal to _____.
b. "Currently, the marginal propensity to save equals zero." (True/False)
c. Currently, the economy _____ (is/is not) in equilibrium. Aggregate expenditure is _____ (greater than/less than) aggregate output.
d. Calculate the value of the multiplier.
e. Unplanned inventory change is _____ (positive/negative).
f. To establish equilibrium, output level will have to _____ (rise/fall) by _____, in which case consumption will _____ (rise/fall) by _____ and saving will _____ (rise/fall) by _____.

Now suppose that the income level (where consumption equals income) is 1,000.
g. When income equals zero, consumption will equal _____ and saving will equal _____.
h. Calculate the formula for the consumption function.
i. Algebraically, confirm your results from (f) above, and calculate the equilibrium income level.

j. Sketch the saving-investment diagram, showing the slope of the saving function, the present income level (1,000) and the equilibrium income level.

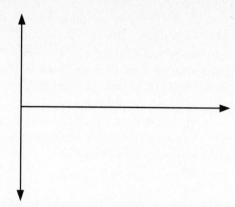

5. a. Fill in the blanks in the following table, based on the model given in the text.

Income	Consumption	Saving	Investment	Expenditures
0				
100	180			
200	260			
300			20	
400				
500				
600				

MPC _____   MPS _____
multiplier = _____

b. The equilibrium output level is _____.
c. Algebraically, determine the consumption function.
d. Confirm your answer to (b) algebraically.
e. When income level is 300, there will be unplanned inventory _____ while, at an income level of 700, inventories will unexpectedly _____ (increase/decrease).
f. Graph the AE function on the 45° line diagram below. Show the income range in which inventories will be rising unexpectedly and the income range in which they will be falling.

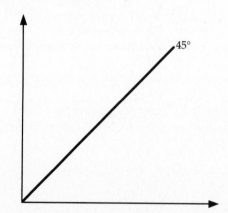

45°

g. If investment increases by 50, by how much would equilibrium output level increase?

h. Consumption and saving would increase by _____ and _____ respectively.

i. The final value of saving would be _____ and investment would be _____.

j. Confirm your results for (g), (h), and (i) algebraically.

k. The economy's equilibrium income level is 850. Suppose that 1,000 is the level of production that would provide full employment. How much more would investment have to rise in order to achieve full employment? _____

6.

> **Graphing Pointer:** Suppose that the consumption function does *not* graph as a straight line, but rather increases at a decreasing rate (flattening off). Given your knowledge of the relationships between consumption, saving, and income, could you now draw the saving function? What sort of slope would it have? What would be happening to the value of the multiplier as income level increased?

7.

> **Graphing Pointer:** We have modeled investment as remaining constant as output level increases. Suppose, more realistically, that investment increases as income level rises. What would happen to the slope of the AE curve? What would happen to the value of the multiplier?

ANSWERS AND SOLUTIONS

ANSWERS TO PRACTICE QUESTIONS

10.

OUTPUT	CONSUMPTION	INVESTMENT	PLANNED AGGREGATE EXPENDITURE	UNPLANNED CHANGE IN INVENTORY
2,000	2,100	400	2,500	−500
3,000	2,850	400	3,250	−250
4,000	3,600	400	4,000	0
5,000	4,350	400	4,750	+250
6,000	5,100	400	5,500	+500
7,000	5,850	400	6,250	+750

16.

NEW EXPENDITURE	NEW INCOME	=	NEW SAVING	+	NEW CONSUMPTION
100.00	100.00	=	20.00	+	80.00
80.00	80.00	=	16.00	+	64.00
64.00	64.00	=	12.80	+	51.20
51.20	51.20	=	10.24	+	40.96
40.96	40.96	=	8.19	+	32.77
.	.		.		.
.	.		.		.
.	.		.		.
500.00	500.00	=	100.00	+	400.00

PRACTICE TEST

I. SOLUTIONS TO MULTIPLE CHOICE QUESTIONS

1. C. See p. 193/619.

2. A. The multiplier formula is 1 / (1 – MPC). See p. 208/634.

3. C. Equilibrium occurs where income equals consumption plus investment, at 6,000. In equilibrium, S = I, so saving must equal 1,000. Alternatively, when income is 6,000 and consumption is 5,000, saving must be 1,000.

4. B. When the income level changes by 1,000 (from 3,000 to 4,000, for example), consumption increases by 800 (from 2,600 to 3,400). The additional 200 is saved. MPS = change in saving/change in income = 200 / 1,000 = .2. The multiplier = 1 / MPS = 1 / .2 = 5.

5. B. If saving rises by 100, consumption must fall initially by 100, given the income level. The multiplier is 5. The final change in equilibrium income is 500 (i.e., 100 × 5). If income falls by 500 and the MPC is .8, consumption will fall by an additional 400. The total decrease in consumption is 500.

6. D. In the equation, "bY" is the portion of consumption that responds to changes in income. When income is zero, consumption is 100.

7. C. When the income level changes by 100 (from 200 to 300, for example), consumption increases by 80 (from 180 to 260). MPC = change in consumption/change in income = 80 / 100 = .8.

8. A. If expenditure increases, then equilibrium income will increase. The multiplier is 5 because MPC is .8. The multiplier equals 1 / (1 – MPC). Income, then, will increase by 500 (i.e., 100 × 5).

9. C. Because the demand for goods has risen, inventory levels will be drawn down.

10. C. MPS is the slope of the saving function. A decrease in MPS requires an increase in MPC. An increase in MPC will cause the slope of the consumption function to become steeper.

11. B. If income increases by 100, our theory assumes that we consume some quantity less than 100 and save some positive quantity.

12. D. Investment is a part of aggregate expenditure. A decrease in investment will decrease AE, shifting the line downward. In equilibrium, S = I. If investment falls, saving must fall too.

13. B. In equilibrium, Y = C + I. See p. 199/625.

14. D. If aggregate output is less than planned aggregate expenditure, then demand is high. Inventory levels will be falling. Because spending is high, saving is low and will be less than planned investment.

15. C. Savings is the accumulation of saving from past periods; it is a stock, while saving is a process (a flow). Saving *always* equals actual investment. When the interest rate falls, saving decreases and consumption increases.

16. A. The slope of the consumption function is irrelevant in this question. Consumption is positive even when income is zero because it is necessary to buy food, housing, and other staples of life. Without income, this is financed by "dissaving."

17. C. When future prospects are less clear, households tend to hold back on purchases, saving more of their current income.

18. A. Firms choose output levels and set up investment programs, but their inventory levels are affected by sales which are dependent upon the whims of their customers.

19. D. An increase in income will not shift the consumption function—there will be a movement along it. If MPC is .6, MPS is .1. A $100 increase in income will generate a $10 increase (100 × .1) in saving.

20. C. Equilibrium income level is 1,000 and planned investment is 100. In equilibrium, consumption must be 900 and saving must be 100. If income falls by 200, consumption falls by 180 (200 × .9) and saving falls by 20 (200 × .1). Saving will be 80.

21. B. The intercept term (a) is 100 because income is zero and C + S must equal this. As income increases from zero to 1,000, saving increases from –100 to 0, an increase of 100. MPS = change in saving/change in income = 100 / 1,000 = .1. MPC = 1 – MPS.

22. D. The multiplier equals 1 / (1 – MPC).

23. C. In equilibrium, saving must equal investment and, therefore, must equal 200. For saving to increase by 300 (from –100 to 200), income must increase by 3,000 (from zero) if MPS is .1.

24. C. Expenditure decreases by 50. The multiplier is 10. Equilibrium output will decrease by 500 (50 × 10). Because MPC is .9, consumption will decrease by 450 (500 × .9). Saving will fall by 50 (500 × MPS), causing saving to be 150 and to be equal to investment.

25. C. $S = Y - C = Y - (100 + .9Y) = -100 + .1Y$.

II. SOLUTIONS TO APPLICATION QUESTIONS

1. a. MPC = .75. Equation 1 tells us that, as income (Y) increases by 100, consumption increases by 75. MPS = .25. Recall that MPC + MPS = 1. Alternatively, as income (Y) increases by 100 and consumption increases by 75, the remaining 25 must be saved.

    b. $S = -300 + .25Y$.

    c. The equilibrium conditions are:

    (1) Planned aggregate expenditure = aggregate output (income)

    $$C + S = C + I$$

    (2) Planned saving = planned investment

    $$S = I$$

    (3) planned investment = actual investment

    (4) unplanned inventory change = 0

    d. If, in equilibrium, equation (1) holds, then (2) must also hold because AE is defined as consumption plus investment and Y is defined as consumption plus saving. Similarly, canceling the "consumptions," we can derive (3). We know that actual investment always equals planned investment plus unplanned inventory change. In equilibrium, unplanned inventory change is zero (5), therefore equation (4) is consistent. If actual investment equals planned investment plus zero, then actual investment equals planned investment.

    e. $Y = C + I$ (in equilibrium)

    $Y = 300 + .75Y + 200 = 500 + .75Y$

    $Y - .75Y = 500$

    $.25Y = 500 \Rightarrow Y = 2,000$.

    f. See the diagram below.

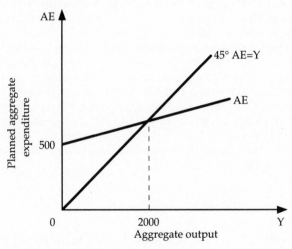

    g. 200 decrease in inventories. Demand (1,400) exceeds production (1,200).

    h. 50 increase in inventories. Production (2,200) exceeds demand (2,150).

    i. At income levels where the AE line is above the 45° line, unplanned inventory change will be negative (e.g., when Y = 1,200); at income levels where the AE line is below the 45° line, unplanned inventory change will be positive (e.g., when Y = 2,200).

    j. $C = 300 + .75Y$. Y = 1,200. $C = 300 + .75(1,200) = 1,200$. $S = Y - C = 0$.

    k. $C = 300 + .75Y$. Y = 2,200. $C = 300 + .75(2,200) = 1,950$. $S = Y - C = 250$.

    l. An autonomous 100-unit increase in expenditure causes a 400 increase in equilibrium income. The multiplier is 4.00.

Check: Multiplier = 1 / (1 – MPC) = 1 / .25 = 4.00

m. $\Delta Y = m \cdot \Delta I$. m = 4 and ΔY = 800, therefore ΔI = 200.

n. Inventories are falling by 100 as producers use previously produced output to meet the unexpected demand.

o.
$$Y = C + I \text{ (in equilibrium)}$$
$$Y = 400 + .75Y + 200 = 600 + .75Y$$
$$Y - .75Y = 600$$
$$.25Y = 600 => Y = 2,400.$$

p. When Y = 2,400, C = 400 + .75(2,400) = 2,200.

q. When Y = 2,400, S = –400 + .25(2,400) = 200.

Check: Y = C + S 2,400 = 2,200 + 200.

r. I is unchanged at 200. Note that, in equilibrium, S = I.

s. Saving has remained unchanged. In equilibrium, S = I, and I has remained unchanged.

2. a. some (probably most, in fact).

b. some.

If you answered "all" for (A) you should have answered "none" for (B). Such answers indicate you're not "typical"—most folks try to set some saving aside. Groups who don't are the young (who may have high initial expenses and low incomes) and the retired (who don't earn much).

c. You probably "agree" with all of these statements.

The "other things" in (i) and the logic behind (iv) will be developed in Chapter 14 (29).

d. If I increase my personal spending by $1, my saving will *decrease* by *exactly* $1. If you missed this one, reread the first few pages of the chapter!

3. a. C + I exceeds C + S because I exceeds S.

b. aggregate expenditure.

c. No.

d. Firms will have to reduce their inventories unexpectedly.

e. Actual investment = planned investment + unplanned inventory change.

f.   15   =   20   +   –5.

4. a. Zero. If consumption equals income, no income can be saved.

b. False. Because MPC equals .9, we can say that MPS equals .1.

c. is not; greater than.

d. 10. Multiplier = 1 / (1 – MPC) = 1 / .1 = 10.

e. negative. Planned aggregate expenditure exceeds aggregate output.

f. rise; 1,000; rise; 900; rise; 100. The "gap" between planned aggregate expenditure and aggregate output is 100. The multiplier is 10. Equilibrium income will fall by 1,000. MPC is .9. Given the increase in income, consumption will increase by 1,000 × .9. MPS is .1. Given the increase in income, saving will increase by 1,000 × .1.

g. 100; –100. If income changes from zero to 1,000, consumption increases by 900 to 1,000 (because MPC is .9). We know, therefore, that consumption is (1,000 – 900) when income level is zero. Because income equals consumption plus saving, saving must equal –100.

h. C = 100 + .9Y.

i.
$$Y = C + I$$
$$= 100 + .9Y + 100$$
$$= 200 + .9Y$$
$$Y - .9Y = 200$$
$$.1Y = 200$$
$$Y = 2,000.$$

j. See the diagram below.

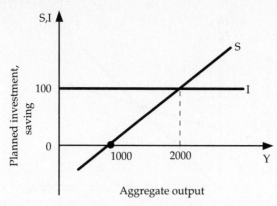

Aggregate output

5. a. See the table below. When income rises by 100 (from 100 to 200), consumption rises by 80 (from 180 to 260). MPC, therefore, is .8. MPC + MPS = 1, therefore MPS = .2. Given MPC, the consumption column can be filled in. Given income and consumption, saving can be derived by subtraction. Investment is assumed to be constant at 20. The expenditure column is derived by adding consumption and investment.

Income	Consumption	Saving	Investment	Expenditures
0	100	−100	20	120
100	180	− 80	20	200
200	260	− 60	20	280
300	340	− 40	20	360
400	420	− 20	20	440
500	500	0	20	520
600	580	20	20	600
700	660	40	20	680
MPC .8		MPS .2		
multiplier = 5				

b. 600. Equilibrium occurs where planned expenditure equals income (and where saving equals investment).
c. C = 100 + .8Y.
d.   Y = 100 + .8Y + 20
   .2Y = 120
   Y = 600.
e. reduction; increase.

f. See the diagram below.

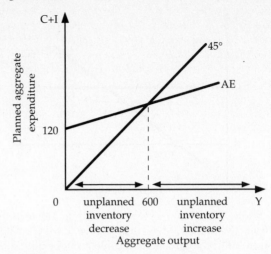

g. 250. The multiplier is 5.
h. 200; 50. Consumption increases by .8 × change in income. Saving increases by .2 × change in income.
i. 70; 70. In equilibrium these two values must be equal.
j. $Y = 100 + .8Y + 70$
    $.2Y = 170$
    $Y = 850$
    $C = 100 + .8Y$
        $= 100 + .8(850) = 780.$
    At Y = 600, C was 580 (See the table above.)
        $S = Y - C = 850 - 780 = 70.$
    At Y = 600, S was 20 (See the table above.)
k. 30. The economy's equilibrium income level is 850, 150 short of the goal. The multiplier is 5, so an autonomous 30-unit increase, multiplied by 5, will hit the target.

6. The slope of the consumption function is MPC and the slope of the saving function is MPS. We know that MPC + MPS equals one. MPC decreases as the slope of the consumption function becomes flatter, so MPS must increase and the slope of the saving function must become progressively steeper. The value of the multiplier is given by the formula: 1 / MPS. As MPS increases, the size of the multiplier will decrease as income level increases. In fact, the effect of this weakened multiplier can be shown graphically. The same vertical increase in aggregate spending will push the economy's equilibrium income level less far when the slope of the AE curve is decreasing.

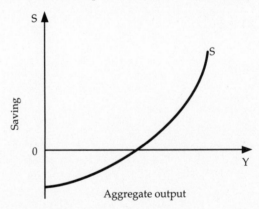

7. The AE function is the total of the consumption function and the investment function. In the original model, the slope of AE is determined solely by the slope of the consumption function—i.e., MPC. However, the slope of the AE curve is properly interpreted as the change in spending (from both sources) that occurs as income changes. If investment also increases, as income increases, the AE curve will become steeper. The value of the multiplier will increase too; in the more complex model we'll be developing in later chapters, the multiplier formulas we have devised are incomplete. In fact, the effect of this strengthened multiplier can be shown graphically. The same vertical increase in aggregate spending will push the economy's equilibrium income level farther as the AE curve becomes steeper.

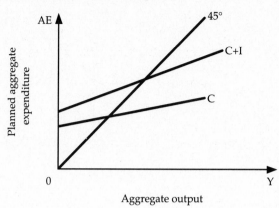

THE GOVERNMENT AND FISCAL POLICY

10

COMBINED TEXT
25

OBJECTIVES: POINT BY POINT

After completing this chapter, you should be able to accomplish the objectives listed below.

General Comment

The basic logic in this chapter is the same as in Chapter 9 (24). Even the Appendix material adds little that's very new. If you're confused, it's a sign to go back *now* and work on Chapter 9 (24) some more.

OBJECTIVE 1: Identify the tools of fiscal policy.

Fiscal policy has three basic tools: government spending (G), taxation, and transfer payments. To simplify matters, our model uses *lump-sum taxes* (which are not related to income). Collectively, taxes and transfers are termed net taxes (T). (page 215/641)

Lump-sum taxes are unusual in the United States. Britain's infamous poll tax, introduced by Margaret Thatcher, was a lump-sum tax—each household, regardless of size, paid the same tax. At the peak of the anti-tax protests, non-payment ran as high as 50% in some areas of the country. Many less developed countries favor lump-sum taxes because there is no need to calculate household income, an important advantage when financial record keeping is rudimentary and/or a large underground economy exists.

PRACTICE

1. Each of the following might be a specific fiscal policy action except
    A. reducing interest rates to stimulate consumer demand.
    B. increasing government spending on military hardware.
    C. easing the eligibility requirements for welfare recipients.
    D. imposing a national sales tax.
    Answer: A. Interest rate changes come under the category of monetary policy.

OBJECTIVE 2: Describe how the inclusion of the government sector affects the aggregate expenditure model.

When the government sector is added to the aggregate expenditure model, government spending is included directly in aggregate expenditure alongside consumption and investment. Consumption and saving are based on disposable (after-tax) income and the equilibrium condition is:

$$Y = C + I + G$$
or
$$S + T = I + G$$

(page 220/646)

Increasing spending or reducing net taxes will increase aggregate expenditures and increase the equilibrium level of production. (page 218/644)

Note: When taxes are "lump-sum," the marginal propensity to consume is not affected. When a tax rate is included in the model, as in Appendix B to this chapter, the MPC value must be modified.

PRACTICE

2. Disposable income is total income
   A. plus transfer payments.
   B. plus net taxes.
   C. minus net taxes.
   D. minus taxes.
   Answer: C. Be careful with the concept of net taxes. This term includes taxes and transfer payments. See p. 216/642.

3. When taxes are lump-sum, tax revenues _____ as income increases.
   A. will increase.
   B. will decrease.
   C. may either increase or decrease depending on the tax rate.
   D. will not change.
   Answer: D. Lump-sum taxes are not related to income. See p. 217/643.

4. When taxes are lump-sum, disposable income _____ as income increases by $100.
   A. will increase by $100.
   B. will increase, but by less than $100.
   C. may increase but by how much depends on the tax rate.
   D. will not change.
   Answer: A. If taxes are lump-sum, no additional taxes will be collected from the additional income. All of the additional income will be disposable income.

5. When the government sector is added to the model, the consumption function formula is
   A. $C = a + b(Y + T)$.
   B. $C = a + b(Y - T)$.
   C. $C = a - b(Y + T)$.
   D. $C = a - b(Y - T)$.
   Answer: B. See p. 218/644. $(Y - T)$ is disposable income.

6. When the government sector is added to the model, it must be true that in equilibrium
   A. $G = T$.
   B. $S = I$.
   C. $S + I = G + T$.
   D. $S + T = I + G$.
   Answer: D. Saving and net taxes are drains on spending (i.e., leakages). Investment and government spending add to spending. In equilibrium, the two forces are equal. Note that "$S = I$" is no longer an equilibrium condition in this expanded model. See p. 220/646.

Use the following table to answer the next four questions. The abbreviations are those used in the textbook.

Y	T	Y_d	C	S	I	G	AE
1,000	200	____	1,060	____	340	400	1,800
2,000	200	____	1,860	____	340	____	____
3,000	200	____	2,660	____	____	____	____
4,000	____	____	____	____	____	____	____
5,000	____	____	____	____	____	____	____
6,000	____	5,800	5,060	____	340	400	5,800

7. Complete the table.
   Answer: See the *Answers and Solutions* section.

8. The marginal propensity to consume is
   A. .6.
   B. .75.
   C. .8.
   D. .85.
   Answer: C. As disposable income changes by 1,000 (e.g., from 1,800 to 2,800), consumption changes by 800 (from 1,860 to 2,660).

9. Equilibrium income level is
   A. 3,000.
   B. 4,000.
   C. 5,000.
   D. 6,000.
   Answer: C. This is where AE = Y, and where S + T = I + G = 740.

10. In equilibrium, the government has a
    A. deficit of 200.
    B. deficit of 240.
    C. surplus of 200.
    D. surplus of 240.
    Answer: A. The government's deficit is 200 because spending (G) is 400 and net tax revenues (T) are 200.

OBJECTIVE 3: Derive and explain the difference between the government spending multiplier and the tax multiplier. Explain how the balanced-budget multiplier result occurs.

The *government spending multiplier* is identical to the expenditure multiplier developed in the previous chapter—if MPC is .75, a one dollar increase in government spending will cause the equilibrium income level to expand by $4. The multiplier is 4. The formula is 1 / MPS. (page 221/647)

The *tax multiplier* is absolutely smaller than the government spending multiplier because, with a tax cut, not all of the resulting increase in disposable income will be spent—some will leak away into saving. The tax multiplier is negative—an *increase* in taxes leads to a *decrease* in production. If MPC is .75, a one dollar increase in tax collections will cause the equilibrium income level to decrease by $3. The tax multiplier is −3. The formula is −MPC / MPS. (page 223/649)

The *balanced-budget multiplier* is *always* equal to one in our model. An equal increase in government spending and net taxes will have a dollar-for-dollar expansionary effect on equilibrium income. The formula is MPS / MPS. (page 225/651)

TIP: In our model, with lump-sum taxes, the (government) spending multiplier and the tax multiplier have a simple numerical relationship. Here are a few common values.

MPC	MPS	SPENDING MULTIPLIER	TAX MULTIPLIER
.50	.50	2.0	−1.0
.60	.40	2.5	−1.5
.75	.25	4.0	−3.0
.80	.20	5.0	−4.0
.90	.10	10.0	−9.0

Given MPC or MPS, if you can work out the regular multiplier, subtract one to get the (negative) tax multiplier. The tax multiplier is **always** negative, not just when taxes increase. If taxes move in one direction, income will always move in the opposite direction. Confirm these values using the tax multiplier formula.

PRACTICE

Use the table you completed for Practice Question 7 to answer the next question.

11. In the table, the government spending multiplier is _____ and the tax multiplier is _____
    A. 4, −3.
    B. 4, 3.
    C. 5, −4.
    D. 5, 4.
    Answer: C. As disposable income changes by 1,000 (e.g., from 1,700 to 2,700), saving changes by 200 (from −60 to 140). MPS is .2. The formula for the government spending multiplier is 1 / MPS, and the formula for the tax multiplier is −MPC/MPS.

12. In the nation of Arbez, which has a government sector, an increase in investment spending of 100 will cause equilibrium income level to increase by 1,000. The government spending multiplier is _____ and the tax multiplier is _____
    A. 5, −5.
    B. 5, −4.
    C. 10, −10.
    D. 10, −9.
    Answer: D. If an increase in investment can be "multiplied" tenfold, then the multiplier must be 10. If so, MPC is .9 and MPS is .1. Note that, with lump-sum taxes, the MPC formulas in Chapter 9 and Chapter 10 are equivalent. The formula for the government spending multiplier is 1 / MPS, so, in this case, the multiplier is 10. The formula for the tax multiplier is −MPC / MPS; the tax multiplier in this case is −9 (−.9 / .1).

OBJECTIVE 4: Analyze the effects on output and unemployment of a change in government spending and/or a change in taxes.

An increase (decrease) in government spending will increase (decrease) planned aggregate expenditure, dollar for dollar. A decrease (increase) in net taxes will also increase (decrease) planned aggregate expenditure—but *not* dollar for dollar. The impacts of the two policy actions are different—the "tax multiplier" is smaller.(page 222/648)

Recall Congress's 1995 "deficit reduction" debate. Republicans called for substantial reductions in government spending programs. Democrats favored hiking taxes. The Republican option would have had the more powerful (negative) economic effect because the government spending multiplier is more powerful.

Caution: When working out the effects of policy actions, take a moment to make sure the result looks sensible. It's easy to forget a negative sign or mess up the arithmetic. Have confidence in your own intuition. If your results don't look right, they probably aren't!

Graphing Pointer: A one-dollar increase (decrease) in government spending or a one-dollar decrease (increase) in net taxes will shift the AE curve vertically upward (downward) but not by the same amount. The shift caused by the tax change will be smaller.

PRACTICE

Use the table you completed for Practice Question 7 to answer the next four questions.

13. The equilibrium income level would be 6,000 if government spending
    A. increased by 200.
    B. increased by 1,000.
    C. decreased by 200.
    D. decreased by 1,000.
    Answer: A. The multiplier is 5. The increase in equilibrium income (ΔY) = $1,000 = \Delta G \times 1 / MPS = 200 \times 5$. See p. 222/648.

14. The equilibrium income level would be 4,000 if net taxes
    A. increased by 200.
    B. increased by 250.
    C. decreased by 200.
    D. decreased by 250.
    Answer: B. The tax multiplier is −4. Decrease in equilibrium income (ΔY) = $1,000 = \Delta T \times -MPC / MPS = 250 \times -4$. See p. 223/649.

15. If government spending increased by 100 and taxes decreased by 100, equilibrium income level would
    A. increase by 100.
    B. increase by 900.
    C. decrease by 100.
    D. not change.
    Answer: B. Split this question into two parts—the effect of the spending change and the effect of the tax change.
    Spending change: $\Delta Y = \Delta G \times 1/ MPS = 100 \times 5 = +500$.
    Tax change: $\Delta Y = \Delta T \times -MPC / MPS = -100 \times -4 = +400$.

16. If government spending decreased by 100 and taxes decreased by 100, equilibrium income level would
    A. increase by 100.
    B. decrease by 900.
    C. decrease by 100.
    D. not change.
    Answer: C. This is a "balanced-budget" change (i.e., $\Delta G = \Delta T$).

Refer to the following diagram to answer the next five questions.

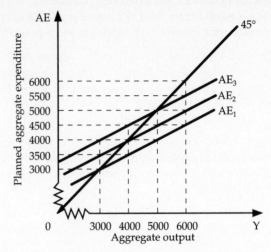

17. If expenditures are as shown by AE_2, the equilibrium income level is
    A. 3,000.
    B. 4,000.
    C. 5,000.
    D. 6,000.
    Answer: B. AE_2 crosses the 45° line at this income level.

18. Given AE_2, if the income level is at 3,000, we know that
    A. government spending is greater than net taxes.
    B. government spending is less than net taxes.
    C. unplanned inventory investment is positive.
    D. unplanned inventory investment is negative.
    Answer: D. Expenditure exceeds production; inventory level will be decreasing.

19. The government spending multiplier is _____ and the tax multiplier is _____
    A. 2, –1.
    B. 2, –3.
    C. 4, –3.
    D. 4, –5.
    Answer: A. As income level rises by 1,000 (from 3,000 to 4,000), planned expenditure rises by 500 (from 3,500 to 4,000). MPC is .5 and MPS is .5.

20. To shift the AE curve from AE_2 to AE_3, we could
    A. increase government spending by 500.
    B. increase government spending by 1,000.
    C. increase net taxes by 500.
    D. increase net taxes by 1,000.
    Answer: A. Increasing taxes will reduce aggregate expenditure—consumers would have less after-tax income to spend. Increasing government spending by 500 will work. Note that the vertical distance between AE_2 and AE_3 is 500.

21. Given AE_2, each of the following policies except _____ would reduce the equilibrium output level to 3,000.
    A. decreasing government spending by 1,000 and decreasing taxes by 1,000.
    B. decreasing government spending by 1,000.
    C. increasing government spending by 500 and increasing taxes by 2,000.
    D. increasing taxes by 1,000.
    Answer: B. The government spending multiplier is 2. $\Delta G \times 1 / MPS = -1{,}000 \times 2 = 2{,}000$. Option A is the balanced-budget case. Option C is quite complex but works as follows: Government spending change = $\Delta G \times 1 / MPS = 500 \times 2 = 1{,}000$. Tax change: $\Delta T \times -MPC / MPS = 2{,}000 \times -1 = -2{,}000$.

22. Given AE$_3$, when income is 4000,
    A. injections exceed leakages by 500.
    B. injections exceed leakages by 1000.
    C. leakages exceed injections by 500.
    D. leakages exceed injections by 1000.
    Answer: A. Demand exceeds production.

OBJECTIVE 5: Explain how the inclusion of the international sector in the model influences the size of the multiplier.

In an economy with an international sector, the size of the multiplier is reduced because more of the economy's spending power is able to "leak away" through U.S. spending overseas.   (page 227/653)

The "opening" of the former Soviet bloc countries, Chinese trade liberalization, and the increasing interdependence of the member states of the European Community are examples of situations where we would expect multipliers to decrease.

> **TIP:** Although the issue of the effect of the international sector seems of only minor importance, it's worthwhile to consider carefully because it goes to the heart of your understanding of multipliers. Recall the two cases we examined in Practice Question 16 in Chapter 9. The strength of the multiplier was determined by the extent of leakage of spending power. That was a general conclusion; it applies here, too.

> **TIP:** The "leakages/injections" equilibrium condition is now:
> $$S + T = I + G + (EX - IM).$$

PRACTICE

23. Until recently, the mountainous nation of Tebit has been cut off from the rest of the world. An active international sector has now been created. Despite this, Tebit has pursued a policy of ensuring that exports equal imports. As a result of its new "openness," Tebit's AE function will
    A. not shift.
    B. become flatter.
    C. become steeper.
    D. shift upward.
    Answer: B. If exports equal imports, their effects on the *level* of planned expenditure cancel out. However, it is the *slope* of the AE function that determines the size of the multiplier and, we know, the multiplier decreases as the economy becomes more open. (By the way, this is a very challenging question!)

OBJECTIVE 6: Define the deficit and explain how it relates to and differs from the federal debt. Describe how the federal government's expenditures and revenues move with the economy. Distinguish between and explain the effects of fiscal drag and automatic stabilizers.

This year's *deficit* is the difference between government spending this year and net tax revenues this year, i.e., G – T. The *federal debt* is the total amount owed by the federal government to the public (because of this year's deficit and those of previous years).   (page 229/655)

Automatic stabilizers (revenue or expenditure items in the federal budget that adjust in magnitude as the level of economic activity changes) operate as the economy moves through the business cycle. During a recession, for instance, when incomes are low, transfer payments increase and partly replace the lost income—spending doesn't fall so much as it otherwise would have. Tax liabilities decrease, too, in such a situation. Automatic stabilizers reduce the severity of fluctuations in the business cycle.

(page 233/659)

Fiscal drag occurs because as the economy expands and/or inflation occurs, incomes rise, pushing taxpayers into higher tax brackets and increasing the average tax rate. Out of each dollar, less is available to spend or save than otherwise would have been the case. The tax structure slows the rate of economic expansion.   (page 233/659)

PRACTICE

24. During the 1980s, the federal budget deficit expanded sharply. Which of the following is not a cause of this expansion?
   A. Government spending (as a percentage of GDP) rose during the 1980s.
   B. Interest payments on the federal debt (as a percentage of GDP) rose during the 1980s.
   C. Personal income tax rates were reduced in 1981.
   D. Transfer payments (as a percentage of GDP) rose during the 1980s.
   Answer: D. See p. 230/656.

25. Automatic stabilizers make the federal deficit _____ during recessions and _____ during expansions.
   A. larger, larger.
   B. larger, smaller.
   C. smaller, larger.
   D. smaller, smaller.
   Answer: B. See p. 233/659.

OBJECTIVE 7: Define the full-employment budget, the structural deficit, and the cyclical deficit.

The *full-employment budget* calculates what the deficit would be, given the structure of current spending and tax programs, if the economy were at full employment. At full employment, the effects on the deficit of cyclical changes should be zero—any deficit that remains is called the *structural deficit*. The *cyclical deficit* is that part of the actual deficit that is caused by cyclical unemployment. At full employment, the actual deficit might be $50 million—this is the structural deficit. If, however, unemployment is currently running at 8%, this indicates the presence of some cyclical unemployment. The deficit is $200 million. The cyclical deficit is $150 million ($200 million − $50 million).   (page 233/659)

PRACTICE

26. At full employment, the federal deficit would be $80 billion. Last year, unemployment was 6.5% and the deficit was $130 billion. This year, however, unemployment is 7.8% and the deficit is $192 billion. This year, the
   A. structural deficit is $62 billion.
   B. structural deficit is $112 billion.
   C. cyclical deficit is $62 billion.
   D. cyclical deficit is $112 billion.
   Answer: D. The structural deficit is $80 billion. The remainder of this year's $192 billion deficit is cyclical. See p. 234/660.

OBJECTIVE 8 (APPENDIX B): Explain how the incorporation of tax rates will influence the multiplier.

When a tax rate is introduced into the model, the formula for the expenditure multiplier must be adjusted—the multiplier's value is reduced (because the leakage of additional spending power is greater than before). Graphically, the consumption function and the AE function become flatter. As income increases, consumption still increases, but at a slower rate, because less income is available as disposable income.

(page 238/664)

PRACTICE

27. In Arboc, the income tax rate is 20% and the MPC is .75. The government spending multiplier is
    A. 2.5.
    B. 3.0.
    C. 3.75.
    D. 4.0.
    Answer: A. The multiplier's formula is $1 / (1 - b + bt)$, where b is MPC and t is the tax rate. In this case, the value is $1 / (1 - .75 + .75(.2))$, or $1 / .4$, which gives a value of 2.5.

28. In Arboc, the income tax rate is 20% and the MPC is .75. The tax multiplier is
    A. −1.5.
    B. −1.875.
    C. −3.75.
    D. −2.75.
    Answer: B. The multiplier's formula is $-b / (1 - b + bt)$, where b is MPC and t is the tax rate. In this case, the value is $-.75 / (1 - .75 + .75(.2))$, or $-.75/.4$, which gives a value of −1.875.

29. In Arboc, the income tax rate is 20% and the MPC is .75. An equal increase of 1,000 in government spending and taxes would cause equilibrium income to
    A. increase by 625.
    B. increase by 1,000.
    C. decrease by 625.
    D. increase by 1,000.
    Answer: A. The government spending multiplier is 2.5 and the tax multiplier is −1.875. The balanced-budget multiplier is .625 (2.5 − 1.875).

30. In Arbez, the income tax rate is 50% and the MPC is .80. To increase equilibrium income by 400, taxes should be
    A. increased by 80.
    B. increased by 300.
    C. decreased by 80.
    D. decreased by 300.
    Answer: D. The tax multiplier's formula is $-b / (1 - b + bt)$, where b is MPC and t is the tax rate. In this case, the value is $-.80 / (1 - .80 + .80(.50))$, or $-.80 / .60$, which gives a value of −1.333. To increase output, taxes should decrease. $\Delta T \times -1.333 = 400$; $\Delta T = -300$.

I. MULTIPLE CHOICE QUESTIONS.

Select the option that provides the single best answer.

_____ 1. MPS is .1. An increase in lump-sum taxes of 100 will
   A. shift the AE function up by 100.
   B. shift the AE function down by 100.
   C. shift the AE function down by 90.
   D. shift the AE curve up by 10.

_____ 2. If MPS is .2, a decrease in government spending of 100 will
   A. increase income by 500.
   B. increase output by 500.
   C. decrease saving by 100.
   D. decrease output by 400.

_____ 3. An increase in government spending of 100 causes the level of output to rise by 250. MPS is
   A. .25.
   B. .4.
   C. .6.
   D. 2.5.

_____ 4. The President wants output to increase by 300. Also, he wants the change in the deficit caused by any policy action to be minimized, and government spending to rise by no more than 75. MPC is .75. Of the following, you would recommend
   A. increasing government spending by 75.
   B. reducing net taxes by 100.
   C. a balanced-budget increase of 300.
   D. a balanced-budget increase of 75.

_____ 5. Government spending rises by a dollar. If taxes were _____, equilibrium production level could remain unchanged.
   A. raised by more than a dollar.
   B. raised by less than a dollar.
   C. cut by more than a dollar.
   D. cut by less than a dollar.

_____ 6. Saving rises from $150 to $190 as income rises from $600 to $800. The marginal propensity to
   A. consume is .8 and the government spending multiplier is 5.
   B. save is .4 and the government spending multiplier is 2.5.
   C. save is .25 and the balanced-budget multiplier is 1.0.
   D. save is .2 and the tax multiplier is −6.

_____ 7. Automatic stabilizers stabilize
   A. taxes.
   B. the deficit.
   C. income.
   D. investment.

_____ 8. The economy is experiencing widespread unemployment. An economist might suggest that the government
   A. decrease taxes.
   B. decrease government spending.
   C. decrease the deficit.
   D. increase investment spending.

_____ 9. There is a sharp fall in investment spending. The Administration could maintain the economy at its current output level by using any of the following measures except _____ government spending and _____ taxes.
   A. raising, lowering
   B. lowering, raising
   C. raising, raising
   D. lowering, lowering
   (Be careful with this one! There is only one correct answer.)

_____ 10. MPC = .8. The Administration wants to raise output by $100 million. It could achieve that goal by doing any of the following except
   A. simultaneously raising government spending by $40 million and cutting taxes by $50 million.
   B. cutting taxes by $25 million.
   C. simultaneously raising government spending by $100 million and raising taxes by $100 million.
   D. raising government spending by $20 million.

_____ 11. All of the following are true except
   A. during a recession, there is a cyclical deficit.
   B. during a recession, there will be a structural deficit.
   C. at full employment, there may be a structural deficit.
   D. at full employment, there is no cyclical deficit.

_____ 12. A budget deficit occurs when
   A. taxes exceed government spending.
   B. total tax receipts exceed total government debt.
   C. transfer payments exceed government spending.
   D. government spending exceeds net tax collections.

Use the following diagram for the next five questions.

The economy is in initial equilibrium at an output level of 5,000. Government spending is fixed at 500 and investment is fixed at 300. Net taxes are 200.

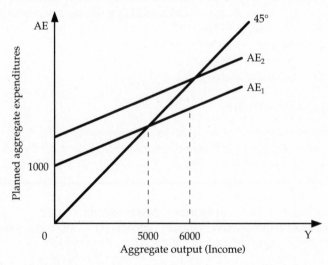

_____ 13. Calculate the marginal propensity to consume.
   A. .60.
   B. .75.
   C. .80.
   D. .85.

_____ 14. Derive the formula for the saving function.
   A. $S = -200 + .20(Y - T)$.
   B. $S = -200 - .20(Y - T)$.
   C. $S = -1000 + .20(Y - T)$.
   D. $S = -1000 - .20(Y - T)$.

_____ 15. Calculate the tax multiplier.
   A. 4.
   B. 5.
   C. −4.
   D. −5.

_____ 16. The government wishes to shift the AE_1 function to AE_2 by changing lump-sum taxes. Taxes should
   A. increase by 200.
   B. increase by 250.
   C. decrease by 200.
   D. decrease by 250.

_____ 17. Given the tax change in the question 16, calculate how much consumption and saving, respectively, must change to attain the new equilibrium.
   A. Consumption increases by 800, saving increases by 200.
   B. Consumption increases by 960, saving increases by 240.
   C. Consumption increases by 1,000, saving increases by zero.
   D. Consumption increases by 1,200, saving decreases by 200.

_____ 18. A tax decrease of $15 billion results in a $60 billion increase in equilibrium income. The government spending multiplier is
   A. −5.
   B. −4.
   C. 4.
   D. 5.

_____ 19. When the government sector is added to the model, the economy can be in equilibrium only when
   A. the government balances its budget.
   B. saving equals investment.
   C. unplanned inventory change is zero.
   D. disposable income is equal to consumption plus saving.

_____ 20. Automatic stabilizers _____ income taxes and _____ government spending during a recession.
   A. increase, increase.
   B. increase, decrease.
   C. decrease, increase.
   D. decrease, decrease.

II. APPLICATION QUESTIONS.

1. a. Use the information below to fill in the gaps in the table. MPC is constant, and investment, government spending, and net exports are determined autonomously. Taxes are lump-sum at a level of 200.

REAL GDP INCOME	CONSUMPTION	PLANNED INVESTMENT	GOVERNMENT SPENDING	NET EXPORTS	AGGREGATE PLANNED EXPENDITURES
0	_____	_____		_____	_____
1,000	1,200	_____	400	_____	_____
2,000	2,000	_____		_____	_____
3,000	_____	300		_____	3,600
4,000	3,600	_____		100	_____
5,000	4,400	_____		_____	_____
6,000	_____	_____		_____	_____
7,000	_____	300		_____	_____

   b. Calculate MPC and MPS.
   c. Determine the equilibrium income level for this economy.

d. If real GDP is 3,000, is unplanned inventory investment positive or negative? Predict how businesses will respond.

e. If real GDP is 7,000, is unplanned inventory investment positive or negative?

f. At which output level is saving zero?

g. At which output level is saving equal to investment?

h. At which output level is saving equal to non-consumption spending?

i. Given your answers above, formulate a rule regarding the level of saving at the equilibrium output level.

j. If government spending fell by 200, would the equilibrium output level fall by more than 200, less than 200, or equal to 200? Use the table to confirm your answer. Describe the pressure that would cause the equilibrium output level to change.

2. You have been called in by the Arbezani Minister of Finance. The full-employment level of output is 124,000 opeks. She tells you that an econometrician has provided the following model of the Arbezani economy. The currency is opeks.

(1) Consumption function: $C = 6,000 + .75Y_d$
(2) Investment function: $I = 11,000$
(3) Government spending: $G = 20,000$
(4) Net taxes: $T = 16,000$
(5) Disposable income: $Y_d = Y - T$
(6) Equilibrium: $Y = C + I + G$

a. Calculate the current equilibrium income level.

b. Determine the value of the government spending multiplier and the tax multiplier.

The Minister, who is extremely concerned about the level of the national debt, is considering two proposals.

Proposal I: Maintain the current level of government spending and increase taxes until the budget is balanced.

Proposal II: Maintain taxes at their present level and decrease federal spending until the budget is balanced.

c. Both policies will be contractionary. Which proposal will have the smaller impact on output and employment?

d. Write a brief to the Minister so that she can answer questions about the relative effects of the two proposals during Ministers' Question Time in Parliament.

Due to rising protests about the level of unemployment, the Minister scraps both of the proposals above and turns her attention to expansionary policies.

e. She is presented with several possible courses of action, listed below, and asks you to evaluate them. In each case, does the proposal restore full employment?

Proposal III: Increase government spending on defense by 8,000 opeks.

Proposal IV: Increase welfare payments by 8,000 opeks.

Proposal V: Increase lump-sum taxes by 4,000 opeks and increase spending on defense by 9,000 opeks.

Proposal VI: Increase welfare payments by 6,000 opeks and reduce lump-sum taxes by 2,000 opeks.

f. Of the proposals that achieve the goal of establishing output at the full-employment level, which is preferred in terms of helping to balance the budget?

g. Of the proposals that achieve the goal of establishing output at the full-employment level, which is preferred in terms of boosting consumption?

3. Use the following information to calculate the multipliers. Assume that taxes are lump-sum.
   a. MPS = .2. The government spending multiplier is _____.
   b. MPC = .95. The government spending multiplier is _____.
   c. MPS = .4. The government spending multiplier is _____.
   d. MPC = .9. The tax multiplier is _____.
   e. MPS = .2. The tax multiplier is _____.
   f. If the government spending multiplier is 8, then the tax multiplier is _____.
   g. If the tax multiplier is −5, then the government spending multiplier is _____.
   h. MPS = .2. The government spending multiplier is _____ and the tax multiplier is _____.

   Using the information from (h) we know that a simultaneous decrease in G and T of $200 each would cause the following total changes in:
   i. Y _____
   j. C _____
   k. S _____
   l. G _____
   m. T _____

4. Use the information in the table to answer the following questions.

Output (Income)	Saving	Planned Investment	Government Spending	Net Taxes	Consumption
1300	150	200	100	50	
1500	200	200	100	50	
1700	250	200	100	50	
1900	300	200	100	50	

   a. Fill in the "consumption" column.
   b. Calculate MPC _____ and equilibrium level of income _____.
   c. Calculate the level of unplanned inventory investment when Y is 1300.
   d. Will the equilibrium level of output (income) increase or decrease if the government were required to balance its budget?
   e. What action could the government have taken to achieve the full employment level of production (2000)?
   f. Calculate the new equilibrium level of output (income) if G increases by 50 and T increases by 50.

5. At the equilibrium output (income) level of 720, the following values occur.
   $$G = 300 \qquad T = 250$$
   $$I = 120 \qquad MPC = .75$$
   $$C = 300$$
   a. Calculate the equilibrium value of saving. _____
   b. Calculate the marginal propensity to save. _____
   c. Calculate the value of the expenditure multiplier. _____
   d. The government deficit now has a value of _____.

   Pessimism occurs in the business community. Planned investment falls by 15. How much of an effect does this have on equilibrium GDP?

   e. GDP will _____ (rise/fall) by _____.
   f. At the original GDP level, unplanned inventories are now _____ (rising/falling).

The Administration attempts to restore the original production level by changing the tax level.

g. Taxes should be _____ (raised/lowered) by _____.

h. After the economy has reached its final equilibrium, the deficit is _____.

i. The final value for consumption is _____.

6. a. Fill in the blanks in the table.

Y	T	Y_d	C	S	I	G	AE
0	20						
100	20				30	10	
200	20					10	
300	20			0		10	
400	20			20	30		

b. Find MPC _____, MPS _____, the government spending multiplier _____, and the tax multiplier _____.

c. Express the consumption function algebraically. _____

d. What is the equilibrium income level? _____

7. Assume the following data for the economy which is in equilibrium at an output level of 480. This example uses the information in the textbook's Appendix B.

G = 150   MPC = 5/7
T = 120   MPS = 2/7
C = 280   t   = .3
S = 80
I = 50

a. Calculate the value of the government spending multiplier. _____

Currently the economy is in a recession. You, as Chairperson of the Council of Economic Advisors, have been asked by how much government spending must be raised to increase equilibrium Y to 550.

b. Calculate the change in output necessary to achieve equilibrium at 550.

c. Use the multiplier to deduce the change in G needed to bring about the above change in equilibrium income.

d. Draw a 45° line picture representing the problem you've just solved.

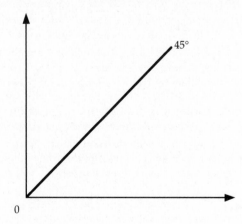

Now government spending has risen, as have taxes. The new level of government spending is the old level plus the policy recommendation you've calculated. The change in taxes can be derived using the tax rate.

  e. What was the deficit originally? _____
  f. How much have tax collections changed? _____
  g. The new deficit is _____.

8. The economy has full employment and a balanced budget. Suddenly, because of a drop in planned investment, there is a recession.
  a. What will happen to the deficit? Explain why.
  b. Has the structural deficit changed, or has the cyclical deficit changed?
  c. Suppose the government responds by increasing government spending and taxes by an equal amount. What will happen to the structural deficit and to the full-employment budget?
  d. If the government is committed to balancing the budget, what will be the consequences of maintaining a balanced budget if automatic stabilizers are present in the economy?

ANSWERS AND SOLUTIONS

ANSWERS TO PRACTICE QUESTIONS

7.

Y	T	Y_d	C	S	I	G	AE
1,000	200	800	1,060	−260	340	400	1,800
2,000	200	1,800	1,860	−60	340	400	2,600
3,000	200	2,800	2,660	140	340	400	3,400
4,000	200	3,800	3,460	340	340	400	4,200
5,000	200	4,800	4,260	540	340	400	5,000
6,000	200	5,800	5,060	740	340	400	5,800

PRACTICE TEST

I. SOLUTIONS TO MULTIPLE CHOICE QUESTIONS

1. C. An increase in lump-sum taxes will decrease consumption and, therefore, shift the AE function downward. If taxes rise by 100, disposable income will fall by 100. If MPC is .9, consumption (and AE) will decrease by 90.

2. C. If MPS is .2, the government spending multiplier is 5. Income will decrease by 500 (100 × 5). If income decreases by 500 and MPS is .2, saving will decrease by 100.

3. B. For an increase in government spending to make output rise by 250, the multiplier must be 2.5. If MPS is .4, the government spending multiplier is 2.5.

4. A. If MPC is .75, the government spending multiplier is 4 and the tax multiplier is −3. If government spending increases by 75, output would increase by 300. The deficit would rise by 75. Reducing taxes by 100 would achieve the required expansion in output, but the increase in the deficit is 100 (greater than with option A). Option C cannot be considered because the maximum increase in government spending allowable is 75. Option D will not work because output would expand by only 75.

5. A. Expenditure rises by a dollar. To neutralize this change, taxes would have to be increased. If taxes are raised by a dollar, consumption would fall, but by less than a dollar. To neutralize the increase in expenditures, taxes will have to increase by more than a dollar.

6. A. If saving increases by 40 as income increases by 200, MPS is .2. MPC, therefore, is .8. When MPS is .2, the government spending multiplier (1 / MPS) is 5.

7. C. See p. 233/659.

8. A. If expenditure increases, equilibrium output will increase. The government can increase government spending and/or cut taxes. Either action will increase the deficit. Investment decisions are made by the private sector.

9. B. To neutralize the effect on AE of the investment decrease, the government wants an action that will make AE increase. Cutting government spending and increasing taxes will certainly not achieve this result. Note that Options C and D may make AE increase—it depends on the relative changes in G and T. See the answer to question 5 above.

10. A. When MPC is .8, the government spending multiplier is 5 and the tax multiplier is −4. If government spending increases by 20, output will increase by 100 (20 × 5). If taxes are cut by 25, output will increase by 100 (−25 × −4). Similarly, the balanced—budget change will achieve the objective. Option A won't. The government spending increase will raise output by 200 (40 × 5), while the tax cut will raise output by a further 200 (−50 × −4).

11. B. The presence or absence of a structural deficit depends on government policy.

12. D. See p. 217/643.

13. C. As income rises by 5,000 (from zero to 5,000), spending rises by 4,000 (from 1,000 to 5,000).

14. A. When Y = 0, autonomous consumption is 200 (Y − I − G), therefore autonomous saving is −200. If MPC is .80, MPS is .20.

15. C. If MPC = .80, the tax multiplier is −4.

16. D. If MPC = .80, the tax multiplier is −4. The desired change in income is +1,000.

17. B. The tax cut will hike consumption autonomously by 250 × .80, or 200. After income has risen by 1,000, consumption will increase by an additional 800 because MPC = .80. The tax cut will hike saving autonomously by 250 × .2, or 50. After income has risen by 1,000, saving will increase by an additional 200 because MPS = .20.

18. D. If a tax decrease of $15 billion results in a $60 billion increase in equilibrium income, the tax multiplier is −4. The tax multiplier formula is −MPC / MPS. MPC = .8 and MPS = .2. The government multiplier formula is 1 / MPS, so the value in this case is 5.

19. C. Option D is not an equilibrium condition—this identity holds whether or not equilibrium is established. Option B was an equilibrium condition in the previous chapter, but is no longer. In equilibrium, leakages (S + T) must equal injections (I + G).

20. C. See p. 233/659.

II. SOLUTIONS TO APPLICATION QUESTIONS

1. a. Refer to the table below.

REAL GDP INCOME	CONSUMPTION	PLANNED INVESTMENT	GOVERNMENT SPENDING	NET EXPORTS	AGGREGATE PLANNED EXPENDITURES
0	400	300	400	100	1,200
1,000	1,200	300	400	100	2,000
2,000	2,000	300	400	100	2,800
3,000	2,800	300	400	100	3,600
4,000	3,600	300	400	100	4,400
5,000	4,400	300	400	100	5,200
6,000	5,200	300	400	100	6,000
7,000	6,000	300	400	100	6,800

b. MPC = .8 and MPS = .2.

c. Aggregate planned expenditures equal real GDP at 6,000.

d. When real GDP = 3,000, aggregate planned expenditures exceed 3,000 (3,600), causing unplanned inventory decumulation. Businesses will respond by hiring more resources and increasing output.

e. When real GDP = 7,000, aggregate planned expenditures are less than 7,000 (6,800), causing unplanned inventory accumulation.

f. Saving is zero when income is 3,000.

g. Saving equals investment (which is constant at 300) when income is 4,500.

h. Saving equals planned non-consumption spending (which is constant at 800) when income equals 7,000.

i. When saving (plus taxes) equals planned non-consumption spending, output will be at its equilibrium level. Leakages must equal injections in equilibrium.

j. Equilibrium output would fall by 1000 to 5,000. At an income level of 5,000, $C + I + G + NX$ equals 4,400 plus 600. The decrease in expenditures will result in unplanned inventory accumulation. Firms will cut production, forcing the equilibrium output level to fall.

2. a. $Y = C + I + G = 6,000 + .75(Y - T) + 11,000 + 20,000 = 37,000 + .75Y - .75T$. But $T = 16,000$, therefore, $Y - .75Y = 37,000 - .75(16,000)$.
$.25Y = 25,000$, therefore, $Y = 100,000$.

b. MPC = .75, therefore the government spending multiplier is 4.0 and the tax multiplier is −3.0.

c. Proposal I is less contractionary.

d. Proposal I: The deficit is currently $20,000 − 16,000$, or 4,000 opeks. A 4,000-opek increase in taxes will initially reduce consumption by 3,000 opeks. Spending will fall by 3,000 opeks.
Proposal II: A 4,000-opek decrease in government spending will reduced aggregate expenditures by 4,000 opeks—a larger initial spending reduction than in Proposal I. Note: The economy will not contract by only 3,000 opeks. With Proposal I, the economy will contract by $3,000 \times 4$, or 12,000 opeks. With Proposal II, the economy will contract by $4,000 \times 4$, or 16,000 opeks.

e. Proposal III is overkill! The multiplier is 4, therefore an autonomous increase in government spending of 8,000 will push the economy past the full-employment output level.
Proposal IV will work. The tax multiplier is −3 and an increase in welfare payments operates in the same way as a reduction in taxes.
Proposal V will work. $\Delta T (4,000) \times -3 = -12,000$. $\Delta G(10,000) \times 4 = 36,000$. The net change in income is $+ 24,000$, which is the amount required.
Proposal VI will work. Welfare is a form of negative tax. $\Delta T(-2,000) \times -3 = 6,000$. Δ welfare $(-6,000) \times -3 = 18,000$. The total change in income is $+ 24,000$, which is the amount required.

f. The deficit $= G - T = 4,000$.
Proposal IV will reduce net taxes by 8,000 and widen the deficit to 12,000.
Proposal V will increase net taxes by 4,000 but increase government spending by 9,000. The deficit will increase by 5,000 opeks.
Proposal VI will reduce net taxes by $6,000 + 2,000$, or 8,000 opeks. The deficit will increase by 8,000 opeks.
Proposal IV and VI are equivalent, but Proposal V is better than either.

g. Proposal IV will reduce net taxes by 8,000 and increase consumption autonomously by 6,000 opeks. As income increases by 24,000, consumption will be induced to increase by an additional 18,000. Total increase in consumption is 24,000 opeks.
Proposal V will increase net taxes by 4,000 and reduce consumption autonomously by 3,000. As income increases by 24,000, consumption will be induced to increase by an additional 18,000. Total increase in consumption is 15,000 opeks.
Proposal VI will increase welfare payments by 6,000 opeks and increase consumption autonomously by 4,500 opeks. The reduction in lump-sum taxes will increase consumption autonomously by 1,500 opeks. As income increases by 24,000, consumption will be induced to increase by an additional 18,000. Total increase in consumption is 24,000 opeks.
Proposal IV and VI have identical effects on consumption.

3. a. 5.   e. −4.   h. 5; −4.   k. −40.
   b. 20.   f. −7.   i. −200.   l. −200.
   c. 2.5.   g. 6.   j. −160.   m. −200.
   d. −9.

4. a. See the table below.

Output (Income)	Saving	Planned Investment	Government Spending	Net Taxes	Consumption
1300	150	200	100	50	1,100
1500	200	200	100	50	1,250
1700	250	200	100	50	1,400
1900	300	200	100	50	1,550

b   MPS is .25, so MPC is .75; Y = C + I + G at an income level of 1,700.

c.   AE = C + I + G = 1,400. If output is only 1,300, inventory is falling by 100.

d.   You can't give a precise numerical answer—it depends on the level at which G and T are equalized—although, in any case, output will decrease because either taxes must increase or government spending must decrease.

    Suppose the budget is balanced at 50. G must fall by 50, and output will fall by 200.

    If G and T are made equal at 100, taxes would have to rise by 50. Output would fall by 150.

e.   Increase government spending by 75 (with a multiplier of 4), decrease net taxes by 100 (with a tax multiplier of −3), or undertake a balanced-budget increase of 300.

f.   This is a balanced-budget change and the balanced-budget multiplier is 1. Income level will increase by 50 to 1,750.

5. a.   In equilibrium, S + T = I + G

    Substituting in numerical values, we get S + 250 = 120 + 300.

    S = 420 − 250 = 170.

  b.   MPS = 1 − MPC = 1 − .75 = .25.

  c.   Multiplier = 1 / MPS = 1 / .25 = 4.

  d.   Deficit = G − T = 300 − 250 = 50.

  e.   Spending change: $\Delta Y = \Delta I \times 1 / MPS = -15 \times 4 = -60$.

  f.   Unplanned inventories are rising. Expenditure has fallen, so unsold stock is accumulating.

  g.   lowered by 20. We want income to rise by 60.

    Tax change: $\Delta Y = 60 = \Delta T \times -MPC / MPS = -20 \times -3$.

  h.   Deficit = G − T = 300 − 230 = 70. Taxes were 250, then were cut by 20.

  i.   The equilibrium income level is unchanged, but disposable income has risen by 20 (because of the tax cut). As MPC is .75, consumption will increase by 15 (20 × .75) to 315.

6. a.   See the table below.

    Saving rises by 20 as income rises by 100. MPS = .2, MPC = .8. This is enough information to complete the saving and consumption columns. Investment is constant at 30, and government spending is constant at 10. Disposable income is Y − T.

Y	T	Y_d	C	S	I	G	AE
0	20	−20	40	−60	30	10	80
100	20	80	120	−40	30	10	160
200	20	180	200	−20	30	10	240
300	20	280	280	0	30	10	320
400	20	380	360	20	30	10	400

  b.   MPC = .8; MPS = .2 (see answer a above); the government spending multiplier is 1 / MPS = 5; the tax multiplier is −MPC / MPS = −4.

  c.   C = 40 + .8(Y − T).

  d.   Equilibrium occurs at 400, where S + T = I + G.

7. a.   The government spending multiplier is 1 / (1 − b + bt), where b = MPC = 5 / 7 and t = .3. The multiplier value is 2.

  b.   Given that the economy is in equilibrium at 480, the President wishes output to increase by 70 (550 − 480).

  c.   Spending change: $\Delta Y = 70 = \Delta G \times 1 / MPS = 35 \times 2.0$. G must increase by 35.

d. See the diagram below.

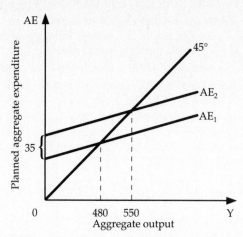

e. Originally, the deficit (G − T) = 150 − 120 = 30.
f. Income has risen by 70. The tax rate is .3. Increase in tax collections = .3 × 70 = 21.
g. Now the deficit (G − T) = (150 + 35) − (120 + 21) = 44.

8. a. A decrease in investment, consumption, or exports will reduce aggregate expenditure and output. As output falls, transfer payments will increase and tax revenues will decrease, opening up a deficit without any explicit government action.
   b. This change has occurred because of the recession—it is a cyclical deficit.
   c. A balanced-budget increase will increase the government's role but leave the size of the structural deficit unchanged. (Note: In the presence of tax rates and other automatic stabilizers, the structural deficit will, in fact, decrease.)
   d. If the government wishes to balance the budget, taxes will have to increase (decrease) more (less) than government spending. Increasing taxes, for example, will depress the economy still further. In this case, there is an incompatibility between balancing the budget and fighting the recession.

THE MONEY SUPPLY AND THE FEDERAL RESERVE SYSTEM

11

COMBINED TEXT

26

OBJECTIVES: POINT BY POINT

After completing this chapter, you should be able to accomplish the objectives listed below.

General Comment

This chapter begins the process of building a model of the financial market that is continued in Chapter 12 (27), where the factors that determine the demand for money holdings and the establishment of money market equilibrium are considered. This model will then be combined with the aggregate expenditure model in Chapter 13 (28). It is important that you develop a good understanding of financial markets at this point.

OBJECTIVE 1: Identify the three functions of money. List the various types of money and the differences among them.

The three functions of money are:
   a.   a medium of exchange (or means of payment),
   b.   a store of value, and
   c.   a unit of account.   (page 242/668)

Before money, there was barter. But because trading goods for goods relies on a double coincidence of wants, barter was inefficient. *Commodity money* (a good that has some value over and above its value as money) was an intermediate stage between barter and the *fiat money* of the modern economy. Gold and cigarettes are examples of commodity money. Dollar bills (Federal Reserve notes) are fiat money—they derive their value from the willingness of individuals to accept them as payment.
                                                                              (page 243/669)

> **TIP:** In this section, it is important to liberate yourself from equating "money" with dollar bills. Try a thought experiment: If dollars (and checks, etc.) disappeared overnight, how would the U.S. economy adapt? What might be used instead of dollars? Which features favor some commodities, such as gold, silver or tobacco, over others, such as fish, cows, or iron?

PRACTICE

1. Money's prime function is as
   A. the standard for credit transactions.
   B. the medium of exchange.
   C. a store of value.
   D. a unit of account.
   Answer: B. The main reason for having money is because it eases the process of exchange. See p. 242/668.

2. In a barter economy,
   A. money functions only as a medium of exchange.
   B. multiple "exchange rates" are likely.
   C. money functions are a medium of exchange and as a store of value.
   D. saving can not occur.
   Answer: B. In a barter economy, there is no money, so Options A and C are incorrect. Saving can occur; saving, recall, is non-consumption. In a barter economy, there will be an exchange rate between apples and corn, another between corn and tobacco, another between tobacco and tomatoes, and so on.

Use the following information to answer the next two questions.

At a flea market, Mary spots some valuable Depression glassware valued at the ridiculously low price of 25¢. She hands over the quarter to secure the item.

3. The price tag on the glassware used money in its role as a
   A. medium of exchange.
   B. store of value.
   C. unit of account.
   D. means of payment.
   Answer: C. Money serves are a way of establishing a consistent way of quoting prices. Money is functioning well in this case—Mary can see that the glassware is undervalued.

4. As Mary hands over the quarter, she is using money in its role as a
   A. medium of exchange.
   B. store of value.
   C. unit of account.
   D. form of credit.
   Answer: A. See p. 242/668.

5. Jack is saving money to buy a new VCR. Money is functioning as a
   A. medium of exchange.
   B. store of value.
   C. unit of account.
   D. standard of deferred payment.
   Answer: B. See p. 243/669.

6. Each of the following is an example of commodity money except
   A. dollar bills.
   B. gold.
   C. cigarettes.
   D. salt.
   Answer: A. Dollar bills have no value other than as dollar bills—they are fiat money. The three commodities have all been used as money. Salt, in fact, is the source of the term "salary."

OBJECTIVE 2: Identify the different measures of the U.S. money supply.

At the heart of the various measures of the money supply is the concept of *liquidity*. The more easily and cheaply an asset can be converted into spending power, the more liquid it is. The most liquid assets are included in M1, the narrowest definition of money. M1, or transactions money, includes notes and coins held by the public, demand deposits, the value of travelers checks, and various checkable accounts. Other assets, such as savings accounts, are called *near monies*. M2 (broad money) includes everything in M1 and near monies such as savings accounts and money market accounts. (page 244/670)

> **TIP:** The definition of M1—notes and coins *held by the public*, demand deposits, the value of travelers checks, and various checkable accounts—prevents "double-counting." When you deposit a dollar bill into your checking account, the money supply doesn't change. The "demand deposit" (checking account) value increases by a dollar, but the "notes and coins *held by the public*" falls by a dollar, because the dollar bill is now held by the banking system, *not* by the public.

PRACTICE

7. Which of the following is not included in M2?
   A. Money-market accounts.
   B. Excess reserves.
   C. Demand deposits.
   D. Savings accounts.
   Answer: B. Excess reserves are not money in any sense. Note that demand deposits are included in M2 because they are included in M1. See p. 245/671.

8. Near monies are
   A. included in the M1.
   B. liquid assets that are close substitutes for transactions money.
   C. stocks, bonds, and collectible artwork.
   D. Federal Reserve notes.
   Answer: B. See p. 245/671.

OBJECTIVE 3: Determine which items are assets and which are liabilities on a bank's balance sheet. Distinguish among total, excess, and required reserves. Describe the process of deposit creation and expansion. Derive and explain the importance of the money multiplier.

> **TIP:** T accounts are used extensively in this chapter. You may never have seen them before. A basic rule to memorize is that "assets go on the left and liabilities go on the right" in a balance sheet.

Bankers have discovered that, because they need only keep a fraction of their total reserves available for withdrawal (*required reserves*), the rest (*excess reserves*) can be loaned out at a profit. Banks create money through these lending activities. When loaned out, the funds advanced to the borrower increase her/his spending power and count as an addition to the money supply. Each bank, therefore, can expand the money supply by the value of its excess reserves. As a whole, the banking system, by recirculating deposits, can expand the money supply by a multiple (the *money multiplier*) of its reserves, the multiple being determined by the fraction of funds that is held as required reserves. In reality, the Federal Reserve establishes a required reserve ratio that determines the maximum size of the money multiplier, which is equal to 1 / (required reserve ratio). (page 249/675)

The following table will help to organize your thoughts on the money creation process. Suppose Alice deposits $1,000 in her bank (Bank A). The required reserve ratio is 20%. Reserves increase by $1,000 (of which $200 are required reserves, which can't be loaned out) and $800 are excess reserves (which can be loaned out). A loan to Jack is made and $800 worth of spending power is released. Jack writes an $800 check to Brenda, who deposits it in her bank (Bank B). Bank A's excess reserves fall to zero when the check is cleared, but it has the $1,000 deposit, $200 in required reserves, and $800 in loans.

Bank B has $800 in deposits, $160 in required reserves, and $640 in excess reserves. The Bank lends $640 to Jill, who writes a check to Chris. Chris deposits the check in Bank C. When Jill's check is cleared, Bank B's excess reserves fall to zero, but it has the $800 deposit, $160 in required reserves, and $640 in loans. And so on.

	New Demand Deposits =	Change in Reserves =	Change in Required Reserves +	Change in Excess Reserves	Change in Loans
A.	1,000	1,000	200	800/0	800
B.	800	800	160	640/0	640
C.	640	640	128	512/0	512
D.	512	512	102.4	409.6/0	409.6
etc.	...	...	...	...	...
Total	5,000		1,000	0	4,000

Points to note:

a. The "change in excess reserves" column contains two steps, the first indicating how much excess reserves increase, the second assuming that all excess reserves have been loaned out and the borrower's check has been honored.

b. It becomes clear, using the table, that the expansion process will continue until all of the original injection of new reserves ($1,000) has been converted into required reserves. At that point the process must stop.

c. The expansion in demand deposit liabilities is balanced on the asset side of the balance sheet by $1,000 of required reserves and $4,000 of loans.

A Circular Flow Diagram: This "leakage" process is similar to that described for the multiplier in Practice Question 16 of Chapter 9. To get an intuitive feel for the money expansion process, you can use a diagram similar to the one presented there. In this case, the "household" sector is split into two parts, borrowers and depositors, but otherwise the argument is similar. In the money creation situation, the leakage occurs when banks retain funds as required reserves. Over and above the leakage of reserves into required reserves, other "leakages," such as holding funds as currency, (either by the borrower or other members of the public) or holdings of excess reserves by the banks, will diminish the strength of the circular flow.

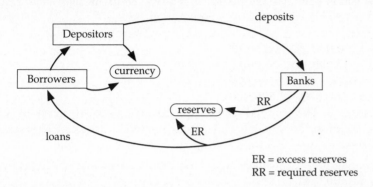

ER = excess reserves
RR = required reserves

> **TIP:** The formula relating commercial bank reserves (RR) and deposits (D) via the required reserve ratio (g) is $D = RR / g$. Memorize it!

A small point. Note that the multiplier refers to the multiple change in *deposits* (which is not the same thing as the money supply). M1 is comprised of deposits and also of notes and coins held by the public. A 10% increase in reserves doesn't necessarily translate into a 10% increase in the money supply. If bank reserves increase because Alice deposits $100 into her checking account, the decrease in currency will partly offset the multiple expansion in deposits.

PRACTICE

9. The basic equation for a bank's balance sheet is
   A. Liabilities = Assets + Net Worth.
   B. Net Worth = Liabilities + Assets.
   C. Assets = Liabilities + Net Worth.
   D. Assets = Liabilities − Net Worth.
   Answer: C. See p. 249/675.

10. Assets are things that are _____; on a balance sheet they are entered on the _____
    A. owned, right.
    B. owned, left.
    C. owed, right.
    D. owed, left.
    Answer: B. See p. 249/675.

Use the following balance sheet for First Union Bank to answer the next three questions. First Union Bank has a reserve ratio of 20%.

Assets		Liabilities	
Reserves	$2,500,000	Checking deposits	6,000,000
Loans outstanding	5,500,000		
Other assets	1,000,000	Net Worth	3,000,000
Total	$9,000,000	Total	$9,000,000

11. First Union Bank has $2,500,000 in reserves, checking deposits of $6,000,000, and a reserve ratio of 20%. First Union has _____ of required reserves and _____ of excess reserves.
    A. $500,000, $2,000,000.
    B. $500,000, $5,500,000.
    C. $1,200,000, $1,300,000.
    D. $1,200,000, $4,800,000.
    Answer: C. The required reserves are calculated relative to the bank's liabilities, therefore $6,000,000 × .2. Total reserves = required reserves + excess reserves.

12. Assuming prudent management, First Union can increase its loans by up to
    A. $1,300,000.
    B. $1,500,000.
    C. $2,000,000.
    D. $3,000,000.
    Answer: A. First Union can increase its loans by the extent of its excess reserves.

13. Assuming all banks have a reserve ratio of 20%, and that the other banks were loaned up initially, the nation's money supply could expand by
    A. $1,300,000.
    B. $6,500,000.
    C. $12,500,000.
    D. $10,000,000.
    Answer: B. The money supply can expand by the extent of the excess reserves ($1,300,000) times the multiplier, which is 1 / .20 = 5.

Use the following balance sheet for First Federal Bank to answer the next two questions.

Assets		Liabilities	
Reserves	$400,000	Checking deposits	$1,000,000
Loans outstanding	$600,000		
Total	$1,000,000	Total	$1,000,000

14. First Federal is fully loaned up. The reserve requirement is
    A. 2.5%.
    B. 40%.
    C. 60%.
    D. 250%.
    Answer: B. If all reserves are required reserves, the requirement is to hold 40% of deposit liabilities.

15. Assume that First Federal is the only bank in the economy and the banking system is closed to foreign banks. The reserve requirement is 40%. Now an additional $100,000 is deposited. The bank can expand its loans up to the point where its total deposits are
    A. $1,100,000.
    B. $1,250,000.
    C. $1,400,000.
    D. $2,000,000.
    Answer: B. Total (required) reserves will be $500,000. The money multiplier is 2.5.

OBJECTIVE 4: Outline the functions of the Fed. Identify the three monetary policy tools of the Fed and how they are adjusted to increase (decrease) the money supply.

The main macroeconomic role of the Fed is to control the money supply and interest rates, but it also oversees the banking system and gives check-clearing and other services. As well as functioning as the bankers' bank, it is the government's bank, the lender of last resort, and a major player in international currency transactions.
(page 254/680)

The primary method used by the Federal Open Market Committee to control the money supply is the manipulation of commercial bank reserves. (Recall that the commercial banks can create deposits only if they have the excess reserves available to support such an expansion.)

The three major tools of monetary policy are:
    a. the required reserve ratio,
    b. the discount rate, and
    c. open market operations, which are the most frequently used and the most precise.
(page 259/685)

To expand the money supply, the Fed can buy government securities (which increases the reserves of the banking system), cut the reserve requirement (which results in the commercial banks having more excess reserves, and thus, greater lending capacity), or cut the discount rate (which reduces the "price" of borrowing funds from the Fed). In each case, the effect is to make more reserves available to the banking system. When these reserves are loaned out, the money supply will increase.
(page 259/685)

> **TIP:** At the outset, the following "trick" will help you to sort out the operation of the monetary policy tools. The discount rate and reserve ratio move in the same direction (both down for an expansionary policy, for example) while, with open market operations, the Fed (B)uys securities to make the money supply (B)igger, and (S)ells them to make it (S)maller.

> **TIP:** Work through the money creation (destruction) process as initiated by an open market purchase (sale) of securities. Remember that the key to changing the money supply is changing commercial bank reserves.

16. The Fed wants to increase the money supply. The most likely monetary policy might include the _____ of bonds by the Fed and the _____ of the discount rate.

    A. purchase, lowering.
    B. purchase, raising.
    C. sale, lowering.
    D. sale, raising.

    Answer: A. Buying securities from the private banks will increase their reserves; cutting the discount rate encourages more borrowing from the Fed.

17. Which of the following instruments is not used by the Fed to change the money supply?

    A. Open market operations.
    B. The discount rate.
    C. The tax rate on interest earnings.
    D. The required reserve ratio.

    Answer: C. Changes in tax rates are undertaken by Congress as part of fiscal policy.

18. U.S. government securities are a(n) _____ of the Fed; Federal Reserve notes are a(n) _____ of the Fed.

    A. asset, asset.
    B. asset, liability.
    C. liability, asset.
    D. liability, liability.

    Answer: B. The securities are claims against the government and owned by the Fed. Federal Reserve notes are issued by the Fed and must be honored by it.

19. Which of the following is not a responsibility of the Fed?

    A. Regulating the banking system.
    B. Clearing interbank payments.
    C. Managing exchange rates.
    D. Issuing new bonds to finance the federal deficit.

    Answer: D. New bonds to finance the deficit are issued by the Treasury.

20. The preferred instrument of monetary policy is

    A. the discount rate.
    B. the required reserve ratio.
    C. open market operations.
    D. the exchange rate.

    Answer: C. See p. 263/689.

21. *Ceteris paribus*, an open market sale of government securities to First Union National Bank will _____ First Union's assets and _____ First Union's liabilities.

    A. increase, increase.
    B. increase, not change.
    C. not change, increase.
    D. not change, not change.

    Answer: D. The composition, but not the level, of First Union's assets will change.

22. First Union National Bank is fully loaned up. Ultimately, an open market sale of government securities to First Union will _____ First Union's reserves and _____ First Union's deposit liabilities.

    A. increase, increase.
    B. increase, decrease.
    C. decrease, increase.
    D. decrease, decrease.

    Answer: D. To buy the securities, First Union must transfer some of its reserves to the Fed. Because reserves have fallen, First Union will be unable to support its original level of demand deposit liabilities.

OBJECTIVE 5: Analyze the Fed's ability to expand or contract reserves and the money supply.

The Fed changes the required reserve ratio infrequently because it is a crude instrument of monetary control. When changes do occur, they tend to exert a powerful effect on the private banks. (page 259/685)

Changes in discount rate help the Fed to "signal" changes in policy, but this policy tool also has some problems. First, the effect of a discount rate change is imprecise. Second, movements in other interest rates may counteract the hoped-for effect of the discount rate change. Moral suasion (threats!) may be used to discourage banks from borrowing heavily from the Fed and then re-lending the reserves. (page 261/687)

Open market operations are a quick, precise, and flexible method of manipulating reserves. (page 263/689)

PRACTICE

Use the following information for the next two questions. The banking system has deposits of $60 million and it is fully loaned up. The required reserve ratio is 25%. Assume no leakages from the banking system occur.

23. If the required reserve ratio is reduced from 25% to 20%, the banking system could
    A. increase loans by $3 million.
    B. increase loans by $12 million.
    C. increase loans by $15 million.
    D. increase loans by $20 million.
    Answer: C. When the ratio is 25%, required reserves are $60 million × .25, or $15 million. When the ratio is 20%, required reserves are $60 million × .20, or $12 million. Because reserves have not changed, this means that the banking system has excess reserves of $3 million. The multiplier is 1 / .20, or 5.

24. The Fed wants deposits to increase to $90 million. The Fed would achieve its goal if it changed the reserve ratio from 25% to
    A. 12%.
    B. 15%.
    C. 16.67%.
    D. 67%.
    Answer: C. When the ratio is 25%, required reserves are $60 million × .25, or $15 million. If the reserve ratio is 16.67, the money multiplier is 1 / .1667, or 6. $15 million × 6 = $90 million.

25. Which of the following is false? Open market operations
    A. are fast and flexible.
    B. are fairly predictable in their impact on the money supply.
    C. are an effective instrument of monetary policy because they are used infrequently.
    D. involve the purchase and sale of pre-existing U.S. government securities.
    Answer: C. Open market operations are the most frequently used tool of monetary policy.

26. Although the required reserve ratio is a tool of monetary policy, it is used infrequently because
   A. only banks that are members of the Federal Reserve System must comply with the requirement, and this discriminates in favor of the many banks that are not members of the Fed.
   B. when the Fed reduces the required reserve ratio, banks will have to "call" some of their loans.
   C. a change in the requirement will take two weeks to have an impact on banks due to lags in bank reporting.
   D. it may take a long time to get Congressional permission to proceed with a change in the ratio.

Answer: C. See p. 260/686. All depository institutions are members of the Fed. Congressional approval of Fed decisions is not required—the Fed is separate from Congress. *Raising* the ratio might result in called loans.

27. Each of the following is a problem associated with the use of the discount rate except that
   A. the discount rate cannot be adjusted quickly.
   B. the impact of a change in the discount rate is imprecise.
   C. the impact of a change in the discount rate can be offset by changes in other interest rates.
   D. the effect of a change in the discount rate on banks' demand for reserves is uncertain.

Answer: A. This rate is established, and can be changed at will, by the Fed.

 PRACTICE TEST

I. MULTIPLE CHOICE QUESTIONS.

Select the option that provides the single best answer.

 1. Each of the following is included in M1 except
   A. Federal Reserve notes.
   B. cash held by the public.
   C. demand deposit accounts.
   D. credit card balances.

2. Which of the following is not a function of money?
   A. A form of speculation.
   B. A medium of exchange.
   C. A unit of account.
   D. A store of value.

 3. Robin Hood borrows $100 in dollar bills from Friar Tuck and deposits it at Citibank. The required reserve ratio is 25%. What is the maximum amount by which the banking system can expand checking accounts?
   A. $500.
   B. $100.
   C. $300.
   D. $400.

 4. Excess reserves equal
   A. demand deposits plus required reserves.
   B. actual reserves minus required reserves.
   C. total reserves minus actual reserves.
   D. demand deposits minus required reserves.

_C_ 5. It is assumed that the money supply curve is _____ it _____ affected by changes in the interest rate.
- A. horizontal, is.
- B. vertical, is.
- C. vertical, is not.
- D. horizontal, is not.

_D_ 6. Checking account deposits at Citibank are Citibank _____; money market accounts at Citibank are Citibank _____
- A. assets, assets.
- B. assets, liabilities.
- C. liabilities, assets.
- D. liabilities, liabilities.

_D_ 7. In a T account, liabilities go on the _____ side and net worth goes on the _____ side.
- A. left, left.
- B. left, right.
- C. right, left.
- D. right, right.

_B_ 8. An increase in the required reserve ratio will
- A. increase the demand for money balances.
- B. reduce the money supply.
- C. increase the value of the money multiplier.
- D. increase the amount of excess reserves.

_A_ 9. The required reserve ratio is 20%. $200 is deposited into a demand (M1) deposit account in the banking system.
- A. Initially, the money supply has changed its composition but not its size.
- B. Eventually, the money supply will increase by $1,000.
- C. Initially, the money supply will increase by $200.
- D. Initially, the money supply will increase by $40.

(Be careful on this one! There is only one correct answer.)

_C_ 10. The FOMC is responsible for all of the following except
- A. setting the discount rate for lending to commercial banks.
- B. establishing and changing the required reserve ratio of the commercial banks.
- C. clearing interbank payments.
- D. deciding whether to buy or to sell U.S. government securities.

Use the following information to answer the next two questions.

The commercial banks are loaned up and have reserves of $500 billion. Now the required reserve ratio is changed from 25% to 10%.

_C_ 11. Initially, excess reserves will
- A. increase by 15%.
- B. decrease by $300 billion.
- C. increase by $300 billion.
- D. increase by $3,000 billion.

_D_ 12. Eventually, the money supply can
- A. increase by 15%.
- B. increase by a multiple of 10.
- C. increase by $1,250 billion.
- D. increase by $3,000 billion.

_A_ 13. Which one of the following pairs of policy actions would definitely *not* increase the money supply?
- A. Open market sales of securities, increasing the discount rate.
- B. Open market sales of securities, reducing the discount rate.
- C. Open market purchases of securities, increasing the discount rate.
- D. Open market purchases of securities, reducing the discount rate.

_D_ 14. The required reserve ratio is 25%. First Union National Bank makes an additional loan of $500,000. If the banking system is holding no excess reserves, then the eventual increase in the money supply will be
- A. zero.
- B. $500,000.
- C. $1,500,000.
- D. $2,000,000.

_C_ 15. If Kristin deposits $5,000 cash into her savings account, then
- A. M1 goes down and M2 goes up.
- B. M1 goes up and M2 goes down.
- C. M1 goes down and M2 stays the same.
- D. M1 stays the same and M2 goes down.

_D_ 16. The value of the money multiplier will be reduced when
- A. recipients of bank loans redeposit the proceeds of their loans into another bank.
- B. each bank holds zero excess reserves.
- C. recipients of bank loans do not keep any of the loan as cash.
- D. the required reserves of the banking system are less than its total reserves.

_D_ 17. The pressure exerted by the Fed on bankers to discourage them from borrowing from the Fed is called
- A. open market operations.
- B. closed market operations.
- C. closing the discount window.
- D. moral suasion.

_B_ 18. The discount rate is the interest rate paid by
- A. the Fed to banks who deposit funds with it.
- B. banks when they borrow from the Fed.
- C. banks when they borrow from each other.
- D. the Fed to the Treasury to buy U.S. government securities.

_A_ 19. Most of the Fed's liabilities are
- A. Federal Reserve notes.
- B. loans made to the private banks.
- C. U.S. government securities.
- D. bank reserves deposited by depository institutions.

_B_ 20. The required reserve ratio is 25% and all banks, whose total reserves are valued at $200 million, are fully loaned up. If the Fed reduces the required reserve ratio to 20%, the banking system could support an additional
- A. $100 million in deposits.
- B. $200 million in deposits.
- C. $400 million in deposits.
- D. $500 million in deposits.

II. APPLICATION QUESTIONS.

1. In the nation of Arboc, the required reserve ratio is 20%. 30% of cash assets end up in foreign accounts. Arbobank (the central bank) buys 500 million opeks of government securities. Calculate how much the money supply will increase. How does the movement of funds to foreign accounts affect the size of the money multiplier?

2. The required reserve ratio is 10%. All banks are "loaned up." Assume that banks lend their excess reserves.
   a. Now First Union discovers an additional $1,000 in excess reserves. Make the final entries on the T account of each of the following banks after deposits have been received, loans made, spending undertaken, and checks cleared. Assume that a borrower from First Union deposits at Second Union, and so on.

First Union			
Assets		Liabilities	
Reserves _____		Deposits _____	
Loans _____			
Second Union			
Assets		Liabilities	
Reserves _____		Deposits _____	
Loans _____			
Third Union			
Assets		Liabilities	
Reserves _____		Deposits _____	
Loans _____			
Fourth Union			
Assets		Liabilities	
Reserves _____		Deposits _____	
Loans _____			

   b. Calculate the extent of overall expansion in the money supply once this process is complete.

3. ArbeFed (the central bank of Arbez) has assets of 1,000 opeks (in the form of government securities). ArbeFed's liabilities are 800 opeks of currency and 200 opeks of deposits by banks in the central bank. All banks are "loaned up" and all currency is held by the public. Assume that no leakages from the banking system occur.
   a. Draw a T account showing ArbeFed's financial position.
   b. The required reserve ratio is 20%. Determine the size of the Arbezani money supply, M1 (currency plus demand deposits).
   c. ArbeFed wishes to increase the money supply to 2,000 opeks by adjusting the reserve requirement.
      i. Would the reserve requirement have to increase or decrease?
      ii. What should the new reserve requirement be?
   d. ArbeFed decides to reduce the money supply by 300, opting for an open market operation.
      i. Should ArbeFed buy bonds or sell bonds on the open market?
      ii. How big should this transaction be if ArbeFed sells to the banking system?
      iii. How big should this transaction be if ArbeFed sells to the public which pays by check?

4. How would each of the following, *ceteris paribus*, affect the M1 and M2 measures of the money supply?
   a. Households move $10 billion of their liquid wealth from demand deposits to money-market deposit accounts.
   b. Households buy $10 billion worth of travelers checks and pay with checks drawn on their checking accounts.
   c. Households cash in $10 billion in large-denomination time deposits and keep the proceeds as cash.

5. List the following assets in terms of their liquidity—i.e., ease and cheapness of conversion into spending power. Put the most liquid first, the least liquid last.

A house; a dollar bill; a car; some IBM stock; a collector's edition plate; a passbook savings account; an individual retirement account.

1. _____   5. _____

2. _____   6. _____

3. _____   7. _____

4. _____

6. Use the following information to calculate the total value of M1 (transactions money) and M2 (broad money) as defined in the text.

Money Market Accounts	50
Credit Cards	403
Stock Market Holdings	1,009
Demand Deposits	140
Federal Reserve Notes held by Public	146
Money Market Mutual Funds	196
Treasury Bills	708
Travelers Checks	20
Checkable Accounts	80
Savings Accounts	300
Treasury Bonds	513
Coins held by the public	10
Gold	73

M1 _____

M2 _____

7. The following table gives several possible required reserve ratios.

Required Reserve Ratio	Money Multiplier	Max. Expansion (Single Bank)	Max. Expansion (Banking System)
10%			
12.5%			
20%			
25%			

a. Calculate the money multipliers and enter the values in the table.

b. Suppose a "loaned up" bank receives a deposit of $100. Given the required reserve ratio, calculate the maximum amount by which the bank could expand its *loans*.

c. In each case, calculate the maximum amount by which the banking system will be able to expand its *deposits*.

8. Suppose that Ace deposits $1,000 into his bank (Bank A), which is fully loaned up. Complete the following table, showing the maximum amount by which deposits, reserves, and loans can increase. Assume that the required reserve ratio is 12.5%.

Bank	New Demand Deposits =	Change in Reserves =	Change in Required Reserves +	Change in Excess Reserves =	Change in Loans
A.					
B.					
C.					
D.					
etc.					
Total					

9. A commercial bank has deposits of $100,000 and total reserves amounting to $31,000. The required reserve ratio is 15%. All other banks are loaned up.
    a. What is the largest loan that this bank can make? _____
    b. What is the value of the money multiplier? _____
    c. If the initial loan is made, what is the maximum expansion that can occur in the money supply if other banks also lend as much as possible? _____

10. Arboc's central bank (Arbobank) holds 2,000 opeks in government securities. The commercial banks have deposited 200 opeks with Arbobank and hold 100 in vault cash. 700 opeks are held as currency by the public. The required reserve ratio is 20%; banks are loaned up.
    a. The money multiplier value is _____.
    b. Calculate Arboc's money supply. _____

    It is felt that the money supply should be increased by 900 opeks. Either an open market operation or a change in the reserve ratio is possible.
    c. If the reserve ratio is changed, what should be the new ratio? _____

    d. If an open market operation is undertaken, it should be a: purchase/sale of _____ opeks.

ANSWERS AND SOLUTIONS

PRACTICE TEST

I. SOLUTIONS TO MULTIPLE CHOICE QUESTIONS

1. D. Federal Reserve notes are the official name for dollar bills. See p. 245/671. From the economist's point of view, credit cards are a means of obtaining a loan, not a means of payment. Payment comes later, when you write a check to Visa or Mastercard.
2. A. See p. 242/668 for a discussion of the functions of money.
3. D. The money multiplier is 4 (1/required reserve ratio). Checking accounts (demand deposits) will increase by 400 (100 × 4). See p. 253/679.
4. B. See p. 251/677. Typically, some of a bank's actual reserves will be excess reserves.
5. C. See p. 266/692.
6. D. Citibank owes depositors the value of their checking accounts; Citibank also owes depositors the value of their money market accounts. Both are liabilities.

7. D. Assets to the left; liabilities to the right. Net worth is the value of the firm (the difference between assets and liabilities).

8. B. Given the reserves of the banking system, if more reserves are required to be held back, the money multiplier (1/required reserve ratio) will decrease and the money supply will decrease. Excess reserves = total reserves − required reserves. As required reserves increase, excess reserves decrease.

9. A. On its own, the deposit has no effect on the money supply. The "currency held outside banks" category decreases by $200; the "demand deposits" category increases by $200. See p. 245/671. Eventually, because the money multiplier is 5, deposits will increase by $1,000, but currency held outside banks has decreased by $200. The net change in the money supply is $800.

10. C. The FOMC is in charge of monetary policy actions. Clearing checks is not a part of monetary policy. See p. 254/680.

11. C. When the banking system is loaned up, all reserves are required reserves. Excess reserves are zero. If the required reserve ratio is 25%, the banking system's reserves must be supporting $2,000 billion (500 billion × 4) in deposits. If the reserve requirement decreases to 10%, only $200 billion will be required, liberating $300 billion as excess reserves.

12. D. If the required reserve ratio is 10%, the banking system's reserves can support $5,000 billion (500 billion × 10) in deposits—an increase of $3,000 billion.

13. A. An open market sale of securities draws reserves away from the private banking system, reducing the money supply. Increasing the discount rate discourages borrowing. Options B and C each contain two conflicting policies-if the expansionary element is stronger (open market purchase, discount rate decrease), the money supply would increase.

14. D. The money multiplier is 4. Each dollar loaned out will be multiplied four times by the banking system as a whole.

15. C. M2 includes all components of M1, so the transfer has no effect on the total value of M2. M1 is reduced because savings accounts are not included in M1.

16. D. When the required reserves of the banking system are less than its total reserves, some excess reserves exist. Excess reserves represent a leakage from the money creation process.

17. D. See p. 262/688.

18. B. See p. 261/687. For your information, the rate charged when banks borrow from each other is the federal funds rate.

19. A. See p. 258/684.

20. B. If the banking system is fully loaned up, all reserves are required reserves. With a required reserve ratio of 25%, total deposits must be $800 million ($200 million × 4). If the Fed reduces the required reserve ratio to 20%, the money multiplier will increase to 5, and the banking system will be able to support $1,000 million of deposits ($200 million × 5)—an increase of $200 million.

II. SOLUTIONS TO APPLICATION QUESTIONS

1. With a required reserve ratio of 20%, the maximum value for the money multiplier is 5. Leakages, however, will reduce this value; flows of reserves overseas is one such leakage. A 500 million opek purchase of securities increases bank system reserves by 500 million opeks. However, domestic reserves will increase by 350 million opeks (500 × .7). Given the multiplier, this increase in reserves will "back" an expansion in the money supply of 1,750 (350 × 1 / .2) million opeks. Effectively, the money multiplier has been reduced from 5 to 3.5—the increase in reserves of 500 million opeks expands the money supply by 1,750 (500 × 3.5) million.

2. a. See the following T accounts.

First Union		
Assets		**Liabilities**
Reserves	−1,000	Deposits _____
Loans	+1,000	

Second Union		
Assets		**Liabilities**
Reserves	+200	Deposits +1,000
Loans	+800	

Third Union		
Assets		**Liabilities**
Reserves	+160	Deposits +800
Loans	+160	

Fourth Union		
Assets		**Liabilities**
Reserves	+128	Deposits +640
Loans	+512	

  b. The money supply can expand by $5,000.

3. a. See the following T account.

ArbeFed		
Assets		**Liabilities**
Securities	1,000	Currency 800
		Deposits of Banks 200

  b. Currency = 800. Because the banking system is fully loaned up and the money multiplier is 5.00, demand deposits are 200 × 5, or 1,000. M1 is 1,800 opeks.

  c. i. The reserve requirement must be decreased to 16.67%.

     ii. The money multiplier is 1 / .1667, or 6. Bank reserves are 200, therefore demand deposits will be 1,200 opeks. Currency remains at 800 opeks.

  d. i. ArbeFed should sell bonds.

     ii. If the central bank sells bonds worth 60 opeks to the banking system and the money multiplier is 5, the money supply will decrease by 300 opeks.

     iii. If the central bank sells bonds worth 60 opeks to the public and the public uses demand deposits from the banking system, banking system reserves will fall by 60. The banking system's reserves are 48 opeks too low (i.e., 60 × .80). Deposits will shrink by an additional 240 opeks (i.e., 48 × 5). Total decrease is 300 opeks.

4. a. Moving funds from DDs to money market deposits: M1, which includes DDs but not money market deposits, would decrease by $10 billion; M2 would remain unchanged.

  b. Moving funds from DDs to travelers checks: M1 and M2 both include both DDs and travelers checks, so each would remain unchanged.

  c. Moving funds from large time deposits to cash: M1 and M2, which include cash but not large time deposits, would increase by $10 billion.

5. A dollar bill; a passbook savings account; some IBM stock; a collector's edition plate; an individual retirement account; a car; a house.

6. M1 is 396—that is, the total of Federal Reserve Notes and coins held by the public, travelers checks, demand deposits, and other checkable accounts; M2 is 942—that is, M1 plus savings accounts, money market mutual funds, and money market accounts.

7. a. See the table below.

Required Reserve Ratio	Money Multiplier	Max. Expansion (Single Bank)	Max. Expansion (Banking System)
10%	10	$90.00	$1,000
12.5%	8	$87.50	$800
20%	5	$80.00	$500
25%	4	$75.00	$400

   b. See the table above.
   c. See the table above.

8. See the table below.

	New Demand Deposits =	Change in Reserves =	Change in Required Reserves +	Change in Excess Reserves -->	Change in Loans
A.	$1,000.00	$1,000.00	$125.00	$875.00/0	$875.00
B.	$ 875.00	$ 875.00	$109.38	$765.62/0	$765.62
C.	$ 765.62	$ 765.62	$ 95.70	$669.92/0	$669.92
D.	$ 669.92	$ 669.38	$ 83.74	$586.18/0	$586.18
	$4,689.46		$586.18	$4103.28/0	$4,103.28
	$8,000		$1,000.00	$7,000.00/0	$7,000.00

9. a. Required reserves are $15,000 and excess reserves are $16,000. The bank can lend out all of its excess reserves—that is, $16,000.
   b. The money multiplier = 1 / required reserve ratio = 1 / .15 = 6.667.
   c. $16,000 × 6.667 = $106,666.67.

10. a. The money multiplier = 1 / required reserve ratio = 1 / .20 = 5.
    b. Bank reserves are vault cash (100) and deposits at the central bank (200). If the banks are loaned up and the multiplier is 5, demand deposits must be 1,500 (300 × 5). The money supply includes currency (700) and demand deposits (1,500) = 2,200 opeks.
    c. To support a money supply of 3,100, with 2,400 opeks of demand deposits (1,500 + 900), using the same quantity of reserves (300), the multiplier must be 8 (2,400 / 300). To get a multiplier of 8, the required reserve ratio must be 12.5%.
    d. If the multiplier is 5, a purchase of 180 opeks will increase the money supply by 900.

THE DEMAND FOR MONEY, THE EQUILIBRIUM INTEREST RATE, AND MONETARY POLICY

12

COMBINED TEXT

27

OBJECTIVES: POINT BY POINT

After completing this chapter, you should be able to accomplish the objectives listed below.

OBJECTIVE 1: Define the interest rate.

The *interest rate* is the annual interest payment expressed as a percentage of the total loan (as opposed to *interest*, which is the charge imposed by a lender on a borrower for the use of funds). *(page 270/696)*

For simplicity, the text assumes that there is only one interest rate and that money earns no interest. Historically, the assumption that money earns no interest was accurate—currency doesn't, and, in previous decades, checking accounts earned no interest.

1. Hansel borrows $50 from Gretel. The loan will last one year. At the end of the year, Hansel will pay Gretel $60. The interest received by Gretel is _____; the interest rate is _____
   A. $10, 10%.
   B. $10, 20%.
   C. $60, 10%.
   D. $60, 20%.
   Answer: B. Interest is the fee charged by Gretel for the use of the $50. The interest rate is the annual interest payment ($10) expressed as a percentage of the loan amount ($50).

OBJECTIVE 2: Describe the trade-off facing households when choosing the quantity of money balances to hold for transactions.

The major reason that individuals choose to hold money balances (the *transaction motive*) stems from the need to buy goods and services. Households face an ever-present problem—the *nonsynchronization of income and spending*—i.e., the mismatch between the receipt of income and the need for expenditures. Income may be a single payment per period while expenditures are ongoing throughout the period. In a two-asset world, an optimal balance can be achieved by transferring some portion of money balances into interest-bearing assets (bonds). If interest rates are high (low), the opportunity cost of holding (non-interest bearing) money is high (low)—less (more) money will be demanded. *(page 271/697)*

> **TIP:** Any time you make a choice, remember that an opportunity cost is involved.

Even as a student with (presumably) limited means, you face the problem described above. Having amassed a bankroll from summer work, how do you allocate your assets? Typically, funds that are less liquid earn higher interest rates, but there may be a "penalty for early withdrawal." Holding all your funds as cash or in a checking account results in an opportunity cost (the interest earnings not obtained). If you could visit the bank only once a month, you would be obliged to hold a fair portion of your assets in readily available form (cash, checkbook). With the convenience of the neighborhood 24-hour ATM, you can cut back on idle cash or assets earning lower interest rates.

PRACTICE

2. In economics, when discussing Tessa's "demand for money," we mean
   A. how much cash Tessa would like to have.
   B. the income that Tessa would need, per time period, to satisfy her minimum living requirements.
   C. how much wealth Tessa would like to have.
   D. the quantity of Tessa's financial assets that she wishes to hold in non-interest-bearing form.
   Answer: D. The meaning of this phrase is quite specific in economics. See p. 271/697.

3. The mismatch between income inflows and spending outflows is known as
   A. the double coincidence of wants.
   B. the want of double coincidence
   C. the nonsynchronization problem.
   D. cash-flow independence.
   Answer: C. See p. 271/697. The mismatch allows us to hold some assets in non-money (interest-earning) form.

4. Thelma receives a $120 check from home each month. This is just enough to meet her spending needs. She deposits the check in her savings account and regularly draws out enough cash to last her 6 days. In a 30-day month, Thelma's average money balance is
   A. $4.
   B. $6.
   C. $12.
   D. $24.
   Answer: C. Thelma makes 5 withdrawals of $24 (120 / 5) each. If she spends her cash evenly, her average holding will be $12 (24 / 2).

5. The optimal money balance will certainly increase if the interest earned on bonds _____ and the costs of switching between bonds and money _____

    A. increases, increase.
    B. increases, decrease.
    C. decreases, increase.
    D. decreases, decrease.

    Answer: C. The lower the interest rate, the lower the opportunity cost of holding money. The higher the transaction cost, the fewer (but bigger) switches would be undertaken. See p. 274/700.

OBJECTIVE 3: Distinguish between the transaction motive and the speculation motive for holding money.

The *speculation motive* for holding money focuses on the negative relationship between bond prices and the interest rate. In a two-asset world, expectations about future bond prices and the interest rate affect money demand. When the interest rate rises, bond prices fall: when the interest rate is expected to rise, bond prices are expected to fall. A low interest rate fosters an expectation of a rise in the rate (and fall in bond prices). If a bond is expected to fall in price, its owner will try to sell it— s/he will wish to hold more money at a lower interest rate than at a higher one.

(page 275/701)

PRACTICE

6. Which statement is false? When the interest rate is higher than normal,
    A. households will expect the interest rate to decrease.
    B. households will expect bond prices to increase.
    C. the opportunity cost of holding money is lower than normal.
    D. households will wish to buy more (interest-bearing) bonds.

    Answer: C. The opportunity cost of holding money is the interest rate.

7. When the interest rate is lower than normal,
    A. bond prices are expected to increase.
    B. bond prices are expected to decrease.
    C. the demand for bonds is higher than normal.
    D. the yield on bonds is higher than normal.

    Answer: B. If the interest rate is lower than normal, we expect it to increase. Because there is a negative relationship between the interest rate and bond prices, we expect bond prices to decrease. With a low interest rate (and yield), the quantity of bonds demanded will be low.

8. There is a temporary excess supply in the money market. Eric will
    A. hold bonds instead of cash. The interest rate should increase in the future, bringing about an increase in the price of bonds.
    B. hold bonds instead of cash The interest rate should decrease in the future, bringing about an increase in the price of bonds.
    C. hold cash instead of bonds. The interest rate should increase in the future, bringing about an increase in the price of bonds.
    D. hold cash instead of bonds. The interest rate should decrease in the future, bringing about an increase in the price of bonds.

    Answer: B. An excess supply in the money market leads Eric to expect a decrease in the interest rate. A decrease in the interest rate causes an increase in the price of bonds. If Eric expects bond prices to rise, he should buy bonds now and sell them after the price increase.

9. Peter bought a bond 4 years ago for $3,000 and sold it yesterday for $2,560. Such a result might have been caused by
   A. a decrease in the reserve requirement by the Fed.
   B. a decline in the level of activity in the economy.
   C. a decrease in the discount rate.
   D. an increase in the overall price level.
   Answer: D. The price of the bond has fallen, implying an increase in the interest rate. Such an interest rate increase must have been caused by an increase in money demand or a decrease in money supply. Money demand increases as the overall price level increases.

OBJECTIVE 4: List the variables that influence the demand for money and indicate in which direction the demand for money will be affected by a change in each of them.

The *transaction motive* shows that money is demanded to finance transactions, and that the demand for money increases when the dollar value of transactions increases. This may happen if prices rise, or it may happen if there is a greater amount of economic activity. An increase in aggregate output or an increase in the price level will shift the money demand curve to the right. The *speculation motive* reinforces the negative relationship between the interest rate and the quantity of money demanded.

(page 276/702)

PRACTICE

10. An increase in the interest rate will _____ the quantity of money demanded for transactions and _____ the quantity of money demanded for speculation.
    A. increase, increase.
    B. increase, decrease.
    C. decrease, increase.
    D. decrease, decrease.
    Answer: D. The change in the interest rate has a negative effect in each case.

11. The demand for money will decrease when
    A. the interest rate increases.
    B. the price level increases.
    C. aggregate output decreases.
    D. the price of bonds is expected to decrease.
    Answer: C. Less money will be demanded if the dollar volume of transactions decreases because of a price level decrease or an output level decrease. Changes (Option A) or expected changes (Option D) in the interest rate don't cause a shift in the position of the demand curve.

12. Each of the following will cause the demand for money to increase except
    A. an increase in aggregate output.
    B. an increase in the average dollar amount of each transaction.
    C. an increase in the transactions cost of switching between money and bonds.
    D. an increase in the money supply.
    Answer: D. An increase in the money supply will affect the interest rate and the quantity of money demanded, but the demand curve will not shift position. Option C will increase money demand: At each interest rate, more idle cash balances will be held.

13. If the price level falls, the money demand curve will
    A. shift to the right.
    B. shift to the left.
    C. become steeper.
    D. become flatter.
    Answer: B. See p. 278/704.

OBJECTIVE 5: Draw a supply and demand diagram of the money market and describe how equilibrium is reached following a demand or supply curve shift.

The money market is modeled quite simply. The money demand curve shows the negative relationship between the quantity of money demanded and the interest rate. Money supply is fixed at a particular level at any point in time—the curve is vertical. The interaction of money supply and money demand establishes an equilibrium interest rate, where quantity demanded equals quantity supplied. If, for example, the demand for money increases, interest rates will rise. At the original interest rate, an excess demand for money occurs. To dissuade individuals from holding cash and to encourage bond purchases, the interest rate must increase.

(page 280/706)

> **Graphing Pointer:** Keep in mind the factors that can shift the money demand curve: aggregate income level and the price level. An increase in either will shift the curve to the right. Changes in the interest rate will cause a *movement along the curve.*

> **Graphing Pointer:** If you are a little rusty on demand and supply analysis, e.g., the difference between a "change in demand" and a "change in quantity demanded", review Chapter 4 now.

One key player in the money market is the Fed, of course, because Fed actions can increase or decrease the money supply. (page 282/708)

> **TIP:** Review the material in Chapter 11 (26) referring to the Fed's three monetary policy instruments, pp. 259–266 (685–692).

PRACTICE

14. If the supply of money increases as a result of an open market _____ of securities by the Fed, the interest rate will _____
    A. purchase, increase.
    B. purchase, decrease.
    C. sale, increase.
    D. sale, decrease.
    Answer: B. The Fed buys bonds to increase the money supply. An increase in the money supply decreases the equilibrium interest rate.

15. If the supply of money decreases as a result of a(n) _____ in the required reserve ratio, the size of money balances will _____
    A. increase, increase.
    B. increase, decrease.
    C. decrease, increase.
    D. decrease, decrease.
    Answer: B. The Fed increases the required reserve ratio to decrease the money supply. A decrease in the money supply increases the equilibrium interest rate and decreases the size of money balances.

16. If the demand for money decreases as a result of a(n) _____ in the price level, the interest rate will _____
    A. increase, increase.
    B. increase, decrease.
    C. decrease, increase.
    D. decrease, decrease.
    Answer: D. As the price level falls, less cash is needed to finance a given level of transactions.

17. If the demand for money increases as a result of an increase in the price level, the money supply will _____ and, ultimately, the size of money balances will _____
   A. increase, increase.
   B. increase, not change.
   C. not change, increase.
   D. not change, not change.
   Answer: D. A change in demand does not cause the supply curve to shift. In equilibrium, demand must equal supply, so the quantity of money demanded will return to its original level (as the interest rate increases).

Use the following diagram to answer the next four questions.

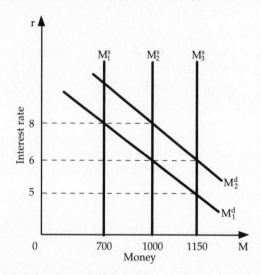

18. The money demand curve is M_1^d and the money supply curve is M_2^s. At an interest rate of 5%, there is an excess
   A. demand of 150.
   B. demand of 300.
   C. supply of 150.
   D. supply of 300.
   Answer: A. At 5%, quantity demanded (1,150) exceeds quantity supplied (1,000).

19. The money demand curve might shift from M_1^d to M_2^d if
   A. the money supply increased.
   B. the interest rate decreased.
   C. the Fed bought bonds in the open market.
   D. the real output level increased.
   Answer: D. The real output level is a determinant of money demand. See p. 279/705.

20. The money supply curve might shift from M_2^s to M_3^s if
   A. the Fed undertook an easy monetary policy such as an open market purchase of securities.
   B. the Fed undertook an easy monetary policy such as an open market sale of securities.
   C. the Fed undertook a tight monetary policy such as an open market purchase of securities.
   D. the Fed undertook a tight monetary policy such as an open market sale of securities.
   Answer: A. The shift from M_2^s to M_3^s is an expansion, caused by an easy money policy. An open market purchase of securities could cause this.

21. The equilibrium interest rate will definitely increase if the money demand curve shifts from _____ and the money supply curve shifts from _____

    A. M_1^d to M_2^d, M_1^s to M_2^s.
    B. M_1^d to M_2^d, M_2^s to M_1^s.
    C. M_2^d to M_1^d, M_1^s to M_2^s.
    D. M_2^d to M_1^d, M_2^s to M_1^s.
    Answer: B. See the diagram.

22. Which of the following pairs of events will definitely result in a decrease in the equilibrium interest rate? A(n) _____ in the level of aggregate output and a(n) _____ in the discount rate.
    A. increase, increase.
    B. increase, decrease.
    C. decrease, increase.
    D. decrease, decrease.
    Answer: D. A decrease in money demand will accompany a decrease in output, while an increase in money supply will accompany a decrease in the discount rate.

23. Which of the following pairs of events will definitely result in an increase in the equilibrium interest rate? A(n) _____ in the price level and an open market _____ of securities.
    A. increase, purchase.
    B. increase, sale.
    C. decrease, purchase.
    D. decrease, sale.
    Answer: B. An increase in money demand will accompany an increase in the price level. An open market sale of securities is a tight monetary policy.

24. Which of the following pairs of actions is the most certain to be a tight monetary policy? A(n) _____ in the required reserve ratio and an open market _____ of securities.
    A. increase, purchase.
    B. increase, sale.
    C. decrease, purchase.
    D. decrease, sale.
    Answer: B. Both actions will reduce the money supply.

OBJECTIVE 6: Discuss the reasoning behind, and the conclusions of, the expectations theory of the term structure of interest rates.

Appendix A: There is not one "interest rate" but rather a whole family of rates. The *expectations theory of the term structure of interest rates* links the behavior of long-term rates to current short-term rates and expected short-term rates. Essentially, long-term rates are based on current short-term rates and expectations about how short-term rates will change in the future. The Fed can influence long-term rates as well as short-term rates, although it has less control over long-term rates.

(page 286/712)

PRACTICE

25. Government securities that take longer than one year to mature are called
    A. Treasury bills.
    B. government bonds.
    C. Federal bonds.
    D. Federal Fund bills.
    Answer: B. See p. 287/713. Bills mature in less than a year, bonds in one or more years.

26. The current interest rate on a one-year bond is 4%. On a similar bond next year the rate is expected to be 6%. According to the expectations theory of the term structure of interest rates, the current rate on a two-year bond is
   A. 2%.
   B. 4%.
   C. 5%.
   D. 10%.
   Answer: C. The two-year rate is the average of the current one-year rate and the one-year rate expected in the future—i.e., (6 + 4) / 2.

27. The current interest rate on a one-year bond is 4%. The current rate on a two-year bond is 7%. According to the expectations theory of the term structure of interest rates, the expected rate on a similar one-year bond next year is
   A. 3%.
   B. 5.5%.
   C. 7%.
   D. 10%.
   Answer: D. The two-year rate (7%) is the average of the current one-year rate (4%) and the one-year rate expected in the future (10%).

28. The Fed reduces the interest rate on Treasury bills by 1%. According to the expectations theory of the term structure of interest rates, the interest rate on 30-year government bonds will
   A. increase by more than 1%.
   B. increase by less than 1%.
   C. decrease by more than 1%.
   D. decrease by less than 1%.
   Answer: D. Rates move together but long-term rates tend to be more stable. See p. 287/713. The difficulty that the Fed experienced in 1992 in moving down 30-year mortgage rates is an example of this sluggishness.

A WORD TO THE WISE

Obviously, Chapters 11 (26) and 12 (27) go together. In Chapter 13 (28), this material will be combined with the earlier macroeconomic model of the goods market. To understand the more complex model, take some time *now* to make sure that you understand the reasoning behind supply and demand in the money market. Why does the money demand curve slope downward? What can shift it? Why is the money supply curve vertical? How will changes in each of the three policy tools affect its position? What is the reasoning behind the move from one equilibrium interest rate to the next? The following Practice Test should help you locate and correct any remaining weak points in your understanding.

 PRACTICE TEST

I. MULTIPLE CHOICE QUESTIONS.

Select the option that provides the single best answer.

_____D_____ 1. A Fed sale of securities to the banks will cause all of the following except
   A. a fall in bank reserves.
   B. an increase in the interest rate.
   C. a fall in the money supply.
   D. a fall in the value of the money multiplier.

_B_ 2. In the demand for money model developed in the text, all of the following are assumed to be true except that
  A. money-cash and checking account balances—earns no interest.
  B. income is received at a completely uniform rate throughout the month.
  C. bonds represent interest-bearing assets of all kinds.
  D. the timing of money inflow and money outflow for household expenses is mismatched.

_D_ 3. The money market is in equilibrium. Now the Fed buys securities. There will be an excess _____ money. This will cause the interest rate to _____
  A. demand for, fall.
  B. supply of, rise.
  C. demand for, rise.
  D. supply of, fall.

_B_ 4. The quantity of money demanded is _____ related to the dollar volume of transactions and _____ related to the interest rate.
  A. positively, positively.
  B. positively, negatively.
  C. negatively, positively.
  D. negatively, negatively.

_C_ 5. A fall in the price level will _____ the demand for money, and a rise in the number of transactions will _____ the demand for money.
  A. increase, increase.
  B. increase, decrease.
  C. decrease, increase.
  D. decrease, decrease.

_C_ 6. Each of the following will make the public wish to hold more money balances except
  A. an increase in the price level.
  B. a decrease in the interest rate.
  C. an increase in the opportunity cost of holding money.
  D. an increase in the dollar volume of transactions.

_B_ 7. The money market is in equilibrium. Now there is an expansion in the money supply. This will cause the interest rate to _____ and the quantity of money demanded to _____
  A. increase, increase.
  B. decrease, increase.
  C. decrease, decrease.
  D. increase, decrease.

_B_ 8. The demand for money is a _____ measure, and the supply of money is a _____ measure.   D
  A. flow, flow.
  B. flow, stock.
  C. stock, flow.
  D. stock, stock.

_A_ 9. When the interest rate rises,
  A. the opportunity cost of holding money increases.
  B. the transactions cost of holding money increases.
  C. the transactions cost of holding money decreases.
  D. the opportunity cost of holding money decreases.

_B_   10. The Fed's ability to control the money supply is due to its ability to
   A. encourage banks not to borrow too heavily.
   B. affect banking system reserves.
   C. sell Treasury bonds at a profit.
   D. buy Treasury bonds at a profit.

_A_   11. The current interest rate on a one-year bond is 8%. On a similar bond next year the rate is expected to rise to 10%, and the year after a similar bond is expected to earn 15%. According to the expectations theory of the term structure of interest rates, the current rate on a three-year bond is around
   A. 8%.
   B. 10%.
   C. 11%.
   D. 15%.

_B_   12. Each of the following will cause an increase in the money supply except
   A. a reduction in the required reserve ratio.
   B. an increase in the demand for money.
   C. a purchase of securities by the Fed from the public.
   D. a purchase of securities by the Fed from the commercial banks.

_D_   13. Given an interest rate increase,
   A. optimal money balances will increase.
   B. optimal money balances will decrease.
   C. the equilibrium supply of money will increase.
   D. the equilibrium supply of money will decrease.

_C_   14. The slope of the money demand curve illustrates the idea that there is
   A. a positive relationship between the interest rate and the quantity of money demanded.
   B. a positive relationship between the price level and the quantity of money demanded.
   C. a negative relationship between the interest rate and the quantity of money demanded.
   D. a negative relationship between the value of transactions and the quantity of money demanded.

_C_   15. The money demand curve will shift right in each of the following cases except when
   A. the price level increases.
   B. the interest rate increases.
   C. the nominal output level increases.
   D. the real output level increases.

_A_   16. Which of the following pairs of events will definitely result in an increase in the equilibrium interest rate? A(n) _____ in the level of aggregate output and a(n) _____ in the required reserve ratio.
   A. increase, increase.
   B. increase, decrease.
   C. decrease, increase.
   D. decrease, decrease.

_A_   17. As the number of economic transactions increases,
   A. more money will be demanded.
   B. less money will be demanded.
   C. more money will be supplied.
   D. less money will be supplied.

_C_ 18. The Fed conducts an open market sale. We would predict each of the following except
  A. a decrease in the money supply.
  B. an increase in the interest rate.
  C. an increase in the price of bonds.
  D. a decrease in the quantity of money demanded.

_D_ 19. If the Fed were to announce that it would follow an "easy" monetary policy over the next few months, we would expect to see each of the following except
  A. an increasing money supply.
  B. open market purchases of securities by the Fed.
  C. falling interest rates.
  D. a rising required reserve ratio.

_B_ 20. When the Fed undertakes open market operations, the interest rate that it controls most closely is the
  A. prime rate.
  B. discount rate.   _C_
  C. federal funds rate.
  D. government bond rate.

II. APPLICATION QUESTIONS.

1. The money market and the bond market are closely intertwined. Explain what will happen to the price of bonds and to money holdings if the Fed changes the interest rate as a result of a decrease in the money supply.

2. Cupro the copper miner earns $1,200 per month and his expenditures (which equal $1,200) proceed at a constant daily rate. Given transactions costs and interest he can earn on savings, he makes 4 trips to the bank each month.
  a. Calculate his average money demand (Md).
  b. Now suppose that the interest rate on Cupro's savings account increases. Predict what will happen to his average money demand.
  c. Now suppose that the bank announces that the withdrawal forms for savings accounts must be notarized (an expensive and time-consuming business). Predict what will happen to Cupro's average money demand.

3. Suppose you are lucky enough to get a monthly paycheck of $1,750 which is automatically deposited at the beginning of each month into a checking account. You will spend the entire $1,750 each month, but you can transfer funds into bonds that earn 1% interest each month. Transferring between bonds and money requires you to pay a $1.50-per-transfer charge. Use the following table (based on those in Appendix B in the textbook) to calculate each of the following:
  a. Your optimal money demand.
  b. The optimal amount of money to transfer each time you go to the automatic teller machine (ATM).
  c. The optimal number of trips to take to the automatic teller machine (ATM).
  d. Your optimal total cost of holding money over the month.

NUMBER OF SWITCHES	AVERAGE MONEY HOLDINGS	AVERAGE BOND HOLDINGS	INTEREST EARNED	COST OF SWITCHING	NET PROFIT
0	_____	_____	_____	_____	_____
1	_____	_____	_____	_____	_____
2	_____	_____	_____	_____	_____
3	_____	_____	_____	_____	_____
4	_____	_____	_____	_____	_____
5	_____	_____	_____	_____	_____
6	_____	_____	_____	_____	_____
7	_____	_____	_____	_____	_____
8	_____	_____	_____	_____	_____

   e. Your income rises to $2,000 per month, the brokerage fee is $2.50, and the interest rate rises to 1%. Predict what will happen to your money demand.

   f. Your income is $1,750, the brokerage fee is $2.50, and the interest rate rises to 5%. Predict what will happen to your money demand.

   g. Your income is $1,750, the interest rate is 1%, and the brokerage fee falls to $1.00. Predict what will happen to your money demand.

4. Maureen buys a $1,000 fixed rate perpetual bond at the going market interest rate of 10%. Note: A perpetual bond (or "consol") is a bond with no maturity date. The payment received on the bond is constant at $100 per year. To calculate the yield on the bond, use the formula:

$$\text{(payment on bond} \times 100\%) / \text{Price of Bond}$$

Initially, the yield on the bond is competitive with the interest rate to be earned elsewhere in the financial market. Suppose now that the market interest rate decreases to 5% (Situation A).

	PRICE OF BOND	PAYMENT ON BOND	YIELD ON BOND	MARKET INTEREST RATE
Initial Purchase	$1000	$100	10%	10%
Situation A	_____	$100	_____	5%
Situation B	_____	$100	_____	20%

   a. What yield must Maureen's bond have to be competitive with other financial assets?

   b. In Situation A, is Maureen's bond attractive or unattractive to potential buyers?

   c. If Maureen decides to sell the bond, which price is fair, relative to the rest of the market?

Suppose the interest rate increases from 10% to 20% (Situation B).

   d. In Situation B, is Maureen's bond attractive or unattractive to potential buyers?

   e. If Maureen decides to sell the bond, which price is fair, relative to the rest of the market?

5. The Arbezani money demand curve is given by the following equation:
$$M^d = 5{,}000 - 10{,}000r + .5Y$$
M^d is money demand, r is the real interest rate, and Y is aggregate income.
   a. Suppose that aggregate income is 3,000. Graph the money demand curve (M_1^d) below. (It's a straight line.)

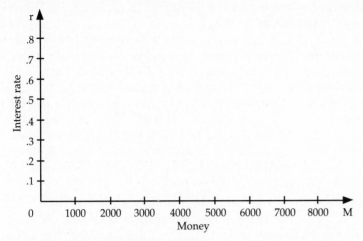

   b. Why does the equation have a negative value for the second term and a positive value for the third term?
   c. At an interest rate of 10% (r = .1), calculate money demand.
   d. At an interest rate of 20% (r = .2), calculate money demand.
   e. Suppose that the equilibrium interest rate is 30% (r = .3). Draw the money supply curve (Ms) on the diagram.
   f. Income rises from Y = 3,000 to Y = 5,000. Draw the new money demand curve (M_2^d) on the diagram.
   g. At the existing interest rate, there is an excess _____ (demand / supply) of money.
   h. The new equilibrium interest rate will be _____.
   i. How much must the money supply increase to restore the original interest rate?
   j. The required reserve ratio in Arbez is 10%. How great an open market purchase or sale of securities should ArbeFed (the central bank) undertake to restore the original interest rate? Purchase / sale of

   _____.

6. Arlene, Charlene, and Darlene each earn and spend $24,000 each year. What is the average money holding in each case?
   a. Arlene is paid yearly. _____
   b. Charlene is paid quarterly. _____
   c. Darlene is paid monthly. _____

7. Will money demand increase (I) or decrease (D) in each of the following cases?
   a. _____ The aggregate price level rises.
   b. _____ New technology makes access to the stock market instantaneous using a home computer.
   c. _____ More credit cards are accepted.
   d. _____ It is arranged nationally that all bills and income will be received on the first day of each month.
   e. _____ The nominal GDP level increases.
   f. _____ Weakening of strict regulation of the financial sector makes buying bonds more risky.
   g. _____ Banks begin to require a $1,000 minimum balance to be kept in checking accounts at all times.

8. The required reserve ratio is 20%. The Fed wants to reduce the money supply by $60 million. Describe an open market operation that will achieve this goal.

Open market _____ (purchase/sale) in the amount of $_____.

9. Graphically, the supply curve for money is _____. The money supply does not depend on the _____ _____ or the level of _____ _____ (both factors that influence the demand for money). In the money market, the equilibrium interest rate is established where the quantity of money supplied equals the quantity demanded. If the interest rate is "too high," the quantity supplied will be _____ (greater/less) than the quantity demanded. To reach equilibrium, the interest rate must _____ (rise/fall). This will happen because, with an _____ (excess demand for/excess supply of) money, households will try to _____ (increase/decrease) their money holdings by _____ (buying/selling) bonds. Those selling bonds will be able to do so at a _____ interest rate.

If the interest rate is "too low," the quantity supplied will be _____ (greater/less) than the quantity demanded. To reach equilibrium, the interest rate must _____ (rise/fall). This will happen because, with an _____ (excess demand for/excess supply of) money, households will try to _____ (increase/decrease) their money holdings by _____ (buying/selling) bonds. Bond issuers will have to offer _____ (higher/lower) interest rates to attract buyers.

10. What happens to the amount of money demanded or supplied in each of the following cases? Draw a separate money demand and money supply graph for each part of this question, label the axes, and show how the change will shift the money demand and/or the money supply curve. Explain any curve shifts in each case. Show initial and final equilibrium interest rate and quantity of money.

a. The Fed sells securities in the open market while the economy is experiencing high inflation.

b. The Fed decreases the required reserve ratio during a recession.

c. During a deep recession, the Fed moves to hold the interest rate constant.

d. A rise in nominal GDP is accompanied by an increase in the discount rate.

e. The Fed conducts an open market purchase of securities and banks begin imposing a $50 charge on all returned checks.

f. The economy moves into a downturn and the commercial banks become more cautious in their lending policies.

ANSWERS AND SOLUTIONS

PRACTICE TEST

I. SOLUTIONS TO MULTIPLE CHOICE QUESTIONS

1. D. When the Fed sells securities to the commercial banks, the banks pay for them with reserves (Option A). As the reserves supporting the money supply fall, the money supply itself will decrease (Option B). As the money supply curve shifts to the left, the interest rate will increase (Option C). The money multiplier is determined by the size of the required reserve ratio, which has not changed.

2. B. Income is assumed to be "bunched up." See p. 271/697.

3. D. When the Fed buys securities, the money supply increases. There will be an excess supply of money at the initial interest rate, causing the interest rate to decrease.

4. B. Individuals need more spending power as their level of transactions increases. The amount of money demanded decreases when the interest rate increases because the interest rate is the opportunity cost of holding money. See p. 275/701.

5. C. When goods can be bought for less, fewer dollars are needed. See p. 278/704.

6. C. An increase in the opportunity cost of holding money is another way of describing an increase in the interest rate.

7. B. As the money supply increases, the interest rate will decrease, causing a movement down along the money demand curve (an increase in quantity demanded).

8. D. Both the demand for and the supply of money are measured at a point in time—clear evidence that they are stock variables. A flow is measured over a period of time.

9. A. Transactions cost includes the time and inconvenience involved in making a transaction and possible explicit costs such as handling fees. The opportunity cost of holding money is the interest rate.

10. B. See p. 282/708.

11. C. The current rate on a three-year bond is approximately the average of the interest rates on the three one-year bonds [(8 + 10 + 15) / 3]. See Appendix A.

12. B. A change in money demand will not affect the money supply. A reduction in the required reserve ratio will increase the money multiplier, increasing the money supply. A Fed purchase of securities will expand the money supply.

13. B. As the interest rate increases, the opportunity cost of holding money increases and, on average, less money will be held. The money supply is vertical—it is unaffected by changes in the interest rate.

14. C. The downward slope shows that the quantity of money demanded decreases as the interest rate increases. Note that it is true that an increase in the price level will increase the demand for money, but this is depicted as a rightward shift of the money demand curve.

15. B. A change in the interest rate causes a movement along the demand curve. Note that nominal output is the price level times real output and that one or the other must have risen for nominal output to increase.

16. A. An increase in the level of aggregate output will increase the demand for money, while an increase in the required reserve ratio will decrease money supply.

17. A. The dollar volume of transactions has a positive relationship with money demand.

18. C. An open market sale will reduce the money supply—see Chapter 11. A decrease in the money supply will drive up the interest rate. When the interest rate increases, the price of bonds decreases.

19. D. Increases in the required reserve ratio are intended to tighten up the money supply.

20. C. See p. 287/713.

II. SOLUTIONS TO APPLICATION QUESTIONS

1. If the Fed decreases the money supply, perhaps through an open market sale of securities, the equilibrium interest rate will increase. At the initial equilibrium interest rate, say 5%, the quantity of money demanded will now exceed quantity supplied—individuals do not have enough funds available to finance their necessary transactions. As a result, individuals will attempt to increase their money holdings by selling off bonds. As the demand for bonds dwindles, bond sellers must increase the reward for holding bonds (the interest rate) to attract customers. This interest rate is the opportunity cost of holding money. As the interest rate rises, the quantity of money demanded falls. The process continues until equilibrium is achieved.

2. a. $M^d = 1/2(1{,}200/4) = 150$.
   b. Cupro's average money demand will fall because he has more incentive to leave idle balances in the form of savings deposits rather than cash.
   c. With notarization of withdrawal forms, the cost involved in converting deposits into cash has increased. Cupro will reduce the number of withdrawals he makes. His average money balance will increase.

3. a. Refer to the table below.

NUMBER OF SWITCHES	AVERAGE MONEY HOLDINGS	AVERAGE BOND HOLDINGS	INTEREST EARNED	COST OF SWITCHING	NET PROFIT
0	$1,750.00	$0.00	$0.00	$0.00	$0.00
1	$875.00	$875.00	$8.75	$1.50	$7.25
2	$583.33	$1,166.67	$11.67	$3.00	$8.67
3	$437.50	$1,312.50	$13.12	$4.50	$8.62
4	$350.00	$1,400.00	$14.00	$6.00	$8.00
5	$291.67	$1,458.33	$14.58	$7.50	$7.08
6	$250.00	$1,500.00	$15.00	$9.00	$6.00

   b–d. Refer to the table above.
   e. Your money demand should rise.
   f. Your money demand should fall.
   g. Your money demand should fall.

4. a. 5%.
   b. Attractive. At the moment, it is yielding 10%, which is better than the market-wide 5%.
   c. The yield should be comparable with the market interest rate, otherwise Maureen is selling too cheaply.
      Yield = Payment on bond × 100% / Price of Bond
      $100 × 100% / Price of Bond = 5%.
      The market price of the bond is $2,000.
   d. Unattractive. At the moment, Maureen's bond is yielding 10%, which is less good than the market-wide 20%.
   e. The yield should be comparable with the market interest rate, otherwise Maureen is asking too high a price.
      Yield = Payment on bond × 100% / Price of Bond
      $100 × 100% / Price of Bond = 20%.
      The market price of the bond is $500.

As shown by the table, there is an inverse relationship between the market interest rate and the price of bonds.

	PRICE OF BOND	PAYMENT ON BOND	YIELD ON BOND	MARKET INTEREST RATE
Initial Purchase	$1000	$100	10%	10%
Situation A	$2000	$100	10%	5%
Situation B	$500	$100	10%	20%

5. a. See the diagram below. When the interest rate is zero, money demand is 6,500. When money demand is zero, $10,000r = 5,000 + 1,500$. $r = .65$, i.e., 65%.

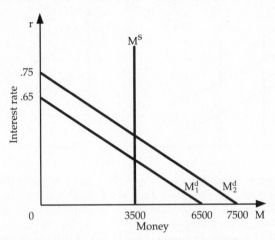

b. All this means is that there is a negative relationship between the demand for money and the interest rate, and a positive relationship between the demand for money and the level of spending in the economy.

c. Money demand = $5,000 − 10,000 (.1) + 1,500 = 5,500$.

d. Money demand = $5,000 − 10,000 (.2) + 1,500 = 4,500$.

e. Money demand = $5,000 − 10,000 (.3) + 1,500 = 3,500$. In equilibrium, the money supply, which graphs as a vertical line, must also be 3,500. See the diagram above.

f. See the diagram above. When the interest rate is zero, money demand is 7,500. When money demand is zero, $10,000r = 7,500$. $r = .75$, i.e., 75%.

g. excess demand. In fact, we can be precise. Money supply = 3,500. Money demand = $5,000 − 10,000 (.3) + 2,500 = 4,500$. There is an excess demand of 1,000.

h. Money supply = 3,500. To restore equilibrium, money demand must be 3,500. Money demand = $5,000 − 10,000 (x) + 2,500 = 3,500$. $x = .40$. The equilibrium interest rate is 40%.

i. $1,000. See the answer to part g.

j. The money multiplier = 1 / required reserve ratio = 10. An open market purchase of $100 would expand the money supply by $1,000.

6. a. Arlene holds an average of $12,000. Average holding = $24,000 / 2. Maximum withdrawal = $24,000 / 1 = $24,000.

b. Charlene holds an average of $3,000. Average holding = $6,000 / 2. Maximum withdrawal = $24,000 / 4 = $6,000.

c. Darlene holds an average of $1,000. Average holding = $2,000 / 2. Maximum withdrawal = $24,000 / 12 = $2,000.

7. a. I. Volume of transactions has a positive effect on money demand.

b. D. The transactions cost of transferring funds has become less, so withdrawals of money will be more frequent but less sizable. See p. 274/700.

c. D. As credit cards are used more, cash will be used less.

d. D. This new national arrangement reduces the problem of nonsynchronization. Money holdings needed to pay the flow of bills will be reduced.

e. I. Volume of transactions has a positive effect on money demand. See p. 278/704.

f. I. There will be more reluctance to hold bonds and less reluctance to hold money.

g. I. This is a transactions cost.

8. The Fed wants the money supply to contract, so an open market sale is called for. The money multiplier = 1 / required reserve ratio = 5. An open market sale of $12 million would reduce the money supply by $60 million.

9. vertical; interest rate; economic activity; greater; fall; excess supply of; decrease; buying; lower; less; increase; excess demand for; increase; selling; higher.

10. See the solutions below.

a. The Fed sale reduces the money supply; the rising price level will increase money demand. The two changes will drive the interest rate higher.

b. The decrease in the required reserve ratio will increase the money supply. Money demand will decrease during the recession. Together, the changes will lower the interest rate.

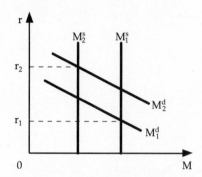

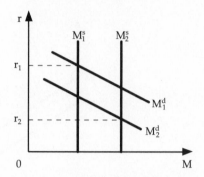

c. During a deep recession, money demand will shift left (decrease). This will decrease the interest rate. The Fed must reduce the money supply to hold the interest rate constant.

d. A rise in nominal GDP will increase the demand for money. An increase in the discount rate will decrease the money supply. Together, the changes will increase the interest rate.

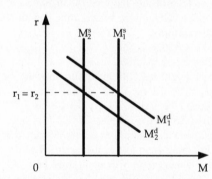

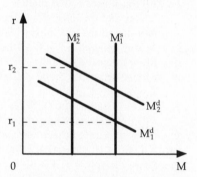

e. The open market purchase of securities will increase the money supply. The $50 bank charge will either encourage individuals to use cash more or to keep more funds in their (M1) checking accounts. The effect on the interest rate is ambiguous.

f. The downturn in the economy will decrease the demand for money; the new caution in lending will increase excess reserves, decrease the money multiplier, and reduce the money supply. The effect on the interest rate is ambiguous.

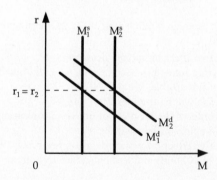

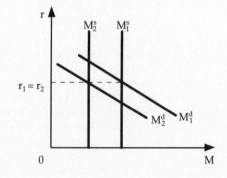

MONEY, THE INTEREST RATE, AND NATIONAL INCOME: ANALYSIS AND POLICY

13

COMBINED TEXT

28

OBJECTIVES: POINT BY POINT

After completing this chapter, you should be able to accomplish the objectives listed below.

General Comment

There's not much in this chapter that is new—it combines material that has been built up independently. The best study tip is to review your notes before beginning this material. If you lose track of the discussion, refer to the earlier chapters.

The most common mistake is to *not* recognize how the goods and money markets influence each other. Think of it this way: If the demand for goods and services is to be met, then output in the goods market must match demand, and this affects the dollar volume of transactions in the economy. Money demand must adjust to this circumstance. The money market must respond by matching the demand and supply of money. Changes in the money market affect the interest rate which impacts on investment decisions in the goods market. And so on.

> **TIP:** The *Answers and Solutions* section in this guide offers more detail and carefully traces through the relationships between the goods market and money market. Think of the "Answers" as additional practice—be sure to verify each step and to verify *why* each incorrect option is incorrect.

> **TIP:** The text is beginning to incorporate some "economic shorthand." It's very useful for you in note-taking, it shows the logical sequence of events, and it summarizes all the steps neatly. For some extra practice, work through each case in the textbook's Table 13 (28).7.

Caution! It is easy to forget, that an economic notation like "—>" represents underlying behavioral relationships that you must understand (rather than just memorize). Take the time to think about each step in these very condensed sequences.

OBJECTIVE 1: Identify the two links between the money market and the goods market. Outline the reasons for the inverse relationship between investment and the interest rate.

There are two links between the goods market and the money market.

  a. Goods market to money market link: Money demand is affected by the price level and the level of real output. A change in the interest rate changes the quantity of money demanded. If planned expenditure increases (decreases) in the goods market, the demand for money will increase (decrease), pushing up (down) the equilibrium interest rate. Because the demand for money depends on the level of economic activity, equilibrium in the money market depends on circumstances in the goods market.   (page 293/719)

  b. Money market to goods market link: If the interest rate rises, planned investment falls—higher borrowing costs make fewer investment projects profitable—and equilibrium output level falls. Because the level of planned aggregate expenditure (which includes planned investment) depends on the interest rate, equilibrium in the goods market depends on circumstances in the money market.   (page 293/719)

There must be a unique combination of output level and interest rate that will give simultaneous equilibrium in both markets.

> **TIP:** There are two main points to note here. First, the two markets are interlinked—the movement to equilibrium in one affects equilibrium in the other. Second, it's a two-way street—changes in the goods market affect the money market, and changes in the money market affect the goods market.

Comment: The text says that there is only one unique combination of r and Y that will equilibrate both markets simultaneously. Don't get this wrong! It doesn't mean that the economy can be in equilibrium only if the interest rate is 8% and output is $3,750 billion, for example. As "given" variables—G, T, or M^s for example—change, so will the specific r and Y values that will ensure equilibrium.

> **TIP:** Follow through the *feedback effects* between the two markets, and you will see that neither the AE nor the money demand curve will settle down to its final equilibrium immediately. As each one adjusts, so the other will adjust a little more. Eventually, they will reach final equilibrium. The diagrams have been drawn to depict the final equilibrium.

PRACTICE

1. The equilibrium interest rate is determined in the _____ market and the equilibrium output level is determined in the _____ market.
    A. goods, goods.
    B. goods, money.
    C. money, goods.
    D. money, money.

    Answer: C. See p. 292/718. In this chapter, we discover that the two markets do not operate in isolation.

2. Which of the following statements is false? *Ceteris paribus,*
    A. an increase in income will reduce the equilibrium interest rate.
    B. an increase in the interest rate will reduce planned investment.
    C. a decrease in money supply will decrease equilibrium output.
    D. when the economy slips into a recession, the interest rate will decrease.

    Answer: A. An increase in income will increase the demand for money, and this will increase the equilibrium interest rate.

3. When the interest rate decreases, the cost of financing investments
_____ and _____ investments projects will be undertaken.
   A. increases, more.
   B. increases, fewer.
   C. decreases, more.
   D. decreases, fewer.
   Answer: C. Lower interest rates mean lower borrowing costs for firms. As costs decrease, more projects become viable. See p. 293/719.

4. A decrease in the interest rate will cause
   A. the money supply curve to shift left.
   B. the money supply curve to shift right.
   C. the planned aggregate expenditure curve to shift up.
   D. the planned aggregate expenditure curve to shift down.
   Answer: C. A decrease in the interest rate will stimulate investment. As investment rises, the AE curve will shift up.

5. Which of the following statements is true? *Ceteris paribus,*
   A. r (up) —> Y (up) —> I (up) —>AE (up).
   B. r (up) —> Y (down) —> I (down) —>AE (down).
   C. r (up) —>AE (down) —>Y (down) —> I (down).
   D. r (up) —>I (down) —>AE (down) —> Y (down).
   Answer: D. See p. 295/721.

6. Which of the following statements is true? *Ceteris paribus,*
   A. Y (up) —> M^s (up) —>r (up).
   B. Y (up) —> M^s (down) —>r (up).
   C. Y (up) —> M^d (up) —>r (up).
   D. Y (up) —> M^d (down) —>r (up).
   Answer: C. See p. 297/723.

OBJECTIVE 2: Distinguish between fiscal policy and monetary policy. Distinguish between a contractionary and an expansionary policy, specifying the tools used in each case.

Expansionary (contractionary) policy is intended to expand (reduce) the equilibrium output level. Expansionary fiscal policy manipulates the economy through increases in the level of government spending and decreases in net taxes—contractionary fiscal policy reverses these changes. Expansionary monetary policy manipulates the economy through increases in the money supply. Tools of expansionary monetary policy include open market purchases, a decrease in the discount rate, and a decrease in the required reserve ratio. (page 297/723)

PRACTICE

7. The main goal of an expansionary fiscal policy is to _____; the main goal of an expansionary monetary policy is to _____
   A. increase output level, increase output level.
   B. increase output level, decrease the interest rate.
   C. decrease the interest rate, increase output level.
   D. decrease the interest rate, decrease the interest rate.
   Answer: A. Any expansionary policy is designed to make the economy grow. As a stepping-stone to achieving this goal, the interest rate may be decreased.

8. A decrease in net taxes intended to change output level in a particular direction is best described as a(n)
   A. expansionary fiscal policy.
   B. contractionary fiscal policy.
   C. expansionary monetary policy.
   D. contractionary monetary policy.
   Answer: A. A reduction in taxes will increase disposable income, consumption, and spending.

Use the diagram to answer the following question. AE_1 is the initial planned expenditure level, AE_2 is an intermediate level, and AE_3 is the final planned expenditure level. r_1 is the initial interest rate.

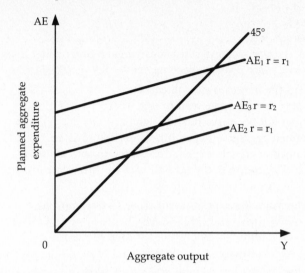

9. Which policy action would produce the changes seen in the diagram?
   A. An open market purchase.
   B. A decrease in net taxes.
   C. An increase in the required reserve ratio.
   D. A decrease in government spending.
   Answer: D. Cutting government spending will cut AE, given the interest rate. As output falls, money demand will fall, the interest rate will increase, and investment spending will increase. Option C is also a contractionary policy, but the interest rate would fall as the economy moved from AE_1 to AE_2. In the diagram it is shown as being constant.

OBJECTIVE 3: Explain when and how the crowding-out effect occurs. Explain the impact of the interest sensitivity of investment demand on the effectiveness of monetary policy.

Expansionary fiscal policy, while raising expenditures, also raises money demand and the interest rate—and the higher interest rate (the cost of borrowing funds) *discourages* planned investment. The policy *crowds out* private sector spending. The more sensitive investment plans are to changes in the interest rate, the greater the crowding out. The presence of the crowding-out effect reduces the potency of fiscal policy and the size of the government spending multiplier. The Fed can restore the potency of fiscal policy by increasing the money supply to prevent the interest rate increase—i.e., by "accommodating." (page 298/724)

> **TIP:** Notice an interesting point with the crowding-out effect—it occurs whether it's government spending or some other variable that's boosting the interest rate. If consumption were suddenly to increase, the extra aggregate expenditure would increase money demand and the interest rate, and investment would be reduced. In the real world, the crowding-out effect reduces not only the government spending multiplier, but the other expenditure multipliers too, even the balanced-budget multiplier.

10. Which of the following statements best describes the operation of the crowding out effect?
    A. G (up) —> Y (up) —> r (up) —> I (down).
    B. G (up) —> Y (up) —> M^d (up) —> r (up) —> I (down).
    C. G (up) —> Y (up) —> M^d (down) —> r (up) —> I (down).
    D. G (up) —> r (up) —> I (up).
    Answer: B. See p. 300/726.

11. An increase in government spending will lead to a(n) _____ in planned aggregate expenditure and a(n) _____ in planned investment.
    A. increase, increase.
    B. increase, decrease.
    C. decrease, increase.
    D. decrease, decrease.
    Answer: B. The government spending increase crowds out investment spending because of a higher interest rate, but, despite this, the expansionary fiscal policy will still cause planned expenditure to increase.

12. The crowding-out effect depends on all of the following except
    A. the interest sensitivity of investment.
    B. how much money demand increases as spending increases.
    C. the slope of the planned investment schedule.
    D. how much the money supply decreases as spending increases.
    Answer: D. Money supply doesn't decrease as spending increases. Note that Options A and C are saying the same thing.

13. An open market sale of securities will be more _____, the _____ the interest sensitivity of investment.
    A. expansionary, greater.
    B. expansionary, less.
    C. contractionary, greater.
    D. contractionary, less.
    Answer: C. An open market sale is a contractionary policy that will increase the interest rate. The effect on planned investment (and aggregate expenditure) will be greater the more interest-sensitive investors are.

OBJECTIVE 4: Outline the issues involved in determining the optimal policy mix.

Because fiscal and monetary policies work in different ways, the effectiveness of policy can be increased if a complementary blend of fiscal and monetary policy could be achieved. Such a mix could, for example, increase output without changing the interest rate.   (page 304/730)

Good examples of effective combinations of policies are mentioned on pp. 301–304 (727–730)—the crowding-out effect of expansionary fiscal policy was forestalled by expansionary monetary policy.

> **TIP:** Fiscal and monetary policies may be coordinated. If the magnitudes of the shifts are unknown, then either the effect on equilibrium output or on equilibrium interest rate *must* be uncertain. Break down the problem into two separate analyses, one for the "fiscal policy change" and the other for the "monetary policy change." In each case, decide the direction of change in output and interest rate, and then add them together.

Example: a net tax decrease and a discount rate decrease.

	Output Change	*Interest Change*
Fiscal Policy Effect	increase	increase
Monetary Policy Effect	increase	decrease
Total effect	increase	uncertain

In this case, where net taxes decrease and the discount rate decreases, we would predict a certain increase in output and an uncertain change in interest.

Note that output and the interest rate will always move in the *same* direction for a given fiscal policy change, but will always move in *opposite* directions for a given monetary policy.

14. The more interest sensitive investment demand is, the _____ effective fiscal policy is and the _____ effective monetary policy is.
    A. more, more.
    B. more, less.
    C. less, more.
    D. less, less.
    Answer: C. If investment is very sensitive to interest-rate changes, fiscal policy effectiveness is reduced because of the crowding-out effect. Monetary policy, whose influence on spending is through changes in the interest rate, is rendered more powerful.

Use the following diagrams to answer the next question.

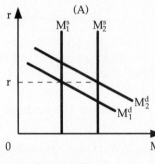
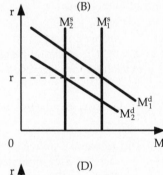
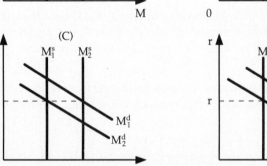
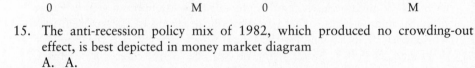

15. The anti-recession policy mix of 1982, which produced no crowding-out effect, is best depicted in money market diagram
    A. A.
    B. B.
    C. C.
    D. D.
    Answer: A. An expansionary fiscal policy increased money demand and an accommodating monetary policy increased money supply to prevent an interest rate increase. See p. 302/728.

16. The government is running a deficit. A new balanced-budget requirement is passed that will take effect next year. This change will make the AE curve shift _____. To maintain the same level of output next year, the central bank should adopt a(n) _____ monetary policy.
    A. up, expansionary.
    B. up, contractionary.
    C. down, expansionary.
    D. down, contractionary.

    Answer: C. To balance the budget, either G must decrease or T must increase—a contractionary fiscal policy. To counteract this, the central bank will have to adopt an expansionary policy.

17. Arboc is in a deep recession, with 35% of its capital not being used. A(n) _____ _____ policy is most likely to be effective in increasing output.
    A. expansionary fiscal.
    B. expansionary monetary.
    C. contractionary fiscal.
    D. contractionary monetary.

    Answer: A. This economy needs an expansionary policy. Investment, with such high underutilization of capital, is unlikely to be responsive to interest rate reductions—the crowding-out effect will be slight. Also, if investment is not responsive to interest rate changes, monetary policy is unlikely to have much effect.

OBJECTIVE 5: List and explain the effect of the determinants of planned investment.

Planned investment depends on the interest rate, expectations about future sales, capital utilization rates (low rates of usage mean low investment), and the cost of capital relative to labor. (page 305/731)

18. Which of the following will cause an increase in planned investment?
    A. an increase in the interest rate.
    B. an increase in the relative cost of labor.
    C. an increase in business pessimism.
    D. a decrease in capital utilization rates.

    Answer: B. If the cost of labor becomes relatively more expensive, the cost of capital becomes relatively less expensive.

OBJECTIVE 6: (Appendix) Explain what is depicted by the IS curve and the LM curve.

The IS/LM model presents the combinations of output and interest rate that will give equilibrium in the goods market (IS) and the money market (LM). The *IS curve* depicts combinations of output and the interest rate that give an equilibrium in the goods market, while the *LM curve* depicts all combinations of output and the interest rate that give an equilibrium in the money market. The IS curve has a negative slope because, in the goods market, a higher interest rate would reduce investment spending and cause a lower equilibrium output level. The LM curve has a positive slope because higher output levels would boost money demand, causing higher interest rates. Policy variables that cause the IS curve to shift are government purchases and net taxes. The policy variable that causes the LM curve to shift is the money supply. Changes in income and the interest rate result in movements along the curves. (page 308/734)

> **Comment:** Do *not* think of the IS and LM curves as aggregate demand and supply curves. In fact, both curves contribute to our understand of the demand side of the economy.

> **Graphing Pointer:** IS/LM gives you a glimpse of a more complex model of the macroeconomy. Aim for an intuitive understanding.

Take each policy variable (G, T, M^s) in turn. First, ask what you would predict if that variable were to increase. [An increase in G, for instance, would cause Y to increase in the *goods market* as a first effect.] Now ask what should be happening in the "other market." [Higher levels of economic activity boost money demand, and the interest rate will rise.] Result: The IS/LM diagram shifts in such a way that Y increases and r increases—this must be represented by a shift right in the IS (goods market) curve. The "other market" curve does not shift.

Repeat this procedure for each case. Also do policy mixes using the procedure outlined in the Tip to Objective 4 above.

> **Graphing Pointer:** You may find it easier to piece together the IS-LM analysis if you incorporate the goods market and money market diagrams explicitly. The following questions are designed to guide you through the analysis.

PRACTICE

Use the following diagram to answer the next four questions. Point A is a point of equilibrium in the goods market, corresponding to AE1 and an interest rate of 8%.

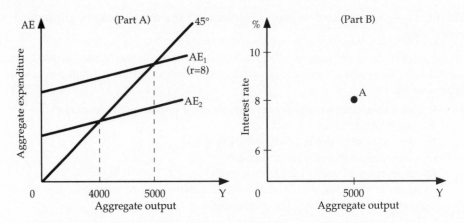

19. In the goods market, the AE curve might shift from AE_1 to AE_2 if the interest rate _____. The IS curve has a _____ slope.
    A. increases, positive.
    B. increases, negative.
    C. decreases, positive.
    D. decreases, negative.
    Answer: B. The AE curve would decrease because planned investment decreases as the interest rate increases.

20. Sketch in the IS curve (IS_1) in Part B of the diagram above.
    Answer: See the *Answers and Solutions* section.

21. The interest rate is 8% and spending is shown by AE_1. If government spending increases, then, at the same interest rate, the equilibrium output level will _____. The IS curve will shift to the _____
    A. increase, right.
    B. increase, left.
    C. decrease, right.
    D. decrease, left.
    Answer: A. An expansionary fiscal policy will increase planned aggregate expenditure and shift the IS curve to the right.

22. Sketch in the new IS curve (IS$_2$) in Part B of the diagram above.
    Answer: See the *Answers and Solutions* section.

Use the diagram below to answer the next four questions. Point B shows equilibrium in the money market, at an interest rate of 8% and an output level of 5,000.

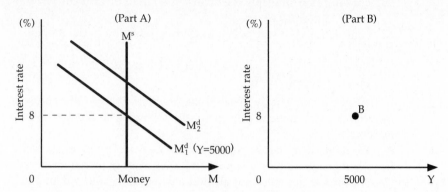

23. In the money market, the money demand curve might shift from M$_1^d$ to M$_2^d$ if the output level _____. The LM curve has a _____ slope.
    A. increases, positive.
    B. increases, negative.
    C. decreases, positive.
    D. decreases, negative.
    Answer: A. As output level increases, money demand increases. The equilibrium interest rate increases—LM has a positive slope.

24. Sketch in the LM curve (LM$_1$) in Part B of the diagram above.
    Answer: See the *Answers and Solutions* section.

25. The interest rate is 8% and money demand is M$_1^d$. If the money supply increases, then, given the output level, the equilibrium interest rate will _____. The LM curve will shift _____
    A. increase, up and to the right.
    B. increase, down and to the left.
    C. decrease, up and to the right.
    D. decrease, down and to the left.
    Answer: C. An expansionary monetary policy decreases the interest rate, given the output level, and shifts the LM curve to the right.

26. Sketch in the new LM curve (LM$_2$) in Part B of the diagram above.
    Answer: See the *Answers and Solutions* section.

PRACTICE TEST

I. MULTIPLE CHOICE QUESTIONS.

Select the option that provides the single best answer.

_____ 1. In each of the following cases we would expect the interest rate to decrease, except when
    A. there is a decrease in the required reserve ratio.
    B. the government increases tax collections.
    C. government spending is increased.
    D. there is a reduction in the level of economic activity.

_____ 2. The feedback effect between the goods market and money market is best illustrated by the situation when, for example,
   A. contractionary monetary policy leads to a reduction in the money supply.
   B. consumption suddenly rises causing a fall in investment due to a rising interest rate.
   C. contractionary fiscal policy leads to a reduction in the money supply.
   D. the value of the money multiplier is reduced due to an increasing required reserve ratio.

_____ 3. If the Fed simultaneously lowered the required reserve ratio and sold government securities, which one of the following would not be a possible consequence?
   A. An increase in money supply and an increase in money demand.
   B. An increase in money supply and a decrease in money demand.
   C. A decrease in money supply and a decrease in money demand.
   D. A rise in the interest rate.
   (Be careful on this one!)

_____ 4. Which of the following would not accompany a fall in the discount rate?
   A. An expansion in the money supply.
   B. A rise in planned investment.
   C. An unplanned rise in inventories.
   D. An increase in aggregate output (income).

_____ 5. The money and goods markets are in equilibrium. Now there is an _expansion_ in the money supply. This will _____ investment and cause the demand for money to _____
   A. reduce, increase.
   B. stimulate, increase.
   C. stimulate, decrease.
   D. reduce, decrease.

_____ 6. An increase in planned aggregate expenditure will make the interest rate _____ while an increase in the money supply will make planned expenditure _____
   A. increase, increase.
   B. increase, decrease.
   C. decrease, increase.
   D. decrease, decrease.

_____ 7. A decrease in net personal income taxes will cause
   A. the LM curve to shift to the left.
   B. the IS curve to shift to the right.
   C. the AE curve to shift downward.
   D. investment to increase.

_____ 8. An increase in money supply will result in _____ output and a _____ interest rate.
   A. higher, lower.
   B. higher, higher.
   C. lower, lower.
   D. lower, higher.

_____ 9. MPC is .8. Which of the following might achieve the goal of increasing output by $200 billion? Assume that some crowding out occurs.
   A. An increase in government spending of $40 billion.
   B. A decrease in taxes of $50 billion.
   C. An increase in government spending of $50 billion.
   D. An increase in government spending and in taxes, each of $50 billion.

_____ 10. An open market purchase of securities by the Fed will cause
  A. the interest rate to fall.
  B. a decrease in the quantity of money demanded.
  C. a shortage of money at the original equilibrium interest rate.
  D. the AE curve to shift down (to the right).

_____ 11. A simultaneous increase in net taxes and open market sale of securities by the Fed will _____ equilibrium output and _____ the interest rate.
  A. increase, decrease.
  B. decrease, have an indeterminate effect on.
  C. decrease, increase.
  D. have an indeterminate effect on, increase.

_____ 12. Planned investment certainly will increase when the interest rate _____ and the cost of labor _____ (relative to the cost of capital).
  A. increases, increases.
  B. increases, decreases.
  C. decreases, increases.
  D. decreases, decreases.

_____ 13. The _____ curve will shift to the _____ if the government cuts taxes.
  A. IS, right.
  B. IS, left.
  C. LM, right.
  D. LM, left.

_____ 14. The _____ curve will shift to the _____ if the Fed buys securities.
  A. IS, right.
  B. IS, left.
  C. LM, right.
  D. LM, left.

_____ 15. Which of the following statements is false? _Ceteris paribus,_
  A. the lower the level of aggregate output, the lower the interest rate.
  B. when the interest rate falls, planned aggregate expenditure increases.
  C. as real output level increases, money demand increases.
  D. as money demand increases, real output level increases.

_____ 16. An open market sale of government securities is a(n) _____ monetary policy. The AE curve will shift _____
  A. expansionary, up.
  B. expansionary, down.
  C. contractionary, up.
  D. contractionary, down.

_____ 17. The intended goal of an expansionary policy
  A. is an increase in the level of aggregate output.
  B. is an increase in the interest rate.
  C. is a decrease in the interest rate.
  D. depends on whether a fiscal policy or a monetary policy is used.

Use the diagram to answer the following question. AE_1 is the initial planned expenditure level, AE_2 is an intermediate level, and AE_3 is the final planned expenditure level. r_1 is the initial interest rate.

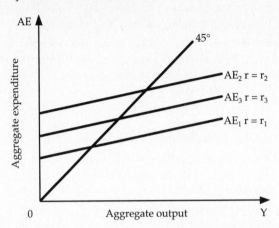

_____ 18. Which policy action would produce the changes seen in the diagram?
A. An open market purchase.
B. A decrease in net taxes.
C. An increase in the required reserve ratio.
D. An increase in government spending.

_____ 19. An increase in government spending will cause a decrease in planned investment, most directly as a result of an increase in
A. aggregate output.
B. the interest rate.
C. the money supply.
D. the price level.

_____ 20. Which circumstance will not strengthen the crowding-out effect?
A. a higher interest-sensitivity of investment.
B. a higher money demand as spending increases.
C. a steeper slope of the AE curve.
D. a greater money multiplier.

_____ 21. Which of the following statements best describes an expansionary monetary policy?
A. M^s (up) —> r (up) —> I (down) —> Y (up) —> r (up) —> M^d (down).
B. M^s (up) —> r (down) —> I (down) —> Y (down) —> M^d (up).
C. M^s (up) —> r (down) —> I (up) —> Y (up) —> M^d (up).
D. M^s (up) —> r (down) —> I (up) —> M^d (up) —> Y (up).

_____ 22. In the presence of a crowding-out effect, a contractionary fiscal policy will result in a _____ in output than if there were no crowding-out effect.
A. larger increase.
B. smaller increase.
C. larger decrease.
D. smaller decrease.

_____ 23. The IS curve has a _____ slope and depicts equilibrium in the _____ market.
A. positive, goods.
B. positive, money.
C. negative, goods.
D. negative, money.

_____ 24. There is a negative relationship between planned investment and the interest rate described by the equation $I = 120 - 10r$. Planned investment will decrease by moving along the curve if
  A. the Fed buys bonds in the open market.
  B. the government increases welfare payments.
  C. entrepreneurs expect sales to decline in the future.
  D. the government cuts back in government spending.

_____ 25. If the Fed buys bonds in the open market at the same time as the government increases government spending, the crowding-out effect will be _____. The _____ interest-sensitive planned investment is, the smaller the crowding-out effect will be.
  A. heightened, more.
  B. heightened, less.
  C. diminished, more.
  D. diminished, less.

II. APPLICATION QUESTIONS.

1. A businesswoman, Kathleen Williamson, hires you as an economic consultant to assist her in her investment decisions.
   a. The government has announced a reduction in income taxes and an increase in welfare benefits. Interpret these policy actions.
      i. Are they expansionary or contractionary?
      ii. How will they affect the interest rate?
      iii. Importantly, how will they affect planned business investment?
      iv. The following IS-LM diagram shows the economy before the policies are initiated. Show how the curve(s) shift(s) in response to the policies.

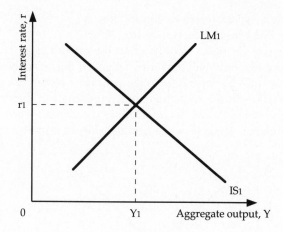

b. Ignore the policy actions in part a. The Fed announces an immediate increase in the reserve requirement and decrease in the discount rate. Interpret these policy actions.
   i. Are they expansionary or contractionary?
   ii. How will they affect the interest rate?
   iii. Importantly, how will they affect planned business investment?
   iv. The following IS-LM diagram shows the economy before the policies are initiated. Show how the curve(s) shift(s) in response to the policies.

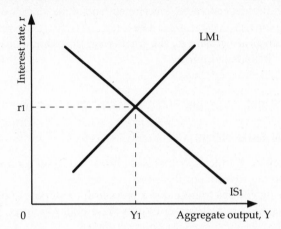

c. Ignore the policy actions in parts a and b. The government initiates an aggressive program of highway construction and inner-city development, effective immediately. Simultaneously, the Fed announces an immediate increase in its purchases of bonds on the open market. Interpret these policy actions.
   i. Are they expansionary or contractionary?
   ii. Is the Fed action accommodating? Why?
   iii. IHow will the policy actions affect the interest rate?
   iv. Importantly, how will they affect planned business investment?
   v. Williamson's business sells to the consumer sector. What other factor(s) ought she to include in determining her investment plans?
   vi. The following IS-LM diagram shows the economy before the policies are initiated. Show how the curve(s) shift in response to the policies.

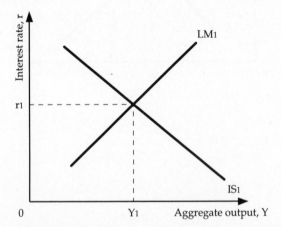

2. a. The Arbocali Minister of Finance (a confirmed believer in the multiplier) notes that the marginal propensity to consume out of income is .8. Because Arboc is presently in a recession, he predicts that a 5 million opek increase in government spending will boost output by 25 million opeks. Although a quite junior official in the Ministry, you believe that he is incorrect. Indicate as many assumptions as you can that he had made to arrive at his prediction.

b. The Minister (also a confirmed believer in IS-LM analysis) suspects that the economy is at some point *above* the LM curve but on the IS curve. This must be a point of disequilibrium. Explain the situation to him.

3. Farview, an economic forecasting firm, has hired you as a promising addition to the staff. Your assignment is to predict the effect of a given economic change on a number of variables, where "+" represents increase, "−" represents decrease, "0" represents no change, and "?" represents ambiguous result. Assume that there are progressive federal income taxes and that the initial change in a variable is the dominant one.

   a. The Fed reduces the discount rate. Predict the effect on:

Y	R	C	S	I	M^s	M^d	FEDERAL DEFICIT
___	___	___	___	___	___	___	___

   b. The government cuts personal income taxes. Predict the effect on:

Y	R	C	S	I	M^s	M^d	FEDERAL DEFICIT
___	___	___	___	___	___	___	___

   c. The capital utilization rate is 70% and firms believe that it should be 85%. Predict the effect on:

Y	R	C	S	I	M^s	M^d	FEDERAL DEFICIT
___	___	___	___	___	___	___	___

   d. There is heightened expectation of an interest rate decrease. Predict the effect on:

Y	R	C	S	I	M^s	M^d	FEDERAL DEFICIT
___	___	___	___	___	___	___	___

4. Determine the effect of each policy and other actions on the following five given variables. Label it (I) if the variable will increase, (D) if it will decrease, (U) if it will remain unchanged, and (?) if the result is ambiguous.

Policy	r	Y	M^s	M^d	I
Increase M^s					
Increase T					
Increase G					
An increase in optimism by entrepreneurs					
Income and payments become better synchronized					

5. Refer to the following diagram to answer this question.

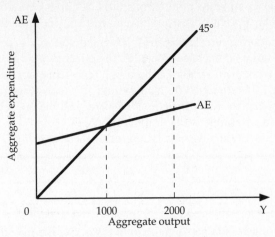

MPC is .8 and the full-employment level of production is 2,000.

a. Draw the money market in equilibrium. Label the curves M_1^d and M_1^s.

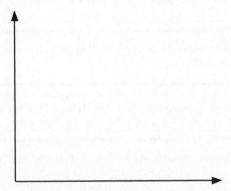

b. Using the *simple* goods market model, by how much would government spending have to change to move the economy to the full-employment equilibrium? Increase/decrease by _____. The government spending multiplier is _____.

c. Similarly, by how much would the tax level have to change to move the economy to full-employment equilibrium? Increase/decrease by _____. The tax multiplier is _____.

d. Similarly, by how much would government spending and tax levels have to increase (balanced-budget change) to move the economy to full-employment equilibrium? Increase by _____. The balanced-budget multiplier is _____.

Suppose we adopt the balanced-budget policy.

e. How much will the AE function shift vertically? Increase/decrease by _____. Show this on the diagram as AE′.

f. Unplanned inventory levels will _____ and output will _____.

g. Show the changes that occur in the money market. Label any new curves clearly.

h. Depict the new AE curve as AE" on the diagram. What has caused the change you've drawn?

i. Is the balanced-budget multiplier still equal to the value given in (d) above?

j. Suppose the Fed acts to prevent the crowding out. Amend your money market picture accordingly.

6. The text provides several examples of "economic shorthand" while tracing through the effects of given changes. Without referring back to the text, test your knowledge by indicating how each variable will change in the examples below. Write "U" if the variable goes up and "D" if the variable goes down as a consequence of the previous step.

   a. Expansionary fiscal policy involving a $100 change in G.

   G (U/D)—> Y (U/D) —> M^d (U/D) —> r (U/D) —> I (U/D) —> Y (U/D)

   b. Expansionary fiscal policy involving a $100 change in T.

   T (U/D)—> Y (U/D) —> M^d (U/D) —> r (U/D) —> I (U/D) —> Y (U/D)

   c. Will the total change in Y be greater in (a) than in (b)? Why or why not?

   d. Expansionary monetary policy.

   Begin by selecting the correct option for each monetary policy tool.

   Open market sale/purchase:]

   Discount rate increase/decrease:] —> M^s (U/D)

   Reserve requirement increase/decrease:]

   —> r (U/D) —> I (U/D) —> Y (U/D) —> M^d (U/D) —> r (U/D)

   e. The effects go in the opposite direction for contractionary policies.

ANSWERS AND SOLUTIONS

ANSWERS TO PRACTICE QUESTIONS

20–22. See the diagram below.

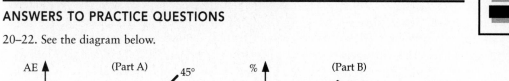

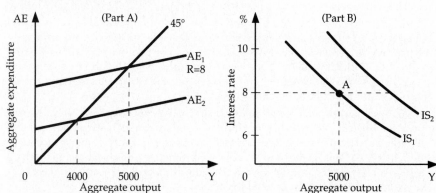

24-26.   See the diagram below.

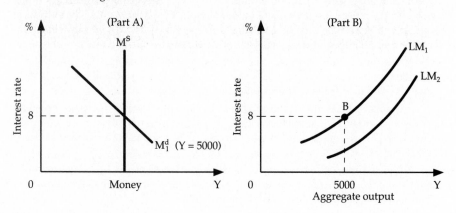

PRACTICE TEST

I. SOLUTIONS TO MULTIPLE CHOICE QUESTIONS

1. C. The increase in government spending is an expansionary policy. Expansionary policies increase money demand and, ultimately, the interest rate.

2. B. Option B correctly traces a feedback between markets. Options A and D are confined to the money market only. Option C is just wrong—the money supply is affected only by monetary policy variables.

3. B. Lowering the required reserve ratio is an expansionary monetary policy; selling securities is a contractionary monetary policy. The net effect on the money supply, therefore, is uncertain. If the money supply increases, the interest rate decreases, and the economy expands. This will increase money demand (Option A). If the money supply decreases, the interest rate increases (Option D), and the economy contracts. This will decrease money demand (Option C).

4. C. The discount rate reduction is an expansionary monetary policy, causing the money supply to increase (Option A) and the interest rate to decrease. An interest rate decrease will stimulate investment (Option B) and aggregate output (Option D). As spending increases, there will be an unplanned decrease in inventory levels.

5. B. The increase in the money supply will decrease the interest rate and stimulate investment. Planned aggregate expenditure will increase, prompting an increased transaction demand for money.

6. A. If planned aggregate expenditure increases, the demand for money will increase, as will the interest rate. An expansion in the money supply, which pushes down the interest rate, will stimulate investment and, therefore, planned aggregate expenditure.

7. B. The IS curve reports changes in the goods market. If net taxes decrease, aggregate expenditure will increase at each interest rate, shifting the IS curve to the right.

8. A. This expansionary monetary policy will reduce the interest rate and raise output.

9. C. If MPC is .8, the expenditure multiplier is 5, and the tax multiplier is –4. (Check Chapter 10 if you can't verify these values.) As noted on p. 303/729, the feedback effect from the money market reduces the size of these multipliers. Options A and B will fall short of $200 billion. The balanced-budget action (Option D) has a maximum increase of $50 billion. Option C may be overkill (we can't tell), but it has the possibility of hitting the $200 billion target.

10. A. An open market purchase will increase the money supply, causing an excess supply at the original interest rate (not Option C) and making the interest rate decrease (Option A). The interest rate decrease will increase the quantity of money demanded (not Option B). This interest rate decrease will stimulate investment and planned aggregate expenditure (not Option D). As planned expenditure increases, there will be an increased transaction demand for money.

11. B. An increase in net taxes is a contractionary policy and a sale of securities is also a contractionary policy. Equilibrium output will decrease. The sale of securities will decrease the money supply, forcing up the interest rate. However, the contraction in output will reduce the transaction demand for money. A decrease in the demand for money will pull down the interest rate. The effect on the interest rate is ambiguous.

12. C. As the interest rate decreases, the cost of new investments decreases and their profitability increases. As the cost of labor increases, employers will use less labor-intensive and more capital-intensive methods of production.

13. A. A change in taxes affects the goods market initially. Planned aggregate expenditure will increase, given the interest rate. At each interest rate, then, the equilibrium output level in the goods market will increase. This is shown as a rightward shift of the IS curve.

14. C. An open market purchase affects the money market initially by increasing the money supply. At the same output level as before, the interest rate will be lower. This is shown as a rightward shift of the LM curve.

15. D. As real output level increases, more money is demanded to finance the increased volume of transactions (Option C). However, as money demand increases, the interest rate rises, and this depresses investment and real output level (Option D). As output decreases, money demand and the interest rate decrease (Option A). Decreases in the interest rate stimulate investment and expenditure (Option B).

16. D. An open market sale reduces the money supply, increases the interest rate, discourages investment, and pushes down the AE curve.

17. A. All expansionary policies are intended to expand equilibrium output level.

18. A. An open market purchase will reduce the interest rate (from r_1 to r_2) and stimulate planned aggregate expenditure through higher investment. As spending increases, money demand increases, pushing up the interest rate (to r_3). Planned expenditure will decrease.

19. B. An increase in government spending will increase aggregate output (Option A), but the most direct reason for the "crowding out" of investment is the interest rate increase. See p. 298/724.

20. D. The size of the money multiplier is irrelevant. As government spending increases, the steeper the AE curve, the greater the initial expansion in spending. Given the spending increase, the more money demand increases, the more the interest rate will increase. The more sensitive entrepreneurs are to interest-rate increases, the greater the decrease in investment.

21. C. See p. 301/727. The higher money supply reduces the interest rate, which stimulates planned investment. As spending increases, money demand increases.

22. D. The crowding-out effect reduces fiscal policy effectiveness. See p. 303/729.

23. C. As the interest rate increases, investment (and aggregate expenditure) decrease, and the equilibrium output level decreases. See p. 308/734.

24. B. A movement along the curve is caused by a change in the interest rate. If the interest increases, investment will decrease. Option A indicates an increase in the money supply and, therefore, a decrease in the interest rate. Option C would shift the curve. Option D is a contractionary policy, reducing income. Option B will expand spending, increasing the demand for money and the interest rate.

25. D. If the Fed increases the money supply the interest rate will decrease. If the government increases government spending, money demand will increase and the interest rate will increase. The effects counteract each other leading to a lesser crowding-out effect. Given the interest rate change, the impact on planned investment will be lower the less influenced are entrepreneurs by the interest rate.

II. SOLUTIONS TO APPLICATION QUESTIONS

1. a. Both actions will stimulate private sector spending—they are similar to an increase in government spending. As the economy expands, money demand will increase, causing an increase in the interest rate. A higher interest rate will reduce planed investment.

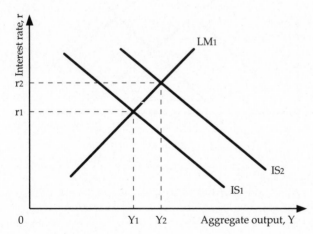

b. The first action is contractionary, while the second is expansionary. The effect on the interest rate is uncertain, therefore the effect on planned investment is uncertain. The LM curve will shift right as a result of the first action and left as a result of the second action. As shown below, the net effect is zero (although, depending on the relative strengths of the policies, the final LM curve could end up either to the left of to the right of LM_1.

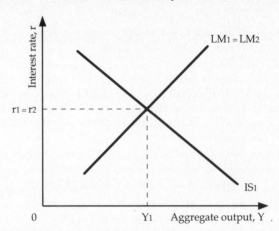

c. Both actions are expansionary. The Fed action is accommodating—the spending initiative will drive up interest rates while the Fed action will reduce them. The effect on the interest rate is uncertain, therefore the effect on planned investment is uncertain. As these policies are expansionary, you should predict higher levels of consumer spending. Even if the interest rate is unchanged, Ms. Williamson's planned investment might rise in expectation of increased sales, higher capital utilization rates, and more optimism about the future. The increased government spending will shift the IS curve to the right while the purchase of bonds will shift the LM curve to the right. Output will increase. The effect on the interest rate depends on the relative strength of the two shifts.

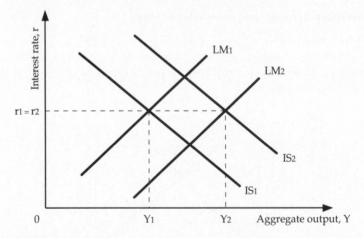

2. a. He has assumed that:
    i.   the marginal propensity to consume value will remain constant as the economy expands;
    ii. the bond-financed expansion in government spending will not provoke an increase in interest rates;
    iii. aggregate supply is horizontal, i.e., that, as aggregate demand increases, no price level increases will occur. (This is discussed in Chapter 14.)
    b. Given the level of output, the interest rate is "too high" and should be less, i.e., there is an excess supply in the money market. Because the economy is currently on the IS curve, there is equilibrium in the output market.

3. a. If the Fed reduces the discount rate, the money supply will increase and the interest rate will decrease. Investment will be stimulated, and aggregate output will increase. Consumption and saving will rise. Higher spending will provoke a higher money demand (which will partially offset the interest rate decrease). A higher level of activity will increase tax collections.

Y	R	C	S	I	M^s	M^d	FEDERAL DEFICIT
+	–	+	+	+	+	+	–

b. If the government cuts personal income taxes, consumption and saving will increase, and aggregate output will rise. Higher spending will increase the demand for money and push up the interest rate. As spending increases, tax collections will rise again somewhat.

Y	R	C	S	I	M^s	M^d	FEDERAL DEFICIT
+	+	+	+	–	0	+	+

c. If the capital utilization rate is too low, firms will reduce investment. As investment falls, output level will decrease. Consumption, saving, and tax collections will fall. The deficit will increase. There is no effect on money supply but money demand will be reduced. This will result in a decrease in the interest rate and a partially offsetting increase in investment.

Y	R	C	S	I	M^s	M^d	FEDERAL DEFICIT
–	–	–	–	–	0	–	+

d. A heightened expectation of an interest rate decrease implies a heightened expectation of a bond price increase. Asset holders will reduce the demand for money and increase the demand for bonds. As there is no change in the money supply, the interest rate will decrease. A decrease in the interest rate will stimulate additional planned investment and raise aggregate output. As output (income) increases, consumption and saving will rise, as will tax collections. The increase in expenditures will cause a partially offsetting increase in money demand and in the interest rate.

Y	R	C	S	I	M^s	M^d	FEDERAL DEFICIT
+	–	+	+	+	0	–	–

4. See the table below.

Policy	r	Y	M^s	M^d	I
Increase M^s	D	I	I	I	I
Increase T	D	D	U	D	I*
Increase G	I	I	U	I	D
An increase in optimism by entrepreneurs	I	?**	U	I	?**
Income and payments become better synchronized	D	I	U	D	I

Examples:

An increase in net taxes is a contractionary fiscal policy. Output level (Y) will decrease because consumers' disposable income is reduced. As output decreases, money demand will decrease. Because there is no monetary policy change, money supply is unchanged and the interest rate is decreased. As the interest rate decreases, planned investment is increased.

* Note the unusual result on investment when net taxes are increased.

An increase in optimism will stimulate planned investment, which will lead spending (and output) to increase. As spending increases, money demand increases and, given the unchanged money supply, the interest rate will increase. This will discourage investment.

** Presumably, the initial increase in investment will be greater than the secondary reduction in investment, although the model is not clear on this.

Better synchronization of income and payments will reduce money demand.

5. a. See the money market diagram below.

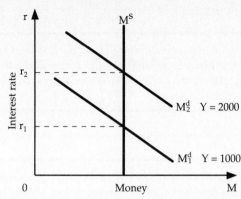

b. MPC is .8, therefore the government expenditure multiplier is 5. To move the economy to the full-employment output level, government spending would have to increase by 200.

c. MPC is .8, therefore the tax multiplier is –4. To move the economy to the full-employment output level, taxes would have to decrease by 250.

d. The balanced-budget multiplier is 1. Increase G and T by 1,000.

e. AE will increase by 200. See the diagram below.

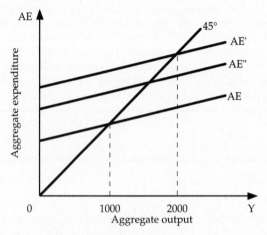

f. Inventory levels will fall and output will rise.

g. See the money market diagram above.

h. See the goods market diagram above. Investment, part of AE, has been driven down somewhat (presumably not by as much as 200!) because of the higher interest rate which has discouraged some investment projects.

i. No. The investment fall has reduced the power of the balanced budget multiplier. (You would get the same sort of result if you had used a straight increase in G or reduction in T.)

j. See the money market diagram in part a above.

6. a. $G\ (U) \longrightarrow Y\ (U) \longrightarrow M^d\ (U) \longrightarrow r\ (U) \longrightarrow I\ (D) \longrightarrow Y\ (D)$.

b. $T\ (D) \longrightarrow Y\ (U) \longrightarrow M^d\ (U) \longrightarrow r\ (U) \longrightarrow I\ (D) \longrightarrow Y\ (D)$.

c. The change will be greater in (a) because the government-spending multiplier is greater than the tax multiplier.

d. Open market purchase:]
    Discount rate decrease:] $\longrightarrow M^s\ (U)$
    Reserve requirement decrease:]
    $\longrightarrow r\ (D) \longrightarrow I\ (U) \longrightarrow Y\ (U) \longrightarrow M^d\ (U) \longrightarrow r\ (U)$.

AGGREGATE DEMAND, AGGREGATE SUPPLY, AND INFLATION

14

COMBINED TEXT

29

OBJECTIVES: POINT BY POINT

After completing this chapter, you should be able to accomplish the objectives listed below.

OBJECTIVE 1: Derive and explain the slope of the aggregate demand curve. Explain what the curve represents.

If the overall price level is allowed to increase, it will raise the interest rate through the increase in the demand for money, and therefore will affect the goods market (through cuts in planned investment and consumption). Equilibrium output falls. There is a negative relationship between the price level and the level of aggregate demand. The *aggregate demand* (AD) curve depicts the negative relationship between the price level and aggregate output. Each point on the curve is a point of equilibrium in both the money market and the goods market.   (page 313/739)

> **TIP:** AS/AD analysis is a powerful, but simple, tool. Note that the AD curve is *not* a market demand curve in any sense. The curve slopes because as the aggregate price level rises, investment and consumption are reduced in the face of a rising interest rate and shrinking wealth. Draw graphs of the money market and goods market on a piece of paper and keep it beside you as you work through the chapter. When price level rises, confirm that the quantity of output demanded decreases.

> **TIP:** Learn the variables! The AS/AD model you are dealing with is quite complex, with many relationships between variables. No variable is determined in isolation-a change in consumption spending will affect the goods market, the money market, wage rates, the interest rate, and the price level. The safest approach is to list and *learn* the determinants of each major variable.

> **TIP:** Don't forget about the factors that affect money demand. As we saw in the previous chapter, money demand is a key link between the goods market and the money market.

Graphing Pointer: Remember that when you shift the aggregate demand curve, the curve moves right or left, not up or down. Ask yourself, if you hold the price level constant, how will the equilibrium level of aggregate output respond to changes in the policy variables (G, T, M^s) or changes in the determinants of consumption and planned investment. Ask the same question when shifting the short-run aggregate supply curve: How will these events affect the amount of aggregate output supplied if the price level does not change.

Comment: Think in terms of the macro meaning of "price." Price refers to the *overall* price level, not to specific prices. To simplify the idea, you might think of the price level as an average price of all the goods and services produced in the economy.

Nominal vs. Real Values: When the price level changes, the distinction between real and nominal values takes on some importance. Nominal variables are affected by price level changes; real variables are not. In this chapter, real output, the real money supply, the real interest rate, etc., are used because it is at that level that the goods and money markets interact.

PRACTICE

1. The level of aggregate output demanded decreases as the price level increases because
   A. higher prices make the interest rate fall.
   B. as prices increase, producers will sell more output.
   C. some goods become relatively more expensive.
   D. the demand for money increases, making the interest rate increase.
   Answer: D. A higher price level means that more money will be demanded, forcing up the interest rate (the cost of borrowing).

2. The best description of the operation of the real wealth effect is that as the price level increases,
   A. the interest rate decreases, making interest earnings decrease. This makes consumption decrease.
   B. the interest rate increases. This makes the cost of investment increase and results in a decrease in planned investment.
   C. profitability increases, encouraging investors to increase planned investment.
   D. the purchasing power of household assets decreases, discouraging consumption.
   Answer: D. See p. 316/742.

3. When the price level decreases, the resulting _____ in the interest rate will _____ investment.
   A. increase, increase.
   B. increase, decrease.
   C. decrease, increase.
   D. decrease, decrease.
   Answer: C. Lower interest rates mean lower borrowing costs for firms.

OBJECTIVE 2: Identify how aggregate demand is affected by monetary and fiscal policy actions.

The AD curve will shift to the right (increase) if there is an increase in government spending or in the money supply, or a decrease in net taxes. Because of greater optimism, consumption or investment could increase and shift the AD curve to the right. One reason why the U.S. economy expanded so slowly during 1993 was that consumer confidence sagged, depressing aggregate demand.   (page 317/743)

PRACTICE

4. A cut in government spending will cause a(n) _____ in aggregate demand, and a decrease in the discount rate will cause a(n) _____ in aggregate demand.
   A. increase, increase.
   B. increase, decrease.
   C. decrease, increase.
   D. decrease, decrease.
   Answer: C. At each price level, a decrease in government spending shifts the AE curve downward—AD will decrease. A discount rate cut increases the money supply and lowers the interest rate—AD will increase.

Refer to the following diagram to answer the next question.

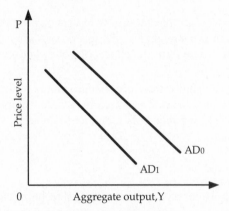

5. The aggregate demand curve would shift from AD_0 to AD_1 if
   A. the government increased welfare payments.
   B. the Fed increased the reserve requirement.
   C. the government cut taxes.
   D. the demand for money decreased.
   Answer: B. A decrease in aggregate demand could be caused by a contractionary monetary policy.

6. The Arbocali Finance Ministry increases both government spending and net taxes by one million opeks. Aggregate demand will
   A. shift to the right.
   B. shift to the left.
   C. remain unchanged, but the price level will increase.
   D. remain unchanged, but the price level will decrease.
   Answer: A. This is a balanced-budget expansionary policy. At the given price level, AE and, therefore AD, will increase.

OBJECTIVE 3: Distinguish between the short run and the long run. Explain why the short-run and long-run aggregate supply curves have the slopes they have. Identify the factors that shift the short-run aggregate supply curve.

The *aggregate supply* (AS) curve shows how the aggregate output supplied by the economy's productive sector responds to changes in the price level.

In the long run, all cost and price-level changes have time to work through the economic system. Wage changes tend to "follow" price changes in the short run but, in the long run, wages have had time to catch up. In the long run, the level of employment (and therefore output) is not influenced by changes in the price level. In the long run, AS is vertical. (page 326/752)

In the short run, as prices rise, producers increase output. The *short-run AS curve* grows steeper at higher output levels because, as the economy approaches full employment, the additional cost incurred in producing more output increases more rapidly. Eventually, when the economy reaches its full productive capacity, the short-run AS curve becomes vertical. (page 320/746)

The short-run AS curve can shift if there are changes in any of the factors affecting the supply decisions of individual firms. These factors include "supply shocks," economic growth or stagnation, shifts in public policy, and natural events, such as weather. (page 323/749)

PRACTICE

7. The aggregate supply curve plots the relationship between
   A. the overall price level and wages—as wages increase, prices increase.
   B. output and supply. As supply increases, more output is available.
   C. the overall price level and the aggregate quantity of output supplied.
   D. equilibrium output and the rate of inflation.
   Answer: C. See p. 319/745.

8. If the economy is in a deep recession, a modest increase in aggregate demand is likely to cause _____ in price and _____ in output level.
   A. an increase, an increase.
   B. an increase, little or no increase.
   C. little or no change, an increase.
   D. little or no change, little or no increase.
   Answer: C. When the economy is in a recession, the short-run AS curve may be horizontal. An increase in demand will increase output with little or no increase in price level. See p. 321/747.

9. The economy is operating at full capacity. The short-run AS curve is _____. An increase in the price level will _____ output.
   A. horizontal, increase.
   B. horizontal, not change.
   C. vertical, increase.
   D. vertical, not change.
   Answer: D. The short-run AS curve is vertical at full capacity—additional price inducement can stimulate no further production.

10. The economy may be working at less than its capacity if there is
    A. cyclical unemployment.
    B. frictional unemployment.
    C. natural unemployment.
    D. structural unemployment.
    Answer: A. Some frictional and structural unemployment is considered necessary and healthy. See p. 321/747.

11. For the short-run aggregate supply curve to have a positive slope
    A. changes in the overall price level must be fully anticipated.
    B. input price changes must be fully anticipated.
    C. changes in the overall price level must lag behind input price changes.
    D. input price changes must lag behind changes in the overall price level.
    Answer: D. See p. 322/748.

12. The aggregate supply curve will be positively sloped in each of the following cases except when input prices change _____ output price changes.
    A. at the same rate as.
    B. more slowly than.
    C. more rapidly than.
    D. not at all in response to.
    Answer: A. See p. 322/748. If input prices change at the same rate as output prices, the changes neutralize each other—relatively, inputs become neither more nor less expensive.

13. Short-run aggregate supply would increase in each of the following cases except
    A. an increase in the female labor-participation rate.
    B. the imposition of an energy tax.
    C. an increase in the stock of capital.
    D. an improvement in the health and nutrition of the labor force.
    Answer: B. An energy tax would raise production costs.

14. Following the double-digit inflation of the 1970s, a growing proportion of American workers have negotiated automatic cost-of-living adjustments (COLAs) in their wage contracts. The effect of this is to make the short-run aggregate supply curve
    A. vertical.
    B. horizontal.
    C. steeper.
    D. flatter.
    Answer: C. The more rapidly input costs can respond to price changes, the less the impact of a price change on output. See p. 322/748.

Refer to the following diagram to answer the next question.

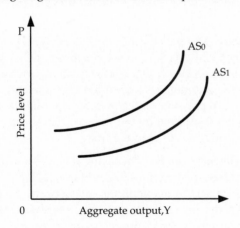

15. Which of the following would shift the U.S. short-run aggregate supply curve from AS_0 to AS_1?
    A. A fall in the number of migrant workers from Mexico.
    B. An increase in income taxes.
    C. An increase in welfare benefits.
    D. An loosening of the restrictions on child labor.

    Answer: D. For AS to shift right (an increase in supply), either more resources must be made available or existing resources must become more productive. Option B has had some supporters—higher taxes reduce after-tax wages and may encourage more work effort to maintain a given standard of living. This argument, though, is weak and is excluded from our model of the macroeconomy.

OBJECTIVE 4: Define potential output.

Potential output is the output level that can be sustained in the long run. Output may be lower (if there is cyclical unemployment, for example) or higher (if resources are being employed overtime), but potential output is that level of production at which the economy could remain over the long run with no pressure for inflation to occur.

(page 327/753)

> **TIP:** The concept is very important. If potential output is the output level that can be sustained in the long run, then any other output level must be only *short-run*. If the AD curve and short-run AS curve intersect at any other level, then economic forces will be exerted to push them to this level.

OBJECTIVE 5: Determine the short-run effect of an expansionary or contractionary fiscal or monetary policy on the equilibrium price level and the inflation rate, and link this to the degree of excess capacity in the economy. Determine the long-run effect of expansionary or contractionary policy.

Short-run equilibrium occurs where AD and short-run AS intersect—goods and money markets are in equilibrium and the desires of demanders and suppliers are met.

(page 326/752)

Fiscal (G, T) or monetary (M^S) policies shift the AD curve. When AS is relatively flat (the economy has substantial "slack"), an expansionary policy will stimulate much additional output in the short run with a relatively small increase in inflation. When AS is relatively steep (the economy is close to full employment), the identical policy will exert a strong upward pressure on the price level with little gain in output. The strength of the multiplier is affected by the slope of the AS curve—the multiplier is much smaller in the second case than in the first.

Fiscal policy is more potent if the Fed "accommodates" by issuing more money to stabilize the interest rate—crowding out can be prevented. Put simply, "accommodation" means that the Fed acts to maintain the interest rate. An expansionary fiscal policy would drive up the interest rate—the Fed increases the money supply in response; a contractionary fiscal policy produces the opposite response. In each case, the impact of the fiscal policy action is *intensified*. The Fed might accommodate if its economic objectives coincided with those of the government. In the long run, neither fiscal nor monetary policy will have any impact on aggregate output because, in the long run, AS is vertical.

(page 328/754)

TIP: Contractionary policies often seem more difficult to work through. In theory, a reduction in government purchases will have simply the reverse effect of an increase. However, working through the effects of contractionary policy actions is an excellent way for you to test your own knowledge. Draw the diagrams too. Compare your conclusions against those in the textbook examples and you'll quickly find out what you know and what you still have to work on.

TIP: The crowding out of investment by increased government spending was first discussed in the previous chapter but it is mentioned again in this chapter. The effect operates through higher interest rates. Using the AS/AD model, you can also think of crowding out occurring a second way—through increases in the price level. An increase in aggregate demand pushes up the price level, money demand, and the interest rate. Ultimately, investment is reduced.

Graphing Pointer: Remember that, graphically, long-run equilibrium is shown by the intersection of three curves (AD, SRAS, LRAS). See the diagram for Questions 19–21. If you shift AD or SRAS and end up at points A, B, C, or D, those points only represent short-run equilibrium. In the long-run, additional adjustments will have to be made.

Comment: The answer to many economic questions is "It depends." This is certainly true with respect to economic policy. Keep in mind that a policy that might be highly successful in one circumstance (a recession, for example) may fail miserably in another. The effectiveness of policy is linked to the multiplier—in our new more complete model the multiplier's value, and the effectiveness of policy, are variable.

PRACTICE

16. Currently, output is substantially less than potential output. Now the Fed buys securities. In the short run we would expect
    A. an unanticipated decrease in business inventories.
    B. an increase in the interest rate because the demand for money has decreased.
    C. a decrease in planned investment because securities are scarcer.
    D. a decrease in production as inflation erodes spending power.
    Answer: A. The Fed action is an expansionary policy. Check Chapter 11(26) if you missed this point. Interest rates fall, planned investment increases, aggregate expenditure and aggregate demand increase, and inventories unexpectedly decrease.

17. An expansionary fiscal policy is most effective when aggregate demand is _____ initially and when the Fed simultaneously _____ the money supply.
    A. high, increases.
    B. high, decreases.
    C. low, increases.
    D. low, decreases.
    Answer: C. The flatter the short-run AS curve, the smaller the increase in price level that will be caused by the fiscal policy (and the smaller reductions in consumption and investment). An "accommodating" monetary policy would help to keep interest rates low, to prevent the crowding out of investment.

18. MPC is .8. In the long run, the most accurate value for the government spending multiplier is _____, and for the tax multiplier the most accurate value is _____
    A. 5, –4.
    B. more than 5, less than –4.
    C. less than 5, more than –4.
    D. zero, zero.
    Answer: D. In the long run, fiscal policy actions have no effect on output level. See p. 331/757.

Use the following diagram to answer the next three questions. The economy is initially at point E.

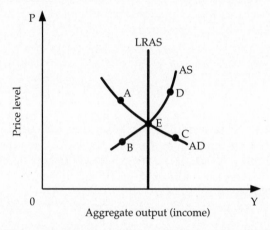

19. In the short run, an increase in energy prices would move the economy to a point such as _____
    A. A.
    B. B.
    C. C.
    D. D.
    Answer: A. An increase in energy prices is a "cost shock" that will shift the short-run AS curve to the left. See p. 323/749.

20. In the short run, an increase in net taxes would move the economy to a point such as _____
    A. A.
    B. B.
    C. C.
    D. D.
    Answer: B. This is a contractionary fiscal policy. Aggregate demand would decrease.

21. In the long run, an increase in money supply would make aggregate demand _____ and short-run aggregate supply _____
    A. increase, increase.
    B. increase, decrease.
    C. decrease, increase.
    D. decrease, decrease.
    Answer: B. A money supply increase is an expansionary monetary policy, designed to shift the aggregate demand curve (to a new equilibrium such as point D). Aggregate supply will shift left, and continue to shift until potential GDP is restored. See p. 326/752.

22. In the long run, an increase in money supply would make aggregate supply shift left because
    A. eventually, all the additional money would be spent.
    B. eventually, input prices would increase because the economy would be working beyond its capacity in the short run.
    C. interest rates would decrease, discouraging investment in factories and infrastructure.
    D. higher prices discourage consumers, and producers cut production when there is a lack of customers.
    Answer: B. With high demand, the economy has been pushed past the potential level of output. There is an upward pressure on costs, which causes the short-run AS curve to shift left.

Use the following information to answer the next three questions. Arbez is in long-run (and short-run) equilibrium. Now the central bank (ArbeFed) increases the money supply. Simultaneously, the government cuts taxes.

23. We would predict a(n) _____ in the price level and a(n) _____ in the output level in the short run.
    A. increase, increase.
    B. increase, decrease.
    C. decrease, increase.
    D. decrease, decrease.
    Answer: A. Both changes are expansionary. AD will shift to the right.

24. To restore long-run equilibrium, the
    A. aggregate demand curve will shift to the right.
    B. aggregate demand curve will shift to the left.
    C. short-run aggregate supply curve will shift to the right.
    D. short-run aggregate supply curve will shift to the left.
    Answer: D. See p. 327/753.

25. Relative to the initial situation, we would predict a(n) _____ in the price level and _____ in the output level in the long run.
    A. increase, an increase.
    B. increase, no change.
    C. decrease, an increase.
    D. decrease, no change.
    Answer: B. The long-run aggregate supply is vertical, therefore, although the price level will change, the initial equilibrium output level will be restored.

OBJECTIVE 6: Define inflation and identify the major sources of inflation. Explain why sustained inflation is believed to be a purely monetary phenomenon.

Inflation, a rise in the overall price level, may be caused by a shift to the right in aggregate demand (*demand-pull inflation*) or by a shift to the left in aggregate supply (*cost-push inflation*). Cost—push inflation results in higher prices and lower production—*stagflation*. Inflation may be fueled by inflationary expectations. If higher prices are expected, suppliers may continue to raise prices even if demand is not increasing. If expansionary fiscal policy is "accommodated" by the Fed (that is, if the Fed issues more money to keep the interest rate constant), the rightward shift in the AD curve is greater than it would have been with only the expansionary fiscal policy, and higher prices ensue. Sustained inflation cannot occur unless the Fed releases additional money into the economy—long-run inflation is a monetary phenomenon.
(page 332/758)

26. Demand-pull inflation occurs when the aggregate _____ curve shifts _____
    A. demand, right.
    B. demand, left.
    C. supply, right.
    D. supply, left.
    Answer: A. An increase in demand will increase the price level. See p. 332/758.

27. If the government undertakes an expansionary fiscal policy, the result will be _____ in the long run than in the short run, and it will be _____ if the Fed accommodates.
    A. more inflationary, more inflationary.
    B. more inflationary, less inflationary.
    C. less inflationary, more inflationary.
    D. less inflationary, less inflationary.
    Answer: A. In the long run, output level doesn't change—all demand increases result in higher prices. When the Fed accommodates an expansionary fiscal policy, it increases the money supply.

28. Which statement is false? An expansionary fiscal policy will be more inflationary
    A. in the long run than in the short run.
    B. if the Fed accommodates than if it doesn't.
    C. in the short run, if the short-run aggregate supply curve simultaneously shifts to the right.
    D. the closer the economy is to full employment.
    Answer: C. If the short-run AS curve shifts to the right, the increase in production will absorb some of the increased demand with less of a price-level increase.

29. If there is an increase in inflationary expectations by firms that causes them to raise their prices, then we would expect the aggregate
    A. demand curve to shift right.
    B. demand curve to shift left.
    C. supply curve to shift right.
    D. supply curve to shift left.
    Answer: D. At each output level, firms will require higher prices than before. See p. 335/761.

30. In the mainly agricultural economy of Arbez there has been an extremely poor harvest because of heavy rains. The central bank initiates an open market purchase of securities. As a result of the policy, we would expect to see output level _____ and price level _____
    A. decrease more than otherwise, increase more than otherwise.
    B. decrease more than otherwise, increase less than otherwise.
    C. decrease less than otherwise, increase more than otherwise.
    D. decrease less than otherwise, increase less than otherwise.
    Answer: C. Aggregate supply is decreasing, reducing output and raising the price level (stagflation). The policy increases aggregate demand. This will stimulate output somewhat by increasing the price level still further.

A Look Ahead

The model that you are learning about has a wide range of applications that will be explored in upcoming chapters. Topics covered in this chapter will be used in a later chapter to explain the similarities and differences among the various schools of economic thought. Also, the closed model developed in this chapter is opened up to include international economic relationships in Chapters 21 (36) and 22 (37).

PRACTICE TEST

I. MULTIPLE CHOICE QUESTIONS.

Select the option that provides the single best answer.

_____ 1. One inflation-fighting policy is to shift AD to the _____ by _____

    A. right, increasing net taxes.
    B. left, decreasing net taxes.
    C. right, increasing government purchases.
    D. left, decreasing government purchases.

_____ 2. Each of the following will make the AD curve shift to the right except
    A. a tax cut.
    B. an open market sale of securities by the Fed.
    C. a decrease in the required reserve ratio.
    D. an increase in government spending.

_____ 3. _Ceteris paribus_, an increase in the price level will cause
    A. the interest rate to fall.
    B. an increase in the quantity of money supplied.
    C. an excess demand for money at the original equilibrium interest rate.
    D. the aggregate demand curve to shift to the left.

_____ 4. Government spending increases and the price of raw materials falls. In an economy with some "slack," we would predict that, in the short run,
    A. price would rise and output would fall.
    B. price would fall and output would rise.
    C. price would rise but the effect on output would be uncertain.
    D. the effect on price would be uncertain but output would increase.

_____ 5. The President abolishes all subsidies to corporations. In the short run, this will cause the price level to _____ and output to _____
    A. increase, increase.
    B. increase, decrease.
    C. decrease, increase.
    D. decrease, decrease.

_____ 6. An increase in the price level will certainly cause the AE curve to shift _____ as the interest rate _____
    A. upward, increases.
    B. upward, decreases.
    C. downward, increases.
    D. downward, decreases.

_____ 7. During an expansionary fiscal policy action, the interest rate _____; during an expansionary monetary policy action, the interest rate _____
    A. increases, increases.
    B. increases, decreases.
    C. decreases, increases.
    D. decreases, decreases.

_____ 8. An increase in government spending will cause
    A. the aggregate demand curve to shift to the right.
    B. the money demand curve to shift to the left.
    C. the AE curve to shift downward.
    D. planned investment to increase.

_____ 9. The _____ curve will shift to the _____ if the Fed buys securities.
   A. AD, right.
   B. AD, left.
   C. AS, right.
   D. AS, left.

_____ 10. A decrease in the price level will _____ money demand and _____ the interest rate.
   A. increase, increase.
   B. increase, decrease.
   C. decrease, increase.
   D. decrease, decrease.

Use the following money market diagram to answer the next two questions.

_____ 11. The government undertakes an expansionary fiscal policy such as a(n) _____. The Fed accommodates by, for example, _____
   A. increase in net taxes, buying securities.
   B. increase in net taxes, selling securities.
   C. decrease in net taxes, buying securities.
   D. decrease in net taxes, selling securities.

_____ 12. Given the policies described in the previous question, which of the following outcomes is possible? Money demand moves from _____ and money supply moves from _____
   A. M_1^d to M_2^d; M_1^s to M_2^s.
   B. M_1^d to M_2^d; M_2^s to M_1^s.
   C. M_2^d to M_1^d; M_3^s to M_2^s.
   D. M_2^d to M_1^d; M_2^s to M_3^s.

_____ 13. In the short run,
   A. input prices are fixed.
   B. output prices are fixed.
   C. input prices respond fully to changes in the overall price level.
   D. input prices do not respond fully to changes in the overall price level.

_____ 14. In the short run, aggregate supply would decrease in each of the following cases except
   A. an increase in the proportion of high school graduates who go on to college.
   B. a deterioration in the nation's infrastructure.
   C. an increase in emigration.
   D. a decrease in the tax rate on business profits.

_____ 15. The economy is currently at the potential output level. An increase in government spending will result in
A. no crowding out of investment.
B. partial crowding out of investment.
C. complete crowding out of investment.
D. partial crowding out of the money supply.

_____ 16. Ultimately, inflation can be sustained from year to year only if
A. the government runs larger and larger deficits each year.
B. government spending increases each year.
C. the money supply is increased each year.
D. private spending increases faster than aggregate supply.

_____ 17. The AD curve is derived by holding constant all of the following except
A. government spending.
B. net taxes.
C. money demand.
D. money supply.

_____ 18. A fiscally-induced increase in aggregate demand will increase prices most sharply when the AS curve is _____ and when the Fed _____ the interest rate constant.
A. flat, holds.
B. flat, does not hold.
C. steep, holds.
D. steep, does not hold.

_____ 19. The natural rate of unemployment rate is 6%. The present unemployment rate is 5%. As time passes, we would expect the
A. long-run aggregate supply curve to shift to the right.
B. long-run aggregate supply curve to shift to the left.
C. short-run aggregate supply curve to shift to the right.
D. short-run aggregate supply curve to shift to the left.

Use the following diagram to answer the next three questions. The economy is in initial long-run equilibrium at point A.

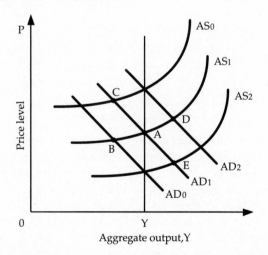

_____ 20. Demand-pull inflation is best represented by the move from
A. A to B.
B. A to C.
C. A to D.
D. A to E.

_____ 21. The price of oil increases. Initially, this will shift the aggregate
  A. demand curve to AD_0.
  B. demand curve to AD_2.
  C. supply curve to AS_0.
  D. supply curve to AS_2.

_____ 22. The price of oil increases. The government initiates a contractionary fiscal policy to offset the inflationary effects of the rising energy prices. This will shift the aggregate demand curve to
  A. AD_0 and intensify the decline in output.
  B. AD_0 and offset the decline in output.
  C. AD_2 and intensify the decline in output.
  D. AD_2 and offset the decline in output.

_____ 23. The price of oil has increased. The government has initiated a contractionary fiscal policy to offset the inflationary effects of the rising energy prices. Given that information, the long-run equilibrium will be restored by
  A. aggregate demand curve shifting to the right.
  B. aggregate demand curve shifting to the left.
  C. short-run aggregate supply curve shifting to the right.
  D. short-run aggregate supply curve shifting to the left.

II. APPLICATION QUESTIONS.

1. The Arbocali economy is initially in long-run equilibrium.
   a. Draw the aggregate demand curve (AD_0), short-run aggregate supply curve (AS_0), and the long-run aggregate supply curve (LRAS). Label equilibrium output and overall price level Y_0 and P_0, respectively.

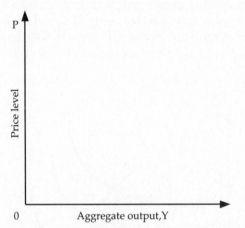

   b. There is a slump in consumer confidence and consumption level falls. Show how the diagram will change. Subscript any new curves "1."
   c. Now the government decreases taxes by an amount equal to the initial decrease in consumption. What will happen to aggregate demand, output, and the price level? Is there an inflationary gap?
   d. Aggregate demand will not shift far enough to the right to restore full employment. Why?
   e. Because the tax cut did not achieve full employment, the government hikes spending by an amount equal to the initial decrease in consumption. Show any curve shifts on the diagram and subscript any new curves "2." How will output and the overall price level change? Show these new levels, with "2" subscripts. Is there an inflationary gap?

The following diagram shows the money market in original equilibrium (before the slump in consumer confidence). The central bank is committed to maintaining the interest rate at 6%.

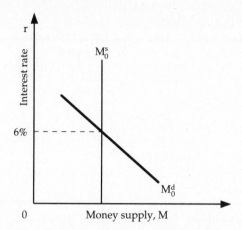

f.   Given the changes in parts a through e above, show how the money market diagram will stand at the end of part e. Subscript any new curves "2." Describe what will happen to the interest rate and to bond prices.

g.   If you've seen IS-LM (Chapter 13/28), you'll know that money market changes can shift the position of the LM curve. In this particular situation, how does the LM curve shift, if at all?

h.   Given the central bank's commitment, what policy action should it choose? How might it implement this policy? Show how the money market diagram will stand immediately after the policy action. Subscript any new curves "3."

i.   What will happen to the AS/AD diagram? Subscript any new curves "3." How will output and the overall price level change? Show these new levels, with "3" subscripts.

j.   Given the changes in the AS/AD diagram, will there be any further change in the money market diagram? If so, what? Subscript any new curves "4."

k.   Describe the central bank's policy response. Is it accommodating? Is it inflationary?

l.   If the central bank had undertaken no expansionary monetary policy, i.e., the money supply curve remained at M_0^s, show on the AS/AD diagram where the economy will reach equilibrium in the long run (point B).

m.   Assuming that the central bank makes no further changes to the money supply, i.e., M_3^s is the final money supply curve, show on the AS/AD diagram where the economy will reach equilibrium in the long run (point C).

n.   "Given an expansionary fiscal policy, an accommodating central bank policy will be more/less inflationary."

2. For each "event," indicate the specific "result" that will occur.
   Result A: increase in aggregate demand.
   Result B: decrease in aggregate demand.
   Result C: increase in aggregate supply.
   Result D: decrease in aggregate supply.

RESULT	EVENT
a. _____	The government cuts personal income taxes.
b. _____	The price of intermediate goods falls.
c. _____	The interest rates rises.
d. _____	Inflationary expectations of firms increase.
e. _____	New, stringent standards for the construction of residential dwellings are enacted.
f. _____	Employer contributions to the social security plan are decreased.

3. Short-run aggregate supply suddenly shifts to the left.
   a. What might have caused this?
   b. Predict how price and output levels will change.
   c. What name is used to describe this phenomenon?
   d. How might the government respond to this supply-side change?
   e. Describe what will happen to the price level and output level if AS shifts to the left and the government pursues an expansionary fiscal policy.

4. a. Draw a goods market diagram and a money market diagram in the space below. Show the equilibrium interest rate (r_0) and output level (Y_0).

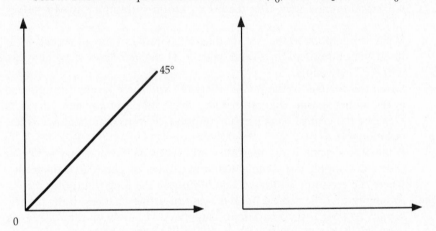

   b. Suppose the price level falls from P_0 to P_1. Show all the curves that shift.
   c. On the diagram below, sketch in the aggregate demand curve. Make your labeling consistent!

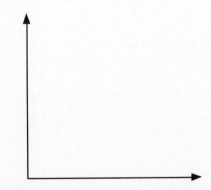

   d. Explain why the AD curve has a negative slope.
   e. Now suppose that the money supply increases. Show how this will affect all the diagrams.

5. In each of the following cases, indicate if the variable will increase (I), decrease (D), or remain unchanged (U).

   a. Assume that the Fed is accommodative and Congress undertakes a contractionary fiscal policy (increasing taxes). Predict how each of the following variables will be affected.

      1. _____ output

      2. _____ the interest rate

      3. _____ the price level

      4. _____ employment

      5. _____ the deficit (government spending – net taxes)

      6. _____ the demand for labor (guess on this one!)

      7. _____ supply of money

   b. Assume that the Fed is not accommodative and Congress increases government purchases. Predict how each of the following variables will be affected.

      1. _____ output

      2. _____ the interest rate

      3. _____ the price level

      4. _____ employment

      5. _____ the deficit

      6. _____ demand for labor

      7. _____ supply of money

   c. Assume that the Fed is accommodative and that investment spending suddenly increases because of an upsurge in business optimism. Predict how each of the following variables will be affected.

      1. _____ planned expenditure (initial change)

      2. _____ demand for money (initial change)

      3. _____ the interest rate (initial change)

      4. _____ the price level

      5. _____ the deficit

      6. _____ demand for labor

      7. _____ supply of money

6. Explain what will happen as a result of the following events. In each case, draw an aggregate demand and short-run aggregate supply diagram showing the initial equilibrium output level (Y_0) and price level (P_0). Show any changes and indicate the final equilibrium output level and price level.

a. The economy is in a recession. Now a reduction in foreign consumption of U.S. products occurs.

b. The economy is operating near full capacity. Now environmental pollution standards are tightened substantially.

c. The economy is in a recession. An increase in government purchases occurs. The Fed tries to maintain the interest rate.

d. The economy is operating near full capacity. An import tax (tariff) is imposed on foreign consumer goods while the Fed tries to maintain the interest rate.

e. The economy is in a recession. Household confidence about the future is reduced. Firms expect greater inflation in the future.

f. The economy is operating near full capacity. Now there is an increase in the price of foreign oil. The Fed attempts to maintain the output level.

PRACTICE TEST

I. SOLUTIONS TO MULTIPLE CHOICE QUESTIONS

1. D. Shifting the AD curve to the left helps to reduce inflation. This may be done by enacting a contractionary policy such as a decrease in government spending or a reduction in the money supply.

2. B. An open market sale of securities is a contractionary policy. A decrease in the money supply will increase the interest rate. This, in turn, will reduce planned investment (and consumption) and cause a lower equilibrium in the goods market.

3. C. As the price level increases, money demand will shift to the right. At the original interest rate, an excess demand will now exist and the interest rate will increase. A change in the price level leads to a movement along the AD curve.

4. D. The fiscal policy action will increase aggregate demand, which will promote increasing prices and increasing output. The price hike for raw materials will make the short-run aggregate supply curve shift to the right, prompting a decrease in prices and an increase in output. Together, the changes will certainly raise output, but the effect on the price level is ambiguous.

5. B. Removing the subsidies increases production costs—the aggregate supply curve will shift left. As supply contracts, price will increase and output will decrease.

6. C. Higher prices reduce consumption and investment because of a higher interest rate and the real wealth effect. Reductions in consumption and investment shift the AE curve downward.

7. B. Higher government spending (or lower net taxes) increase aggregate demand and money demand, and therefore, the interest rate. An increased money supply reduces the interest rate and increases aggregate demand. Note that money demand will increase, partly offsetting the decrease in the interest rate.

8. A. Increased government spending crowds out investment as aggregate demand rises.

9. A. If the Fed buys securities then, *at the same price level*, the money supply will increase and the interest rate will decrease. Planned investment and consumption will increase, shifting the AD curve to the right.

10. D. One of the factors affecting money demand is the price level. See p. 313/739.

11. C. Cutting taxes is an expansionary policy. It will push up the interest rate. To prevent this, the Fed must expand the money supply—the most frequent method is buying securities.

12. A. An expansionary fiscal policy will cause money demand and the interest rate to increase. If the Fed accommodates, it will act to maintain the interest rate at its original level. The Fed must increase the money supply to do this.

13. D. See pp. 322–323 (748–749), especially Footnote 3 on p. 323/749.

14. D. The tax rate cut will increase the (self-interested) incentive to produce. Note that an increase in college students will reduce the labor force in the short run; in the long run, because of better *human* capital, aggregate supply would increase.

15. C. The policy action will not be effective. Each additional dollar of government spending will reduce investment spending by a dollar. See p. 330/756. Note that some consumption spending, rather than investment spending, may be lost if consumption is interest-sensitive.

16. C. To have sustained inflation, the money supply must expand. Option A is only possible, ultimately, if the Treasury prints money to cover the government's debts.

17. C. When the price level changes, government spending, net taxes, and the money supply need not change. Money demand, however, will, causing reductions in planned investment.

18. C. A given expansionary fiscal policy will be augmented if the Fed expands the money supply to hold the interest rate constant. The closer to capacity the economy is (the steeper the AS curve), the more inflationary the result.

19. D. Production level is higher than the full employment level. To compensate, the short-run aggregate supply curve will shift to the left.

20. C. The moves from A to B and from A to E represent decreases in the price level. The move from A to C is caused by a shift in the position of the short-run aggregate supply curve.

21. C. Oil is an input. Production costs rise, affecting the supply side of the economy.

22. A. A contractionary policy will shift the aggregate demand curve to the left.

23. C. The economy is in short-run equilibrium below potential GDP. Input prices will fall.

II. SOLUTIONS TO APPLICATION QUESTIONS

1. a. See the diagram below.

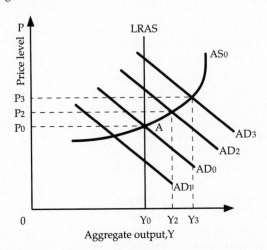

b. See the diagram above. Aggregate demand will shift to AD_1.

c. Aggregate demand will increase as consumer's disposable income increases and therefore, output and the overall price level will increase. Output is less than full-employment output therefore there is no inflationary gap.

d. The tax multiplier is less than the multiplier for consumption.

e. See the diagram above. Aggregate demand will shift to AD_2. Recall that the demand curve shift reflects both the government spending increase and the tax cut. Output and overall price level will both increase. The inflationary gap is the distance Y_0Y_2.

f. Money demand, M_0^d, is based on the initial (full-employment) level of expenditures. When the consumption decrease, tax increase, and government spending increase have taken place, aggregate demand will be at AD_0. Money demand will increase to M_2^d. The interest rate will rise; bond prices will fall. Check Chapter 12/27 if you're unsure about this.

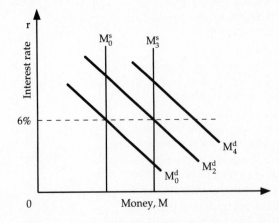

g. LM doesn't shift! The net effect of the consumption, tax, and government spending changes will be to shift IS right. There will be a movement up along the LM curve as income level and the interest rate increase.

h. The bank should increase the money supply by buying bonds, cutting the discount rate, or cutting the reserve requirement. Money supply will shift to M_2^s. See the diagram above.

i. AD will shift further to the right to AD_3. See the diagram above. The price level will increase.

j. Higher expenditures will result in higher money demand (M_4^d). See the diagram above. The interest rate will increase.

k. If the central bank wishes to maintain its target interest rate of 6%, it will be obliged to increase the money supply once more. Central bank actions are both accommodating and inflationary.

l. See the diagram below.

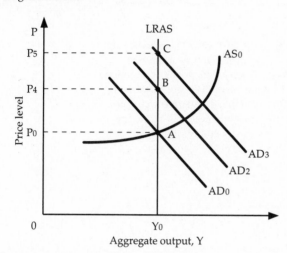

m. See the diagram above.

n. Given an expansionary fiscal policy, an accommodating central bank policy will be more inflationary, as we can see from the diagram above.

2. a. A   c. B   e. D
    b. C   d. D   f. C

Note: Some of these "shocks" may affect both AD and AS curves. The above answers are for the single strongest change.

3. a. Many possible factors could be given. Increases in oil prices have been one major factor. Increased government red tape, poor weather, emigration, or war are other factors.

    b. As the short-run AS curve shifts left, the economy will experience a rising price level and decreasing output.

    c. Stagflation. See p. 334/760.

    d. The traditional response has been to increase demand (through increased government spending, reductions in taxes, or an expansionary monetary policy). A more recent approach, which is discussed in Chapter 19 (34), has been to expand supply (by reducing tax rates to encourage greater work effort).

    e. The price level will certainly increase, while output level might fall, rise, or remain unchanged, depending on the relative strengths of the shifts.

4. a. See the diagrams below.

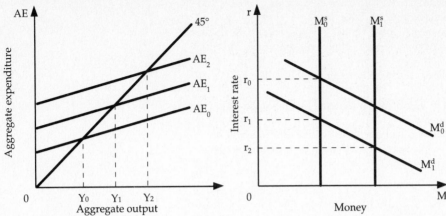

b. See the diagrams above. Money demand will shift to the left (M_1^d). The interest rate will fall to r_1. The interest rate decrease will boost planned investment, and AE will increase to AE_1. Note that this feedback process between the goods and money markets could continue for a while—the money demand curve (M_1^d), for instance, is based on an equilibrium income level that changes as planned investment changes.

c. See the diagram below. The AD curve is AD_1. At P_0, income level was Y_0. At the new, lower, price level P_1, the level of demand that provides equilibrium in goods and money markets simultaneously is Y_1.

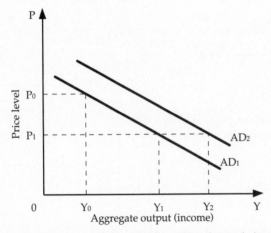

d. A fall in price level means that less money will be demanded to purchase planned expenditures. The interest rate will fall from r_0 to r_1. At a lower interest rate more investment will occur, increasing AE from AE_0 to AE_1. The real level of output rises in response to a fall in price level.

e. See the diagrams above. Money supply moves from M_0^s to M_1^s. The interest rate falls to r_2. Investment and AE will increase, say to AE_2. At the given price level, P_1, the aggregate demand curve will shift to the right, from AD_1 to AD_2. (There will be further adjustments as money demand increases—in the interests of brevity, these have been ignored.)

5. In each of the following cases, the strengths of the effects will depend on the point at which the short-run AS curve intersects the AD curve.

    a. 1. D   2. U   3. D   4. D
        5. D   6. D   7. D

        Explanation: An increase in taxes is a contractionary fiscal policy that will reduce the after-tax income of households. AD will shift to the left. Output and the price level will decrease—both changes will reduce money demand. As money demand decreases, the interest rate will decrease. The Fed's accommodative policy will be to reduce the money supply so that the interest rate will be unchanged. Note that this is an additional contractionary policy. As output decreases, the demand for labor by firms will decrease and there will be cyclical unemployment. Government spending has not changed but taxes have risen, so the deficit will decrease. Note that if we have tax rates and transfer payments in our economy, rising unemployment will reduce net taxes somewhat.

b. 1. I   2. I   3. I   4. I
    5. I   6. I   7. U

Explanation: An increase in government spending is an expansionary fiscal policy that will make AD shift to the right. Output and the price level will increase—both changes will increase money demand. As money demand increases, the interest rate will increase. The Fed is not accommodative, so the money supply will be unchanged. As output increases, the demand for labor by firms will increase and there will be more employment. Government spending has increased but taxes have not changed, so the deficit will increase. Note that if we have tax rates in our economy, an expanding economy will increase net taxes somewhat.

c. 1. I   2. I   3. I   4. I
    5. D   6. I   7. I

Explanation: An increase in optimism will lead to greater planned investment and the AE curve will shift upward. This will make AD shift to the right. Short-run AS (which is based on existing capital) will not shift. Output and the price level will increase—both changes will increase money demand. Initially, as money demand increases, the interest rate will increase. The Fed's accommodative policy will be to increase the money supply so that the interest rate will be unchanged ultimately. Note that this is an additional expansionary policy. As output increases, the demand for labor by firms will increase and there will be more employment. Government spending has not changed but, given automatic stabilizers, net taxes will increase, so the deficit will decrease.

6. Note: Some of these "shocks" may affect both AD and AS curves. The following answers are for the single strongest change.

a. The decrease in foreign consumption will shift the AD curve to the left. In a recession, the fall in price level will be small; the main contraction will be in output.

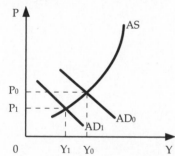

b. The new pollution standards will increase production costs and the AS curve will shift to the left, raising price and reducing output. Stagflation results.

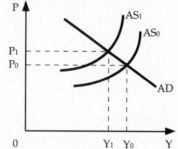
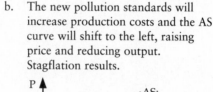

c. The increase in government purchases will shift AD to the right and raise the interest rate. The Fed will have to increase the money supply, which will increase AD even more. In a recession, the price level increase will be small; the main expansion will be in output.

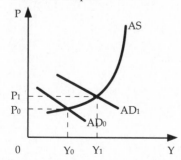

d. A tariff makes foreign consumer goods more expensive—demand for domestic goods will rise, moving AD rightward and raising the interest rate. The Fed will expand the money supply, which will increase AD even more. The main effect will be to raise the price level.

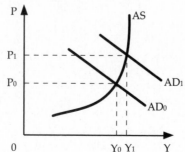

e. Low consumer confidence will cause reduced consumption and a decreasing AD curve. If firms expected greater inflation, AS will shift left. Both effects reduce output; the effect on the price level is ambiguous. Basically, a bad situation has become worse.

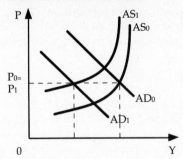

f. If foreign oil (which is an input) rises in price, AS will shift to the left. To maintain the output level, the Fed would have to expand the money supply and shift the AD curve to the right. Both effects are inflationary.

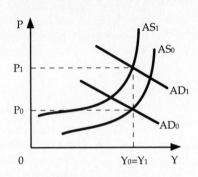

THE LABOR MARKET, UNEMPLOYMENT, AND INFLATION

15

COMBINED TEXT

30

OBJECTIVES: POINT BY POINT

After completing this chapter, you should be able to accomplish the objectives listed below.

General Comment

The textbook has addressed the issue of unemployment before. This chapter, however, isn't simply a re-run of previous material. Make a list of the theories relevant to unemployment. In most cases, this is new material. Note that the theories are not mutually exclusive.

OBJECTIVE 1: Interpret a diagram representing the classical view of the labor market and explain the beliefs of the classical economists.

Classical economists argued that wages adjust freely to clear the labor market. During economic upswings, workers accept higher wages and, in downturns, accept lower wages. Unemployment shouldn't persist—the wage rate should adjust until equilibrium is restored. A low wage, after all, is better than nothing. Price level changes would cause rapid changes in wages, implying a vertical aggregate supply curve. The classical economists saw little role for active fiscal or monetary policy. Persistent (involuntary) unemployment is not possible in such a model; events during the Depression showed that the model was implausible.   (page 343/769)

> **TIP:** Keep in mind that the critical assumption of the classical economists is that wages are perfectly flexible. Keynesians, on the other hand, believe in the presence of "stickiness" in wages.

PRACTICE

1. _____ unemployment is the type that increases during recessions.
   A. Frictional.
   B. Structural.
   C. Cyclical.
   D. Natural.
   Answer: C. Cyclical unemployment varies with the business cycle. See p. 343/769.

Use the following diagram of the classical labor market to answer the next three questions.

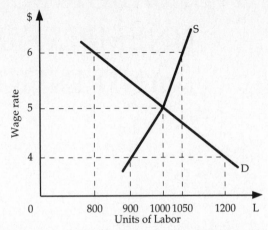

2. At a wage rate of _____ there is an excess _____ labor of 300.
   A. $4, demand for.
   B. $4, supply of.
   C. $6, demand for.
   D. $6, supply of.
   Answer: A. When the wage rate is low, firms increase quantity demanded and workers reduce quantity supplied. At $4, the excess demand is 300 (1,200 – 900).

3. If workers increase the value that they place on nonmarket activities, then the labor _____ curve will shift to the _____
   A. demand, right.
   B. demand, left.
   C. supply, right.
   D. supply, left.
   Answer: D. Changes in workers' preferences will affect the labor supply curve. In this case, at each wage rate, less labor would be supplied.

4. In the diagram above, the equilibrium wage is _____. If workers increase the value that they place on nonmarket activities, then the equilibrium wage will _____
   A. $4, increase.
   B. $5, increase.
   C. $5, decrease.
   D. $6, decrease.
   Answer: B. Equilibrium occurs at the wage rate where quantity demanded equals quantity supplied. The change in preferences will shift the supply curve to the left.

5. If the price level in the economy decreases, the labor _____ curve will

   _____
   A. demand, increase.
   B. demand, decrease.
   C. supply, increase.
   D. supply, decrease.
   Answer: B. Because the output of workers is worth less, firms will demand fewer workers at each wage rate.

6. The government introduces a "guaranteed living standard" program, a plan whereby all citizens, whether they work or not, receive a check equal to twice the poverty line. We would predict that the
    A. labor demand curve will shift right and the wage will increase.
    B. labor demand curve will shift left and the wage will decrease.
    C. labor supply curve will shift right and the wage will decrease.
    D. labor supply curve will shift left and the wage will increase.
    Answer: D. The opportunity cost of leisure has decreased—fewer citizens will seek jobs.

7. In Arboc, most workers have labor contracts that lock in the wage rate for a period of 3 years. In Arbez, however, wages are renegotiated every month. Fiscal policy will be more effective in _____; monetary policy will be more effective in _____
    A. Arboc, Arboc.
    B. Arboc, Arbez.
    C. Arbez, Arboc.
    D. Arbez, Arbez.
    Answer: A. Policy actions are most effective when the short-run aggregate supply curve is relatively flat. The more responsive input prices are to changes in economic conditions, the less impact policy actions will have.

OBJECTIVE 2: Distinguish among the theories explaining wage stickiness. Relate wage stickiness to persistent unemployment.

TIP: To help yourself organize the material in this and the next objective, note that there are four broad explanations of unemployment:
a.   Sticky wage theories,
b.   Efficiency wage theories,
c.   Imperfect information, and
d.   Minimum wage laws.

Several theories suggest that wages may be "sticky."
a. The *implicit contract* explanation suggests that workers and employers share an unspoken "understanding" that cutting wages is not one of the rules of the game.
(page 347/773)
b. The *relative-wage* theory says that any group of workers will resist wage cuts unless convinced that similar groups are also experiencing them.
(page 348/774)
c. *Explicit contracts* attempt to insulate both workers and employers from short-term changes in the economy. Workers (at least the senior workers who may command the bulk of the workers' bargaining power) may prefer layoffs to wage cuts. Also, layoffs are clear "evidence" that the firm has too much labor. Cuts in wages and prices are far more difficult to monitor.   (page 348/774)

TIP: One fairly obvious reason why workers and employers sign contracts is so that they can avoid the costs of renegotiation. After all, would you like to haggle over your wage every morning before work?

8. The _____ explanation is not included among the "sticky wage" theories of unemployment.
   A. social contract.
   B. efficiency wage.
   C. relative-wage.
   D. explicit contract.
   Answer: B. See p. 349/775.

9. During a recession, workers in the construction industry are laid off because of an unspoken agreement between employers and workers. This is consistent with the _____ explanation of unemployment.
   A. social contract
   B. efficiency wage.
   C. relative-wage.
   D. explicit contract.
   Answer: A. See p. 347/773.

10. During a recession, workers in the construction industry in the Northeast are laid off because they are unwilling to accept a wage cut unless they know that similar workers elsewhere are also experiencing such cuts. This is consistent with the _____ explanation of unemployment.
    A. social contract.
    B. efficiency wage.
    C. relative-wage.
    D. explicit contract.
    Answer: C. See p. 348/774.

OBJECTIVE 3: Outline the efficiency wage theory, the role of imperfect information in the wage adjustment process, and the possible effects of a minimum wage law.

The following theories suggest that an above-equilibrium wage may be set. Persistent unemployment is a consequence.

The *efficiency wage theory* argues that worker productivity rises as the wage rate rises. Employers may choose to set the wage rate above the equilibrium to increase morale and productivity, to reduce turnover and retraining, and to establish and retain an experienced pool of workers.   (page 349/775)

Imperfect information about future price behavior can cause wages to be set too high (or too low). Because of the complexity of the wage-setting process and of the economy itself, unemployment may persist if the wage rate is set too low.
                    (page 350/776)

Minimum wage legislation may cause unemployment for inexperienced or less productive workers whom it isn't profitable to hire at the minimum wage. Simply put, such workers cost too much, produce too little, and won't be hired.
                    (page 350/776)

> TIP: With the profusion of theories, it's easy to miss the point of this section. The point is that economists are trying to explain why unemployment persists in the real world.

PRACTICE

11. Marley and Scrooge find that the costs of screening, hiring, and training workers is substantial. To reduce labor turnover, they pay higher-than-average wages. Their behavior is consistent with the _____ explanation of unemployment.
    A. minimum wage.
    B. efficiency wage.
    C. imperfect information.
    D. cost effectiveness.
    Answer: B. See p. 349/775.

12. If, due to imperfect information, firms set the wage above the market-clearing level,
    A. wages will decrease rapidly, as unemployed workers seek jobs.
    B. wages will not fall, as many workers will be available at that wage.
    C. the government will set a minimum wage to prevent unemployment.
    D. wages may adjust slowly because of the complexity of the labor market.
    Answer: D. The more complex the labor market and the more changeable the economy, the more difficult it is to determine the "correct" wage rate.

13. Refer to the diagram used in question 2 above. If the government imposed a minimum wage of $4,
    A. unemployment would be zero.
    B. unemployment would be 100 (1,000 – 900).
    C. unemployment would be 250 (1,050 – 800).
    D. unemployment would be 300 (1,200 – 900).
    Answer: A. The equilibrium wage is $5. Setting a minimum wage that is less than $5 will have no impact on the labor market.

OBJECTIVE 4: Use the AS/AD model to explain the Phillips Curve "trade-off" as it appeared in the 1950s and 1960s and to explain why the relationship collapsed in the 1970s and 1980s.

The AS/AD diagram shows that an increase in aggregate demand leads to higher output (and employment). The unemployment rate would fall and inflation would occur: There would be an apparent trade-off between unemployment rate and inflation rate that is reflected in the *Phillips Curve*. In the 1960s, this relationship seemed so stable that many believed that unemployment and inflation were affected by the same single factor—the level of demand. The analysis rested on the fact that the AS curve had been fairly stable. In the 1970s and 1980s, supply-side factors (particularly the price of oil and higher inflationary expectations) became more volatile and the stable inflation-unemployment relationship collapsed. (page 351/777)

> **TIP:** It's tempting to dismiss the Phillips Curve as irrelevant, but, following that logic, one would have to dismiss the demand curve because things other than the price level can change. The Phillips Curve suggests, *ceteris paribus*, that with rising aggregate demand, as the economy approaches full employment, the costs of increasing production increase. Employers will try to pass these cost increases on by raising prices, moving up along the aggregate supply curve. When unemployment is high, the argument is reversed.

> **TIP:** Import prices didn't change much during the 1950s and 1960s as noted in the text. There is a second point, though, that's worth keeping in mind. The foreign sector of the economy (exports and imports) has become much more significant and a greater source of potential instability. Imports accounted for only about 6% of GDP in 1960; by 1993, the number was approaching about 11%.

Graphing Pointer: First, the Phillips Curve is a descriptive graph—it simply plots the annual association of the inflation rate and the unemployment rate. Next, develop the Phillips Curve as an analytical graph. Draw an AS/AD diagram and indicate the equilibrium value of the price level and aggregate output. Beside this diagram, set up a Phillips Curve diagram (with inflation rate on the vertical axis and unemployment rate on the horizontal axis) and plot a point which corresponds to the inflation rate and unemployment rate at equilibrium in the AS/AD figure. Now, draw an increase in AD (don't move the AS curve). This shift will result in a higher price level and an expansion in aggregate output. On your Phillips Curve diagram, plot a point corresponding with the higher inflation rate and lower unemployment rate. As you continue to shift the AD you will trace out the Phillips Curve. (Once this is completed and comprehended, shift the AS curve and observe that you are now "off" the Phillips Curve which you constructed.)

PRACTICE

14. Which factors led to the breakdown of the Phillips Curve in the 1970s?
    A. Supply-side policymakers reduced business taxes, which made the aggregate supply curve shift to the left.
    B. Adverse "supply shocks" such as the oil price increase of 1973–1974 made the aggregate supply curve shift to the left.
    C. Government spending resulted in large deficits and high inflation.
    D. The aggregate demand curve shifted to the left following the end of hostilities in Vietnam.
    Answer: B. As the AS curve shifted to the left, stagflation (rising inflation and rising unemployment) occurred. Reduced business taxes (Option A) would make the aggregate supply curve shift to the right.

15. If the AS curve is stable, there will be a _____ relationship between the inflation rate and the unemployment rate when the AD curve shifts to the right and a _____ relationship when the AD curve shifts to the left.
    A. positive, positive.
    B. positive, negative.
    C. negative, positive.
    D. negative, negative.
    Answer: D. Higher (lower) demand increases (decreases) the inflation rate and decreases (increases) the unemployment rate.

16. Evidence from 1970 to 1994 suggests that there is _____ relationship between inflation and unemployment.
    A. no particular.
    B. a weak negative.
    C. a strong negative.
    D. a weak positive.
    Answer: A. See p. 354/780.

17. In the 1970s, increasing inflation became a fact of life. This expectation shifted the AS curve to the _____ and shifted the Phillips Curve to the _____
    A. right, right.
    B. right, left.
    C. left, right.
    D. left, left.
    Answer: C. As we saw in the previous chapter, the AS curve will shift to the left as firms expect increased inflation. The Phillips Curve will shift right. See p. 356/782.

18. The Fed increases the money supply. Assuming no changes in expectations, this policy would result in a(n) _____ in the unemployment rate and a(n) _____ in the inflation rate.
    A. increase, increase.
    B. increase, decrease.
    C. decrease, increase.
    D. decrease, decrease.
    Answer: C. The policy will shift AD to the right, increasing output and employment which decreases the unemployment rate and increases inflation.

OBJECTIVE 5: Explain why a vertical AS curve implies a vertical (long-run) Phillips Curve. Link the vertical Phillips Curve to the concept of the natural rate of unemployment and comment on the effectiveness of fiscal and monetary policy.

If the long-run AS curve is vertical, then the long-run Phillips Curve is also vertical. Changes in fiscal or monetary policy will have no long-run impact on output level or unemployment rate. Expansionary fiscal and monetary policies will have no long-run effect except to fuel inflation—in the long run, unemployment will gravitate to the *natural rate of unemployment* and output will remain at potential GDP level. The *natural rate of unemployment* is the sum of frictional and structural unemployment

(page 359/785)

PRACTICE

19. The natural rate of unemployment is the sum of
    A. frictional and cyclical unemployment.
    B. frictional and structural unemployment.
    C. cyclical and structural unemployment.
    D. frictional, cyclical, and structural unemployment.
    Answer: B. See p. 359/785.

20. If the Phillips Curve is vertical in the long run, then an increase in the money supply from year to year will _____ the unemployment rate and will _____ the inflation rate.
    A. increase, increase.
    B. increase, not change.
    C. not change, increase.
    D. not change, not change.
    Answer: C. Fiscal or, in this case, monetary policies will not affect the natural rate of employment or the unemployment rate in the long run. However, as we saw in the previous chapter, persistent increases in the money supply fuel inflation.

21. Currently, the unemployment rate is greater than the natural rate of unemployment. In the long run, the natural rate will be attained if policymakers
    A. increase the money supply.
    B. decrease the money supply.
    C. do nothing.
    D. do all of the above.
    Answer: D. This is a trick(y) question! In the long run it doesn't make any difference what policymakers do (or don't do). The natural rate of unemployment will prevail in the long run in any and all circumstances. Note that an argument could be made that doing nothing is preferable because it might shorten the economy's period of adjustment.

Comment

In this chapter and the previous one you've been given a number of theories concerning the causes of unemployment and inflation. Notice that the list of causes isn't the same for both. Unemployment and inflation aren't opposite sides of the same problem (as the Phillips Curve might suggest), but rather, different problems. If you need proof, think about stagflation, where both problems occur simultaneously. This new view, that the two problems need to be addressed separately, is an important development in the thinking of economists and policymakers.

PRACTICE TEST

I. MULTIPLE CHOICE QUESTIONS.

Select the option that provides the single best answer.

_____ 1. In the classical model, it is always true that there will be full employment (no involuntary unemployment) because
A. workers will bid wages downward if necessary.
B. wages are sticky.
C. employers set wages.
D. unions and employers have equal bargaining strength.

_____ 2. The existence of sticky wages suggests that
A. workers hold most of the bargaining power in wage negotiations.
B. wages will be constant over the business cycle.
C. some unemployment is caused by workers' and firms' unwillingness to negotiate wage cuts.
D. nominal wages are eroded during a period of inflation.

_____ 3. If firms expect higher prices next quarter, the labor _____ curve will shift to the _____
A. supply, right.
B. supply, left.
C. demand, right.
D. demand, left.

_____ 4. Which of the following reasons is given as an explanation why labor markets do not always clear?
A. Workers have better price information than employers.
B. The total demand for labor has fallen.
C. Workers are reluctant to accept a lower wage relative to other similar groups of workers.
D. The supply of labor has fallen.

_____ 5. The relative-wage explanation of sticky wages fails to recognize that
A. the cost of information is virtually zero.
B. firms are not willing to cut wages even when there is a recession.
C. search costs are virtually zero.
D. workers don't have perfect information about wages in similar industries.

_____ 6. Which of the following will lead to an increase in inflation?
A. a price hike by foreign oil producers.
B. an open market sale of securities by the Fed.
C. a cut in government spending.
D. an increase in the demand for money.

Use the following diagram, showing the demand for and supply of teenage labor, to answer the following question.

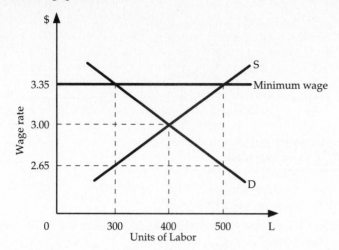

_____ 7. The government has imposed a minimum wage of $3.35 per hour. Unemployment would be
    A. 500.
    B. 300.
    C. 200.
    D. 400.

_____ 8. Which of the following is most likely to cause stagflation?
    A. falling prices on imported oil.
    B. an increase in the money supply.
    C. a decrease in the money supply.
    D. rising prices on imported oil.

_____ 9. The Phillips Curve has broken down since the early 1970s because of all of the following except
    A. inflationary expectations became variable.
    B. rising import prices became a significant feature of the economy.
    C. aggregate demand was more variable than before.
    D. the _ceteris paribus_ assumptions, under which the analysis was made, were infringed.

_____ 10. The Phillips Curve in the 1960s showed that
    A. the inflation rate and the price level were positively related.
    B. increases in wages and unemployment were positively related.
    C. the unemployment rate and the inflation rate were negatively related.
    D. the money supply and the interest rate were negatively related.

_____ 11. When the economy is at the natural rate of unemployment there is
    A. no structural unemployment.
    B. no frictional unemployment.
    C. some cyclical unemployment.
    D. some frictional and structural unemployment.

_____ 12. The classical economists' model of the labor market is consistent with a
    A. horizontal aggregate demand curve.
    B. horizontal aggregate supply curve.
    C. vertical aggregate demand curve.
    D. vertical aggregate supply curve.

_____ 13. Many economists today believe that the Phillips Curve is _____ in the short run and _____ in the long run.
  A.   downward sloping, vertical.
  B.   vertical, downward sloping.
  C.   upward sloping, vertical.
  D.   vertical, upward sloping.

_____ 14. If the AD curve is stable, there will be a _____ relationship between the inflation rate and the unemployment rate when the AS curve shifts to the right, and a _____ relationship when the AS curve shifts to the left.
  A.   positive, positive.
  B.   positive, negative.
  C.   negative, positive.
  D.   negative, negative.

_____ 15. The large shifts to the left of the AS curve in the 1970s were caused mainly by
  A.   increasing government deficits.
  B.   substantial increases in the money supply.
  C.   increases in the price of imported raw materials.
  D.   aggressive labor union activity during 1973–1977.

Use the following diagram to answer the next five questions. The economy is initially at point E. Point E represents the rate of unemployment that is the natural rate.

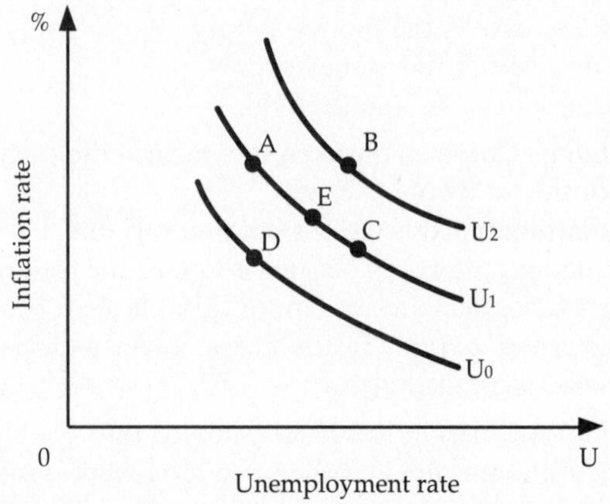

_____ 16. An increase in government spending would move the economy to point
  A.   A.
  B.   B.
  C.   C.
  D.   D.

_____ 17. A move from point E to point D is most likely to be caused by
  A.   a decrease in the inflationary expectations of firms.
  B.   a decrease in the money supply.
  C.   an increase in the price of imported oil.
  D.   an adverse supply shock, such as bad harvests.

_____ 18. An increase in the price of imported raw materials would move the economy to point
  A.   A.
  B.   B.
  C.   C.
  D.   D.

_____ 19. If point E represents the rate of unemployment that is the natural rate, then at point A, actual output _____ potential output, and structural and frictional unemployment rates are _____

    A. exceeds, positive.
    B. exceeds, negative.
    C. is less than, positive.
    D. is less than, negative.

_____ 20. In the long run, the Phillips Curve will pass through
    A. points A, E, and C.
    B. points D, E, and B.
    C. point E only.
    D. none of these points because the long-run Phillips Curve is vertical.

II. APPLICATION QUESTIONS.

1. The small nation of Arboc is at point A on its Phillips Curve. Inflation is expected to be 0%. The natural rate of unemployment is 6.0%.

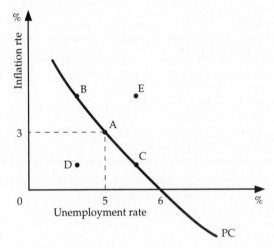

    a. If the natural rate of unemployment is 6% and the expected inflation rate is 0%, what sort of macroeconomic action could have moved the economy to point A?

What will happen to the price level and output in each of the following cases? In each case, will the factor in question affect the inflation rate and unemployment rate as a simple Phillips Curve would predict? Using point A as a reference, how would the economy move in the short run?

    b. A severe hurricane destroys the sugar cane crop, the main agricultural crop in this predominantly rural economy.
    c. The Arbocali government passes a new environmental protection law that requires producers to decrease emission of atmospheric pollutants.
    d. In anticipation of a war with neighboring states, the Arbocali government increases its military spending by 50%.
    e. Legislation is passed making it more difficult to unionize and making union activity such as picketing illegal.
    f. Consumer confidence in the economy is undermined because of a change in government.

Now suppose that none of the changes above took place. The economy will not remain at point A in the long run.

    g. Explain why the economy will not remain at point A.
    h. Suppose actual inflation remains 3%. Explain how the economy will adjust in the long run.
    i. Sketch in the long-run Phillips Curve.

2. Macrovia has a population of 160,000 citizens. Because of a highly sophisticated computerized job placement program, frictional and structural unemployment runs at a constant 10,000. The nation's labor demand and supply curve are $Q_D = 120 - W$ and $Q_S = 5W$, respectively. Q is the quantity of labor supplied or demanded in thousands of workers, W is the wage in sponduliks, the local currency.

   a. Calculate the equilibrium wage, the level of employment, and the unemployment rate in Macrovia.

   b. Calculate the size of the labor force and the participation rate.

   c. The Secretary of Labor is under pressure to introduce a minimum wage. If the minimum wage is set at 22 sponduliks (a 10% increase), calculate the effect on employment, unemployment, the labor force, the unemployment rate and the participation rate.

3. Use the following table to answer this question. Columns (1) and (2) give information about the short-run aggregate supply curve for Arboc. Column (3) shows total employment at different output levels. There are 200,000 workers in the total labor force. Normally 10,000 workers are structurally and frictionally unemployed.

(1) OVERALL PRICE LEVEL	(2) AGGREGATE OUTPUT	(3) TOTAL EMPLOYMENT	(4) OUTPUT DEMANDED	(5) OUTPUT DEMANDED	(6) OUTPUT DEMANDED	(7) OUTPUT DEMANDED
4.60 opeks	2,550	191,000	100	800	1,400	2,200
4.50 opeks	2,500	190,000	400	1,100	1,700	2,500
4.40 opeks	2,400	189,000	700	1,400	2,000	2,800
4.30 opeks	2,300	188,000	1,000	1,700	2,300	3,100
4.20 opeks	2,000	184,000	1,300	2,000	2,600	3,400
4.10 opeks	1,600	178,000	1,600	2,300	2,900	3,700
4.00 opeks	1,000	168,000	1,900	2,600	3,200	4,000

   a. Based on the behavior of the aggregate supply curve, potential GDP is _____ and the natural rate of unemployment is _____%.

   b. Draw the short-run aggregate supply (SRAS) curve below.

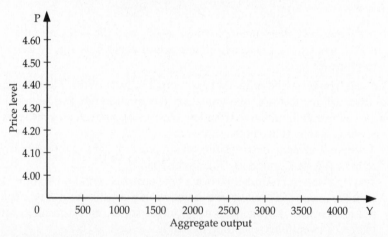

   c. Currently, aggregate demand is shown by columns (1) and (4). Graph this AD curve (AD_1). Equilibrium overall price level is _____ and equilibrium output is _____. The unemployment rate is _____%.

d. The central bank, Arbobank, undertakes an expansionary monetary policy, an open market _____ (purchase/sales) of securities. Aggregate demand curve will shift to the _____ (right/left). The new curve is described by columns (1) and (5). Graph this AD curve (AD_2). Equilibrium overall price level is _____ and equilibrium output is _____. Employment has increased by _____. The unemployment rate is _____%. Cyclical unemployment is _____%. The inflation rate is _____%.

e. If the central bank had undertaken a more expansionary monetary policy, AD would have shifted further, as described by columns (1) and (6). Graph this AD curve (AD_3). Equilibrium overall price level is _____ and equilibrium output is _____. Employment has increased by _____. The unemployment rate is _____%. Relative to the original price level, the inflation rate is _____%.

f. If the central bank had undertaken a still more expansionary monetary policy, AD would have shifted further, as described by columns (1) and (7). Graph this AD curve (AD_4). Equilibrium overall price level is _____ and equilibrium output is _____. Employment has increased by _____. The unemployment rate is _____%. Relative to the original price level, the inflation rate is _____%.

4. For each "event" affecting equilibrium inflation rate and unemployment rate, indicate the specific "result" that will occur.

Result A: inflation increases, unemployment increases.
Result B: inflation decreases, unemployment decreases.
Result C: inflation decreases, unemployment increases.
Result D: inflation increases, unemployment decreases.

	RESULT	EVENT
a.	_____	The government raises personal income taxes.
b.	_____	The price of imported final goods falls.
c.	_____	The interest rate rises.
d.	_____	The price of imported intermediate goods rises.
e.	_____	New, stringent standards for the construction of residential dwellings are enacted.
f.	_____	Environmental pollution standards are tightened substantially.
g.	_____	A reduction in foreign consumption of U.S. products occurs.
h.	_____	Employer contributions to the social security program are decreased.
i.	_____	The imposition of an import tax (tariff) on foreign consumer goods.
j.	_____	An increase in government purchases occurs.
k.	_____	There is an increase in the price of foreign oil.
l.	_____	Households prefer to save more.
m.	_____	An increased demand for new machinery or construction.
n.	_____	Inflationary expectations increase.

5. For each pair of events, work out what will happen to aggregate demand and/or aggregate supply, and then predict the impact on the inflation rate and unemployment rate. Assume that each given change (there are two changes in each case) will affect *only* aggregate demand *or* aggregate supply, but not both curves. Note: As you saw in Chapter 4, if both demand and supply curves shift, the effect on at least one variable must be uncertain.

Result A: inflation change uncertain, unemployment increases.
Result B: inflation change uncertain, unemployment decreases.
Result C: inflation decreases, unemployment change uncertain.
Result D: inflation increases, unemployment change uncertain.

RESULT	EVENTS
a. _____	The government raises business taxes and the Fed conducts open market purchases of securities.
b. _____	Inflationary expectations of firms are reduced and government spending is increased.
c. _____	The Fed raises the discount rate and foreign oil becomes much more expensive.
d. _____	The government imposes a new sales tax on consumer goods and decreases employer contributions to the social security program.
e. _____	Government trims back on defense spending and gives more generous depreciation allowances for industrial firms.

ANSWERS AND SOLUTIONS

PRACTICE TEST

I. SOLUTIONS TO MULTIPLE CHOICE QUESTIONS

1. A. If there is an excess supply of workers—i.e., unemployment—workers will accept lower wages. See p. 343/769.
2. C. See p. 347/773.
3. C. Employers will demand more labor if it is thought that the value of workers' output will increase. See p. 344/770.
4. C. This is the relative-wage explanation of unemployment. See p. 348/774. With respect to Option A, it is believed that employers generally have better information about prices.
5. D. See p. 348/774. From the discussion in this section of the chapter it is clear that price and wage information is imperfect.
6. A. The oil price hike will affect production costs and push the AS curve to the left, raising the price level. Options B and C are contractionary policies. In Option D, the demand for money will increase as a consequence of a price increase.
7. C. At the minimum wage level, quantity supplied is 500 and quantity demanded is only 300.
8. D. The classic examples are the oil price increases of the 1970s.
9. C. If aggregate demand became more (or less) variable, the Phillips Curve would not break down. The relationship developed as a result of aggregate demand changes.
10. C. The Phillips Curve revealed a negative relationship between the inflation rate and the unemployment rate.
11. D. The natural rate includes both structural and frictional unemployment.
12. D. See p. 345/771. As prices rise, wages rise to keep pace, and the level of employment is stable.

13. A. There is a trade-off between inflation and unemployment in the short run but, as wages adjust to catch up with rising prices, the natural rate of unemployment will be restored.

14. A. Higher (lower) supply decreases (increases) the inflation rate and decreases (increases) the unemployment rate.

15. C. The major raw material to show price increases was oil. Options A and B would shift aggregate demand. Option D is a fiction.

16. A. The spending increase is an expansionary fiscal policy that will shift the AD curve to the right. The unemployment rate will decrease and the inflation rate will increase—a move along the Phillips Curve.

17. A. The move from E to D represents a decrease in inflation and unemployment. This will occur if the AS curve shifts to the right, as will happen when firms expect less inflation.

18. B. The rise in the price of raw materials (imported or otherwise) will shift the AS curve to the left.

19. A. Point A represents unemployment that is lower than the natural rate, indicating that production is extremely high. Structural and frictional unemployment, although low, can't be negative!

20. C. The long-run Phillips Curve is vertical, to be sure. However, because the unemployment rate shown at point E is the natural rate, the long-run Phillips Curve will pass through this point.

II. SOLUTIONS TO APPLICATION QUESTIONS

1. a. An increase in aggregate demand would decrease unemployment and increase inflation in the short run.
   b. Aggregate supply will shift left. Price level will increase and output will decrease. The negative relationship between the inflation rate and the unemployment rate will be absent. There would be a move off the existing Phillips Curve to point E.
   c. Aggregate supply will shift left. Price level will increase and output will decrease. The negative relationship between the inflation rate and the unemployment rate will be absent. There would be a move off the existing Phillips Curve to point E.
   d. Aggregate demand will increase causing the price level to increase and output to increase. There would be a move along the existing Phillips Curve to point B.
   e. Aggregate supply will increase causing the price level to decrease and output to increase. The inflation rate will decrease and the unemployment rate will decrease. There would be a move off the existing Phillips Curve to point D.
   f. Aggregate demand will decrease causing the price level to decrease and output to decrease. The inflation rate will decrease and the unemployment rate will increase—a movement along the Phillips Curve to point C.
   g. There is a mismatch between the actual inflation rate (3%) and the expected inflation rate (0%). The Phillips Curve is based on a particular level of inflationary expectations. In the long run, the actual inflation rate and the expected inflation rate must be equal. Either expectations must increase, which would shift the Phillips Curve to the right, or the actual inflation rate must decrease.
   h. If actual inflation remains at 3%, the Phillips Curve will shift to the right (as expectations change). This shift will continue until expectations equal reality. When the expected inflation rate exceeds the actual future inflation rate, real wages will rise, unemployment will increase, and output will decrease. The short-run aggregate supply curve will shift to the left.
   i. The long-run Phillips Curve is vertical at an unemployment rate of 6%.

2. a. In equilibrium, $Q_D = Q_S$. $300 - W = 5W$. $120 = 6W$, therefore $W = 20$. When $W = 20$, employment is 100, i.e., 100,000. Frictional and structural unemployment run at a constant 10,000. There is no cyclical unemployment. Unemployment rate = $5 / 110 = 4.55\%$.
   b. Labor force = 100,000 employed + 10,000 unemployed = 110,000.
      Participation rate = labor force × 100% / population = 110,000 / 160,000 = 68.75%.

c.   If $W = 20$, $Q_D = 120 - (22) = 98$ and $Q_S = 5(22) = 110$.

Employment will decrease from 100,000 to 98,000.

Frictional and structural unemployment remain at 10,000, but an additional 12,000 individuals will be seeking work. Total unemployed is 22,000.

The labor force has increased by 10,000 to 120,000.

The unemployment rate, which is unemployed $\times$ 100% / labor force, will be 22,000 $\times$ 100% / 120,000, or 18.33%.

Participation rate = labor force $\times$ 100% / population = 120,000/160,000 = 75%.

3.   a.   Structural and frictional unemployment run at 10,000. The natural rate of unemployment is 10,000 / 200,000 or 5%. When 190,000 workers are employed, the output level is 2,500. The maximum output level is 2,500. Note that the maximum value of output for the short-run AS curve can be greater than the potential output level.

    b.   See the diagram below.

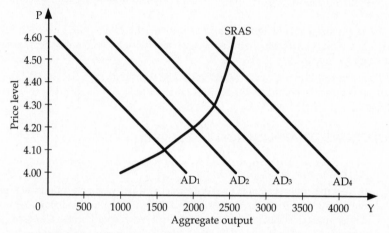

    c.   The equilibrium price level (where AD = AS) is 4.10 opeks and equilibrium output is 1,600. The unemployment rate is 11%.

    d.   purchase; right. Price level is 4.20 opeks, and output level is 2,000. Employment has risen by 6,000 workers. 8% of workers remain unemployed. Because structural and frictional unemployment are at 5%, cyclical unemployment must be 3%. The price level has risen from 4.10 opeks to 4.20 opeks, therefore the inflation rate is 2.44%.

    e.   Price level is 4.30 opeks, and output level is 2,300. Employment has risen by 4,000 workers. 6% of workers remain unemployed. The price level has risen from 4.10 opeks to 4.30 opeks, therefore the inflation rate is 4.88%.

    f.   Price level is 4.50 opeks, and output level is 2,500. Employment has risen by 2,000 workers. 5% of workers remain unemployed. The price level has risen from 4.10 opeks to 4.50 opeks, therefore the inflation rate is 9.76%.

4.   a. C   e. A   i. D   m. D
    b. C   f. A   j. D   n. A
    c. C   g. C   k. A
    d. A   h. B   l. C

Compare these results with those obtained in Application questions 2 and 6 in the preceding chapter.

Note: Some of these "shocks" may affect both aggregate demand and aggregate supply. The above answers are for the single strongest change.

5.   a.   D. An increase in business taxes will shift the AS curve to the left, while the open market purchase will increase the money supply and shift the AD curve to the right. Both shifts are inflationary, but the effect on output (and on the unemployment rate) is ambiguous.

    b.   B. As firms come to expect less inflation, they will be willing to produce more at any given price level—AS will shift to the right. The increase in government spending is expansionary and will shift the AD curve to the right. Both shifts will expand output and reduce unemployment, but the effect on the inflation rate is ambiguous.

c. A. As oil increases in price, the AS curve will shift to the left. The Fed action is contractionary and will shift the AD curve to the left. Both shifts will reduce output and increase unemployment, but the effect on the inflation rate is ambiguous.

d. C. The sales tax will reduce consumption, and the AD curve will shift to the left. The reduction in employer contributions to social security will reduce the costs of production—AS will shift to the right. Both shifts will reduce inflation, but the effect on output (and on the unemployment rate) is ambiguous.

e. C. The cutback in defense spending will reduce aggregate demand. The increased depreciation allowances will increase the profitability of firms and encourage more production. In fact, this is a typical "supply-side" policy. See Chapter 19 (34). AS will shift to the right. Both shifts will reduce inflation, but the effect on output (and on the unemployment rate) is ambiguous.

DEFICIT REDUCTION, STABILIZATION POLICY, AND MACRO ISSUES ABROAD

16

COMBINED TEXT

31

OBJECTIVES: POINT BY POINT

After completing this chapter, you should be able to accomplish the objectives listed below.

GENERAL COMMENT

This chapter contains an assortment of topics, none of which is worth a chapter on its own, but each of which is interesting. It gives you a good opportunity to review your understanding of the macroeconomic model that Case and Fair have constructed and to analyze the economics behind your own political beliefs.

OBJECTIVE 1: Outline the relationship between the federal deficit and the federal debt. Indicate the difference between debt owed by a household and debt owed by the government.

The *federal deficit* (G – T) is the difference between government tax receipts and expenditures. The *federal debt* is the accumulation of all previous deficits (minus surpluses). Just like a household, when the government incurs debt it must borrow and pay interest on the loans. Unlike a household, though, the government can refinance loans by issuing new bonds—this process could continue indefinitely. If "crowding out" of private investment is a consequence of the federal deficit, future standards of living could be lower because expansion of the capital stock has been restricted. (page 364/790)

> **TIP:** Increases in government spending (G) and decreases in net taxes (T) will increase the deficit. Expansionary fiscal policies, therefore, increase the deficit. However, expansionary monetary policies reduce the deficit. Why? Lower interest rates stimulate investment, boost aggregate income, and increase tax receipts.

Note that, given no change in government policy, the recession of 1990–91 would have had an expansionary impact on the deficit. Lower incomes mean lower income tax receipts, and longer unemployment lines mean larger unemployment benefit payouts.

PRACTICE

1. Which of the following statements about the deficit and debt is true
   A. The federal debt is the total of all previous federal budget deficits.
   B. Almost 40% of the federal debt is held by foreigners.
   C. A decrease in the deficit will result in a decrease in the debt.
   D. The federal debt is an asset of the private sector.
   Answer: D. See p. 365/791. Note that the government would have to run a surplus, not just reduce the deficit, to decrease the debt (Option C). Option A is incorrect—the debt is the net total of all previous deficits minus previous surpluses.

2. By the end of 1994, the debt was approximately _____ of GDP.
   A. 5.0%.
   B. 18.7%.
   C. 23.2%.
   D. 51.7%.
   Answer: D. See p. 365/791.

3. _____ is the largest single element of the federal budget, followed by _____ (second) and _____ (third).
   A. Interest payments, national defense, social security payments.
   B. National defense, social security payments, interest payments.
   C. National defense, interest payments, social security payments.
   D. Interest payments, social security payments, national defense.
   Answer: B. See p. 366/792.

4. In 1996, the government announces the slashing of Social Security benefits beginning in 1999. *Ceteris paribus,* such a policy would _____ the deficit before 1998. Total government obligations would _____
   A. reduce, increase.
   B. reduce, decrease.
   C. have no effect on, increase.
   D. have no effect on, decrease.
   Answer: D. See p. 369/795.

OBJECTIVE 2: Outline the objectives and drawbacks of the Gramm-Rudman-Hollings (GRH) Bill and the proposed balanced-budget amendment of 1995. Use the concept of the deficit response index to demonstrate the effects on the deficit of a cut in government spending.

Pressure for deficit reduction legislation led to the 1986 *Gramm-Rudman-Hollings Bill,* which set targets for the maximum deficit values in successive years. Failure to meet the targets would trigger across-the-board cuts in spending programs. In fact, the targets were "moved" when it became clear that they would not be met!

(page 369/795)

GRH is over-simple. To remove a deficit of $20 billion doesn't require a government spending cut of $20 billion, but rather a greater reduction because spending cuts have a negative impact on tax revenues. A spending cut reduces aggregate output and, therefore, tax receipts. Lower tax receipts widen the deficit again. The *deficit response index* measures how much a one dollar cut in income will reduce the deficit.

(page 371/797)

Deficit targeting is an automatic destabilizer, calling for spending cuts or tax hikes when economic activity decreases. Such contractionary action would further aggravate the recession. Only aggressive expansionary action by the Fed or increased confidence by the private sector could offset this effect.

(page 373/799)

> **TIP:** Review Chapter 25 to see that private sector saving must finance investment and public sector borrowing. When deficits increase, there is less left over for private sector investment.

> **TIP:** The DRI is a tricky concept. Take the time to work through the text-book's example carefully. Try it again with your own numbers.

Comment: The government multiplier approaches zero as the (short-run) aggregate supply curve becomes steeper.

PRACTICE

5. The effectiveness of GRH is best summarized by which of the following?
   A. GRH succeeded in its objective, and the deficit has been reduced.
   B. GRH succeeded in its objective, but the deficit remains high.
   C. GRH failed in its objective, but the deficit has been reduced.
   D. GRH failed in its objective, and the deficit remains high.
   Answer: D. The size of the deficit remains an important issue.

6. Each of the following is a partial explanation for the fact that the federal deficit increases during a recession except
   A. a decrease in output results in more government transfer payments to households.
   B. a decrease in output causes personal income tax revenues to decrease (because taxable income decreases during an economic slowdown).
   C. a decrease in output results in expansionary fiscal policy.
   D. a decrease in output causes decreases in tax revenues collected from corporations.
   Answer: C. The government may not choose to enact expansionary fiscal policies during a recession.

7. The multiplier is 2.5. Investment spending falls by $200 million causing taxes to fall by $100 million. The deficit response index is _____.
   A. .5.
   B. .2.
   C. −.2.
   D. −.5.
   Answer: C. Output will decrease by $500 million (200 × 2.5). DRI = change in deficit/change in income = 100 / −500 = −.2.

8. In the U.S. economy, the government wishes to cut the deficit by $50 billion. This could be achieved by _____ government spending by _____ $50 billion.
   A. increasing, more than.
   B. increasing, less than.
   C. decreasing, more than.
   D. decreasing, less than.
   Answer: C. A spending cut of exactly $50 billion reduces equilibrium income by some multiple (perhaps 1.4). As income falls, net taxes decrease, partly offsetting the deficit-reducing effect of the spending cut.

9. The balanced-budget amendment would have been destabilizing because, if the economy dips into a recession, the legislation would require _____ in government spending and/or _____ in net taxes.
   A. increases, increases.
   B. increases, decreases.
   C. decreases, increases.
   D. decreases, decreases.
   Answer: C. See p. 371/797.

10. Deficit targeting is in effect when the economy is hit by a negative demand shock. The deficit will _____ . By acting to balance the budget, government policy will make aggregate demand decrease _____

    A. increase, more.
    B. increase, less.
    C. decrease, more.
    D. decrease, less.

    Answer: A. See Figure 16/31.3.

11. Arboc and Arbez are neighboring economies. The deficit response index in each is –.2. The government spending multiplier in Arboc is 2; the government spending multiplier in Arbez is 4. An equal decrease in government spending of $20 (million) in each economy would result in a

    B. smaller reduction in the deficit in Arbez.
    C. bigger increase in the deficit in Arbez.
    D. smaller increase in the deficit in Arbez.

    Answer: B. Arboc: $\Delta Y = -\$20 \times 2 = -\$40$. Change in deficit $= \Delta Y \times DRI = -\$40 \times -.2 = \$8$. The deficit decreases by $\$20 - \$8$, or $\$12$. Arbez: $\Delta Y = -\$20 \times 4 = -\$80$. Change in deficit $= \Delta Y \times DRI = -\$80 \times -.2 = \$16$. The deficit decreases by $\$20 - \$16$, or $\$4$.

OBJECTIVE 3: State the goals of the Fed (as discussed in this chapter) and explain the rationale behind the policy of "leaning against the wind."

The Fed seeks to maintain high output, high employment levels, and low inflation. When aggregate demand is high (low), the Fed will reduce (increase) the money supply. The Fed often "leans against the wind," which means that it moves to offset fluctuations in the economy.

The central banks of other nations have goals (and policy tools) similar to those of the Fed. Following the reunification of Germany in 1989, the German government incurred very sizable deficits and borrowed heavily. Inflation was feared. The Bundesbank adopted an extremely restrictive monetary stance, raising interest rates far above those of its European Union partners, to choke off excessive spending, as can be seen from Figure 16/31.8.

Any deficit reduction strategy makes an assumption about the behavior of the Fed. The Fed might move to compensate for cuts in government spending by reducing the interest rate, or it might not. In the former case, the deficit reduction strategy would be more successful because tax collections would not fall.

(page 374/800)

PRACTICE

12. The Fed is most likely to increase the money supply when output is _____ and inflation is _____

    A. high, high.
    B. high, low.
    C. low, high.
    D. low, low.

    Answer: D. An increase in the money supply is an expansionary policy. The Fed is most likely to stimulate the economy when output is low. Given the Fed's concern about inflation, an easy money policy is more likely when inflation is low.

13. There is a negative demand shock. The Fed "leans against the wind." We would expect the money supply to _____. The interest rate will decrease _____ than otherwise.
    A. increase, more.
    B. increase, less.
    C. decrease, more.
    D. decrease, less.
    Answer: A. To compensate for the demand shock, the Fed would undertake an expansionary policy. The initial shock would reduce money demand and the interest rate. The increased money supply will make the interest rate reduction greater.

14. Congress introduces a deficit-reduction program. If the Fed "leans against the wind," output will be _____ than otherwise and net taxes will be _____ than otherwise.
    A. greater, greater.
    B. greater, smaller.
    C. smaller, greater.
    D. smaller, smaller.
    Answer: A. "Leaning against the wind" means that the Fed offsets other economic changes. The deficit-reduction package is contractionary, so the Fed's policy will be expansionary, causing output to fall less. Net taxes will fall less.

15. The short-run aggregate supply curve shifts to the left. Inflation will _____. If the Fed decreases the money supply, it indicates that the Fed believes low output to be a _____ problem than high inflation.
    A. increase, greater.
    B. increase, lesser.
    C. decrease, greater.
    D. decrease, lesser.
    Answer: B. The decrease in aggregate supply will cause stagflation. A contractionary policy is designed to dampen inflation, but it will aggravate the decrease in output. See p. 375/801.

Use the following information to answer the next three questions. Arboc's central bank, Arbobank, is committed to maintaining output close to full employment, a situation that currently exists. Suddenly, Arboc experiences sharply higher prices for its imported steel (an important input it cannot make itself).

16. The shock experienced by Arboc is best described as a
    A. positive demand shock.
    B. positive supply shock.
    C. negative demand shock.
    D. negative supply shock.
    Answer: D. Negative shocks reduce output. If the price of an input increases, it will have an adverse effect on supply—this is *stagflation*.

17. Given the shock experienced by Arboc, Arbobank "leans against the wind." The Fed will _____ the money supply. Aggregate demand will _____.
    A. increase, increase
    B. increase, decrease
    C. decrease, increase
    D. decrease, decrease
    Answer: A. To stimulate output the Fed will increase the money supply which will make the aggregate demand curve shift to the right.

18. If Arbobank had taken no action, then in the long run, the inflation rate would have been _____ it was in the initial situation. In the long run, the policy of leaning against the wind will make the inflation rate _____ it was in the initial situation.
   A. higher than, higher than.
   B. higher than, the same as.
   C. the same as, higher than.
   D. the same as, the same as.

   Answer: C. If Arbobank had taken no action, Chapter 29 tells us that the AS curve would have shifted to the right (i.e., back to its original position) with no effect on prices. The central bank's action, however, has met a price-increasing decrease in supply with a price-increasing expansion in demand.

OBJECTIVE 4: Distinguish the three types of time lag in stabilization policies. Discuss the problems time lags cause for stabilization policy.

Fiscal and monetary *stabilization policies* are intended to smooth out fluctuations in output, employment, and prices, but policy actions do not operate immediately. There are *time lags*. Economists distinguish three:

   a. the *recognition lag* is the time between the development of a problem and its recognition.
   b. the *implementation lag* is the time necessary to hammer out and enact a policy following the recognition of the problem. Implementation lags tend to be shorter for monetary policy than for fiscal policy.
   c. the *response lag* is the time it takes for the economy to react to the policy action. Response lags tend to be longer for monetary policy than for fiscal policy. (page 380/806)

A case ("the fool in the shower") can be made that stabilization policies actually destabilize the economy because, by the time a policy is taking effect, the problem it is designed to address (rising unemployment, for example) may have been replaced by another (inflation, for example) for which the policy is completely inappropriate. (page 378/804)

The conventional wisdom has been that post-1945 stabilization policy has reduced the size of business cycles (relative to their magnitude in the 1930s and before). Interestingly, more recent studies have found that the size of the business cycle may have been unaffected by stabilization policy.

   Comment: The main differences in terms of time lags between fiscal and monetary policy are at the implementation stage (where monetary policy can be almost instantaneous and fiscal policy lumberingly slow) and the response stage (where fiscal policy tends to work more quickly).

   The problems of policy effectiveness have led some economists to call for the complete abandonment of stabilization policy.

   Comment: GDP is measured neither continuously nor with great accuracy. At the beginning of 1994, the Fed predicted the economy's performance for the year: economic growth of 3%, inflation of 3% and unemployment of 6.5%. In fact, in 1994, economic growth was 4%, inflation was 2.7% and unemployment was 5.6%.

PRACTICE

19. Stabilization policy attempts to
   A. stabilize the federal budget.
   B. minimize changes in the money supply and interest rates.
   C. minimize changes in the levels of output and prices.
   D. increase the size of automatic stabilizers.

   Answer: C. See p. 377/803.

20. The response lag is shorter for
    A. fiscal policy, because changes in, say, government spending have an immediate impact on aggregate demand.
    B. fiscal policy, because monetary policy requires approval by a minimum of 75% of the Federal Reserve Board.
    C. monetary policy, because open market operations are very easy to perform.
    D. monetary policy, because money (currency, demand deposits) must be used in almost all transactions.
    Answer: A. See p. 380/806.

21. Implementation lags tend to be _____ for monetary policy than for fiscal policy; response lags tend to be _____ for monetary policy than for fiscal policy.
    A. shorter, shorter.
    B. shorter, longer.
    C. longer, shorter.
    D. longer, longer.
    Answer: B. See pp. 379–380 (805–806).

22. The "fool in the shower" analogy argues that
    A. we should leave the economy to adjust on its own to cure fluctuations.
    B. the government and the Fed should coordinate policy actions throughout the business cycle.
    C. policymakers must provide alternating periods of stimulus and restraint to keep the economy from stagnating.
    D. given time lags, expansionary policies are required to stabilize the economy.
    Answer: A. See p. 378/804.

OBJECTIVE 5: Compare the business cycle experiences of Europe and Japan with those of the United States. Provide four reasons for the persistence of high unemployment in the European countries.

In general, Japanese business cycles have been relatively mild with low inflation and unemployment rates, and robust growth. Signs of weakness appeared in the early 1990s. Japan responded to these signs by "leaning against the wind." At the opposite end of the spectrum, the United Kingdom suffered quite severe recessions in the early 1980s and 1990s with negative GDP growth. In 1991–93, the Bank of England responded by easing monetary policy and lowering interest rates. Similar patterns were exhibited by the other European economies.   (page 382/808)

A phenomenon peculiar to Europe is persistently high unemployment rates even when the economy is prospering. Reasons suggested include:
    a. generous welfare benefits that reward inactivity,
    b. declining employability as the period of unemployment lengthens,
    c. artificially high wages due to union power, and
    d. policies that have not been sufficiently expansionary.

Comment: In Britain, unemployment averaged about 3.5% during the 1970s; in the 1980s, it averaged above 9.0%, partly because of the contractionary policies of the Thatcher government. The perplexing issue is that, when the contractionary policies were released, unemployment remained high.

PRACTICE

23. Each of the following might result in the persistently high unemployment rates exhibited in Europe in the 1980s except
    A. increased unemployment benefits.
    B. decreases in union negotiating power that decrease the wage and discourage workers.
    C. timid expansionary policies that have not been aggressive enough in stimulating the economy.
    D. declines in work skills due to extended periods of unemployment.
    Answer: B. See p. 384/810.

POLICY PROBLEMS

This chapter is excellent in pointing out the problems faced by policymakers. It's easy to think that we should be able to "fine tune" the economy, efficiently curing inflation, unemployment, output, the deficit, and so on. (Economists used to believe so, too.) But time lags, lack of coordination between Congress and the Fed, political considerations, slippages in the economy, and the ticklish problem of expectations conspire to make policy much more like a blunt instrument than a surgeon's scalpel.

PRACTICE TEST

I. MULTIPLE CHOICE QUESTIONS.

Select the option that provides the single best answer.

_____ 1. The multiplier is 1.8 and the deficit response index is –.15. The government cuts spending by $100 million. The Fed "leans against the wind." Net taxes will fall by _____ and the deficit will fall by _____
    A. more than $27 million, more than $73 million.
    B. more than $27 million, less than $73 million.
    C. less than $27 million, more than $73 million.
    D. less than $27 million, less than $73 million.

_____ 2. Expansionary monetary policies _____ the deficit and expansionary fiscal policies _____ the deficit.
    A. increase, increase.
    B. increase, decrease.
    C. decrease, increase.
    D. decrease, decrease.

_____ 3. The multiplier is 2 and the deficit response index is –.3. The government cuts spending by $100 million. Taxes will
    A. rise by $200 million.
    B. fall by $200 million.
    C. rise by $60 million.
    D. fall by $60 million.

_____ 4. The multiplier is 1.6 and the deficit response index is –.2. The government cuts spending by $50 million. Taxes will fall by _____ and the deficit will fall by _____
    A. $80 million, $34 million.
    B. $80 million, $16 million.
    C. $16 million, $34 million.
    D. $34 million, $16 million.

5. Government spending decreases. If the Fed "leans against the wind," interest rates will be _____ than otherwise and the deficit will be _____ than otherwise.
   A. higher, greater.
   B. higher, smaller.
   C. lower, greater.
   D. lower, smaller.

6. The implementation lag is the length of time between _____ and _____
   A. the recognition of a problem, the resolution of the problem.
   B. the recognition of a problem, the development and enactment of a remedy.
   C. the development of a problem, its ultimate resolution.
   D. the development of a problem, the development and enactment of a remedy.

7. The multiplier is 2. The government cuts spending by $100 million. Taxes fall by $50 million. The deficit response index is
   A. .5.
   B. −.5.
   C. .25.
   D. −.25.

8. Because the change occurs directly in aggregate demand, the _____ lag for fiscal policy is _____ than that for monetary policy.
   A. implementation, shorter.
   B. implementation, longer.
   C. response, shorter.
   D. response, longer.

9. The multiplier is 1.6. The government cuts spending by $50 million. The deficit falls by $40 million. The deficit response index is
   A. .125.
   B. −.125.
   C. .25.
   D. −.25.

10. GRH is recognized as an automatic destabilizer because
    A. during a recession, it required tax cuts if the deficit target had not been met.
    B. during a boom, it required spending increases if the deficit target had not been met.
    C. during a recession, it required contractionary fiscal measures if the deficit target had not been met.
    D. during a recession, it required expansionary fiscal measures if the deficit target had not been met.

11. The government implements a tax cut. If the Fed "leans against the wind," it will undertake
    A. an expansionary monetary policy to increase interest rates.
    B. an expansionary monetary policy to decrease interest rates.
    C. a contractionary monetary policy to increase interest rates.
    D. a contractionary monetary policy to decrease interest rates.

12. The federal deficit is a _____; the federal debt is a _____
    A. flow, flow.
    B. flow, stock.
    C. stock, flow.
    D. stock, stock.

_____ 13. The European Community imposes a ban on agricultural imports from the United States. From the U.S. point of view, this is best described as a
  A. positive demand shock.
  B. positive supply shock.
  C. negative demand shock.
  D. negative supply shock.

_____ 14. The economy is expanding. If the Fed "leans against the wind," we should expect open market _____ resulting in a _____ interest rate than would otherwise have been the case.
  A. purchases, higher.
  B. purchases, lower.
  C. sales, higher.
  D. sales, lower.

Use the following information to answer the next two questions. Noil and Regit are two neighboring economies. Noil imposes a tariff on consumer goods imported from Regit. In retaliation, Regit imposes a similar tariff on Noilian oil (an input which Regit does not produce itself).

_____ 15. Noil's tariff is a negative _____ shock for Regit. Regit's federal deficit will _____
  A. demand, increase.
  B. demand, decrease.
  C. supply, increase.
  D. supply, decrease.

_____ 16. Noil's tariff will _____ unemployment in Regit. Regit's tariff will _____ the effect of the Noilian tariff.
  A. increase, intensify.
  B. increase, offset.
  C. decrease, intensify.
  D. decrease, offset.

II. APPLICATION QUESTIONS.

1. a. "The less negative the deficit response index, the more effective a government spending cut will be in reducing the deficit." True or false? Explain.
   b. "The Gramm-Rudman-Hollings legislation, if applied as originally intended, would have operated as an additional automatic stabilizer." True or false? Explain.
   c. "If the Fed expands the money supply during a period of substantial excess capacity, the government deficit will be reduced." True or false? Explain.

2. The economy is at the full-employment output level. The budget deficit is currently $240 million. Evidence shows that the government spending multiplier is 1.5 and that, for each $1 decrease in GDP, net tax revenues decrease by 20¢. The Congress decides to balance the budget by cutting government spending by $240 million.
   a. Calculate the effect on GDP.
   b. Calculate the effect on net taxes.
   c. Calculate the effect on the deficit.
   d. Calculate the size of the deficit following the policy action.
   e. In terms of the AS / AD diagram, describe what the government's policy action has done to the curves, to prices, and to unemployment.
   f. If policymakers make no other changes, what will happen, qualitatively, to the deficit? Why? Can you give numbers to support your view?

g. Policymakers are too impatient to wait for the long run. Can you calculate how much government spending would have to be cut in order to balance the budget immediately. (We know it must be a cut of more than $240 million.)

Congress returns to its original proposed cut of $240 million. This will be inadequate to balance the budget.

h. What sort of policy action could the Fed take to help balance the budget?
i. Given the three tools of monetary policy, indicate in which direction each would have to change in order to effect the desired policy?

3. The "insider-outsider theory" has been developed to explain the persistently high unemployment rates in Europe. Union members are insiders—they control wage negotiations and get the first choice of jobs. Nonunion members are outsiders—they receive any additional jobs. Any worker who is unemployed for a specified period of time is no longer eligible to be a union member. Following is a simple model to explain how long-term unemployment might occur.

The demand for labor (Q_D) is given by $Q_D = 600,000 - 20W$, where W is the wage. As a simplifying assumption, the total supply of labor (Q_S) is assumed to be fixed at 500,000. We will ignore frictional and structural unemployment.

a. Determine the equilibrium wage and the unemployment rate.
b. Now suppose that 400,000 workers unionize and negotiate a wage contract that will give them the highest possible wage without any unemployment of their members. Determine the equilibrium wage.
c. Determine the unemployment rate.

Now suppose that contractionary monetary policies produce a recession (as happened in Europe in the early 1980s) and that 40,000 workers lose their jobs. These workers are no longer eligible to be union members.

d. Calculate the number of union members and the number of outsiders.
e. The "insiders" negotiate a new wage contract that will give them the highest possible wage without any unemployment of their members. Determine the equilibrium wage.
f. Determine the unemployment rate.

Now the economy begins to expand, causing the demand for labor to increase. The new demand for labor (Q_D) is given by $Q_D = 700,000 - 20W$. (Graph this to verify that this is a rightward shift of the labor demand curve.)

g. Given the new labor market environment, the "insiders" negotiate a new wage contract that, again, will give them the highest possible wage without any unemployment of their members. Determine the equilibrium wage.
h. Determine the unemployment rate.
i. Analyze the plausibility of the "insider-outsider" model.

4. Suppose the economy is described by the following model.
   (1) $C = 280 + .8Yd$
   (2) $I = 400$
   (3) $G = 800$
   (4) $T = -400 + .2Y$
   (5) $Yd = Y - T$

a. Calculate the equilibrium income level (where $Y = C + I + G$).
b. Calculate the government deficit (D) where deficit $= G - T$.
c. The expenditure multiplier is _____.
d. Given the initial model, suppose that, suddenly, investment falls by $50. Calculate the change in the equilibrium income level.
e. How will this investment change affect the deficit?
f. The deficit response index in this model is _____.
g. Given the initial model, to achieve a balanced budget through a cut in government spending, GDP would have to fall by _____.
h. To achieve this GDP cut with a reduction in government spending, G must fall by _____.

i. Given the initial model, suppose that this year's deficit target is 200. Suddenly, as we saw above, investment falls by $50. To restore the deficit target of 200, government spending would have to _____ (rise/fall) by _____.

j. The investment change and the government spending change together would make income _____ (rise/fall) by _____.

5. Suppose that the budget is required by law to be balanced.
   a. What will happen to production and output if investment spending falls?
   b. What will happen to tax receipts?
   c. What will happen to public transfer payments?
   d. Bearing these factors in mind, what must now be happening to the budget?
   e. What would you recommend, given the balanced budget requirement that demands equality between government spending and net tax receipts?
   f. What would your obligatory policy recommendation do to an economy already experiencing recession and growing unemployment?

6. Congress cuts government spending by $50 to reduce the deficit. If the spending multiplier has a value of 2, aggregate output will _____ (rise/fall) by _____. If the deficit response index is –.1, taxes will _____ (rise/fall) by _____ and the deficit will _____ (increase/decrease) by _____. If the multiplier has a value of 1.4, however, aggregate output would _____ (rise/fall) by _____. If the deficit response index is still –.1, taxes will _____ (rise/fall) by _____ and the deficit will _____ (increase/decrease) by _____. We can conclude that a given cut in government spending will be more effective in reducing the deficit the _____ (larger/smaller) the value of the spending multiplier.

ANSWERS AND SOLUTIONS

PRACTICE TEST

I. SOLUTIONS TO MULTIPLE CHOICE QUESTIONS

1. C. If the Fed takes no action, the $100 million cut in spending will result in a $180 million reduction in output. The DRI indicates that the deficit will increase by $27 million (–.15 × –180 million) as net taxes decrease by $27 million. The net change in the deficit is $73 million (100 – 27). If the Fed "leans against the wind," this reduces the size of the output decrease and reduces the size of the tax decrease (less than $27 million). The deficit will be reduced, therefore, by more than $73 million.

2. C. An expansionary monetary policy increases spending and income—net taxes increase and the deficit decreases. An increase in government spending or a decrease in net taxes results in an immediate increase in the deficit. Unless the DRI is more negative than –1.00, the deficit will increase.

3. D. Output decreases by $200 million (2 × $100 million). As output decreases, net taxes decrease by $60 million (–.3 × $200 million).

4. C. Output decreases by $80 million (1.6 × $50 million). As output decreases, net taxes decrease by $16 million (–.2 × $80 million). The net change in the deficit is $34 million (50 – 16).

5. D. A cut in government spending (which is contractionary) will provoke a compensating increase in the money supply. The interest rate will decrease as a result. Output and net taxes will decrease less than otherwise.

6. B. See p. 379/805.

7. D. Output decreases by $200 million (2 × $100 million). As output decreases, net taxes decrease by $50 million (DRI × $200 million). DRI = –.25.

8. C. See p. 379/805.

9. B. Output decreases by $80 million (1.6 × $50 million). The net change in the deficit is $40 million (50 – 10). Net taxes, therefore, decrease by $10 million (DRI × $80 million). DRI = –.125.

10. C. GRH requires across-the-board spending cuts, even during a recession.

11. C. A tax cut will increase disposable income and encourage higher consumption spending. A contractionary monetary policy is called for. A contractionary monetary policy will reduce the money supply and increase interest rates.

12. B. A flow is measured over a period of time—the deficit is for a particular year. A stock is measured at a point in time—the debt is measured, say, on December 31st.

13. C. Demand for American output has decreased—the AD curve has shifted to the left.

14. C. The Fed will dampen demand by raising the interest rate. An open market sale would be a suitable contractionary policy.

15. A. Regit's exports to Noil will decrease, i.e., there is less demand for Regitani production. As output falls, net taxes will decrease.

16. A. When demand decreases in Regit, output will decrease and layoffs will occur. By hiking the cost of a production input, the Regitani authorities have caused a negative supply shock, which will shift the aggregate supply curve to the left.

II. SOLUTIONS TO APPLICATION QUESTIONS

1. a. True. If output falls by $1 billion, the deficit response index indicates how much the deficit will increase as a result. If the DRI were zero, the deficit would not change at all. If, to reduce the deficit, government spending were cut and it was this that prompted the decline in output, and the DRI were zero, there would be no offsetting increase in the deficit. See p. 371/797.

   b. False. GRH would have been destabilizing, calling, for example, for cuts in government spending during a recession. See p. 373/799.

   c. True. An expansionary monetary policy will increase output and employment. Net taxes will be increased, reducing the deficit.

2. a. $\Delta GDP = \Delta G \times$ multiplier $= -\$240$ million $\times 1.5 = -\$360$ million.

   b. ΔNet taxes $= \Delta GDP \times .2 = -\$360$ million $\times .2 = -\$72$ million.

   c. $\Delta D = \Delta G - \Delta T = (-\$240 - -\$72)$ million $= -\$168$ million.

   d. The deficit has been reduced by $168 million, from $240 million to $72 million.

   e. The AD curve has shifted to the left. The new intersection of AD and the short-run AS curve is $360 million below the full-employment output level where the vertical LRAS curve is located. The overall price level is lower and, as output has been reduced, unemployment is higher.

   f. In the long run the economy will move back to the full-employment output level—the short-run aggregate supply curve will shift to the right. As output expands (by $360 million), net taxes will increase by $360 million times .2, or $72 million. The budget will be balanced.

   g. $\Delta D = \Delta G - \Delta T = \Delta G - .2\Delta GDP. \Delta GDP = 1.5\Delta G.$
   $\Delta D = \Delta G - .2(1.5)\Delta G = \Delta G - .3\Delta G = .7\Delta G. \Delta D = \$240$ million.
   $.7\Delta G = \$240$ million, therefore $\Delta G = \$342.8571$ million.
   Government spending must be cut by $342,857,143.

   h. The Fed would need to undertake an expansionary monetary policy.

   i. Open market purchases of bonds, a reduction in the discount rate, or a reduction in the reserve requirement.

3. a. In equilibrium, $Q_D = Q_S$, therefore $600,000 - 20W = 500,000$. $W = 5000$.
   All workers have a job, therefore the unemployment rate is zero. Note that we are ignoring frictional and structural unemployment.

   b. In equilibrium, $Q_D = Q_S$, therefore $600,000 - 20W = 400,000$. $W = 10,000$. Note that employers may go along with this arrangement in order to avoid costly strikes.

   c. The unemployment rate $= 100,000 \times 100\% / 500,000 = 20\%$.

   d. There are now 360,000 union members and 140,000 nonunion workers.

   e. In equilibrium, $Q_D = Q_S$, therefore $600,000 - 20W = 360,000$. $W = 12,000$.

   f. The unemployment rate $= 140,000 \times 100\% / 500,000 = 28\%$. Note that contractions in the economy raise wages and increase unemployment.

   g. In equilibrium, $Q_D = Q_S$, therefore $700,000 - 20W = 360,000$. $W = 17,000$.

   h. The unemployment rate remains at 28% even when the economy is expanding.

   i. Some of our simplifying assumptions are too simple. Total labor supply and union labor supply are unlikely to be perfectly vertical. However, the arrangement specified is clearly in the best interests of union members. Employers may benefit through fewer disruptions and the development of a skilled, motivated (union) labor force. Outsiders lose of course but, with Europe's generous unemployment benefits, may be compensated sufficiently not to protest.

4. a. $Y = C + I + G$
$= 280 + .8(Y - T) + 400 + 800$
$= 1{,}480 + .8(Y + 400 - .2Y)$
$= 1{,}480 + .8Y + 320 - .16Y$
$.36Y = 1{,}800$
$Y = 5{,}000.$

b. $G - T = 800 + 400 - .2(5{,}000) = 200.$

c. multiplier $= 1 / (1 - MPC) = 1/(1 - .64) = 2.7778.$
Note: A simple way to get MPC is to conduct the following "thought experiment." If income (Y) increases by 100, taxes will increase by 20 (.2Y). Disposable income will increase by 80. Consumption increases by 64 (.8Yd). As income changes by 100, consumption changes by 64.

d. The new equilibrium level of income may be calculated by changing the value of I as follows:
$Y = C + I + G$
$= 280 + .8(Y - T) + 350 + 800$
$= 1{,}430 + .8(Y + 400 - .2Y)$
$= 1{,}430 + .8Y + 320 - .16Y$
$.36Y = 1{,}750$
$Y = 4{,}861.11$, so income decreases by 138.89.
Alternatively, $\Delta Y = \Delta I \times$ multiplier $= -50 \times 2.7778 = -138.89.$

e. $G - T = 800 + 400 - .2(4{,}861.11) = 227.78$ The deficit increases by 27.78.

f. DRI $= \Delta D / \Delta Y = 27.78 / -138.89 = -.20.$

g. GDP must decrease by 1,250.
Thought experiment: A 100 dollar cut in spending will reduce income by 277.78.
Taxes will fall by 55.56 (277.78 × .2). The deficit will be decreased by 44.44.
To reduce the deficit by 200, income must decrease by 1,250.

h. To achieve this change in income, government spending must decrease by 450.
$\Delta Y = \Delta G \times$ multiplier $= -1{,}250 = -450 \times 2.778.$
Check: $G = 350$ (800 − 450)
$T = -400 + .2(3{,}750) = 350.$

i. When I decreases by 50, Y equals 4,861.11, so income decreases by 138.89. The deficit increases by 27.78.
We want the deficit to decrease by 27.78.
A 100 dollar cut in spending will reduce the deficit by 44.44. A 62.5 decrease in spending will achieve a 27.78 decrease in the deficit.

j. $Y = C + I + G$
$= 280 + .8(Y - T) + 350 + 737.5$
$= 1{,}367.5 + .8(Y + 400 - .2Y)$
$= 1{,}480 + .8Y + 320 - .16Y$
$.36Y = 1{,}687.5$
$Y = 4{,}687.5$ Income will decrease by 312.5.
Check: $G = 737.5$ (800 − 62.5)
$T = -400 + .2(4{,}687.5) = 537.5$
$G - T = 737.5 - 537.5 = 200.$

5. a. Less demand, rising inventories, cutbacks in production and employment.

b. Personal and corporate income tax revenues will fall, as will sales tax revenues.

c. Welfare payments and unemployment compensation will be rising.

d. It will be experiencing a deficit.

e. Cut spending or increase taxes.

f. Make the situation worse.

6. fall; 100; fall; 10; decrease; 40; fall; 70; fall; 7; decrease; 43; smaller.

HOUSEHOLD AND FIRM BEHAVIOR IN THE MACROECONOMY

17

COMBINED TEXT

32

OBJECTIVES: POINT BY POINT

After completing this chapter, you should be able to accomplish the objectives listed below.

OBJECTIVE 1: State the reasoning behind the life-cycle hypothesis, explaining why it is an extension of the Keynesian theory of consumption.

The *life-cycle theory* argues that current income is not the only determinant of consumption, as Keynes had suggested. Permanent income—i.e., current *and* expected future income—is important, as is wealth. The household's long-range goal is to maintain a fairly stable level of consumption over the life cycle. It accomplishes this goal by dissaving in low-income periods of the life cycle (young and old) and accumulating a "nest egg" during the prime earning years. The more permanent a change in income is perceived to be, the more consumption/saving behavior will adjust. Temporary "blips" in income will have little effect on consumption. Note that, if it is permanent income that affects consumption, we get a conclusion that, at first glance, seems unusual. If Jill's income unexpectedly increases (she finds $100), the theory suggests that her consumption pattern will not change—she will save the money rather than spend it. (page 391/817)

Jack and Jill, who have identical current income levels, should have identical consumption levels according to the simple Keynesian view. But, according to the life-cycle theory, if Jack's permanent income is higher than Jill's, Jack will spend more of his current income, perhaps even borrowing against expected future income.

> **TIP:** Remember that your course is macroeconomics! During this chapter it is easy to end up thinking about the consumption and labor supply decisions of individual households and firms, rather than aggregate behavior. The point of this chapter is to increase your understanding of aggregate consumption behavior by investigating the basis for individual decisions. For example, unexpected changes in inventories will affect our macroeconomic model on the supply side, and changes in consumption will have an impact on aggregate demand.

PRACTICE

1. _____ is the proportion of income households spend on consumption.
   A. Average propensity to consume.
   B. Marginal propensity to consume.
   C. The consumption ratio.
   D. The standard of living.
   Answer: A. See p. 391/817.

2. Keynes said that consumption _____ as current income increases, and that APC _____ as income increases.
   A. increases, increases.
   B. increases, decreases.
   C. decreases, increases.
   D. decreases, decreases.
   Answer: B. Households with more income spend more, but they save a larger percentage of their income. If so, APC must decrease as income increases. See p. 391/817.

3. Permanent income is
   A. the total income earned during one's lifetime.
   B. after-tax income.
   C. the income left after all unavoidable bills have been paid.
   D. the average level of one's expected future income stream.
   Answer: D. See p. 393/819.

4. The _____ theory states that consumption and saving decisions are based on _____
   A. Keynesian, permanent income only.
   B. Keynesian, current and expected future income.
   C. life-cycle, current income only.
   D. life-cycle, current and expected future income.
   Answer: D. Keynesian consumption theory singles out current income; the life-cycle theory focuses on income expected throughout the life cycle.

OBJECTIVE 2: Distinguish between the substitution effect and the income effect. Relate these effects to the factors affecting the supply of labor.

There is a trade-off between hours of work and hours of leisure. According to the *substitution effect,* if the real wage rate rises, the opportunity cost of leisure increases, and work will be substituted for leisure. However, at higher real wage rates, more income is earned and households may prefer to reduce work-time to consume leisure—this is the *income effect.* Usually, the substitution effect dominates—higher wages lead to an increase in the quantity of labor supplied.

(page 394/820)

The microeconomic model argues that consumption and labor supply decisions are made together. Accordingly, wage rates, prices, and preferences determine both consumption and the amount of labor supplied. The wage rate of importance is the *real wage rate.*

(page 394/820)

> **Comment:** As in previous chapters, the distinction between real and nominal variables is important. Nominal wage is how many dollars you earn; real wage is how much those dollars are worth at the store. The real wage (and income) is what is significant when deciding how much to spend and how much to work.

Other factors that influence household behavior are:
a. expected future real wages,
b. wealth,
c. current and expected nonlabor income,
d. the interest rate, and
e. current and expected tax rates and transfer payments.   (page 394/820)

Greater wealth and nonlabor income discourage labor supply and increase consumption. The same holds true for higher tax rates (assuming that the substitution effect dominates) and more generous transfer payments. A higher interest rate will also discourage current consumption by rewarding saving.   (page 396/822)

> **TIP:** Note that a change in wealth or nonlabor income has an income effect on labor supply but that the substitution effect is absent.

The substitution effect discourages consumption when the interest rate rises—the opportunity cost of spending a dollar (i.e., saving it and earning interest) is higher. If the household owns positive wealth, a higher interest rate translates into higher income—the income effect operates to stimulate consumption. If the household is in debt, a higher interest rate makes it poorer—the income effect operates to depress consumption.   (page 397/823)

Tax rates and transfer payments affect consumption and the labor-supply decision. To increase labor supply, tax rates and transfers should be reduced, assuming that the substitution effect is dominant. Lower tax rates, which increase disposable income, will increase consumption and stimulate labor supply, while lower transfers will reduce consumption and stimulate labor supply.   (page 398/824)

> **TIP:** Remember that you might find exceptions to each of the cases mentioned. Exceptions do not prove the theory wrong. What is being described are the general relationships that apply most of the time for most households.

> **TIP:** Analysis using income and substitution effects is daunting at the beginning but this method of looking at the household's decision making process provides rich results—stick with it!

Comment: Both income and substitution effects are present any time that a wage change occurs, although usually the substitution effect will dominate. Note, too, that income and substitution effects are not limited to influencing only labor supply through wage rates—consumption and saving are also affected. Also, income and substitution effects are felt when there are changes in the interest rate or tax rates.

PRACTICE

5. There is a real wage decrease. The income effect will lead to a(n) _____ in the quantity of labor supplied, and the substitution effect will lead to a(n) _____ in the quantity of labor supplied.
    A. increase, increase.
    B. increase, decrease.
    C. decrease, increase.
    D. decrease, decrease.
    Answer: B. Income has decreased, given the number of hours worked. Workers are poorer and, therefore, will work more hours. The opportunity cost of leisure has decreased. Workers will more readily substitute leisure for labor.

6. The main variable that determines the trade-off between working and non-labor activity is
   A. the real wage rate.
   B. current household income.
   C. current and expected household income.
   D. the interest rate.
   Answer: A. Each of the listed factors is important in determining the preferred balance between labor and leisure, but the key variable is the wage rate. See p. 394/820.

7. There is a wage increase. If the substitution effect dominates the income effect, the quantity of labor supplied will _____ and leisure will _____
   A. increase, increase.
   B. increase, decrease.
   C. decrease, increase.
   D. decrease, decrease.
   Answer: B. Typically, the substitution effect is the stronger effect. Higher wages typically result in more work-time and less leisure.

8. Mr. Micawber is in debt. The interest rate increases. The substitution effect will _____ his consumption level, and the income effect will _____ his consumption level.
   A. increase, increase.
   B. increase, decrease.
   C. decrease, increase.
   D. decrease, decrease.
   Answer: D. The opportunity cost of consumption has increased—Micawber will substitute saving for consumption. As a debtor, a higher interest rate makes Micawber poorer; poorer individuals consume less.

9. Ebenezer Scrooge receives unexpected wealth. As a result, his consumption will _____ and his labor supply will _____
   A. increase, increase.
   B. increase, decrease.
   C. decrease, increase.
   D. decrease, decrease.
   Answer: B. Scrooge is richer; richer individuals consume more. Richer individuals also wish to have more leisure time. See p. 396/822.

10. The government cuts unemployment benefits. As a result, consumption will _____ and labor supply will _____
    A. increase, increase.
    B. increase, decrease.
    C. decrease, increase.
    D. decrease, decrease.
    Answer: C. See p. 398/824.

11. Increased tax rates reduce after-tax income. If the tax rate increases and the change is thought to be permanent, the effect on current consumption will be _____ and the effect on labor supply will be _____ than if the tax rate increase is thought to be temporary.
    A. greater, greater.
    B. greater, smaller.
    C. smaller, greater.
    D. smaller, smaller.
    Answer: A. A temporary change in circumstances can be ridden out without changing behavior very much. In the face of a permanent change, behavior will be affected more. See p. 398/824.

OBJECTIVE 3: Outline the implications of employment constraints on the consumption and labor-supply decisions of households.

If the economy is fully employed, the supply of labor is not constrained—workers seeking jobs will find them. In an economy suffering from unemployment, workers are restricted in the hours they actually work because they are on short-time or have been laid off. The actual number of hours worked depends less on the number of hours that households supply and more on how many they can get. Because the number of hours worked is no longer a variable households control, it is reasonable to argue that, if current income increased, so would current consumption. This was the original Keynesian position. The Keynesian theory is thought to apply well during periods of unemployment.   (page 399/825)

The Smith household needs to spend $1,000 a month to maintain an adequate standard of living, but it is severely constrained (by part-time employment) to spending only $600. Expected future income is not an important factor-changes in current income will determine current consumption.

> **Comment:** The distinction between durable and nondurable goods is rather fuzzy. Are clothes durable or nondurable, for example? A rule of thumb is to classify a good as durable if it lasts longer than three years and as nondurable if it doesn't.

> **Comment:** The housing investment diagram shows why "housing starts" are considered a good "leading" indicator of economic fluctuations. Notice that housing investment sagged substantially before each of the recessions and that the recovery did not begin until housing investment had risen strongly.

PRACTICE

12. The number of hours that the Smiths would work if they could is the
    A. constrained supply of labor.
    B. unconstrained supply of labor.
    C. actual supply of labor.
    D. planned supply of labor.
    Answer: B. See p. 399/825.

13. The Smiths are limited to a lesser level of employment than they would have chosen. We should expect each of the following except that
    A. saving will decrease.
    B. the average propensity to consume will decrease.
    C. the Smiths' income will decrease.
    D. the Smiths will work longer hours.
    Answer: B. APC will rise as income level decreases.

OBJECTIVE 4: Describe the factors that influence the decisions of firms regarding employment and investment in plant and equipment.

Firms must make decisions about their usage of capital and labor. When it buys new plant and equipment, the firm is making a commitment that may affect its production capacity for many years. The firm must choose whether to increase output by adopting a relatively capital-intensive or labor-intensive method of production. The relative costs of the inputs will clearly be an important factor in the choice of technology.   (page 404/830)

Expectations about sales and profits also play a major role in investment choices. Keynes named the entrepreneur's feelings about the firm's prospects "animal spirits." Because expectations are subject to much uncertainty, rapid changes in investment are likely, making this a particularly volatile component of GDP. The *accelerator effect* is the name given to the tendency to postpone investment during slumps and to expand it rapidly during upturns. As a buffer against fluctuations in production (caused by fluctuations in sales), firms may hold excess labor and/or capital. Sharp shifts in the levels of capital stock and employment cause adjustment costs—in some cases, it may be cheaper to maintain excess inputs. (page 406/832)

> **TIP:** Underpinning the discussion of the behavior of the firm is the assumption of profit maximization. If you've done the microeconomic course, take some time to review your notes. If you've never heard of profit maximization, a (very brief) outline is given here.
>
> The goal of firms is assumed to be profit maximization. To achieve this goal, firms make decisions at the margin. Will this additional unit of output draw in more revenue than it costs to produce? If not, it shouldn't be produced. Will this extra unit of an input (a machine or worker) pay its way? If not, it shouldn't be hired. By hiring inputs until the final unit of each input just breaks even, and by producing until the final unit of output just pays its way, the firm will maximize profits.

> **TIP:** Think of the two types of investment as different kinds of activities. Firms often use inventory investment in response to short-term fluctuations in demand, as a buffer between production and sales. This may occur almost "accidentally," i.e., without conscious planning. Investment in plant and equipment is different in nature, representing reflections on the long-term trends in the firm's operation.

PRACTICE

14. The firm can add to its capital stock by
    A. purchasing additional raw materials.
    B. reducing its inventory levels.
    C. investing in plant and equipment.
    D. hiring additional labor capacity.
    Answer: C. Investment is the addition to the capital stock. The capital stock can be increased by buying more plant and equipment or by accumulating additional inventory. See p. 404/830.

15. Technology X uses 10 units of capital and 20 units of labor. If Technology Y is relatively more capital-intensive, it might use
    A. 5 units of capital and 5 units of labor.
    B. 5 units of capital and 10 units of labor.
    C. 20 units of capital and 40 units of labor.
    D. 40 units of capital and 100 units of labor.
    Answer: A. A method of production is relatively more capital-intensive the greater the ratio of capital to labor. Options B and C have the same level of capital intensity as Technology X (1:2). Option D is less capital-intensive.

16. Technology Z is labor intensive. An expansion in output is likely to _____ the demand for labor and _____ the demand for capital.
    A. increase, increase.
    B. increase, decrease.
    C. decrease, increase.
    D. decrease, decrease.
    Answer: A. The demand for additional machines for workers should increase, albeit only modestly. See p. 405/831.

17. An entrepreneur who is feeling very confident about the future is likely to
    A. invest in more capital-intensive methods of production.
    B. invest in more labor-intensive methods of production.
    C. hold excess supplies of labor and capital.
    D. reduce excess capacity.
    Answer: C. In anticipation of good times (and high production) ahead, the entrepreneur will be reluctant to reduce capacity.

OBJECTIVE 5: Discuss the role of inventories in the output decision and describe the trade-off involved in reaching the optimal level of inventories.

Inventory is unsold production. Inventory investment occurs when production exceeds sales. Holding inventories involves both a cost and a benefit for the firm. Too low an inventory might mean lost sales, but too high an inventory involves storage costs and the tying up of funds that could be earning interest. The *optimal level of inventories* is at the point of balance between these two concerns. Sales tend to be more variable than production, and inventories can be used to smooth out the mismatch between the two, resulting in lower adjustment costs.   (page 408/834)

A clear example of the smoothing function of inventories can be seen in fireworks manufacturing. Typically, sales have one peak—just before the Fourth of July—but production may occur for many months before. Inventories accumulate to prevent a rush of production at the last moment. Inventories, though, represent payments to inputs that have already been made, and there are risks and storage costs. These may be high in the case of fireworks.

TIP: In a way, saving operates for the household in the same way that inventories operate for the firm. Inventories allow the firm to smooth its production in the face of fluctuating sales; saving (and dissaving) permits the household to smooth consumption and maintain a stable standard of living in the face of fluctuating income.

PRACTICE

18. Stock of inventories (end of period) equals stock of inventories (beginning of period)
    A. plus production plus sales.
    B. plus production minus sales.
    C. minus production plus sales.
    D. minus production minus sales.
    Answer: B. See p. 408/834.

19. If the sales of the Caledonian Curling Stone Company are less than expected, inventories will be
    A. higher than expected and future production will increase.
    B. higher than expected and future production will decrease.
    C. lower than expected and future production will increase.
    D. lower than expected and future production will decrease.

    Answer: B. Unsold production will be greater than expected. This is a signal that the firm's production level is too high. See p. 408/834.

20. The desired, or optimal, level of inventories is the level at which the extra cost in lost sales from _____ inventories by a small amount is just equal to the extra gain (in interest revenue and _____ storage costs).
    A. increasing, increased.
    B. increasing, decreased.
    C. decreasing, increased.
    D. decreasing, decreased.
    Answer: D. See the discussion on p. 408/834.

I.   MULTIPLE CHOICE QUESTIONS.

Select the option that provides the single best answer.

_____ 1. According to the life-cycle theory, Jill's APC will be less than one
   A.   when Jill is young.
   B.   when Jill is in her prime earning years.
   C.   when Jill is old.
   D.   both when Jill is young and when she is old.

_____ 2. According to the microeconomic model, which of the following certainly will make labor supply increase?
   A.   A decrease in nonlabor income.
   B.   An increase in wealth.
   C.   An increase in tax rates.
   D.   An increase in the nominal wage rate.

_____ 3. Three major and interlinked economic decisions of households are
   A.   how much to work, how much to invest, and how much to save.
   B.   how much to consume, how much to invest, and how much to work.
   C.   how much to work, how much to consume, and how much to save.
   D.   how much to produce, how much to invest, and how much to borrow.

_____ 4. According to the permanent income view, the household's estimate of its permanent income will be affected by all of the following except
   A.   a tax hike viewed as temporary.
   B.   an annual merit raise.
   C.   institutional changes, for example in the social security system.
   D.   a tax hike viewed as permanent.

_____ 5. Capacity constraints imply all of the following except that
   A.   firms may be unable to meet unexpected increases in demand.
   B.   the economy may be unable to raise production levels if it is at full employment.
   C.   increasing output may be increasingly costly.
   D.   increasing output is possible without increasing prices.

_____ 6. The nominal wage increases and the price level remains constant. The income effect tells us that
   A.   workers' opportunity cost of each hour of leisure has increased.
   B.   workers' opportunity cost of each hour of leisure has decreased.
   C.   workers' opportunity cost of each hour of leisure has remained constant.
   D.   workers can afford to work fewer hours.

_____ 7. An increase in nonlabor income (such as transfer payments) will _____ consumption and _____ the labor supply.
   A.   increase, increase.
   B.   increase, decrease.
   C.   decrease, increase.
   D.   decrease, decrease.

_____ 8. The labor-force participation rate for prime-age males is _____, and is _____ than that of prime-age females.
   A.   rising, greater.
   B.   rising, smaller.
   C.   falling, greater.
   D.   falling, smaller.

9. During an economic expansion, we would expect _____ to expand most rapidly.
   A. services, such as those of a dentist.
   B. services, such as those of a manicurist.
   C. consumer durables, such as groceries.
   D. consumer durables, such as CD players.

10. Holding inventory causes the firm to
    A. reduce storage costs.
    B. lower its productive capacity.
    C. increase its ability to meet unexpected demand.
    D. smooth its sales pattern.

11. An increase in expected future sales will have a _____ effect on investment, and an increase in the cost of labor will have a _____ effect.
    A. positive, positive.
    B. positive, negative.
    C. negative, positive.
    D. negative, negative.

12. An increase in expected future sales will have a _____ effect on employment, and an increase in the cost of labor will have a _____ effect.
    A. positive, positive.
    B. positive, negative.
    C. negative, positive.
    D. negative, negative.

13. The _____ the expected decline in sales and the _____ the adjustment cost, the greater the amount of excess labor that will be held.
    A. shorter, smaller.
    B. shorter, greater.
    C. longer, greater.
    D. longer, smaller.

14. Investment depends on each of the following except
    A. expected future sales.
    B. the accelerator effect.
    C. the cost of capital.
    D. the cost of labor.

15. According to the life-cycle theory, the main determinants of consumption include all of the following except
    A. current disposable income.
    B. expected future income.
    C. nominal wages.
    D. wealth.

16. Lower income tax rates will _____ consumption and _____ labor supply if the substitution effect is dominant.
    A. increase, increase.
    B. increase, decrease.
    C. decrease, increase.
    D. decrease, decrease.

17. The "discouraged worker" effect is most noticeable among _____ during a recession
    A. prime-age males.
    B. prime-age females.
    C. non-prime-age workers.
    D. males aged between 25 and 54.

_____ 18. Miss Faversham has a sudden increase in wealth. The substitution effect will _____ her consumption and _____ her labor supply.

A. increase, increase.
B. increase, have no impact on.
C. have no impact on, increase.
D. have no impact on, have no impact on.

Use the following diagram to answer the next two questions. "Income" refers to disposable (after-tax) income.

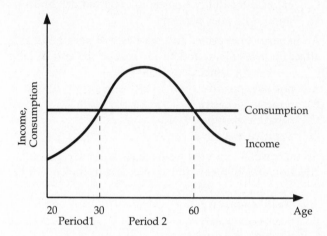

_____ 19. In the diagram above, average propensity to consume is _____ in Period 1, and the household is _____

A. high, saving.
B. high, borrowing.
C. low, saving.
D. low, borrowing.

_____ 20. In the diagram above, average propensity to consume is _____ in Period 2, and the average propensity to save is _____

A. greater than 1, positive.
B. greater than 1, negative.
C. less than 1, positive.
D. less than 1, negative.

II. APPLICATION QUESTIONS.

1. As the "baby boomers" age, what will happen to the national saving rate, according to the life-cycle model?

2. Suppose that there is an increase in the hourly cost of child care for Jan's toddler, Teddy. How might this affect Jan's labor-supply decision? What are the income and substitution effects? How do they apply to Jan?

3. Forty-year old Simon Simple is a life-long resident of the state of South Virginia—he has frequently observed that nothing could induce him to leave his home state. Simon is a highly skilled lathe operator employed in the furniture industry. He has some wealth and no debts. Indicate how each of the following circumstances will affect Simon's current consumption and saving.

   a. Simon is told that a long-lost relative has left him a large bequest. The bequest, however, is to be kept in a trust and Simon will not be able to withdraw funds from it until he is 50 years old.

   b. Simon's doctor tells him that Simon has an amazingly healthy constitution and should easily expect to live until he is in his nineties. This prediction, which adds an additional 20 years to Simon's expected life span, does not influence Simon's plan to retire at age 60 in order to perfect his fishing skills.

c. Simon, who is a taxpayer, reads a reliable newspaper report that South Virginia's state government's budget deficit is much worse than had previously been thought. A substantial tax increase next year and in subsequent years now seems inevitable.

d. Because of foreign competition, which is thought likely to become increasingly intense in future years, Simon's employer has announced that, after the end of this year, no overtime work will be allowed and that, indeed, workers must anticipate reduced work weeks.

4. Arbez has the following consumption function: C = 400 + .8Y.
    a. What is the marginal propensity to consume in Arbez? _____
    b. Calculate APC when income is:

1,000 _____	2,000 _____	3,000 _____

    c. At which income level will saving be:

zero _____	positive _____	negative _____

    d. Based on (c), formulate a rule relating saving and the value of APC.
    e. When APC is greater than 1.0, suggest two ways that a household might finance its consumption.

5. Arboc and Arbez are neighboring nations. In each of the following cases, in which economy would we expect to see higher levels of inventory investment? Why?
    a. Aggregate demand in Arbez is very stable, but aggregate demand in Arboc is highly variable and unpredictable.
    b. The interest rate is historically lower in Arboc than in Arbez.
    c. Arboc has begun to move away from manufacturing toward an economy that is more oriented to production of services. Arbez remains based in manufacturing.

6. Jack and Jill both earn $30,000 this year. Jack expects his income to increase by $2,000 every year over the next 5 years. Jill expects her income to decrease by $2,000 every year over the same period. Who should have the higher APC? Why?

7. Bill and Ben have identical current incomes.
    a. Bill has more wealth than Ben. Who should have the higher level of consumption? _____. Who will tend to work more? _____.

    b. Bill receives dividend payments, but Ben doesn't. Who will have the higher level of consumption? _____. Who will tend to work more? _____.

    c. Personal income tax rates are cut in the state where Bill lives, but not in the state where Ben lives. Who should have the higher level of consumption? _____. Who will tend to work more? _____.

    d. As a new member of a credit union, Bill is eligible for a lower interest rate on loans. Who should have the higher level of consumption? _____.

    e. The President pledges "no new taxes." Bill believes him; Ben doesn't. Who should have the higher level of consumption? _____ Who will tend to work more? _____.

    f. Bill spends more of his current income than Ben does (but not all of it). Now interest rates increase. Who is more likely to increase his savings? _____.

g. Bill and Ben return to school. Bill attends a business school, while Ben embarks on a degree in theology. Who should have the higher consumption level today? _____.

8. Here are two production functions for the Caledonian Curling Stones Company.

Output	—Mix 1—		—Mix 2—	
	K	L	K	L
11	6	1	2	7
12	7	3	3	10
13	9	5	4	14
14	12	7	5	20
15	15	9	6	26
16	21	11	7	32

a. The firm wishes to produce 14 units of output. Capital costs $4/unit and the labor costs $2/unit. Which input mix will be chosen?

b. At this output level, will this still be the cheaper method if the input prices change to $2 and $4, respectively?

c. As the rental cost of capital falls from $4 to $2, investment _____ from _____ units to _____ units, and there is a _____ (positive/ negative) effect on employment.

9. a. Use the following table to calculate APC and MPC.

Income	Consumption	APC	MPC
1,000	1,500		
2,000	2,200		
3,000	2,900		
4,000	3,600		
5,000	4,300		

b. Will APC ever be less than MPC in this model? Why?

ANSWERS AND SOLUTIONS

PRACTICE TEST

I. SOLUTIONS TO MULTIPLE CHOICE QUESTIONS

1. B. During the prime earning years, Jill's earnings (Y) will be more than her consumption (C). APC is C / Y. See p. 391/817.

2. A. As workers' nonlabor income decreases, they will wish to work more. Note that an increase in tax rates has an ambiguous result—the income effect will stimulate the supply of labor, but the substitution effect will dampen it. See p. 398/824.

3. C. See p. 390/816. Note that, when deciding how much of current income will be consumed, the household is simultaneously determining how much will be saved.

4. A. A temporary change will have no permanent effect. See p. 393/819.

5. D. At the macroeconomic level, consider the shape of the short-run aggregate supply curve in answering this question.

6. D. If the nominal wage increases with no change in the price level, the real wage has increased. An increase in the real wage will increase labor income. As income increases, the income effect tells us, the demand for leisure time will increase, reducing work time. The substitution effect refers to the opportunity cost of the leisure/labor decision—in this case, the opportunity cost increased.

7. B. As household wealth increases, consumption increases. The desire to work will decrease. Note that there is no substitution effect in this case. See p. 395/821.

8. C. See p. 402/828.

9. D. Groceries are nondurables. Consumer durables, the purchases of which may be postponed during an economic slowdown, are purchased more vigorously during an economic expansion. See p. 401/827.

10. C. The firm does not have to match production to sales as closely when inventory is present. Production levels can be smoother, therefore.

11. A. If sales are expected to increase, the firm will wish to expand production capacity. As labor costs rise, machinery becomes relatively less expensive (and more attractive).

12. B. If sales are expected to increase, the firm will wish to expand its productive capacity, including its labor force. The more expensive workers are, the fewer the firm will wish to employ.

13. B. If a decline in sales is expected to last a long time, the relative cost involved in laying off workers becomes less. The smaller the cost of hiring and firing workers, the less excess labor will be held.

14. B. The accelerator effect is the consequence, not the cause, of investment.

15. C. The wage is an important part of income, but the nominal wage is less of a consideration than the real wage and is, in any case, included in the more general term "income."

16. A. As the tax rate decreases, after-tax income increases, increasing consumption. As after-tax income increases, the opportunity cost of not working increases-the substitution effect would lead us to work more. Note that the income effect would lead us to work less, but the question assumes that the substitution effect is stronger.

17. C. Non-prime-age workers tend to be more "marginal" members of the labor force. See the graph on p. 403/829.

18. D. Changes in nonlabor income and wealth have only income effects. The opportunity cost of leisure (the substitution effect) remains untouched.

19. B. Consumption exceeds income, therefore this household must be borrowing.

20. C. APC is consumption divided by income. In Period 2, consumption is less than income; the remaining income is saved. Note that average propensity to consume plus the average propensity to save equals one. See p. 392/818.

II. SOLUTIONS TO APPLICATION QUESTIONS

1. The "baby boomers" are presently in their prime earning years. They should be saving for retirement. Current consumption, therefore, should be low relative to current income—i.e., APC is less than 1 and the national saving rate is comparatively high. As the baby boomers age and begin to retire, their income will decrease more sharply than their consumption levels—they will be dissaving—and the national saving rate will decrease.

2. The increase in child-care costs will have an income effect and a substitution effect for Jan. In effect, Jan's hourly wage rate has decreased. The substitution effect indicates that the opportunity cost of not working (staying home and caring for Teddy) has decreased—Jan may supply less labor. The income effect goes in the opposite direction. The increase in the cost of child care (and the effective wage decrease) has made Jan poorer. The poorer one is, the greater the need to work. Jan, therefore, is driven to supply more labor. Whether Jan works longer hours or chooses to stay home more will depend on the relative strengths of the two effects.

3. a. Consumption will increase (saving will decrease). Although he cannot access the funds, Simon's permanent income has increased.
   b. Consumption will decrease (saving will increase). Simon must eke out his lifetime earnings over a longer period.
   c. Consumption will decrease (saving will increase). Simon's expectation is that his after-tax income will be decreased in future years. This news reduces his lifetime income.
   d. Consumption will decrease (saving will increase). Simon's expectation is that his income will be decreased in future years. This news reduces his lifetime income.

4. a. .8. MPC is the rate at which consumption changes as income changes. If income increases by 1,000, consumption will change by 800.

    b. 1.2; 1.0; .933. See the table below.

Income	Consumption	APC
0	400	—
1,000	1,200	1.200
2,000	2,000	1.000
3,000	2,800	.933

    c. 2,000; 3,000; 1,000. Saving = income − consumption.

    d. When APC is greater than 1.0, saving is negative (dissaving occurs). When APC is less than 1.0, saving will occur.

    e. The household could borrow, reduce accumulated savings, or receive wealth transfers (from parents, for example).

5. a. Arboc will hold higher stocks of inventories because the danger of inadequate stock is greater there.

    b. Arboc. The interest rate is a major cost of holding inventories.

    c. Arbez. It is impossible to hold inventories of services.

6. Jack should have the higher APC because his consumption will be higher. It will be higher because his expected future income is greater. Jill will be saving more today, in anticipation of bad times to come.

7. a. Bill; Ben. Bill will be able to finance more consumption out of his wealth. Ben is poorer. The income effect (which discourages work) will be less strong for Ben.

    b. Bill; Ben. Dividend payments are nonlabor income. The higher one's income, the less one tends to work.

    c. Bill; Bill. Bill's after-tax income has increased; Ben's has not. With more income, Bill will consume more. Assuming that the substitution effect dominates, Bill will work extra hours. Ben has no incentive to work extra hours because his tax rate did not change.

    d. Bill. The cost of borrowing has decreased for Bill.

    e. Bill will have the higher level of consumption. Bill's expectations about his future real income are more optimistic than Ben's. Ben is likely to work more now.

    f. Bill is more likely to increase savings. The substitution effect is similar for both, but the income effect of the increased interest rate will be greater for Ben. Higher future income will encourage Ben to indulge in greater current consumption. Because the income effect is smaller for Bill, his savings are more likely to increase.

    g. The business school graduate (Bill) should expect a higher future income stream, and so his current consumption level should be higher than that of the theology student (Ben).

8. a. Mix 2 will be chosen; it will cost $60 [(5 × $4) + (20 × $2)] instead of Mix 1's $62 [(12 × $4) + (7 × $2)].

    b. Mix 1 will have a total cost of $52 [(12 × $2) + (7 × $4)], while Mix 2 costs $90 [(5 × $2) + (20 × $4)].

    c. As the rental cost of capital falls from $4 to $2, investment increases from 5 units to 12 units, and there is a negative effect on employment (as the firm substitutes away from the relatively expensive input).

9. a. See the table.

Income	Consumption	APC	MPC
1,000	1,500	1.50	—
2,000	2,200	1.10	.7
3,000	2,900	0.97	.7
4,000	3,600	0.90	.7
5,000	4,300	0.86	.7

   b. No. APC will become closer to MPC but it can never be less than MPC. As long as the marginal value is less than the average, the average will decrease.

FURTHER TOPICS IN MACROECONOMIC ANALYSIS

18

COMBINED TEXT

33

OBJECTIVES: POINT BY POINT

After completing this chapter, you should be able to accomplish the objectives listed below.

General Comment

This chapter contains an assortment of topics, but each of which is interesting and quite topical. It gives you a good opportunity to review and to check your understanding of the macroeconomic model that Case and Fair have constructed over the past several chapters.

OBJECTIVE 1: Using the income and substitution effects, analyze how the tools of fiscal policy influence the decisions of households regarding consumption and labor supply.

Tax and government spending changes have differing impacts on the economy, depending on whether households and firms perceive them as temporary or permanent. A permanent change in taxes or government spending will have a more powerful economic impact because the permanent income of households and/or the investment environment of firms has been fundamentally altered. A temporary policy change will have less of an impact on consumption and investment because, although current income is affected, future expected income is not.   (page 417/843)

A change in tax rates has both an income effect and a substitution effect on labor supply and consumption. A reduction in tax rates causes an increase in disposable income (leading to a reduction in labor supply as workers favor increased leisure—income effect) and a simultaneous increase in the opportunity cost of leisure (because the marginal hour of work now yields a higher disposable income—substitution effect). The net effect of the two opposing tendencies is uncertain—labor supply and consumption may increase or decrease. With a lump-sum tax reduction, the influence of the substitution effect is absent—labor supply, therefore, would certainly decrease.   (page 419/845)

A fall in nonlabor income results in a pure income effect on consumption and labor supply. Consumption will fall and labor supply will rise.

> **TIP:** The first part of the chapter makes extensive use of the income and substitution effects. If you're still hazy on the application of this important item in your economic tool kit, go back to the previous chapter.

PRACTICE

1. A temporary tax cut will have _____ on household behavior than a permanent tax cut.
   A. more of an effect.
   B. less of an effect.
   C. the same effect.
   D. no effect.
   Answer: B. Temporary changes can be ridden out without having to make significant changes in behavior. See p. 418/844.

2. If social security entitlements are cut, and this is seen as a permanent reduction in benefits, personal saving for retirement will _____ and current consumption will _____
   A. increase, increase.
   B. increase, decrease.
   C. decrease, increase.
   D. decrease, decrease.
   Answer: B. The cut reduces the expected lifetime (permanent) income of households. Poorer households consume less today and need greater private saving for use during retirement. See p. 419/845.

3. Of the following, the most effective way of increasing the supply of labor is
   A. an increase in personal tax rates.
   B. a decrease in personal tax rates.
   C. an increase in personal taxes by a lump-sum amount.
   D. a decrease in personal taxes by a lump-sum amount.
   Answer: C. The lump-sum tax change affects income, but not the trade-off between work and leisure. A lump-sum decrease would increase household after-tax income—richer households would reduce their labor supply. A lump-sum increase, on the other hand, would unambiguously increase the supply of labor. With tax rate changes, there are two conflicting effects. The income effect of a tax rate increase will increase labor supply, but the substitution effect will reduce it.

4. The trusted and reliable president of Arbez, President Truth, announces a tax increase that is to be a "temporary" sacrifice. The Arbocali president, President Slick Dickie, who is considered unscrupulous and dishonest, also announces a tax increase that is to be a "temporary" sacrifice. Permanent income will _____ in Arbez.
   A. increase more.
   B. increase less.
   C. decrease more.
   D. decrease less.
   Answer: D. The claim that the Arbocali tax cut is a temporary necessity is less likely to be believed. Taxpayers will suspect a permanent hike. Their permanent income, then, will decrease more than that of Arbezani taxpayers.

OBJECTIVE 2: Describe two channels through which changes in the interest rate can affect aggregate demand.

Monetary policy operates through two channels. From previous chapters we know that, if the Fed changes the interest rate, planned investment changes. The interest rate is the opportunity cost of consumption—changes in the interest rate will affect consumption and saving. A higher interest rate should encourage saving (and discourage consumption). (page 420/846)

> **Comment:** Which elements of consumption are more likely to be affected by interest rate changes? The durable-goods sector (cars, refrigerators, etc.) is by far the most affected portion of consumption spending.

PRACTICE

5. The greater the interest-bearing wealth of households, the _____ the _____ on consumption of an interest rate change.
   A. stronger, income effect.
   B. stronger, substitution effect.
   C. weaker, income effect.
   D. weaker, substitution effect.
   Answer: A. As interest rates increase, the nonlabor income earned increases. The greater the wealth holdings, the stronger the income effect will be.

6. The Fed cuts the money supply. The income effect will _____ consumption; the substitution effect will _____ consumption.
   A. increase, increase.
   B. increase, decrease.
   C. decrease, increase.
   D. decrease, decrease.
   Answer: B. A decrease in the money supply will increase the interest rate. Interest earning will increase-richer households will increase consumption. According to the substitution effect, the opportunity cost of consumption has increased-consumption will decrease.

OBJECTIVE 3: Explain why fiscal and monetary policies will be less effective during periods of high output.

The effectiveness of (demand-side) policy and the size of the multiplier are affected by the slope of the short-run aggregate supply curve—the steeper the slope, the less effective policy will be and the smaller the multiplier will be. At low output levels, firms are likely to be holding a fair amount of excess capital and excess labor. An expansionary policy may allow these resources to be used more fully with little increase in wages or prices. Near full employment, however, expansionary impulses will result in an upward pressure on input costs and prices as firms scramble to hire increasingly scarce resources. (page 420/846)

PRACTICE

7. Policy will have a larger effect when
   A. inventory is high and much excess capacity is present.
   B. inventory is high and little excess capacity is present.
   C. inventory is low and much excess capacity is present.
   D. inventory is low and little excess capacity is present.
   Answer: C. See p. 420/846.

OBJECTIVE 4: Analyze the macroeconomic effects of a fall in stock prices using the life-cycle theory.

The 1987 stock market crash, which wiped out a part of households' wealth, was expected to generate a recession. In theory, falling wealth should have meant less consumption spending. Expectations by firms of falling consumption spending should have led to the postponement of investment spending. The predicted slump didn't materialize, however, perhaps because of the prompt action of the Fed, which pushed interest rates downward to stimulate spending and as a signal that the recession would be resisted. (A fortuitous boom in export sales, caused by the depreciation of the dollar, also helped support demand during this period.) (page 421/847)

> **TIP:** Caution! Be careful not to slip back into the old habit of equating "investment" with financial transactions such as the purchase of stock.

8. If there is a fall in stock prices that is perceived as permanent, consumption
   will _____ and planned investment will _____
   A. increase, increase.
   B. increase, decrease.
   C. decrease, increase.
   D. decrease, decrease.
   Answer: D. See p. 421/847. Planned investment will decrease as firms anticipate
   permanent reductions in consumption spending and an economic downturn.

OBJECTIVE 5: Explain the relationship between bond prices and the interest rate.

There is a negative relationship between bond prices and the interest rate. The interest payment on a bond (the coupon) is fixed. Therefore, for an existing bond to
remain attractive, the price of acquiring the right to the coupon must vary. As the
market interest rate increases, the price of the bond must fall to make the "reward"
from buying the bond competitive with the going interest rate.   (page 422/848)

PRACTICE

9. The payment on a bond is called the
   A. maturity.
   B. coupon.
   C. interest rate.
   D. yield.
   Answer: B. See p. 422/848.

10. Which of the following statements about a bond is true?
    A. The interest rate on a bond is fixed at the time of issue and cannot vary
       during the life of the bond.
    B. If the market interest rate is higher today than when a bond was first
       issued, a seller who bought the bond when it was issued will make a
       capital gain.
    C. The yield on a bond will increase as its price increases.
    D. When the market interest rate increases, bond prices decrease.
    Answer: D. See p. 422/848.

OBJECTIVE 6: Describe the relationship between the productivity of labor and the holding of excess labor by firms.

In the short term, labor productivity—total output divided by the number of hours
worked—may be a misleading guide to the economy's performance because business
cycles affect the measurement. Although workers are still capable of producing just
as much as before, productivity falls in an economic slowdown because firms tend
to hold excess labor. Output fluctuates much more than employment over the
business cycle. Productivity also follows the cycle. In the long run, productivity
measures, such as GDP per capita, are less misleading.   (page 426/852)

PRACTICE

11. Which of the following statements is true?
    A. Employment fluctuates more than output over the business cycle, causing high productivity during periods of high output and low productivity during periods of low output.
    B. Employment fluctuates more than output over the business cycle, causing high productivity during periods of low output and low productivity during periods of high output.
    C. Employment fluctuates less than output over the business cycle, causing high productivity during periods of high output and low productivity during periods of low output.
    D. Employment fluctuates less than output over the business cycle, causing high productivity during periods of low output and low productivity during periods of high output.

    Answer: C. By holding onto excess labor during downturns and by having existing employees work more during upswings, employment remains fairly stable. When output is high, therefore, productivity is high.

OBJECTIVE 7: State Okun's Law and list the "slippages" that make the "law" unstable.

Simple macroeconomic relationships are seldom reliable—the Phillips Curve is one example. *Okun's Law*—which attempts to link output and the unemployment rate in a stable relationship—is another. Okun's Law is flawed because output depends on more than just the total number of workers who are employed.

(page 428/854)

Three "slippages," all of which vary over the course of the business cycle, occur between a change in output and a change in the unemployment rate. First, as output increases, firms utilize their excess capacity and/or offer overtime rather than increase their labor force. Second, some persons hold more than one job—in general, the number of jobs exceeds the number of employed workers. New jobs (and expanded production) may be filled by currently employed workers—the unemployment rate will not be affected. Finally, with higher production, discouraged workers may be attracted back into the ranks of the officially unemployed, actively seeking work but swelling the unemployment rate.

PRACTICE

12. Okun's Law states that the unemployment rate
    A. increases by three percentage points for every 1% increase in GDP.
    B. increases by one percentage point for every 3% increase in GDP.
    C. decreases by three percentage points for every 1% increase in GDP.
    D. decreases by one percentage point for every 3% increase in GDP.

    Answer: D. As production increases, the unemployment rate decreases. See p. 428/854.

13. Which of the following is NOT a "slippage" between an increase in output and a decrease in the unemployment rate?
    A. The relationship between the change in output and the utilization by firms of their excess capacity.
    B. The relationship between the change in output and the increase in overtime work.
    C. The relationship between the change in the number of jobs and the change in the number of workers employed.
    D. The relationship between the change in output and amount of frictional unemployment.

    Answer: D. Okun's Law looks at the effect of changes in output on the unemployment rate through the business cycle—i.e., cyclical unemployment.

14. When production increases, discouraged workers may _____ the ranks of the officially unemployed. This will _____ the unemployment rate.
    A. enter, increase.
    B. enter, decrease.
    C. leave, increase.
    D. leave, decrease.
    Answer: A. Higher production offers the prospect of jobs where none were before.

15. As output increases by 1%, the number of jobs tends to increase by less than 1%. In part, this is because
    A. firms expand output by expanding the number of hours worked by workers who are already on the payroll.
    B. discouraged workers enter the labor force.
    C. discouraged workers leave the labor force.
    D. firms reduce the quantity of excess capital.
    Answer: A. See p. 428/854. The presence or absence of discouraged workers (Options B and C) has no effect on the number of jobs created.

16. Although Okun's Law has been proved incorrect, it is true to state that there is a _____ relationship between the changes in GDP and the unemployment rate.
    A. positive and stable.
    B. positive but unstable.
    C. negative and stable.
    D. negative but unstable.
    Answer: D. As output increases, the unemployment rate decreases, but the trade-off depends on so many factors that it is unstable.

OBJECTIVE 8: Indicate how changes in each of the factors affecting the multiplier influence the size of the multiplier.

The real-world multiplier is smaller (1.4) and less immediate than that suggested by the marginal propensity to consume. Various factors dampen the effect of an increase in, for example, government spending. Automatic stabilizers offset pressures for change. The interest rate may rise, crowding out investment and consumption. Prices, instead of output, may rise, especially if the economy is close to full employment. If output is low initially, firms may be holding excess labor and capital, or a large stock of inventories, which could be used to meet higher demand without much of a rise in employment or investment. The consumption response of households may be lukewarm if the new income is considered temporary, and businesses may not be tempted to launch new investment programs. Finally, if a portion of the extra income "leaks" overseas to buy imports, domestic production will not feel the benefit. (page 429/855)

> **TIP:** Although the discussion of the size of the multiplier is placed at the end of the chapter, it's true that all of the material in this chapter contributes to this section. Go back and reread the earlier sections and note how the discussions of policy effectiveness, the relationship between productivity and the business cycle, and the "slippages" between output and unemployment all build toward the final section on the reduced size of the real-world multiplier.

17. The greater the crowding-out effect, the _____ the multiplier; the smaller the percentage of imports, the _____ the multiplier.
    A. larger, larger.
    B. larger, smaller.
    C. smaller, larger.
    D. smaller, smaller.
    Answer: C. Given an increase in government spending, the effect on aggregate expenditure will be less, the more significant the crowding-out effect. The smaller the leakage of spending power abroad, the greater the amount retained for recycling through the economy's circular flow.

18. _____ is the policy with the greatest multiplier.
    A. A permanent increase when inventory levels are high.
    B. A permanent increase when inventory levels are low.
    C. A temporary increase when inventory levels are high.
    D. A temporary increase when inventory levels are low.
    Answer: B. See p. 430/856.

19. Automatic stabilizers _____ the multiplier; the more interest-sensitive planned investment, the _____ the multiplier.
    A. increase, larger.
    B. increase, smaller.
    C. decrease, larger.
    D. decrease, smaller.
    Answer: D. See p. 430/856.

20. A stock market crash will have a greater economic impact, the _____ the portion of household wealth held as stock and the _____ permanent the crash is expected to be.
    A. larger, more.
    B. larger, less.
    C. smaller, more.
    D. smaller, less.
    Answer: A. Permanent changes have a greater impact than temporary ones.

PRACTICE TEST

I. MULTIPLE CHOICE QUESTIONS.

Select the option that provides the single best answer.

_____ 1. During a slump, labor productivity will _____ and the amount of excess labor held by a firm will _____
    A. increase, increase.
    B. increase, decrease.
    C. decrease, increase.
    D. decrease, decrease.

_____ 2. The actual multiplier is smaller than the theoretical multiplier because of all of the following reasons except that as spending increases,
    A. the interest rate rises and reduces investment spending.
    B. producers may increase prices instead of output.
    C. transfer payments tend to increase.
    D. excess labor may be pressed into service, with no change in employment.

_____ 3. Common stock holdings are
  A. insured by the Federal Reserve.
  B. regulated by the Federal Reserve.
  C. a part of the wealth of households.
  D. issued to pay for the federal deficit.

_____ 4. Because of the ability of firms to _____ the number of hours worked per worker, employment _____ increase as rapidly as does output during an upswing.
  A. increase, does.
  B. increase, does not.
  C. decrease, does.
  D. decrease, does not.

_____ 5. _Ceteris paribu_s, when the interest rate increases, bond prices _____. As a result, consumption will _____
  A. increase, increase.
  B. increase, decrease.
  C. decrease, increase.
  D. decrease, decrease.

_____ 6. A "temporary" lump-sum income tax increase will _____ output by _____ than a "permanent" tax increase of an equal amount.
  A. increase, more.
  B. increase, less.
  C. decrease, more.
  D. decrease, less.

_____ 7. Productivity of labor
  A. is higher in the short run than in the long run.
  B. is lower in the short run than in the long run.
  C. measures the marginal product of labor.
  D. measurements are less accurate in the short run than in the long run.

_____ 8. A decrease in nonlabor income will cause consumption to _____ and labor supply to _____
  A. increase, increase.
  B. increase, decrease.
  C. decrease, increase.
  D. decrease, decrease.

_____ 9. One reason why an increase in output might not lead to an increase in employment is that
  A. any additional jobs may be filled by teenagers who aren't counted in labor statistics.
  B. any additional jobs may be filled by workers who already have jobs.
  C. the rate of growth in production may be greater than the marginal productivity of workers.
  D. the rate of growth in production may be less than the marginal productivity of workers.

_____ 10. Consumption spending increases. If the Fed increases the discount rate, then the interest rate will be _____ than otherwise and the multiplier will be _____ than otherwise.
  A. higher, greater.
  B. higher, smaller.
  C. lower, greater.
  D. lower, smaller.

_____ 11. As the interest rate rises, planned investment _____ and saving _____

    A. increases, increases.

    B. increases, decreases.

    C. decreases, increases.

    D. decreases, decreases.

_____ 12. Each of the following changes will reduce the size of the multiplier except:

    A. the portion of additional income spent on foreign goods decreases.

    B. tax rates increase.

    C. households become more doubtful about the longevity of "permanent" tax reductions.

    D. entrepreneurs become more sensitive to changes in the interest rate.

_____ 13. The Fed increases the discount rate. The money supply will _____. The wealth of bondholders will _____.

    A. increase, increase.

    B. increase, decrease.

    C. decrease, increase.

    D. decrease, decrease.

_____ 14. The government spending multiplier is likely to be smaller during periods of _____ output and _____ unemployment.

    A. high, high.

    B. high, low.

    C. low, high.

    D. low, low.

_____ 15. Each of the following is a transfer payment except

    A. dividends.

    B. welfare.

    C. unemployment benefits.

    D. social security payments.

_____ 16. If corporate taxes are decreased, dividends are likely to increase. As dividends increase, households will _____ consumption and _____ labor supply.

    A. increase, increase.

    B. increase, decrease.

    C. decrease, increase.

    D. decrease, decrease.

_____ 17. A bond pays a coupon of $6 per $100 of face value. The current yield on new bonds of similar risk and maturity is 10%. The current price of the bond

    A. is certainly higher than its face value.

    B. is certainly lower than its face value.

    C. may be higher than its face value-it also depends on the extent of capital gains or losses.

    D. may be lower than its face value-it also depends on the extent of capital gains or losses.

_____ 18. Arbocorp issues bonds worth 1,000,000 opeks and 600,000 shares of one-opek stock.

    A. Household wealth increases by 400,000 opeks.

    B. Household wealth increases by 600,000 opeks.

    C. Household wealth increases by 1,000,000 opeks.

    D. Household wealth increases by 1,600,000 opeks.

_____ 19. Although Okun's Law is flawed, it is roughly true that the unemployment rate
  A. increases by more than 1% for every 1% increase in GDP.
  B. increases by less than 1% for every 1% increase in GDP.
  C. decreases by more than 1% for every 1% increase in GDP.
  D. decreases by less than 1% for every 1% increase in GDP.

_____ 20. The Fed decreases the reserve requirement. Bond holders will experience a
  A. capital gain and consumption will increase.
  B. capital gain and consumption will decrease.
  C. capital loss and consumption will increase.
  D. capital loss and consumption will decrease.

II. APPLICATION QUESTIONS.

1. In each of the following cases, predict what will happen to consumption, labor supply, planned investment, the overall price level, output, and employment.
   a. While the Arbocali economy is operating at full employment, the Arbocali central bank (Arbobank) increases the discount rate.
   b. The Arbezani economy is in a deep recession. The government hikes government spending.
   c. The Noilian economy is in a deep recession. The government increases welfare benefits.

2. In 1992, the U.S. economy was struggling to shake off the Gulf War recession. President Bush announced that taxpayers could reduce the amount of tax taken from their paychecks. The same total tax contribution would be due at the end of the tax year, but less would have to be paid during the year. This offer was intended to increase disposable income and stimulate household spending. How would you have responded?

3. In each of the following cases, determine whether the factor will make the size of the Arbezani government spending multiplier higher or lower than would otherwise be the case. Assume an expansionary policy.
   a. Due to the Arboc-Arbez Free Trade Agreement, trade is liberalized and Arbez buys more Arbocali imports.
   b. ArbeFed, the central bank, is committed to a policy of maintaining the interest rate at its current level.
   c. The Arbezani economy is in a recession (as opposed to close to full employment).
   d. Arbezani firms have low inventory levels.
   e. The government's action is viewed as temporary.
   f. Costs of inventory storage have decreased.
   g. Households become more sensitive to interest rate changes because of a high burden of credit card debt.
   h. A new Arbezani law is passed requiring all wage contracts to include automatic cost of living adjustments.

4. Arboc and Arbez are two neighboring economies. In each of the following cases, indicate which nation will experience the greater change in output. As always, "_ceteris paribus_" applies.
   a. Arbez enacts a temporary 10% reduction in taxes while Arboc enacts a permanent 10% reduction.   _____
   b. Arbez reduces tax rates in such a way that the average household receives a $1,000 tax break while Arboc gives each household a lump-sum tax credit worth $1,000.   _____
   c. Arboc and Arbez both expand their money supply by 5%. Arboc is in a high-output situation while Arbez is in a low-output situation.

   _____

d. Arboc and Arbez raise government spending by 10%. Inventory levels are higher in Arbez. _____

e. Arboc and Arbez raise government spending by 10%. The tax structure is more progressive in Arbez. _____

f. Each economy experiences a 10% increase in exports to the United States. Arboc tends to import more from overseas. _____

g. Both economies expand their money supply by 5%. Arboc buys relatively fewer nondurable goods and is more service-oriented than Arbez.

_____

h. The joint Arboc-Arbez stock market (Arbestock) suffers a catastrophic collapse. Arbocalis hold less of their wealth in stocks than do Arbezanis.

_____

i. The joint Arboc-Arbez stock market (Arbestock) suffers a catastrophic collapse. The Arbocalis by nature tend to be more pessimistic than their Arbezani neighbors. _____

5. Imagine a 30-year bond issued by HAL Corp. It has a face value of $1,000 and a fixed coupon payment of $100.

a. What is the interest rate on this bond? _____ (Suppose that this is the market interest rate too.)

b. Now the market interest rate moves to 5%. Is HAL's bond attractive or unattractive, and why?

c. What is happening to the demand for this bond?

d. What will happen to the supply of this bond flowing onto the market?

e. Predict what will happen to the price of the bond, based on demand and supply behavior.

f. Formulate a rule relating movements in the interest rate and bond prices.

ANSWERS AND SOLUTIONS

PRACTICE TEST

I. SOLUTIONS TO MULTIPLE CHOICE QUESTIONS

1. C. Although output level is falling, firms tend to retain extra workers during a slump to avoid the costs of rehiring them during the recovery. Each worker is producing less, so productivity decreases. See p. 426/852.

2. C. Transfers, such as welfare payments, decrease as workers leave the unemployment rolls and are hired.

3. C. Stock is an asset that has some value. As such, it is part of household wealth. The stock market crash of 1987 resulted in the obliteration of billions of dollars of wealth.

4. B. Part-time workers can be made full-time, and full-time workers can be offered overtime. The firm does not need to increase the number of workers it employs—only the number of hours that they are employed.

5. D. An increase in the interest rate is accompanied by a decrease in bond prices. See p. 422/848. Wealth has decreased and, because the household is poorer, consumption will decrease.

6. D. A temporary tax increase will reduce after-tax income temporarily. As a result, households will reduce consumption less than if the tax increase had been permanent. The decrease in consumption will cause a decrease in output.

7. D. See p. 427/853.

8. C. As households become poorer, consumption will be scaled back, especially on postponable purchases of durable goods, and a greater quantity of labor will be supplied. If you are still uncertain on these points, review the previous chapter.

9. B. "Employment" refers to the number of persons with jobs, not the number of jobs.

10. B. An increase in the discount rate is a contractionary monetary policy. As the money supply decreases, the interest rate increases. A higher interest rate discourages consumption and investment.

11. C. The higher the interest rate, the higher the cost of financing capital expansions, and the higher the opportunity cost of consumption.

12. A. The portion of income spent on foreign goods is "imports." This represents a leakage of spending power. The smaller the leakage, the greater the multiplier.
    See p. 430/856. If households become more skeptical about the permanence of tax reductions, they are coming to think that permanent income will be lower than was previously believed. As permanent income decreases, consumption decreases.

13. D. An increase in the discount rate reduces the money supply. The interest rate increases. As the interest rate increases, the price of bonds and, therefore, the wealth of bondholders decrease.

14. B. When output is high, the economy is close to capacity. Increases in government spending will result in an increase in the aggregate price level, which will reduce the size of the multiplier.

15. A. Dividends are payments of profits made to the risk-taking owners of a corporation.

16. B. Households have more spending power. Labor supply decreases as nonlabor income increases.

17. B. If the current yield is greater than 6%, the price of the bond must have fallen to less than $100 (because the coupon is fixed). We can conclude this with certainty, without knowing the extent of the capital loss.

18. D. Stocks and bonds are both assets that add to the wealth of households.

19. D. See p. 428/854.

20. A. A decrease in the reserve requirement is an expansionary monetary policy. The interest rate will decrease. An interest rate decrease will result in an increase in bond prices (a capital gain). As wealth increases, bond holders will increase consumption.

II. SOLUTIONS TO APPLICATION QUESTIONS

1. a. This is a contractionary monetary policy. The interest rate will increase, resulting in lower investment. The effect on consumption is ambiguous—if the income effect dominates, consumption will increase; if the substitution effect dominates, consumption will decrease. The effect on labor supply is similarly ambiguous. As aggregate demand decreases, the overall price level and output will decrease although, because we are operating on the steep part of the Arbocali aggregate supply curve, price will decrease more significantly than output. Employment will decrease.

   b. The government spending increase will shift the aggregate demand curve to the right. Because we are operating on the relatively flat portion of the AS curve, aggregate output and employment will increase substantially while the overall price level will increase less vigorously. If firms are holding excess labor, the expansion in employment will be less marked. The interest rate will increase, reducing (crowding out) planned investment. The effect on consumption is ambiguous—if the income effect dominates, consumption will increase; if the substitution effect dominates, consumption will decrease.

   c. This is an expansionary fiscal policy. Consumption will increase and the labor supply will decrease. The increase in aggregate demand will increase the price level (a little, because we are on the relatively flat portion of the AS curve) and increase output (a lot). Employment should increase, unless firms already have excess labor. Higher output levels should prompt greater investment although this increase is likely to be partly offset by the operation of the crowding out effect.

2. The President's scheme was largely unsuccessful in stimulating consumption. Most tax-payers, who were already lacking in confidence, saw the tax reduction as temporary and were concerned that they would have a larger tax bill at the end of the year. Some of those households which were finding it difficult to make ends meet took the opportunity to "spend now and pay later."

3. a. The multiplier will be lower. A greater portion of any injection of spending power by the government will be removed from the Arbezani economy.

   b. The multiplier will be higher. There will be no crowding out effect to offset the government spending change.

   c. The multiplier will be higher during a recession. Close to full employment, further expansion is likely to be cramped by supply bottlenecks, i.e., close to full employment the economy is operating on the steep portion of the AS curve.

   d. The multiplier will be higher. If inventories are high, there is less need to hire extra workers and generate additional spending power.

   e. The multiplier will be lower. Firms will be less likely to step up investment plans and expand production if the source of the economy's growth is temporary. Households are more likely to save any "bonus" income received as a cushion against hard times in the future.

   f. The multiplier will be lower. Inventories will be higher than otherwise so, when the government enacts its policy, there is less need to increase production and hire more workers.

   g. The multiplier will be lower. An expansion in government spending increases the interest rate. If households are concerned about debt repayments, they will reduce their current purchases.

   h. The multiplier will be lower. The more rapidly input prices respond to changes in output prices, the less firms will be willing to expand employment opportunities and production.

4. a. Arboc. A permanent change will have more of an impact on behavior than a temporary change that will soon disappear.

   b. Arbez. The Arbezani tax break affects the real wage; the Arbocali lump-sum tax credit is an increase in nonlabor income. The income effect is the same in both cases, but there is no substitution effect with the lump-sum tax credit. The tax rate reduction will encourage a greater quantity of labor to be supplied because the opportunity cost of leisure is now higher in Arbez. If the labor supply does increase, the economy will expand more.

   c. Arbez. If Arbez is farther from the potential output level, where full employment occurs, it is on the flatter portion of the short-run aggregate supply curve. An increase in aggregate demand will produce less of an increase in the aggregate price level. In Arboc, the increase in demand will cause more substantial wage and price increases.

   d. Arboc. With high inventory levels in Arbez, the need to increase employment to meet the increased demand will be less. In Arboc, employment will rise more significantly, distributing extra income through the economy.

   e. Arboc. Tax rates rise more sharply in Arbez. As income expands in response to the increase in government spending, more will be drawn off in taxes in Arbez. The multiplier will be smaller as a result.

   f. Arbez. Additional exports will stimulate both economies, but the expenditure multiplier is lower in Arboc because more of its spending power "leaks" abroad in the form of imports.

   g. Arbez. In the face of an expansionary monetary policy, spending will increase more in Arbez, which buys more durable goods. During an expansion, durable goods, which are postponable, tend to expand more rapidly than nondurables or services.

   h. Arbez. If the Arbezanis hold a large portion of their wealth in the stock market, the crash will have a significant negative impact on household wealth. Consumption spending will decrease more in Arbez.

   i. Arboc. Two factors may enter in this case. First, Arbocali entrepreneurs may cut back investment in Arboc in the expectation of a recession. Their "animal spirits" are low. Second, Arbocali consumers, dreading a long-lasting reduction in their wealth, will reduce consumption spending.

5. a. The rate is (coupon × 100%) / face value = ($100 × 100%) / $1,000 = 10%.
    b. The bond is attractive because it is paying an interest rate (10%) that is higher than the market rate (5%).
    c. Demand for this attractive bond will increase.
    d. Supply will decrease. Why sell such a high-yielding bond? Note the difference between the supply of this bond (a flow) versus the total number in existence at any point in time (a stock).
    e. The price of the bond should rise to more than $1,000. In fact, if the market interest rate remains at 5% and we recall that the coupon is a fixed value, the price must increase to $2,000 to make the rate on this bond equal to the market interest rate—i.e., 100 / 2,000 equals 5%.
    f. As the market rate falls (rises), the price of bonds rises (falls).

DEBATES IN MACRO-ECONOMICS: MONETARISM, NEW CLASSICAL THEORY, AND SUPPLY-SIDE ECONOMICS

19

COMBINED TEXT

34

OBJECTIVES: POINT BY POINT

After completing this chapter, you should be able to accomplish the objectives listed below.

General Comment

This chapter exposes some of the controversies that have boiled up within macro-economics. It should alert you to the fact that no single model is accepted by all economists. Economics, unlike the physical sciences, is not governed by a set of undeniable laws. The model that is preferred often has as much to do with the prevailing philosophical attitude as it does with tested theories. A political dimension may be detected too. The activist "demand-side" Keynesian view is fairly liberal; the supply-side theory was a major plank of Ronald Reagan's presidential campaign in 1980; Milton Friedman, the most famous monetarist, attracted the attention of Presidents Nixon and Ford; and the new classical economics advocates a "hands-off" approach to government intervention in the economy.

OBJECTIVE 1: Outline the assumptions of the quantity theory and discuss the rationale for policy actions advised by monetarists that distinguish them from Keynesians.

The AS/AD model is essentially *Keynesian*: Keynesians believe that the money market and goods market are linked; it is possible for cyclical unemployment to persist; and government policy can influence economic activity. More recently, "Keynesianism" has come to be associated with "activist" fiscal and monetary policy.   (page 436/862)

The *quantity theory (monetarist)* view of the economy relates the money supply (M) to nominal GDP (PY). On average, each dollar must be used a given number of times to buy all the goods produced; this given number is the velocity of money (V) and it is assumed to be (practically) constant. The central idea of the quantity theory is captured in the equation of exchange:

$$MV = PY$$

Given V, any change in M must cause a change in PY. If the economy tends to remain close to full employment (another part of the monetarist view), then sustained changes in M must show up as changes in the price level rather than as changes in output—inflation is caused solely by excessive growth in the money supply. To the extent that velocity is not constant—and there is, in fact, a positive relationship between velocity and the interest rate—the monetarist view is weakened.   (page 438/864)

Keynesians support coordinated fiscal and monetary policy actions to stabilize the economy; monetarists argue for a "money growth rule"—the money supply should grow at a steady rate, equal to the long-term growth rate of the economy. If this is done, inflation is avoided. (page 441/867)

> **TIP:** As you study monetarism, focus on the "MV = PY" formula, which is sometimes called the "equation of exchange."

> **TIP:** In equilibrium, money demand (M^d) must equal money supply (M), therefore, in equilibrium, $M^d = M = PY/V$. One can think of an increase in velocity as being the equivalent of a decrease in money demand, and *vice versa*.

> **TIP:** In terms of prior money demand/money supply diagrams, monetarists hypothesize a steep, inelastic money demand curve.

> **TIP:** Much of the difference between the Keynesian and monetarist schools of thought can be seen as a difference in time horizons. Keynesians function in the short run—sticky wages and cyclical unemployment are to be expected. Monetarists take a longer view—the AS curve is vertical and changes in aggregate demand have no effect on output (Y), changing only the price level (P).

PRACTICE

1. In 1995, nominal GDP was $5,951 billion. The money supply (M1) was about $967 billion. Velocity was approximately
   A. .162.
   B. .0615.
   C. 6.154.
   D. 16.25.
   Answer: C. V = nominal GDP (PY) / M.

2. The money stock is $400 million, the price level is $2, and velocity is 5.
   A. Real GDP is 2,000 million.
   B. Real GDP is 1,000 million.
   C. Nominal GDP is 160 million.
   D. Nominal GDP is 1,000 million.
   Answer: B. In the equation MV = PY, Y stands for real GDP.

3. Monetarists advocate
   A. a coordinated fiscal and monetary policy.
   B. a coordinated demand-side and supply-side policy.
   C. a policy of steady, slow growth in the money supply.
   D. an activist stabilization policy to control inflation and a passive stabilization policy to control unemployment.
   Answer: C. See p. 441/867.

4. Which of the following statements is false?
   A. Velocity can be affected by institutional factors, such as the frequency of payments to workers.
   B. Velocity can be affected by the development of new methods of payment of bills.
   C. The quantity theory is strengthened if the demand for money is dependent on the interest rate.
   D. A 10% increase in M, coupled with a reduction in V, will result in a less than 10% increase in nominal GDP.
   Answer: C. The quantity theory is weakened if V is not constant. V will vary if the demand for money is interest-sensitive. See p. 439/865.

5. Which of the following is not a valid argument suggesting that velocity may not be constant?
   A. Velocity increases as the interest rate increases.
   B. Velocity will change if there is a change in the frequency with which workers are paid.
   C. Velocity increases as the supply of money increases.
   D. Velocity will change if the banking system becomes more efficient.
   Answer: C. As the money supply increases, the interest rates decreases. The opportunity cost of holding money decreases, and there is an increase in the quantity of money demanded. For the same level of transactions, velocity will decrease. Note that institutional factors affect the demand for money (Options B and D).

6. "Strict" monetarists claim that most of the inflation experienced in the U.S. economy over the past 20 years could have been avoided if
   A. the federal government deficit had been reduced.
   B. the Fed had not expanded the money supply so rapidly.
   C. income taxes had not been reduced to stimulate labor supply.
   D. the banking industry had not been deregulated, because deregulation has increased velocity.
   Answer: B. For monetarists, inflation is purely a monetary phenomenon.

7. Monetarists believe that the demand for money depends primarily on
   A. the interest rate.
   B. the level of nominal GDP.
   C. consumption expenditures.
   D. the overall price level.
   Answer: B. Nominal GDP is PY. Option D is covered by the more general Option B.

8. In general, evidence since 1960 suggests that velocity
   A. has been fairly constant.
   B. has been increasing.
   C. has been decreasing.
   D. decreased in the first part of the period and increased in the second part of the period.
   Answer: B. See the diagram on p. 440/866.

OBJECTIVE 2: State the assumptions of the new classical macroeconomic theory, especially the role of expectations, and describe the model's policy conclusions. Outline the reasoning behind the real business cycle theory.

The *new classical macroeconomics* has combined the assumption of *rational expectations* (a hypothesis that states that the individual forms expectations by incorporating all available information into a "true model" of the economy) with the *Lucas supply function.* Having rational expectations doesn't mean that one will be perfectly correct in one's predictions—the Lucas supply function tells us that price "surprises" (mismatches between the actual price level and the expected price level) can occur that will affect output—but it does mean that individuals will adjust for expected changes. The conclusion is that anticipated changes in government policy won't be a surprise, won't affect output, and won't affect employment. The issue boils down to one question—do individuals have a true model of the economy and are they well informed? (page 442/868)

The assumptions of real business cycle theory lead to a vertical AS curve, even in the short run, therefore, fluctuations in output must be caused only by shifts of the AS curve (supply shocks).

PRACTICE

9. According to the Lucas supply function, when the _____ price level is greater than the expected price level, production will _____
   A. actual, increase.
   B. actual, decrease.
   C. previous, increase.
   D. previous, decrease.
   Answer: A. Firms and workers find their own price (or wage) to be higher than expected and produce more. See p. 445/871.

10. When there is a mismatch between the expected price level and the actual price level, the difference is called a(n)
    A. rational expectation.
    B. irrational expectation.
    C. price surprise.
    D. untrue model.
    Answer: C. See p. 445/871.

11. According to the new classical economists, which of the following will affect output?
    A. An expansionary and anticipated fiscal policy.
    B. An expansionary and anticipated monetary policy.
    C. A contractionary and unanticipated fiscal policy.
    D. A contractionary and anticipated monetary policy.
    Answer: C. Only unanticipated policy actions will be effective.

12. The Lucas supply function states that real output depends on the difference between
    A. the actual output level and the potential output level.
    B. the actual price level and the expected price level.
    C. the actual price level and the equilibrium price level.
    D. the actual output level and the expected output level.
    Answer: B. See p. 445/871 for a discussion of the Lucas supply function.

13. Given rational expectations, unemployment is due to
    A. announced expansionary policies, whether fiscal or monetary.
    B. announced contractionary policies, whether fiscal or monetary.
    C. deficient aggregate demand within the private sector.
    D. unpredictable shocks.
    Answer: D. If an event can be predicted, it will have no impact on the real economy.

14. Which of the following statements about expectations is false?
    A. The traditional treatment of expectations is flawed in that it is inconsistent with the microeconomic assumption that individuals are forward-looking.
    B. The traditional treatment of expectations is flawed in that it is inconsistent with the microeconomic assumption that individuals are rational.
    C. The rational-expectations hypothesis assumes that errors in forecasting future inflation are systematic.
    D. The rational-expectations hypothesis assumes that errors in forecasting future inflation are random.
    Answer: C. If individuals use all available information with the true model, overestimates and underestimates will be randomly distributed.

15. The major argument against the rational-expectations hypothesis is that
    A. it requires households and firms to know too much.
    B. it is inconsistent with the assumptions of microeconomics.
    C. it assumes that expectations are formed rather naively.
    D. it assumes that information collection is costless.
    Answer: A. See p. 446/872.

16. According to the real business cycle theory, which of the following does not cause business cycles?
    A. A change in labor productivity.
    B. A change in the money supply.
    C. A change in the size of the labor force.
    D. A change in the real quantity of the capital stock.
    Answer: B. A change in money supply will affect aggregate demand; the other options will affect the supply side of the economy.

OBJECTIVE 3: Outline the reasoning behind supply-side policies and summarize the evidence about the "supply-side experiment" of the 1980s.

Supply-side economics came to prominence in the early 1980s and, in opposition to the traditional Keynesian "demand-side" policies, advocated policies designed to affect aggregate supply. Policies were intended to increase the incentives to supply labor, to save, and to invest. Personal tax rates were reduced and tax credits were given for investment. Additionally, government regulation of the private sector was lessened. Essentially, such measures were attempts to shift the aggregate supply curve, which would combat inflation and unemployment simultaneously. (page 448/874)

The *Laffer Curve*, which relates tax rates and tax revenues, was a key part of this strategy. Its shape suggests that, if taxes are prohibitive, cuts in tax rates will increase tax collections as well as *increase* incentives to work. (This was an attractive theory for a president committed to reducing the federal deficit while cutting tax rates.) Studies have found little evidence to support the supply-side theory. (page 448/874)

> **Comment:** Changes in taxes are acceptable policy options for the demand-side Keynesians and for the supply-siders. The effect of the tax cut is viewed differently. A Keynesian economist would see the tax cut boosting consumption and, thus, aggregate demand, while a supply-side economist would emphasize the effect on labor supply.
>
> An investment tax credit should increase investment (demand-side) and productive capacity (supply-side)—again, the difference between the two views is one of emphasis. The Keynesian would believe that the stronger and more immediate effect would be felt through a change in aggregate demand, while the supply-side economist would argue that the most immediate effect would be felt in aggregate supply.

PRACTICE

17. Supply-side economists argued that the government should focus on policies designed
    A. to stimulate demand.
    B. to stimulate supply.
    C. to discourage demand.
    D. to discourage supply.
    Answer: B. See p. 448/874.

18. According to the Laffer Curve, as tax rates increase, tax revenues will
    A. increase.
    B. decrease.
    C. increase and then decrease.
    D. decrease and then increase.
    Answer: C. See p. 448/874.

19. Which of the following is a potential supply-side policy?
    A. An increase in government spending.
    B. An increase in depreciation allowances for businesses intended to encourage investment.
    C. Increases in the employer contributions to the social security program.
    D. Increases in welfare benefits.

    Answer: B. Greater depreciation allowances will stimulate additional investment and greater aggregate supply. Note that the increase in planned investment will also increase aggregate demand.

20. Supply-side cuts in personal tax rates and increases in investment incentives would
    A. increase aggregate demand only.
    B. increase aggregate supply only.
    C. increase aggregate demand and aggregate supply.
    D. decrease aggregate demand and increase aggregate supply.

    Answer: C. Cutting tax rates and providing investment incentives would increase labor supply and the capital stock, but would also increase consumption and planned investment spending.

Endpoint: Comparisons of the Keynesian, Monetarist, New Classical, and Supply-Side Models

Here are a few of the differences between the models that you've seen. Use these generalizations to help you sort out the different views and, perhaps, to find the one you feel is most accurate.

Factor	Keynesian	Monetarist	New Classical	Supply-Side
Prices	rigid	flexible	flexible	flexible
Do markets clear?	no	yes	yes	yes
Expectations	adaptive	adaptive	rational	adaptive
Policy preferences	demand-side fiscal and monetary policy	demand-side monetary policy	"hands-off"— no anticipated policy will work	supply-side fiscal policy

Note: "Adaptive" expectations is the name given to the traditional view of how expectations are formed, as described on p. 443/869 in the textbook. Individuals adapt their expectations based on what has gone before. Proponents of the forward-looking rational expectations hypothesis term such adaptive behavior "backward-looking."

The models in this chapter can all be interpreted in terms of the AD/AS diagram. Keynesianism focuses on the short-run diagram and manipulation of aggregate demand. Monetarism also focuses on movement of aggregate demand (ultimately through changes in the money supply), but the long run arrives more quickly. Supply-side economics also claims that policy actions can shift the economy—by moving the aggregate supply curve. Again, markets are competitive and responsive, and the long run arrives rapidly. New classical economists argue that government intervention is destabilizing. With rational expectations, the economy achieves potential output rapidly.

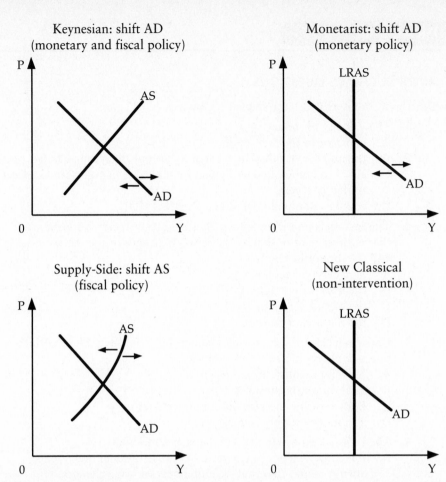

Keynesian: shift AD
(monetary and fiscal policy)

Monetarist: shift AD
(monetary policy)

Supply-Side: shift AS
(fiscal policy)

New Classical
(non-intervention)

The debate about price surprises and employment can be quite difficult to follow. The table below will help you to grasp the main ideas.

| Price level | Inflation | | wage/hour | hrs worked | Reward/hour | |
	expected	actual			expected	actual
1.00	0%	0%	10.00	8	10	10
1.00	0%	0%	11.00	9	11	11
1.10	0%	10%	11.00	9	11	10
1.10	10%	10%	11.00	8	10	10

Suppose an economy that neither has nor expects inflation. The price level is $1.00.

The first two rows of numbers represent the supply of labor that will occur at two different wage levels. Given the price level, the worker will work 8 hours for a nominal wage of $10.00 per hour and 9 hours for $11.00 per hour. What is the real wage in each case?

The next row shows that, unexpectedly, prices have jumped 10%. Employers can now offer higher (nominal) wages. Employment increases because workers are "fooled" into thinking that their real wage has risen to 11 units/hour. Eventually, when workers discover that their real reward is only 10 units/hour, the quantity of labor supplied will decrease.

Conclusion: A price surprise can cause production and employment levels to change.

I. MULTIPLE CHOICE QUESTIONS.

Select the option that provides the single best answer.

_____ 1. The velocity of money is
   A. constant in the real world.
   B. the number of times an average dollar bill changes hands per year.
   C. equal to nominal GDP divided by the value of goods and services traded in a year.
   D. equal to nominal GDP divided by real GDP.

_____ 2. The macroeconomic viewpoint that believes velocity is constant and that a direct relationship exists between growth of the money stock and the rate of inflation is
   A. new classical economics.
   B. classical economics.
   C. the quantity theory.
   D. the Keynesian theory.

_____ 3. Under which of the following assumptions could we state that inflation is a purely monetary phenomenon?
   A. Velocity is constant.
   B. Real output is constant.
   C. Both velocity and real output are constant.
   D. The money supply is constant.

_____ 4. The rational expectations hypothesis assumes that
   A. full employment always occurs because rational individuals always realize that they should adjust to wage changes.
   B. there is no unanticipated inflation.
   C. decision-makers have a theoretical model of how the economy works.
   D. individuals are able to predict future inflation rates accurately.

_____ 5. According the supply-side economic theory, the most important effect of a cut in personal income tax rates would be
   A. increased consumption spending.
   B. increased personal saving.
   C. increased number of hours worked.
   D. decreased tax revenues.

_____ 6. The Laffer Curve shows the relationship between tax rates and
   A. inflation.
   B. tax revenues.
   C. the federal deficit.
   D. national income.

_____ 7. Lucas hypothesized that aggregate _____ is reduced when the expected price level is _____ the actual price level.
   A. demand, greater than.
   B. demand, less than.
   C. supply, greater than.
   D. supply, less than.

_____ 8. According to monetarists, inflation has persisted because
   A. the Fed has accommodated the federal deficit by cutting the rate of growth of the money supply.
   B. aggregate supply has failed to expand adequately because of regulation and tax laws.
   C. aggregate supply has risen quite sharply despite government regulation and tax laws.
   D. the Fed has accommodated the federal deficit through expansionary monetary policy actions.

_____ 9. The new classical macroeconomic view developed because traditional economics
   A. unrealistically assumed that individuals have perfect knowledge of the future.
   B. failed to assume that, on average, individuals can accurately predict future events.
   C. assumed that individuals do not learn from errors in forecasts.
   D. assumed that consumers have less information than producers.

_____ 10. According to the Lucas supply function,
   A. anticipated expansionary fiscal policy actions can increase production.
   B. unanticipated expansionary fiscal policy actions can increase production.
   C. anticipated expansionary monetary policy actions can increase production.
   D. anticipated contractionary fiscal policy actions can increase production.

_____ 11. The Fed increases the money supply. As the interest rate decreases, the quantity of money demanded _____ and the velocity of money _____
   A. increases, increases.
   B. increases, decreases.
   C. decreases, increases.
   D. decreases, decreases.

_____ 12. The Fed increases the money supply by 10%; the interest rate decreases. Because velocity decreases, the _____ in nominal GDP will be _____
   A. increase, more than 10%.
   B. increase, less than 10%.
   C. decrease, more than 10%.
   D. decrease, less than 10%.

_____ 13. M2 is _____ than M1; the measure of velocity based on M2 will be _____ than the measure of velocity based on M1.
   A. larger, larger.
   B. larger, smaller.
   C. smaller, larger.
   D. smaller, smaller.

_____ 14. Which of the following schools of thought is not directly opposed to use of fiscal policy to manipulate the macroeconomy?
   A. Keynesian.
   B. Monetarism.
   C. Rational expectations.
   D. New classical.

_____ 15. The velocity of money is the ratio of
   A. nominal GDP to the stock of money.
   B. real GDP to the stock of money.
   C. stock of money to real GDP.
   D. the stock of money to nominal GDP.

_____ 16. When inflation is increasing and expectations are formed rationally, individuals will
   A. consistently overestimate inflation.
   B. consistently underestimate inflation.
   C. estimate inflation correctly every time.
   D. estimate inflation correctly on average, with randomly distributed errors.

_____ 17. Supply-siders argued that a cut in tax rates would _____ the amount of taxable income and _____ tax revenues.
   A. increase, increase.
   B. increase, decrease.
   C. decrease, increase.
   D. decrease, decrease.

_____ 18. According to the real business cycle theory, a beneficial productivity shock would _____ the real interest rate and _____ the price level.
   A. increase, increase
   B. increase, decrease
   C. decrease, increase
   D. decrease, decrease

II. APPLICATION QUESTIONS.

1. In Arbez a simple proportional tax is imposed on wages. Tax revenues (T) are:
$$T = t \times W \times L$$

where t is the tax rate, W is the gross hourly wage rate, and L is the total supply of labor in hours.

The after-tax wage is $\quad W_n = (1 - t)W$

Suppose that W = $6, L = 10,000, and t = .3.
   a. Calculate tax revenues.
   b. What is the net hourly wage?
   c. Now suppose that the tax rate is reduced to .25. For tax revenues to remain unchanged, how much must the labor supply increase (assuming that the gross hourly wage rate doesn't change)?
   d. Calculate the new net hourly wage.
   e. Elasticity of labor supply is $\%\Delta L \div \%\Delta W_n$. Calculate the numerical value of the elasticity of labor supply.
   f. Interpret the meaning of the elasticity number you've calculated with respect to the plausibility of reducing taxes while maintaining the same level of tax collections.

2. a. Calculate the values for PY and write them in the table below. This is a short-run aggregate supply schedule.

P	Y	PY	MV30	MV45
$0.50	50			
$1.00	60			
$2.00	70			
$3.00	80			
$4.00	90			
$5.00	100			
$6.00	110			

b. Suppose that velocity (V) is constant and equal to 8, and that the money supply is equal to $30. Complete the MV30 column of the table.

c. In equilibrium, calculate the nominal GDP level, the price level, and the real output level.

d. Now the Fed increases the money supply to $45 (a 50% increase). Velocity remains constant. Complete the MV45 column of the table.

e. In equilibrium, calculate the nominal GDP level, the price level, and the real output level is.

Can you see that the MV30 and MV45 columns represent the dollar value of expenditures at different levels of the money supply? For a monetarist, this is the same thing as an aggregate demand curve!

Our supply schedule is short-run—monetary policy actions have an effect on output. In the long run, however, a monetarist would claim that a ten percent increase in money supply would result in a ten percent increase in prices and in wages; real wage and output level would be unaffected by price changes. Aggregate supply is vertical in the long run!

3. Rational expectations theorists claim that the traditional (Keynesian) view of the formation of expectations about inflation leads to systematic mistakes. If formed rationally, expectations will not make systematic mistakes.

Let EP_t = Expected price level (this time period)
P_t = Price level (this time period)
EP_{t+1} = Expected price level (next time period)

Suppose that individuals are backward-looking, following the formula $EP_{t+1} = EP_t + .5(EP_t - P_t)$ when they form their expectations.

Calculate the expected price level in the table below.

Year	0	1	2	3	4	5	6	7	8	9
Price Level	100	100	110	121	131	142	126	115	107	100
Expected Price Level	100	___	___	___	___	___	___	___	___	___

Graph the values for the expected price level and the price level on the graph.

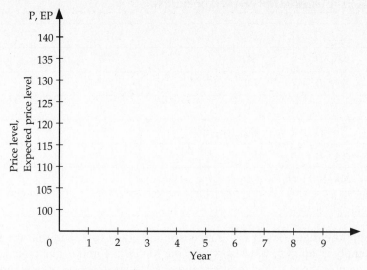

4. a. In the diagram below, why are tax collections zero at point A?

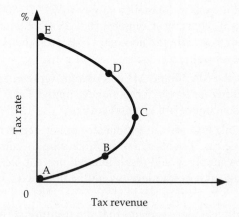

b. Why are tax collections zero at point E?
c. At which point on the curve did Laffer believe the economy was in the early 1980s?
d. What policy action was called for?
e. Assuming spending programs remained unchanged, what effect would this have had on the budget deficit?
f. What effect did Laffer believe this sort of move would have on the supply of labor?
g. If the tax rate was at point B, and the same policy was pursued, what would have happened to the deficit and the supply of labor?

PRACTICE TEST

I. SOLUTIONS TO MULTIPLE CHOICE QUESTIONS

1. B. This is a good, easy-to-understand definition of velocity. Note that it does not require velocity to be constant.

2. C. The "quantity" in the quantity theory refers to the quantity of money in the economy. See p. 438/864.

3. C. In the equation MV = PY, if V and Y are both constant, then an increase in P (inflation) can be caused only by an increase in M.

4. C. It is assumed that each individual knows the "true model" that generates inflation. We may not have perfect information, however, and our expectations may not be completely accurate. Given price surprises, deviations from full employment will occur.

5. C. If the tax rate is cut, after-tax take-home pay increases. The substitution effect would encourage workers to supply more labor. The income effect would partly offset the substitution effect, but supply-siders believe that the substitution effect would dominate.

6. B. See p. 448/874.

7. C. A mismatch between the expected and the actual price level affects supply. If the actual price level is greater than the expected price level, each firm believes that the actual price it is able to charge is "high," and so it increases production. Each worker believes that the wage s/he earns is "high," and works more.

8. D. Monetarists believe that inflation is a purely monetary phenomenon.

9. B. See p. 442/868. Note that individuals do learn from errors but, because consumers remain backward-looking, errors can persist.

10. B. Anticipated changes will have no effect on the economy, according to the rational-expectations hypothesis.

11. B. See p. 439/865.

12. B. Given MV = PY, the decrease in V partly offsets the 10% increase in M. The right-hand side of the equation will increase, but by less than the full 10%.

13. B. M2 includes M1 and other assets, such as passbook savings accounts. Given the value of GDP, if we define V as PY / M, V will decrease the larger the value of M.

14. A. See p. 437/863.

15. A. See p. 437/863.

16. D. The rational-expectations hypothesis does not claim that expectations will always be correct. It does claim that no systematic error will be made.

17. A. According to the Laffer Curve, a reduction in tax rates will encourage more labor supply and, therefore, more income that can be taxed. Despite lower tax rates, tax revenues will increase.

18. D. The AS curve will shift right.

II. SOLUTIONS TO APPLICATION QUESTIONS

1. a. Tax revenue = $t \times W \times L = .3 \times \$6 \times 10,000 = \$18,000$.
    b. The net wage (after tax) = $(1 - t)W = .7 \times \$6 = \$4.20$.
    c. It must change from 10,000 to 12,000. Tax revenue = $t \times W \times L = .25 \times \$6 \times 12,000 = \$18,000$.
    d. The net wage (after tax) = $(1 - t)W = .75 \times \$6 = \$4.50$.
    e. $\%\Delta L = 2,000 / (10,000 + 12,000) = .09091$
       $\%\Delta Wn = .30 / (4.20 + 4.50) = .03448$
       $\%\Delta L / \%\Delta Wn = .09091 / 03448 = 2.6363$
    f. This elasticity coefficient indicates that labor supply would have to be very elastic for the government to undertake the tax cut and hope to avoid having tax revenues decrease. Essentially, the after-tax wage has increased by 3.448%. To accomplish its goal of maintaining tax revenues, the government must encourage a 9.091% increase in hours worked.

2. a. See the table below.

P	Y	PY	MV30	MV45
$0.50	50	$ 25	$240	$360
$1.00	60	$ 60	$240	$360
$2.00	70	$140	$240	$360
$3.00	80	$240	$240	$360
$4.00	90	$360	$240	$360
$5.00	100	$500	$240	$360
$6.00	110	$660	$240	$360

b. See the table above. In each case, M × V = 30 × 8 = 240.
c. Nominal GDP = $240, price level = $3.00, output = 80. Recall that, in equilibrium, MV = PY.
d. See the table above. In each case, M × V = 45 × 8 = 360.
e. Nominal GDP = $360, price level = $4.00, output = 90.

3. Example of calculations
Year 2: EPt+1 = EPt + .5(Pt − EPt) = 100 + .5(100 − 100) = 100
Year 3: EPt+1 = EPt + .5(Pt − EPt) = 100 + .5(110 − 100) = 105
Year 4: EPt+1 = EPt + .5(Pt − EPt) = 105 + .5(121 − 105) = 113
Year 5: EPt+1 = EPt + .5(Pt − EPt) = 113 + .5(131 − 113) = 122
Year 6: EPt+1 = EPt + .5(Pt − EPt) = 122 + .5(142 − 122) = 132
Year 7: EPt+1 = EPt + .5(Pt − EPt) = 132 + .5(126 − 132) = 129

Year	0	1	2	3	4	5	6	7	8	9
Price Level	100	100	110	121	131	142	126	115	107	100
Expected Price Level	100	100	100	105	113	122	132	129	122	114.5

In the graph below, note that individuals systematically underestimate increases in the price level and then overestimate them when the price level decreases.

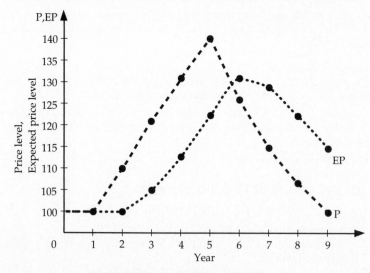

4. a. Tax collections are zero because the tax rate is zero.
b. If all income were taxed away, there would be no incentive to earn income. Income (and tax collections) would fall to zero.
c. Point D. Laffer felt that tax rates were acting as a disincentive to work.
d. Reduce tax rates, moving from point D toward point C.
e. The deficit would have fallen because tax revenues would have increased.
f. Because after-tax pay was rising, labor supply would have risen, according to Laffer.
g. If the tax rate were reduced from point B, the supply of labor should still have risen, but, because of shrinking tax revenues, the deficit would have increased.

ECONOMIC GROWTH AND PRODUCTIVITY

20

COMBINED TEXT

35

OBJECTIVES: POINT BY POINT

After completing this chapter, you should be able to accomplish the objectives listed below.

OBJECTIVE 1: Define economic growth and identify the sources of economic growth.

Economic growth is an increase in real per capita GDP resulting in improved standards of living. This chapter is concerned with what causes the upward trend. Production is limited by the resources and technology that the economy possesses. Growth occurs when more resources become available or when current resources are used more efficiently. In terms of the production possibility frontier, the maximum levels of production shift to the right as the resource base expands and/or technology improves.   (page 455/881)

Growth can take place in two ways: either the economy discovers new resources or it uses its given resources more efficiently. Growth occurs, then, through:

a. an increase in resources,
    i. labor supply
    ii. physical capital
    iii. human capital

b. the discovery of new ways to combine resources more efficiently—to increase their productivity,
    i. technological change
    ii. other advances in knowledge
    iii. economies of scale.

> **TIP:** Economies of scale will show up again in Chapters 23 (38) and 24 (39), which cover some of the same material as Chapter 20 (35). You may have met this concept in a microeconomics course. Case and Fair cover economies of scale in Chapter 9 of their Principles of Microeconomics textbook. Take this opportunity to recall how average costs are determined and how a firm is able to spread out its fixed costs by producing more output. The higher the overheads are, the greater production must be to spread out these costs.

PRACTICE

1. Economic growth is defined as an increase in
   A. real output.
   B. consumption per household.
   C. economic well-being.
   D. the rate at which inventions occur.
   Answer: A. Growth is difficult to measure—the accepted yardstick is real GDP (or real GDP per capita).

2. When we draw a production possibility frontier (ppf), we assume that
   A. the quantity of capital available increases as we move along the ppf.
   B. the quantity of capital available increases and the quantity of labor decreases as we move along the ppf.
   C. the quantity of labor available increases as we move along the ppf.
   D. the quantity of capital and labor is fixed.
   Answer: D. It is assumed that the resource base and technology are fixed. Changes in any one of these constraints will cause the ppf to shift position.

3. Graphically, economic growth can be represented by a
   A. rightward shift of the aggregate demand curve.
   B. leftward shift of the aggregate demand curve.
   C. rightward shift of the production possibility frontier.
   D. leftward shift of the production possibility frontier.
   Answer: C. Economic growth is, indeed, an expansion in an economy's possible levels of production. See p. 456/882.

4. A production possibility frontier shows
   A. how much of a good will be produced as the price of the good changes.
   B. all the combinations of two goods that can be produced when all resources are being used efficiently.
   C. all the combinations of two resources that can be produced efficiently.
   D. how much of a product can be produced as additional units of input are added to the production mix.
   Answer: B. See the diagram on p. 456/882.

5. Which of the following is an incorrect statement about the term "capital"?
   A. Capital has no effect on the productivity of labor.
   B. Capital yields services to people over a period of time.
   C. The act of producing capital goods may involve a sacrifice in terms of current consumption.
   D. The addition to the stock of capital is called investment.
   Answer: A. Capital can be combined with labor to make workers more productive.

6. Colleen and Bill construct a net out of vines so that they can trap fish. Having never done this before, they find that they are "learning by doing." Colleen and Bill are
   A. acquiring physical capital only.
   B. acquiring human capital only.
   C. acquiring physical capital and human capital.
   D. acquiring a consumption good.
   Answer: C. The net is a tool that should increase their ability to catch fish—it is physical capital. By learning as they work, Colleen and Bill are increasing their human capital.

OBJECTIVE 2: Explain the information presented by an aggregate production function. Describe the circumstances that cause diminishing returns and relate this concept to the work of Malthus and Ricardo.

A production function relates combinations of inputs to the maximum level of output of a good; an *aggregate production function* does the same thing for national output in the entire economy. Increases in the quantity and quality of resources and increases in productivity cause the output level to rise.   (page 457/883)

As additional units of a resource (e.g., labor) are added to a fixed quantity of other resources, after some point, their productivity will begin to decline. When capacity constraints begin to make themselves felt, *diminishing returns* result. This phenomenon was the reason for the gloomy predictions of Malthus and Ricardo.

> **TIP:** The usual assumption made is that diminishing returns go into effect immediately. Each additional unit of a resource will experience diminishing returns when added to a fixed quantity of other resources. Also, note that diminishing returns apply to any resource, not just labor.

PRACTICE

7. Malthus and Ricardo were concerned that the fixed supply of _____ would lead to diminishing returns.
   A. capital.
   B. technology.
   C. labor.
   D. land.
   Answer: D. See p. 458/884.

8. In Arbez, the capital stock is fixed. Because of immigration, the supply of labor increases. As diminishing returns set in, we should expect output to _____ and average labor productivity to _____
   A. increase, increase.
   B. increase, decrease.
   C. decrease, increase.
   D. decrease, decrease.
   Answer: B. As additional resources are added, output should increase, but more slowly. As diminishing returns set in, average productivity will decline. See p. 458/884.

9. Malthus and Ricardo believed that, in order to provide enough food for a rapidly growing population, farmers would have to cultivate _____ productive land _____ intensively.
   A. more, more.
   B. more, less.
   C. less, more.
   D. less, less.
   Answer: C. Presumably, the best land was already under cultivation, with less good land left unexploited. This land would have to be pressed into service and farmed intensively.

10. Diminishing returns to labor will occur if
    A. capital accumulation takes place, given the supply of labor.
    B. there is technological change, given the supply of labor.
    C. the labor supply grows more rapidly than the capital stock.
    D. the labor supply gains additional skills.
    Answer: C. See p. 458/884.

OBJECTIVE 3: List the six factors that affect growth.

There are six factors that lead to growth:

a. increases in the supply of labor, caused by immigration, maturity of the population, and improved health,

b. increases in physical capital (plant and equipment),

c. increases in human capital, caused by education, on-the-job training, and improved health,

d. technological change,

e. other advances in knowledge, and

f. economies of scale. (page 457/883)

PRACTICE

11. An increase in human capital will _____ labor productivity and _____ output.
    A. increase, increase.
    B. increase, decrease.
    C. decrease, increase.
    D. decrease, decrease.
    Answer: A. See p. 460/886.

12. As industries increase in size, they derive cost savings called
    A. innovations.
    B. inventions.
    C. external economies of scale.
    D. cost depreciations.
    Answer: C. As industries expand, "overheads" might be reduced—for example, by training or educational programs for employees—or the creation of a pool of skilled labor in a region.

13. Arboc has experienced growth, although the quantity of its inputs has remained unchanged. This growth must have been caused by
    A. random shocks to the economic system.
    B. an increase in the productivity of inputs.
    C. an increase in imports.
    D. a decrease in imports.
    Answer: B. If the quantity of resources is unchanged but more output is produced, productivity must have increased. Labor productivity is defined as output/labor. Changes in imports are irrelevant. If Arboc had imported extra machinery, for example, the quantity of capital in Arboc would have changed.

14. An industrial consultant enters a car factory and reorganizes the layout of the assembly line. Without changing the amount of capital or the number of workers, car production can be increased by 10%. This change is
    A. both labor-saving and capital-saving.
    B. labor-saving but not capital-saving.
    C. capital-saving but not labor-saving.
    D. neither labor-saving nor capital-saving.
    Answer: A. Each worker and each unit of capital is more productive than before.

OBJECTIVE 4: Outline the strategies proposed to increase the growth rate.

Although, since the mid-nineteenth century, the United States has achieved a record of growth that would be the envy of most nations, there has been some concern since the 1970s that the growth rate—and, more particularly, labor productivity—was slowing down. Proposed public policies to correct sagging growth included policies intended to:

a. improve the quality of education and training,
b. increase the saving rate (through changes in tax laws),
c. increase investment (through investment tax credit schemes),
d. increase research and development (through subsidization),
e. reduce government regulation of industry, by allowing increased (and decreased) competition and a smaller degree of supervision on pollution and health issues, and
f. involve the government in a coordinated *industrial policy* of targeting specific industries for preferential treatment.   (page 466/892)

The growth rate and productivity have improved since the mid 1980s.

> **TIP:** Notice that monetary growth is not one of the variables listed as affecting long-term economic growth. The point is that changes in the quantity of money might influence production in the short term, but that monetary expansions, boosting aggregate demand, will ultimately run up against the supply-side constraint. Pumping up the money supply might enhance short-term growth but also might breed inflation. Unanticipated inflation, which heightens risk and lessens the willingness of individuals to make long-term commitments, might have an adverse effect on investment. (Remember, too, that during rapid inflation individuals may prefer to buy goods rather than save a currency that is losing its spending power.)

Comment: Society can accumulate capital only through net investment, and investment in future production can occur only if current consumption is given up. Saving then is the basis for growth. This key point can be applied both to the accumulation of physical capital and also to investment in human capital.

PRACTICE

15. According to Denison, approximately _____ of U.S. growth in output from 1929 to 1982 was due to increases in factors of production.
    A. 20%.
    B. 25%.
    C. 50%.
    D. 75%.
    Answer: C. See p. 465/891.

16. According to Denison, the contribution of education and training to growth has
    A. increased steadily since 1929.
    B. increased at first and then decreased since 1929.
    C. decreased steadily since 1929.
    D. remained constant since 1929.
    Answer: D. See p. 468/894.

17. Which of the following has not been advanced as a way of increasing the rate of growth in the United States?
   A. Increasing the rate of consumption spending.
   B. Cutting government regulation of industry.
   C. Encouraging additional research and development.
   D. Implementing an industrial policy.
   Answer: A. Increasing the rate of consumption spending requires that the saving rate be decreased. One of the key determinants of growth is the economy's willingness to forego current consumption.

OBJECTIVE 5: Summarize the arguments for and against continued economic growth.

Growth is not a universally accepted goal; there are costs and benefits. The benefits are obvious—more leisure and material possessions—but costs are present too. Growth may be accompanied by pollution and other "bads" that adversely affect the quality of life and alienate the worker. Big business, it is argued, may induce demand for its products rather than respond to market demands. Rapid growth may deplete the world's resources while widening the gap between the "haves" and the "have-nots." As is usually the case in economics, the decision to encourage or discourage growth involves trade-offs. (page 470/896)

PRACTICE

18. Supporters of growth claim all of the following except that
   A. growth gives more choices.
   B. growth saves time.
   C. growth improves the standard of living.
   D. growth reduces income inequalities.
   Answer: D. In fact, it is one of the anti-growth arguments that growth increases income inequality.

19. Which of the following arguments is not made by opponents of economic growth?
   A. Growth requires an unfair distribution of income.
   B. Growth rapidly depletes the world's finite resources.
   C. The net impact of growth on the quality of life is beneficial.
   D. Growth encourages the creation of artificial needs.
   Answer: C. Opponents of growth argue that increased growth removes many beneficial, if unmeasurable, aspects of life.

20. Which statement is true?
   A. For poor nations, redistribution of existing income is a fast track to growth.
   B. For poor nations, growth is the only hope for improvement in the standard of living in the long run.
   C. Growth benefits all groups of society equally.
   D. Advocates of economic growth argue that growth equals progress.
   Answer: B. See p. 471/897.

I. MULTIPLE CHOICE QUESTIONS.

Select the option that provides the single best answer.

_____ 1. Modern economic growth refers to a period of rapid growth in
A. nominal GDP.
B. per capita real GDP.
C. nominal per capita GDP.
D. real GDP.

_____ 2. The law of diminishing returns suggests that increases in the
_____, *ceteris paribus*, may not lead to increased
_____
A. stock of capital, employment.
B. number of workers, output per capita.
C. number of workers, efficiency of capital.
D. stock of capital, money supply.

_____ 3. The ability of technological change to affect productivity depends on both
A. the discovery and implementation of new technology.
B. the stock of capital and the acceptance of new technology.
C. the number of new patents and the quality of the workforce.
D. the willingness of the workforce to accept change and the overall level of macroeconomic activity.

_____ 4. _____ generally enhances labor productivity. An increase
in _____ can increase _____
A. Competition, output, income.
B. Competition, population, output.
C. Training, capital, income.
D. Capital, capital, output.

_____ 5. The amount of capital accumulation is limited ultimately by
A. the interest rate.
B. marginal tax rates.
C. disposable (after-tax) income.
D. the saving rate.

_____ 6. In general, economic growth will occur where there are additions to
A. the labor force.
B. per capita nominal income.
C. the stock of money.
D. import purchases.

_____ 7. A public policy strategy designed to increase productivity might include which one of the following?
A. Increased regulations on industrial pollution.
B. Tax breaks on interest income.
C. Tax incentives to increase consumption spending.
D. Increases in college tuition.

_____ 8. Each of the following has been suggested as a likely reason for the decline in the growth rate of labor productivity in the 1970s except
A. relatively low saving rates.
B. government regulations.
C. reductions in investment spending.
D. reductions in educational standards.

_____ 9. Each of the following has been proposed as a major anti-growth argument except
A. the increased creation of "needs."
B. the reduction in the quality of life.
C. the increased choices available to the economy.
D. the uneven distribution of benefits across the community.

_____ 10. Economic growth will occur in each of the following cases except through
A. an increase in the quantity of labor.
B. an increase in the quality of labor.
C. an increase in the quantity of money.
D. an increase in the quantity of physical capital.

_____ 11. Pro-growth supporters argue that growth allows a society to allocate resources
A. to only those industries that produce goods without pollution.
B. to compete against unfair foreign imports.
C. to produce goods that households want.
D. to increase government regulation.

_____ 12. The introduction of robots is a
A. labor-saving invention.
B. labor-saving innovation.
C. capital-saving invention.
D. capital-saving innovation.

_____ 13. Malthus and Ricardo were concerned that there would be insufficient food because of the fixed supply of land. They failed to foresee the effect of _____ on agricultural production.
A. additional labor supply.
B. technological improvements.
C. diminishing returns.
D. erosion.

_____ 14. An increase in the capital/labor ratio will
A. increase the productivity of capital.
B. increase the productivity of labor.
C. increase the productivity of labor and capital.
D. decrease the productivity of labor and capital.

_____ 15. A hallmark of economies experiencing modern economic growth is
A. a stable capital to labor (K / L) ratio.
B. an increasing capital to labor (K / L) ratio.
C. a decrease in public capital.
D. a decreasing capital to labor (K / L) ratio.

II. APPLICATION QUESTIONS.

1. The following tables present data on three economies: Arbez, Arboc, and Aneyh. Complete the tables. What do the data tell you about the causes of growth?

ARBEZ PERIOD	L	K	Y	Y/L	GROWTH RATE OF OUTPUT
1	100	300	520.00	____	
2	110	304	546.00	____	____
3	119	307	578.76	____	____
4	123	312	596.12	____	____

ARBOC PERIOD	L	K	Y	Y/L	GROWTH RATE OF OUTPUT
1	100	300	520.00	____	
2	105	309	551.20	____	____
3	111	317	589.78	____	____
4	114	327	619.27	____	____

ANEYH PERIOD	L	K	Y	Y/L	GROWTH RATE OF OUTPUT
1	100	300	520.00	____	
2	105	304	540.80	____	____
3	111	307	567.84	____	____
4	114	312	579.20	____	____

2. Which countries do you think provide the most development assistance per capita? You'll need to guess here. Rank the following nine *alphabetized* countries, ("1" being the least generous and "9" being the most generous), then check the *Answers and Solutions* section to see if your intuition is As a guide, the percentage of GDP given as aid by the nine countries is included *in ascending order* in the third column. It is not meant to suggest that Canada contributes .23% of its GDP, for instance.

COUNTRY	RANKING	PERCENTAGE OF GDP
Canada	____	.23
Denmark	____	.32
France	____	.48
Netherlands	____	.72
Norway	____	.85
Saudi Arabia	____	.89
Sweden	____	1.01
United Kingdom	____	1.20
United States	____	4.52

3. Ethiopia is one of the world's very poorest nations, with a GDP per capita of only $110 in 1992. By contrast, GDP per capita for the United States was $23,240 in the same year. In other words, the average U.S. citizen earns 211.27 times as much as the average Ethiopian. Use your intuition to pair the "multiplier" from the "Selection" column with the appropriate country, then check the *Answers and Solutions* section.

COUNTRY	MULTIPLIER	SELECTION
Ethiopia	211.27	211.27
Bangladesh	_____	105.64
Canada	_____	74.97
Colombia	_____	17.47
India	_____	6.70
Israel	_____	3.09
Japan	_____	1.76
Mexico	_____	1.31
Norway	_____	1.12
Saudi Arabia	_____	.90
Switzerland	_____	.82
United Kingdom	_____	.64

4. How will each of the following affect the long-run measured growth rate in the nation of Noil?
   a. Noil's Ministry of the Environment imposes more stringent environmental regulations on businesses.
   b. The government increases spending on education. The additional spending is financed by a tax on consumers.
   c. The government pledges to trim the deficit by reducing the size of the Noilian army.
   d. The government pledges to trim the deficit by cutting expenditures on education.
   e. Noil opens its borders to migrant workers from Regit.

5. There are two neighboring economies—Formica and Klorofill. Each economy has an identical production possibility frontier (ppf), as shown below. Currently at F1, Formica prefers to produce investment goods while Klorofill, currently at K1, prefers a relatively high rate of consumption.

   Note: The ppfs are drawn as (constant-cost) straight lines merely for simplicity.

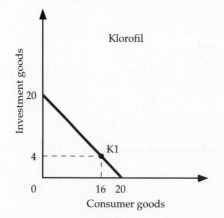
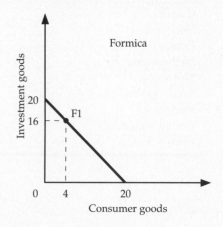

Suppose that each economy was in a recession last time period. In fact, each economy produced 4 units of consumer goods and 4 investment goods.

a.   In Klorofill's case, the economy has moved to K1. How would you represent this change on an AS/AD diagram? In Formica's case, the economy has moved to F1. How would you represent this change on an AS/AD diagram?

Let us assume that the depreciation rate in each economy is 4 machines per year.

b.   What is happening to the capital stock in Klorofill this year? In Formica?

c.   Describe the effect on the Klorofillian ppf. Describe the effect on the Formican ppf.

d.   Describe how Klorofill's AS/AD diagram will differ from that of Formica, as time passes.

Let us assume that the depreciation rate in each economy is 5 machines per year.

e.   What is happening to the capital stock in Klorofill this year? In Formica?

f.   Describe the effect on the Klorofillian ppf. Describe the effect on the Formican ppf.

g.   Describe the differences in choices faced by Klorofillians and Formicans as time passes.

6.   Write down the six factors that cause growth in the table below and match each with one of the following examples.

Letter	Factor

Examples

A.   the construction of a new, larger, factory

B.   improvements in health

C.   the implementation of a newly discovered production process

D.   decreasing production costs as plant size increases

E.   managerial skills

F.   immigration

ANSWERS AND SOLUTIONS

PRACTICE TEST

I.   SOLUTIONS TO MULTIPLE CHOICE QUESTIONS

1.   B. See the marginal definition on p. 455/881.

2.   B. If, as extra workers are added to productive activity, diminishing returns set in, output will still rise, but less rapidly. Five percent more workers might increase output by four percent. Accordingly, the average output of workers will decrease.

3.   A. New technology must be discovered, but this on its own will not increase productivity. The new ideas must be incorporated into the productive process.

4.   D. Capital is usually a complement for labor. Additional capital increases the productivity of each worker.

5.   D. See p. 468/894.

6.   A. Growth occurs when inputs increase or improve, or technology changes.

7. B. If the rate of saving (non-consumption) is the ultimate constraint on growth, measures to encourage saving will encourage growth. Option C clearly moves in the opposite direction. Option A makes production more difficult while Option D reduces inputs in the future (i.e., human capital).

8. D. See p. 466/892.

9. C. See the list of arguments on p. 472/898.

10. C. Money, by itself, is not a productive resource. Robinson Crusoe, on his island, would have had little use for dollar bills except, perhaps, to kindle a fire.

11. C. The ultimate goal of growth is to give people the things they want.

12. B. See p. 463/889.

13. B. Improved technology (better planting and harvesting techniques, improved fertilizers, more hardy and better-yielding hybrids) has allowed farmers to increase production while reducing the amount of land under cultivation.

14. B. An increase in the capital/labor ratio means that each worker has more equipment with which to work. Labor productivity will increase. The productivity of capital will decrease because additional capital is being added to a given stock of labor. See Table 3 in the textbook.

15. B. See p. 460/886.

II. SOLUTIONS TO APPLICATION QUESTIONS

1. See the tables below.

ARBEZ PERIOD	L	K	Y	Y/L	GROWTH RATE OF OUTPUT
1	100	300	520.00	5.20	
2	110	304	546.00	4.96	5.00%
3	119	307	578.76	4.86	6.00%
4	123	312	596.12	4.85	3.00%

ARBEZ PERIOD	L	K	Y	Y/L	GROWTH RATE OF OUTPUT
1	100	300	520.00	5.20	
2	105	309	551.20	5.25	6.00%
3	111	317	589.78	5.31	7.00%
4	114	327	619.27	5.43	5.00%

ARBEZ PERIOD	L	K	Y	Y/L	GROWTH RATE OF OUTPUT
1	100	300	520.00	5.20	
2	105	304	540.80	5.15	4.00%
3	111	307	567.84	5.12	5.00%
4	114	312	579.20	5.08	2.00%

The growth rate is greatest in Arboc. Compared with Aneyh, whose rate of growth in labor resources is identical, Arboc is superior in output/labor ratio. Compared with Arbez, Arboc's Y/L ratio is increasing, while that of Arbez is decreasing. However, Arbez is growing more rapidly than Aneyh because Arbez's labor force is expanding more rapidly.

2. The donor countries are ranked from least generous (1) to most generous (9). Perhaps it is not surprising that Saudi Arabia, with a surplus of petro—dollars, ranks so high, but the low position of the United States, in terms of GDP *per capita*, is remarkable—Norwegians contribute almost five times as much, as a percentage of GDP. In fact, the Scandinavian countries are consistently generous.

COUNTRY	RANKING	PERCENTAGE OF GDP
Canada	4	.48
Denmark	6	.89
France	3	.72
Netherlands	7	1.01
Norway	8	1.20
Saudi Arabia	9	4.52
Sweden	5	.85
United Kingdom	2	.32
United States	1	.23

3. It is worthy of note that, although the United States citizen is still among the very highest income earners in the world, a few countries have leap-frogged ahead (those with multipliers having a value of less than one).

COUNTRY	MULTIPLIER	GDP PER CAPITA (U.S. DOLLARS)
Ethiopia	211.27	110
Bangladesh	105.64	220
Canada	1.12	20,710
Colombia	17.47	1,330
India	74.97	310
Israel	1.76	13,220
Japan	.82	28,190
Mexico	6.70	3,470
Norway	.90	25,820
Saudi Arabia	3.09	7,510
Switzerland	.64	36,080
United Kingdom	1.31	17,790

4. a. More stringent environmental regulations on businesses will reduce the measured growth rate. Profits will be reduced and less investment will occur.

b. The growth rate will rise because of additional investment in human capital and because the tax on consumption will encourage households to save more.

c. The growth rate will increase because, with a reduced deficit, national saving will be greater and interest rates will be lower. Private investment will be encouraged.

d. The effect on the growth rate is uncertain. A reduced deficit will encourage investment (see part c, above), but lower educational expenditure represents a reduction in human capital investment (see part b, above). The growth rate will increase if there is a greater return on private investment or on education.

e. Immigration increases the labor force and may reduce the capital to labor ratio. If so, productivity will decrease. However, the Regitani workers may be highly skilled (human capital) which will increase the capital to labor ratio. In addition, the migrants may be more highly motivated to succeed. If so, productivity would increase and Noil would benefit from the influx.

5.   a.   The AD curve has moved to the right by the same amount in each case.
     b.   The capital stock in Klorofill is stationary, with 4 new machines being produced and 4 existing machines wearing out. In Formica, the capital stock is increasing by 12 (i.e., 16 – 4).
     c.   Klorofill's ppf is stationary; Formica's ppf is shifting outward as its productive resources increase.
     d.   Klorofill's AD curve will remain stationary with consumption at 16 units and investment at 4 units. Productive capacity is not increasing, therefore the aggregate supply curve will not shift. In Formica, aggregate supply will increase to match expansions in aggregate demand because of the expanding resource base.
     e.   The capital stock in Klorofill is declining, with 4 new machines being produced and 5 existing machines wearing out. In Formica, the capital stock is increasing by 11 (i.e., 16 – 5).
     f.   Klorofill's ppf is shifting inward; Formica's ppf is shifting outward as its productive resources increase.
     g.   As time passes, the Klorofillians will be forced to cut back their standard of living. Currently, their resource base is shrinking. To prevent this they will have to increase investment good production at the expense of consumer good production. The Formicans face no such hard choice—their ppf is shifting outward so they can increase consumption and investment levels.

6.   A.   an increase in physical capital.
     B.   an increase in human capital.
     C.   technological change.
     D.   economies of scale.
     E.   an advance in knowledge.
     F.   an increase in the supply of labor.

INTERNATIONAL TRADE, COMPARATIVE ADVANTAGE, AND PROTECTIONISM

21

COMBINED TEXT

36

OBJECTIVES: POINT BY POINT

After completing this chapter, you should be able to accomplish the objectives listed below.

OBJECTIVE 1: Distinguish between an open and a closed economy. Distinguish between a trade surplus and a trade deficit.

In open economies such as the United States, aggregate expenditures are affected by the presence of exports and imports. We have seen international trade steadily increase in importance throughout the last several decades. If exports exceed imports, the country runs a *trade surplus*. In the oil—expensive years of the 1970s and 1980s, the value of imports into the United States increased to over 12% of GDP, and the United States began to experience *trade deficits*—that is, its imports exceeded its exports. (page 481/907)

> **TIP:** Learn the difference between exports and imports. Imports are foreign-produced goods consumed here. Exports are domestically-produced goods sold to customers overseas. Imports and exports are not opposites; they are determined by different factors.

Comment: The two terms, "balance of payments" and "balance of trade", are not synonymous. The balance of trade refers only to exports and imports of goods, while the balance of payments includes all international transactions.

PRACTICE

1. The U.S. trade _____ reached a _____ in the late 1980s.
   A. surplus, peak.
   B. surplus, minimum.
   C. deficit, peak.
   D. deficit, minimum.
   Answer: C. See the table on p. 481/907.

OBJECTIVE 2: Distinguish between absolute advantage and comparative advantage and explain the logic behind the theory of comparative advantage. Given a particular two-country, two-good situation, calculate which country will trade which good and indicate the feasible range for the terms of trade.

The *theory of comparative advantage* provides the rationale for free trade. Given a two-country, two-good world, and assuming that the countries have advantages in the production of different goods, Ricardo showed that both trading partners could benefit from specialization in the production of the good in which they have the comparative advantage. Each country should specialize in the production of that good in which it has a comparative advantage and trade its surplus. Production and welfare will be maximized. Country A is said to have an *absolute advantage* if it can produce a unit of output with fewer resources than Country B. Comparative advantage, though, is a relative concept. Country A will have a *comparative advantage* in whichever good it can produce comparatively cheaper. Specialization and trade allow a country to consume more than it can produce of a good.   (page 482/908)

> **TIP:** If you're like most individuals, you'll need several numerical examples to strengthen your grasp of pure trade theory. The Applications below take you through all the steps included in the text. Review Application questions 2, 7 and 10 in Chapter 2 of this manual. They will lead you through the opportunity cost concept that underlies the theory of comparative advantage.

> **TIP:** Comparative advantage hinges on the concept of opportunity cost. (Take a little time to go back and review the material you learned in Chapters 1 and 2.) The producer (person, firm, or country) with the lowest *opportunity cost* will hold the comparative advantage in that product. Don't be misled—absolute advantage is irrelevant.

> **Graphing Pointer:** Using the production possibility frontier (ppf) diagram, trade will be advantageous if the ppf's have differing slopes. Differing slopes means that a comparative advantage exists—i.e., that the relative costs of production differ. Even though Country A may be more efficient in producing both goods—an absolute advantage—it is the *comparative* advantage of Country A that will establish the preferred pattern of specialization and trade. The country with the flatter curve has an advantage in the good on the horizontal axis.

Given that specialization occurs, *the terms of trade* (the "price" of the traded commodities) must be negotiated. For trade to be beneficial, the "price" of the exported good (in terms of the imported good) must be greater than its cost of production. A range of terms of trade will exist. The deal cut within this range will depend on the relative negotiating strengths of the two partners.   (page 488/914)

PRACTICE

Refer to the following table to answer the next four questions. The table shows the possible output levels from one day of labor input.

	ARBEZ	ARBOC
Wheat	12 bushels	6 bushels
Cloth	12 yards	12 yards

2. Arbez
   A. has an absolute advantage in the production of cloth.
   B. has an absolute advantage in the production of wheat.
   C. has a comparative advantage in the production of cloth.
   D. should export cloth to Arboc.
   Answer: B. Arbez can produce absolutely more wheat per worker than Arboc can.

3. The opportunity cost of one bushel of wheat in Arboc is
   A. ½ yard of cloth.
   B. 2 yards of cloth.
   C. 6 yards of cloth.
   D. 12 yards of cloth.
   Answer: B. 6 bushels would cost 12 yards of cloth, therefore 1 bushel costs 2 yards of cloth.

4. Which of the following statements is false?
   A. Arboc has an absolute advantage in the production of wheat.
   B. Arbez should export wheat to Arboc and import cloth from Arboc.
   C. The opportunity cost of wheat is twice as high in Arboc as in Arbez.
   D. The opportunity cost of a yard of cloth in Arbez is one bushel of wheat.
   Answer: A. Arboc is half as productive per worker as Arbez in wheat production.

5. Arboc and Arbez decide to specialize according to the law of comparative advantage and trade with one another. We would expect that
   A. the trade agreement will be somewhere between 1 bushel of wheat for 1 yard of cloth and 1 bushel of wheat for 2 yards of cloth.
   B. the trade agreement will be somewhere between ½ a bushel of wheat for 1 yard of cloth and 2 bushels of wheat for 1 yard of cloth.
   C. Arboc will benefit from trading with Arbez, but Arbez will not benefit from trading with Arboc.
   D. Arboc will specialize in the production of wheat and Arbez will specialize in the production of cloth.
   Answer: A. The Arbezani opportunity cost of 1 bushel of wheat is 1 yard of cloth. Arboc's opportunity cost of 1 bushel of wheat is 2 yards of cloth.

6. The ratio at which exports are traded for imports is known as
   A. the exchange rate.
   B. the trade balance.
   C. the balance of exchange.
   D. the terms of trade.
   Answer: D. See p. 488/914.

Use the following diagrams, which show the production possibility frontiers (ppf's) for Malaysia and Sri Lanka, to answer the next nine questions.

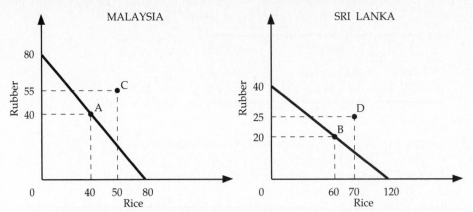

7. Which of the following statements is true?
   A. Malaysia has an absolute advantage in the production of rubber; Sri Lanka has an absolute advantage in the production of rice.
   B. Sri Lanka has an absolute advantage in the production of rubber; Malaysia has an absolute advantage in the production of rice.
   C. Malaysia has an absolute advantage in the production of both goods.
   D. Sri Lanka has an absolute advantage in the production of both goods.
   Answer: A. See p. 482/908.

8. Which statement is false?
   A. In Malaysia, the opportunity cost of one unit of rubber is one unit of rice.
   B. In Malaysia, the opportunity cost of one unit of rice is one unit of rubber.
   C. In Sri Lanka, the opportunity cost of one unit of rubber is three units of rice.
   D. In Sri Lanka, the opportunity cost of one unit of rice is three units of rubber.
   Answer: D. The Sri Lankan opportunity cost of one unit of rice is a third of a unit of rubber.

9. Which of the following statements is true?
   A. Malaysia has a comparative advantage in the production of rubber; Sri Lanka has a comparative advantage in the production of rice.
   B. Sri Lanka has a comparative advantage in the production of rubber; Malaysia has a comparative advantage in the production of rice.
   C. Malaysia has a comparative advantage in both goods.
   D. Sri Lanka has a comparative advantage in both goods.
   Answer: A. See p. 483/909.

10. Given that Malaysia and Sri Lanka decide to trade,
    A. Malaysia should specialize in the production of rubber; Sri Lanka should specialize in the production of rice.
    B. Malaysia should specialize in the production of rice; Sri Lanka should specialize in the production of rubber.
    C. Malaysia and Sri Lanka should each devote half their resources to the production of each commodity.
    D. Malaysia should specialize in the production of rubber; Sri Lanka should produce some rice but continue to produce some rubber.
    Answer: A. Malaysia's comparative advantage lies in rubber production; Sri Lanka's lies in rice.

11. Before trade, Malaysia produced at Point A on its ppf and Sri Lanka produced at Point B. Given complete specialization based on comparative advantage, total rubber production has risen by _____ and total rice production has risen by _____.
    A. 80, 120.
    B. 120, 80.
    C. 40, 60.
    D. 20, 20.
    Answer: D. Total rubber production was 60 (40 + 20); now it is 80. Total rice production was 100 (40 + 60); now it is 120.

12. After trade, Malaysia is consuming at Point C and Sri Lanka is consuming at Point D. Malaysia is exporting _____ units of rubber and Sri Lanka is exporting _____ units of rice.
    A. 80, 100.
    B. 55, 70.
    C. 25, 50.
    D. 15, 10.
    Answer: C. Malaysian rubber production is 80, and domestic consumption is 55, leaving 25 for export. Sri Lankan rice production is 120, and domestic consumption is 70, leaving 50 for export.

13. After trade, Malaysia is consuming at Point C and Sri Lanka is consuming at Point D. Malaysia is importing _____ units of rice and Sri Lanka is importing _____ units of rubber.
    A. 80, 100.
    B. 50, 25.
    C. 25, 50.
    D. 15, 10.
    Answer: B. See the answer to the previous question. In a two-country world, Country A's exports are Country B's imports.

14. Which statement is true?
    A. Only Sri Lanka will benefit if the terms of trade are set at 1 : 2, rubber to rice.
    B. Only Malaysia will benefit if the terms of trade are set at 1 : 2, rubber to rice.
    C. Both countries will gain if the terms of trade lie between 3 : 1 and 1 : 1, rubber to rice.
    D. Both countries will gain if the terms of trade lie between 1 : 1 and 1 : 3, rubber to rice.
    Answer: D. Check these values against the opportunity cost values you calculated in question 8. Also note the correct value of the rubber : rice ratio in question 12.

15. Which statement is false? If the terms of trade are set at
    A. 1 : 1, rubber to rice, only Sri Lanka will gain.
    B. 1 : 2, rubber to rice, both countries will gain.
    C. 1 : 3, rubber to rice, only Malaysia will gain.
    D. 1 : 4, rubber to rice, both countries will wish to produce rice.
    Answer: D. If the terms of trade are set at 1 : 4, rubber to rice, rubber is relatively valuable and can cover its opportunity cost in both countries. Both will wish to produce rubber.

OBJECTIVE 3: Calculate the limit values of the exchange rate in a given example and relate the exchange rate to the notion of comparative advantage. Describe how changes in the exchange rate can affect trade flows.

Trade flows are affected by comparative advantage and by the exchange rate (the "price" of the domestic currency in terms of a foreign currency). There will be some range of exchange rates that will permit mutually beneficial specialization and trade.

(page 489/915)

The distribution of benefits from trade depends on the exchange rate. To buy foreign goods one must hold foreign currency, which is bought and sold in the foreign exchange market. If the value of the dollar changes, the relative attractiveness of the foreign goods will be affected. A strengthening yen will increase the price tag of a Toyota for a U.S. buyer, but the price tag of the domestically-produced Chrysler will not change—the relative attractiveness of the Toyota will decline. Tourists watch exchange rates keenly—a stronger dollar is good news because each dollar will buy more foreign currency and, therefore, more foreign goods and services (which have, in that sense, become cheaper).

The previous comparative advantage material (in Chapter 2) was based on production capabilities—supply is important; demand is absent. By incorporating prices, the demand side of the market can be represented.

> **TIP:** Remember that an increase in the value of the dollar means that foreign goods cost U.S. citizens less (imports increase), but U.S. goods cost foreigners more (exports fall). Choose a foreign country and currency and make up your own example.

PRACTICE

16. The exchange rate is one British pound equals $1.75. If the exchange rate changes to one British pound equals $1.50, we can conclude that, for a British buyer, a U.S. car has become _____ expensive and, for a U.S. buyer, a British cashmere sweater has become _____ expensive.
    A. more, more.
    B. more, less.
    C. less, more.
    D. less, less.
    Answer: B. Each pound is worth less U.S. currency—British buyers are becoming poorer. The opposite is true for U.S. buyers of British goods.

17. As the exchange rate changes from one British pound equals $1.50 to one British pound equals $2.00, British traders will gain _____ from trade with the United States, and American traders will gain _____ from trade with the United Kingdom.
    A. more, more.
    B. more, less.
    C. less, more.
    D. less, less.
    Answer: B. Each pound is worth more U.S. currency. British producers, selling the same amount of exports, will be able to claim more U.S. goods than before.

Use the following table, which shows the domestic prices per unit of steel and corn in Slovakia and Slovenia, to answer the next three questions.

	SLOVAKIA	SLOVENIA
Steel	20 koruna	48 tolars
Corn	30 koruna	87 tolars

18. If the exchange rate is 1 koruna = 1 tolar, then
    A. Slovakia will import both steel and corn.
    B. Slovenia will import both steel and corn.
    C. Slovakia will import steel and Slovenia will import corn.
    D. Slovakia will import corn and Slovenia will import steel.
    Answer: B. In Slovenia, the domestic prices of steel and corn are 48 tolars and 87 tolars, respectively. The imported prices are 20 tolars and 30 tolars, respectively.

19. If the exchange rate is 1 koruna = 3 tolars, then
    A. Slovakia will import both steel and corn.
    B. Slovenia will import both steel and corn.
    C. Slovakia will import steel and Slovenia will import corn.
    D. Slovakia will import corn and Slovenia will import steel.
    Answer: A. In Slovakia, the domestic prices of steel and corn are 20 koruna and 30 koruna, respectively. The imported prices are 16 koruna and 29 koruna, respectively.

20. Two-way trade will occur only if the price of the koruna is between
    A. 1.0 tolars and 3.0 tolars.
    B. 1.5 tolars and 2.4 tolars.
    C. 2.4 tolars and 2.9 tolars.
    D. 1.5 tolars and 3.0 tolars.
    Answer: C. If the exchange rate is 1 koruna = 2.4 tolars, no trade in steel will occur. If the exchange rate is 1 koruna = 2.9 tolars, no trade in corn will occur. Between these rates, Slovakia will import steel and Slovenia will import corn.

OBJECTIVE 4: Provide an intuitive explanation of the Heckscher-Ohlin theorem.

The *Heckscher-Ohlin theorem* builds on the theory of comparative advantage by focusing on the differing factor endowments of countries. Some countries seem more labor-abundant (India, China) while others are more capital-abundant (United States, Japan). The Heckscher-Ohlin theorem states that a country will specialize in and export that good whose production calls for a relatively intensive use of the input that the country has in abundance: India should export labor-intensive goods and import capital-intensive goods, for example. (page 492/918)

The assembly of audiocassettes requires a large stock of semi-skilled cheap labor with little capital. This favors Mexico. Research into the capabilities of fiber optics requires a large stock of expensive capital. This favors the United States. The production of timber requires an abundant stock of forest land—a requirement that Canada meets.

PRACTICE

21. We observe that Arbez produces wooden ornaments (a labor-intensive activity), and that Arboc produces plastic containers (a capital-intensive activity). Which of the following statements is true?
    A. Arbez has more labor than Arboc; Arboc has more capital than Arbez.
    B. Arboc has more labor than Arbez; Arbez has more capital than Arboc.
    C. Labor is relatively abundant in Arbez.
    D. Labor is relatively abundant in Arboc.
    Answer: C. Assuming that the two countries are being rational, Arbez is producing the good in which it has a comparative advantage.

OBJECTIVE 5: Define a tariff, an export subsidy, and a quota. Outline, using a demand and supply analysis, the costs involved in the imposition of a tariff.

Tariffs, export subsidies, and quotas are examples of trade barriers. *Tariffs* are taxes on imports, designed to force up their price; *export subsidies* are government payments to U.S. exporters, intended to make them more competitive overseas; *quotas* are limits on the quantity of imports. *Dumping* is meant to price competitors out of the market; having achieved market domination, the firm can then raise prices. (page 493/919)

22. A tariff imposed on imported French wine will cause the U.S. price of French wine to _____ and U.S. production of wine to _____
    A. increase, increase.
    B. increase, decrease.
    C. decrease, increase.
    D. decrease, decrease.
    Answer: A. The tax will push up the price of the import. This will increase the demand for substitutes.

Use the following diagram to answer the next three questions. The diagram shows the American demand for and supply of T-shirts. The world price is $4 per shirt.

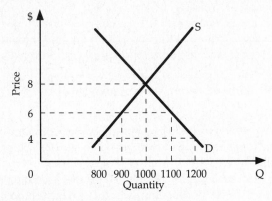

23. In an unrestricted open market, the U.S. will
    A. export 400 T-shirts.
    B. export 200 T-shirts.
    C. import 400 T-shirts.
    D. import 200 T-shirts.
    Answer: C. At a price of $4, there is an excess U.S. demand of 400.

24. The garment industry successfully lobbies Congress to impose a $2 per shirt tax on imports. Now the U.S. will
    A. export 400 T-shirts.
    B. export 200 T-shirts.
    C. import 400 T-shirts.
    D. import 200 T-shirts.
    Answer: D. An excess demand remains that must be met from overseas.

25. The government will collect _____ in tariff revenues.
    A. $100.
    B. $200.
    C. $400.
    D. $800.
    Answer: C. The government collects $2 per shirt on each of the 200 imported shirts.

OBJECTIVE 6: Give the arguments advanced for and against protection. Describe the costs involved in permitting free trade.

The case for free trade is based on the theory of comparative advantage. Trade benefits the participants. Welfare increases if trade flows are allowed to follow their "natural" pattern; obstacles, such as tariffs and quotas, reduce that welfare. Higher-cost production results. (page 497/923)

The argument in favor of protection is based on the observation that efficient foreign competition will result in job loss for domestic workers and lost production. Individual arguments for protection from foreign competition may include claims that cheap foreign labor is "unfair," that national security must be protected, that trade encourages dependency on foreigners, that we need to let infant industries develop, and that, if the dollar is overvalued, domestic producers will be hurt. Some of these arguments are simply false, and others are misused.   (page 499/925)

PRACTICE

26. Which of the following is not an argument used by protectionists?
    A. Infant industries need support until they are strong enough to compete.
    B. Restricting trade builds up dependency on other counties.
    C. Protection is needed in the light of unfair foreign practices, in order to ensure a level playing field.
    D. Cheap foreign labor makes competition unfair.
    Answer: B. See p. 499/925.

PRACTICE TEST

I. MULTIPLE CHOICE QUESTIONS.

Select the option that provides the single best answer.

_____ 1. According to the textbook, _____ of all cars and _____ of all consumer electronics bought in the United States are produced abroad.
    A. 50%, 50%.
    B. 50%, 80%.
    C. 80%, 50%.
    D. 80%, 80%.

_____ 2. A country imports less than it exports. It has
    A. an export subsidy.
    B. a tariff quota.
    C. a trade surplus.
    D. a trade deficit.

_____ 3. Relative to Arboc, Arbez has a comparative advantage in the production of goat milk. We can say that Arbez
    A. uses fewer resources to produce goat milk than does Arboc.
    B. must also have an absolute advantage in the production of goat milk.
    C. is the producer with the lower opportunity cost of producing goat milk.
    D. should diversify into other products rather than trade with the high-cost, inefficient Arbocalis.

_____ 4. In Arbez/Arboc trade, an increase in the exchange rate of the Arbezani currency (the bandu) relative to that of the Arbocali currency (the opek) means that
    A. Arbezani goods will appear to be relatively cheaper to the Arbocalis.
    B. Arbocali goods will appear to be relatively cheaper to the Arbezanis.
    C. Arbez will lose any comparative advantage that it had.
    D. Arbez will experience a decreasing trade deficit.

_____ 5. The Heckscher-Ohlin theorem states that Arbez will have a(n) _____ advantage in the production of a good that uses its relatively _____
   A. absolute, scarce input intensively.
   B. absolute, abundant input intensively.
   C. comparative, abundant input intensively.
   D. comparative, scarce input intensively.

_____ 6. Two goods are produced, pins and needles. Jill has a comparative advantage in the production of pins. Relative to Jack, and with the same resources,
   A. Jill is better at producing pins than at producing needles.
   B. Jill is better at producing both pins and needles.
   C. Jill can produce pins more efficiently than Jack.
   D. Jill can produce more pins than Jack.

_____ 7. Jill chooses to trade pins for needles with Jack. It is likely that
   A. Jill's gains equal Jack's losses.
   B. pins are more expensive than needles.
   C. each trader receives goods that he or she values more highly than those he or she gives up.
   D. neither trader can gain more than the other.

For questions 8–10, assume that Arbez and Arboc have the same amount of resources and similar preferences for goat milk and bananas. The table shows the number of labor hours needed to produce 1 liter of goat milk and 1 kilo of bananas.

	Arbez	Arboc
Goat Milk	.3	.6
Bananas	.5	.2

_____ 8. According to the table above,
   A. Arbez has a comparative advantage in the production of both goods.
   B. Arbez has a comparative advantage in the production of bananas, and Arboc has a comparative advantage in the production of goat milk.
   C. Arbez has a comparative advantage in the production of goat milk, and Arboc has a comparative advantage in the production of bananas.
   D. Arboc has a comparative advantage in the production of both goods.

_____ 9. According to the table, one unit of labor hours produces
   A. 3 liters of goat milk in Arbez and 6 liters in Arboc.
   B. 5 kilos of bananas in Arbez and 2 kilos in Arboc.
   C. 2 kilos of bananas in Arbez and 5 kilos in Arboc.
   D. 6 liters of goat milk in Arboc and 2 kilos of bananas in Arboc.

_____ 10. For trade to occur, the terms of trade might be
   A. 2 liters of goat milk for 1 kilo of bananas.
   B. 1 liter of goat milk for 4 kilos of bananas.
   C. 1 liter of goat milk for .7 of a kilo of bananas.
   D. 3 liters of goat milk for 1 kilo of bananas.

_____ 11. Tariffs and quotas are economically inefficient because
   A. the government does not collect any revenues under a tariff.
   B. imports rise and this reduces the welfare of consumers.
   C. producers are saved from the pressure of foreign competition.
   D. domestic prices must be reduced.

_____ 12. Which of the following is an argument in favor of increased protection?
A. U.S. consumers have become too dependent on foreign countries for their luxury goods.
B. National defense can be jeopardized if strategic supplies are produced by foreigners.
C. Running a persistent trade deficit is unhealthy and must be avoided.
D. Higher tariffs increase the welfare of U.S. consumers.

_____ 13. Each of the following is a trade barrier except a(n)
A. flexible exchange rate.
B. quota.
C. export subsidy.
D. tariff.

_____ 14. Statement 1: A country with an absolute advantage in the production of a good will also have a comparative advantage.
Statement 2: A country with a comparative advantage in the production of a good will also have an absolute advantage.
Statement 1 is _____; Statement 2 is _____
A. true, true.
B. true, false.
C. false, true.
D. false, false.

_____ 15. A tariff _____ increase the government's tax receipts; a quota _____ increase the government's tax receipts.
A. does, does.
B. does, does not.
C. does not, does.
D. does not, does not.

_____ 16. In Tokyo, a Big Mac sells for 500 yen. The dollar : yen exchange rate is one dollar per 125 yen. The price of the Big Mac in dollars is
A. 500.
B. .25.
C. 4.
D. 5.

_____ 17. In Tokyo, a Big Mac sells for 500 yen. The exchange rate changes from one dollar for 125 yen, to one dollar for 250 yen. The price of the Big Mac in dollars
A. has increased.
B. has decreased.
C. has not changed.
D. has doubled.

_____ 18. The Heckscher-Ohlin theorem explains the pattern of trade by focusing on
A. comparative advantage.
B. absolute advantage.
C. relative factor endowments.
D. exchange rate variations.

_____ 19. As the exchange rate changes from one British pound equals $1.50 to one British pound equals $1.00, the terms of trade shift _____ the United States. American traders will gain _____ from trade with the United Kingdom.
A. in favor of, more.
B. in favor of, less.
C. against, more.
D. against, less.

_____ 20. We would expect a tariff imposed on an import to _____ the price of the import and to _____ the price of domestic substitutes for the import.
   A. increase, increase.
   B. increase, not affect.
   C. decrease, decrease.
   D. decrease, not affect.

II. APPLICATION QUESTIONS.

1. The Arbezani Minister of Trade, a firm believer in the Heckscher-Ohlin theorem, asks your advice regarding some recent changes within the Arbezani economy. In each case, he wishes to know whether or not the Heckscher-Ohlin explanation of trade flows will be strengthened. Arbez has established a free-trade region with its sole trading partner, Arboc.
   a. Arbezani unions in a substantial number of industries lobby successfully for increased restrictions on movement between industries, e.g., longer apprenticeships, work permits, drug testing of new entrants into an industry.
   b. It has been discovered that Arbez and its trading partner, Arboc, have identical endowments of all resources.
   c. Nationalistic Arbezani politicians, concerned about the loss of sovereignty caused by a free-trade area, have successfully passed restrictions on the flow of labor and other inputs between Arbez and Arboc.

2. The nations of Noil and Regit produce loaves and fishes. The labor supply is 12,000 labor units per year in Noil while, in Regit, the labor supply is 72,000 labor units per year. Assume that labor is the only input and that costs are constant within each economy. The costs of producing loaves and fishes, in labor units, are given in the following table.

UNITS OF LABOR SUPPLY NEEDED TO PRODUCED 1 UNIT OF:	NOIL	REGIT
Loaves	2	3
Fishes	1	3

   a. Calculate the maximum output levels of loaves and fishes for each economy and enter your results in the following table.

MAXIMUM UNITS PRODUCED:	NOIL	REGIT
Loaves	_____	_____
Fishes	_____	_____

   b. Draw the production possibility frontiers for each nation.

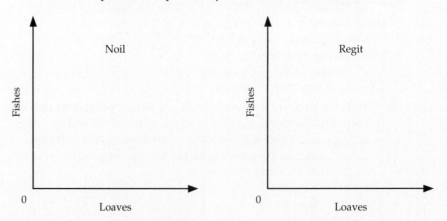

c. When questioned about the possibility of establishing trade between the two nations, the Regitani Minister of Trade states his government's official line—the proposal is ludicrous because Regit has an advantage in the production of each good. Is the Regitani view correct?

In both nations, the custom is to consume two loaves with each fish.

d. Assume that no trade takes place. Calculate the annual production of loaves and fishes that will most satisfactorily meet demand in each country separately. Also determine the total production of loaves and fishes for the two countries without trade.

MAXIMUM UNITS PRODUCED:	NOIL	REGIT	TOTAL
Loaves	____	____	____
Fishes	____	____	____

e. Yielding to pressure, the Regitani government opens its borders to trade with Noil. Based on comparative advantage, which good should Noil specialize in producing? Explain.

f. Assuming that specialization and trade flows are dictated by comparative advantage, determine the quantity of loaves and fishes that can be produced.

g. Suppose that the terms of trade are established at 1 fish = 2 loaves. Determine the consumption of loaves and fishes in each country.

UNITS CONSUMED:	NOIL	REGIT
Loaves	____	____
Fishes	____	____

h. Has trade been mutually beneficial in this case?

i. Suppose that the terms of trade are established at 1 fish = 1 loaf. Determine the consumption of loaves and fishes in each country.

UNITS CONSUMED:	NOIL	REGIT
Loaves	____	____
Fishes	____	____

j. Has trade been mutually beneficial in this case?

k. Suppose that the terms of trade are established at 2 fishes = 1 loaf. Determine the consumption of loaves and fishes in each country.

UNITS CONSUMED:	NOIL	REGIT
Loaves	____	____
Fishes	____	____

l. Has trade been mutually beneficial in this case?

m. Determine the "price" of a loaf (in terms of fish) necessary to have mutually beneficial two-way trade.

3. The domestic price of Arbocali cloth is 4 opeks a yard. The domestic price of Arbezani leather is 12 bandu per hide. Arboc sells cloth to Arbez and Arbez sells hides to Arboc. The opek : bandu exchange rate is 2 opeks per bandu. The exchange rate is flexible.

Ignoring transportation and other such costs, calculate the price in Arbez of a yard of imported Arbocali cloth and the price in Arboc of an imported Arbezani hide.

4. Use the diagrams below to answer this question.

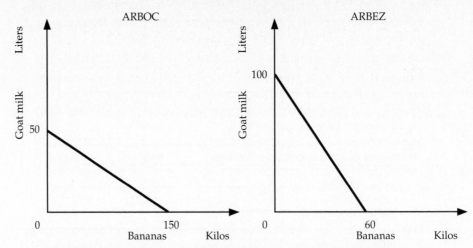

a. What is the opportunity cost of one kilo of bananas in Arboc?
b. What is the opportunity cost of one kilo of bananas in Arbez?
c. Which country has a comparative advantage in the production of bananas?
d. What is the opportunity cost of one liter of goat milk in Arboc?
e. What is the opportunity cost of one liter of goat milk in Arbez?
f. Which country has a comparative advantage in the production of goat milk?
g. If the terms of trade were 1.0 liter of goat milk/kilo of bananas, which country would want to export goat milk?
h. If the terms of trade were 3 liters of goat milk/kilo of bananas, Arboc should produce _____ and Arbez should produce _____.
i. Suppose that the terms of trade were 1 kilo of bananas/1.5 liters of goat milk. _____ would export bananas and _____ would export goat milk.

5. Arboc and Arbez produce wine and cheese, and each has constant costs of production. The domestic prices for the two goods are given in the table. At the moment 1 Arbocali opek is traded for 1 Arbezani bandu.

	Arboc	Arbez
wine	40 opeks	120 bandu
cheese	20 opeks	30 bandu

a. Which country has a comparative advantage in cheese production?
b. Which country has a comparative advantage in wine production?
c. At the present exchange rate (1 opek = 1 bandu), will two-way trade occur? Explain.
d. Which country will have a balance of trade deficit?
e. What should happen to the value of the opek, relative to the bandu?
f. If the exchange rate is 1 opek = 2 bandu, what would happen to trade?
g. Cheese making is capital-intensive, and wine making is labor-intensive. Which country should have the relatively abundant supplies of labor, if the Heckscher-Ohlin theory is correct?
h. If the exchange rate is 1 opek = 4 bandu, what would happen to trade?

6. Here are the domestic demand and supply schedules for diapers.

Price	Quantity Demanded	Quantity Supplied
$6	800	1,100
$5	1,000	1,000
$4	1,200	900
$3	1,400	800
$2	1,600	700

a. Graph the demand and supply curves.

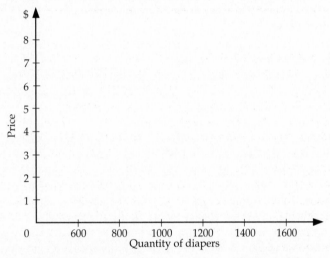

b. The equilibrium price is $_____ and quantity is _____.

c. The world price for diapers is $3. Show this on the diagram as Pw. What will be the levels of domestic consumption and domestic production?

In order to preserve employment, diaper manufacturers contend successfully that theirs is an "infant industry" and should be protected.

d. A tariff is imposed that raises the price of imported diapers to $4. Show this on the diagram as Pt.

e. The tariff causes an increase in price and an increase in domestic production of _____ units. Consumption will fall to _____ units.

f. Imports will be _____ units. The tariff will yield $_____ in tax revenues.

g. Shade in the areas representing the net welfare loss caused by the tariff.

h. The loss in welfare is $_____.

ANSWERS AND SOLUTIONS

PRACTICE TEST

I. SOLUTIONS TO MULTIPLE CHOICE QUESTIONS

1. B. See p. 480/906.
2. C. See p. 481/907.
3. C. Arbez might be relatively inefficient in producing both goods but relatively less inefficient in producing goat milk. Because Arbez has a comparative advantage in producing goat milk, its opportunity cost of producing goat milk must be less.
4. B. As the Arbezani currency becomes more powerful, Arbocali goods will become cheaper when calculated in terms of the Arbezani currency.
5. C. See p. 492/918.
6. A. Remember that comparative advantage is a relative concept. It requires that we compare two producers and two goods.
7. C. In voluntary trade, we expect each trader to gain something more than s/he traded.
8. C. Goat milk is relatively cheap to produce in Arbez and bananas require relatively few resources in Arboc. In a two-good, two-country situation, one party can never have a comparative advantage in both goods.
9. C. .5 labor hour gives 1 kilo of bananas in Arbez—1 hour gives 2 kilos. .2 labor hour gives 1 liter of milk in Arboc—1 hour gives 5 liters.
10. C. The terms of trade must lie in the range from 1 liter of goat milk : $\frac{3}{5}$ kilo of bananas to 1 liter of goat milk : 3 kilos of bananas. If Arbez has 6 hours of labor, it could produce 20 liters of goat milk or 12 kilos of bananas—a ratio of 1 : $\frac{3}{5}$. If Arboc has 6 hours of labor, it could produce 10 liters of goat milk or 30 kilos of bananas—a ratio of 1 : 3.
11. C. Tariffs impose welfare losses in two ways. Consumers pay a higher price and, as mentioned in this question, marginal producers are allowed to survive. Option B is incorrect—imports don't increase, they decrease. See p. 497/923.
12. B. The national security argument is persistent.
13. A. See p. 493/919 for a discussion of trade barriers.
14. D. A country may have an absolute advantage in the production of Good A and Good B; it may have a comparative advantage in the production of Good A and, therefore, a comparative disadvantage in Good B. Similarly, a country with a comparative advantage in the production of Good A might be less efficient than its partner in producing either good.
15. B. A tariff is a tax that provides revenues; a quota merely restricts the number of units that may be imported.
16. C. 125 yen equal $1. 500 yen equal $4.
17. B. 125 yen equal $1. 500 yen equal $4. 250 yen equal $1. 500 yen equal $2.
18. C. See p. 492/918.
19. A. Dollars are becoming relatively more valuable.
20. A. A tariff will drive up the price of the import, increasing demand for domestic substitutes whose price will then increase.

II. SOLUTIONS TO APPLICATION QUESTIONS

1. a. Heckscher-Ohlin assumes that inputs are mobile within an economy. Such restrictions will work against Heckscher-Ohlin because, as an economy begins to specialize and trade, it will wish to reallocate inputs.
   b. According to Heckscher-Ohlin, comparative advantage is dependent upon differences in factor endowments. No differences in factor endowments, no comparative advantage: no comparative advantage, no trade. Arbez and Arboc should have no basis for trade.
   c. The new restrictions should not affect the pattern of trade. The Heckscher-Ohlin

theorem assumes that inputs are not mobile between countries.

2.

a.

MAXIMUM UNITS PRODUCED:	NOIL	REGIT
Loaves	6,000	24,000
Fishes	12,000	24,000

b. See the following diagrams.

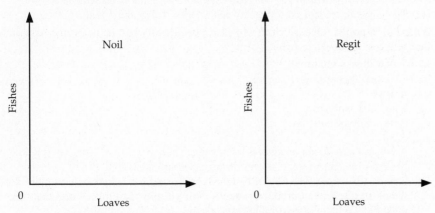

c. The Regitani view is mainly incorrect. Regit does have an absolute advantage in the production of both loaves and fishes, but it does not have a comparative advantage in both, and it is comparative advantage that determines whether or not trade is advantageous.

d.

MAXIMUM UNITS PRODUCED:	NOIL	REGIT	TOTAL
Loaves	4,800	16,000	20,800
Fishes	2,400	8,000	10,400

e. Noil should produce fishes. In Noil, the cost of producing 1 loaf is 2 fishes while the cost of producing 1 loaf in Regit is 1 fish. Loaves are less costly in Regit. Regit has a comparative advantage in loaves; Noil has a comparative advantage in fishes.

f. Noil can produce 12,000 fishes and Regit can produce 24,000 loaves.

g.

UNITS CONSUMED:	NOIL	REGIT
Loaves	12,000	12,000
Fishes	6,000	6,000

Noil can produce 12,000 fishes and export 6,000, earning 12,000 loaves in return. Regit can produce 24,000 loaves and export 12,000, earning 6,000 fishes in return.

h. Trade has benefited Noil, but Regit has a lower standard of living than it had before trade!

i.

UNITS CONSUMED:	NOIL	REGIT
Loaves	8,000	16,000
Fishes	4,000	8,000

Noil can produce 12,000 fishes and export 8,000, earning 8,000 loaves in return. Regit can produce 24,000 loaves and export 8,000, earning 8,000 fishes in return.

j. Trade has benefited Noil, but Regit's standard of living is unchanged.

k.

UNITS CONSUMED:	NOIL	REGIT
Loaves	4,800	16,000
Fishes	2,400	8,000

Noil can produce 12,000 fishes and export 9,600, earning 4,800 loaves in return. Regit can produce 24,000 loaves and export 4,800, earning 9,600 fishes in return.

l. Trade has benefited Regit, but Noil's standard of living is unchanged.

m. The terms of trade need to be between 1 loaf = 1 fish and 1 loaf = 2 fish.

3. A yard of imported Arbocali cloth will cost 2 bandu in Arbez. An imported Arbezani hide will cost 24 opeks in Arboc.

4. a. $\frac{1}{3}$ of a liter of goat milk.

   b. $1\frac{2}{3}$ liters of goat milk.

   c. Arboc.

   d. 3 kilos of bananas.

   e. $\frac{6}{10}$ of a kilo of bananas.

   f. Arbez.

   g. Arbez, because it can produce a liter of goat milk at a cost of less than one kilo of bananas and, therefore, can gain through this specialization.

   h. bananas, bananas. One kilo of bananas can be sold for 2 liters of goat milk. Both Arboc and Arbez can produce bananas more cheaply than this ($\frac{1}{3}$ of a liter of goat milk and $1\frac{2}{3}$ liters of goat milk, respectively).

   i. Arboc, Arbez. One kilo of bananas can be sold for 1.5 liters of goat milk. Arboc can produce bananas more cheaply than this ($\frac{1}{3}$ of a liter of goat milk) and so will produce bananas. One liter of goat milk can be sold for $\frac{2}{3}$ kilo of bananas. Arbez can produce goat milk more cheaply than this ($\frac{6}{10}$ of a kilo of bananas) and so will produce goat milk.

5. a. Arbez. Wine is four times as expensive as cheese in Arbez, but only twice as expensive in Arboc.

   b. Arboc. Each country must have a comparative advantage in one of the goods.

   c. No. Because Arboc can produce both goods more cheaply, the Arbezanis will import both. The Arbocalis will not wish to buy either Arbezani product.

   d. Arbez, because it has some imports and zero exports.

   e. The Arbocali currency (the opek) should be heavily demanded (by Arbezanis seeking to buy Arbocali goods). The demand for the bandu will be low. The opek will rise in value; the bandu will fall in value.

   f. At a price of 30 bandu (15 opeks), Arbezani cheese will now be cheaper than Arbocali cheese (at a price of 20 opeks). Arboc will import cheese. Arbez will continue to import Arbocali wine. At a price of 40 opeks (80 bandu), Arbocali wine is still cheaper than that produced in Arbez (at a price of 120 bandu).

   g. Arboc.

   h. At a price of 30 bandu (7.50 opeks), Arbezani cheese will be cheaper than Arbocali cheese (at a price of 20 opeks). Arboc will import cheese.

   At a price of 40 opeks (160 bandu), Arbocali wine will be more expensive than that produced in Arbez (at a price of 120 bandu). Arboc will import wine.

   Arboc will have a trade deficit and Arbez a surplus.

6. a. See the diagram below.

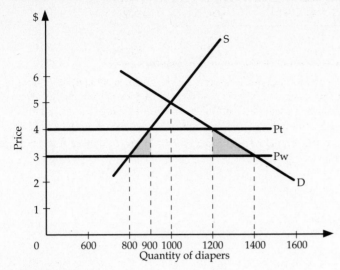

b. $5, 1000.
c. See the diagram above. 1400, 800.
d. See the diagram above.
e. 100, 1200.
f. 300, $300.
g. See the diagram above.
h. $(50 + 100).

OPEN-ECONOMY MACROECONOMICS: THE BALANCE OF PAYMENTS AND EXCHANGE RATES

22

COMBINED TEXT

37

OBJECTIVES: POINT BY POINT

After completing this chapter, you should be able to accomplish the objectives listed below.

OBJECTIVE 1: Outline the components comprising the balance of payments and distinguish between the current account and the capital account.

When goods, services, or assets are bought and sold, or transfer payments are made internationally, currencies flow between nations. These flows of foreign exchange (that is, all currencies other than that of the home country) are recorded in the *balance of payments.* (page 506/932)

The balance of payments, which must "balance" (equal zero) is split into two parts:
a. the *current account*, which includes imports and exports of goods and services (and net transfer payments) and
b. the *capital account*, which includes the "export" and "import" of U.S. and foreign assets—i.e., capital inflows and capital outflows.

If, on the current account, total credits are greater than (less than) total debits, the economy has a current account surplus (deficit). Funds from a current account surplus can be used to buy foreign assets, such as Treasury bills or real estate. A current account deficit must be financed by attracting funds from overseas (capital inflows) by selling American assets (capital). The current and capital accounts must sum to zero.

> **TIP:** Any transaction that brings in foreign exchange is a credit item; any transaction causing a loss of foreign exchange is a debit.

> **TIP:** The capital account is difficult to conceptualize. The easy way into this topic is to imagine a nation (Japan) with a current account surplus. What happens to the extra foreign earnings? The Japanese can use the funds to buy U.S. assets and companies. A nation that runs a current account deficit is overspending. To raise the foreign currency needed to buy imports, the U.S. must sell off some of its assets. Counterintuitively perhaps, capital inflows are rather like exports (in the sense that we're "exporting" IOUs), and capital outflows can be thought of as similar to imports (funds flow out to "import" foreign securities).

> **TIP:** A Japanese purchase of an American factory in Texas is a capital *inflow* for the United States (funds flow in). An American purchase of a Brazilian coffee plantation is a capital *outflow* for the United States (funds flow out). Focus on which country receives payment, not which receives the asset.

PRACTICE

1. Imports account for about _____ of U.S. GDP.
   A. less than 5%.
   B. less than 10%.
   C. more than 10%.
   D. more than 15%.
   Answer: C. The proportion is approximately 12%, in fact.

2. The price of Arboc's currency in terms of that of Arbez is the
   A. foreign exchange.
   B. exchange rate.
   C. balance of payments.
   D. currency ratio.
   Answer: B. See p. 506/932.

3. The balance of payments is split into the
   A. current account and the merchandise trade account.
   B. capital account and the foreign exchange account.
   C. capital account and the current account.
   D. current account and foreign exchange account.
   Answer: C. See p. 507/933.

4. Which of the following would be included in the current account?
   A. The purchase by an American citizen of stock in the Japanese company Sony.
   B. The sale by an American citizen of a French government security.
   C. The sale of an American-built computer to Germany.
   D. The sale of IBM stock to a German citizen.
   Answer: C. This is an export.

5. An increase in "foreign private assets in the United States" means that
   A. American citizens have increased their holdings of foreign private assets.
   B. American citizens have decreased their holdings of foreign private assets.
   C. citizens of foreign countries have increased their holdings of American private assets.
   D. citizens of foreign countries have decreased their holdings of American private assets.
   Answer: C. The phrase "foreign private assets" means assets of the U.S. private sector (e.g., an American company like IBM) held by foreigners.

6. Which of the following is not an item in the capital account?
   A. Change in private U.S. assets abroad.
   B. Change in U.S. government assets abroad.
   C. Net investment income.
   D. Change in foreign private investment in the United States.
   Answer: C. See Table 1 on p. 508/934. Items in the current account show income from earnings (on exports, investments abroad), expenditures (on imports), transfers, and investment income—no financial or real productive assets change hands. It is the capital account that shows the effects of the purchase or sale of financial and real productive assets.

OBJECTIVE 2: Incorporate imports and exports into the AE diagram and explain how imports affect the size of the expenditure multiplier.

When exports and imports are incorporated into the macroeconomic model, exports represent an increase in the amount of expenditures on domestically produced goods and services while imports reduce the amount of expenditures on domestically produced goods and services.

In the open economy, AE = C + I + G + EX − IM

Foreign demand for American goods is influenced mainly by foreign factors—exports are assumed to be constant as domestic (U.S.) output increases. Imports, however, increase as U.S. income increases. The marginal propensity to import (MPM) is positive. The expenditure multiplier is smaller in an open economy than it is in a closed economy because imports represent a leakage of spending power away from domestically produced goods.

In the open economy, the multiplier formula is 1 / [1 − (MPC − MPM)].

(page 511/937)

PRACTICE

Use the following information to answer the next three questions. In the closed economy of Arbez, the marginal propensity to consume is .75. Arbez opens its borders to trade and finds that its marginal propensity to import is .15.

7. The Arbezani multiplier was _____ for the closed economy and is _____ for the open economy.
    A. 4, 2.5.
    B. 4, 10.
    C. 5, 2.5.
    D. 5, 10.
    Answer: A. In the closed economy, the multiplier is 1 / [1 − MPC]. In this case, 1 / [1 − MPC] = 1 / [1 − .75] = 4. In the open economy, the multiplier is 1 / [1 − (MPC − MPM)]. In this case, 1 / [1 − (MPC − MPM)] = 1 / [1 − (.75 − .15)] = 1 / .4 = 2.5. In general, the open-economy multiplier is less than the closed economy multiplier, so Options B and D must be incorrect.

8. Arbez finds that net exports are zero. As a result of world trade, the Arbezani economy has become _____ stable. If the economy expands, Arbez will experience a trade _____
    A. more, surplus.
    B. more, deficit.
    C. less, surplus.
    D. less, deficit.
    Answer: B. In the open economy, the multiplier is smaller. Shifts in the components of planned aggregate expenditure will result in smaller changes in equilibrium income level—the economy is more stable. Currently, exports and imports are equal. An economic expansion will increase imports (MPM is .15), but exports, which depend on foreign demand, will not change and a trade deficit will occur. Note: This is a very difficult question.

9. The Arbezani government increases government spending by 100. Equilibrium output will _____ and net exports will _____ (Hint: Use the open-economy multiplier.)
    A. increase by 100, increase by 15.
    B. increase by 100, decrease by 15.
    C. increase by 250, increase by 37.5.
    D. increase by 250, decrease by 37.5.
    Answer: D. As G increases, the economy will expand by 250 because the multiplier is 2.5—see question 9. Exports do not change, but imports will increase. MPM is .15, so imports will increase by 250 × .15, or 37.5, and net exports (EX − IM) will decrease.

10. The quantity of U.S. exports depends directly on
    A. the output level in the United States.
    B. the output level in the other countries.
    C. the size of the multiplier in the United States.
    D. the size of the multiplier in other countries.

    Answer: B. The demand for our exports depends on output (income) level of foreign purchasers. A *change* in their income will affect our exports through their marginal propensity to import and their multiplier.

11. Arboc opens its economy to world trade. Its net exports are negative. Compared with its AE function before world trade, the function now will be
    A. higher and steeper.
    B. higher and flatter.
    C. lower and steeper.
    D. lower and flatter.

    Answer: D. Net exports are negative, so the level of expenditure on domestic goods is lower than before. Because the marginal propensity to import is a positive value, some part of any increase in income will be spent abroad, so the rise in domestic expenditures will be less—a flatter function.

OBJECTIVE 3: List the variables that influence exports and imports. Outline how the trade feedback effect and the price feedback effect operate.

The factors that influence domestic demand (wealth, the interest rate, after-tax real wage) also affect imports. Import demand is sensitive to the relative price of imports—we would buy more Volvos if they were cheaper.

U.S. exports to Germany are affected by the same factors that influence the other elements of demand in Germany (wealth of German consumers, German interest rates, after-tax real wage in Germany) and relative prices. Germans will buy more Volkswagens and more Fords if German interest rates decrease.

In the European Union, it is often said that Germany is the "engine of European growth." When Germany prospers, so do its trading partners; when Germany falters, the rest of Europe falters too. Some Canadians and Mexicans have worried that, with the implementation of the North American Free Trade Agreement (NAFTA), the Canadian and Mexican economies will become "prisoners" of the United States. Clearly, events in one economy can have international repercussions (feedback effects).

Two feedback effects operate in the open economy.
a. The *trade feedback effect.* Increased U.S. imports cause expansion in the export sectors of foreign economies. More prosperity abroad will stimulate increased imports from the U.S.. Similarly, increases in U.S. exports will expand the U.S. economy, causing more foreign goods to be imported and, ultimately, will result in increased prosperity overseas and at home. (page 515/941)

> **TIP:** Frequently, the media and our own intuition present trade as a "you-win-so-I-lose" situation. The trade feedback effect shows that, on a level playing field, trade benefits both participants.

b. The *price feedback effect.* Higher import prices cause aggregate demand and/or aggregate supply to shift, causing higher prices for domestically produced goods, including exports. Accordingly, the price increase is passed on when exports occur. Changes in the price of imports cause changes in the price of exports, and vice versa. (page 516/942)

> **TIP:** Notice that a one dollar increase in exports will cause imports to increase, but by less than a dollar. Although some of the export earnings will be used to buy imports, some will be used to buy domestically produced goods and some will be saved.

To remember the price feedback effect, simply remember the impact of high oil prices in the 1970s. High import prices affected aggregate supply and forced U.S. companies to sell their exports at high prices. A worldwide stagflation (recession and higher prices) developed.

PRACTICE

12. The trade feedback effect shows that
    A. an increase in economic activity in the United States results in an increase in the U.S. net exports.
    B. an increase in U.S. imports results in an increase in U.S. exports.
    C. an increase in U.S. imports reduces the imports of other countries.
    D. an increase in U.S. exports reduces the imports of other countries.
    Answer: B. See p. 515/941.

13. U.S. exports tend to increase when
    A. economic activity abroad is relatively low.
    B. U.S. prices are relatively low.
    C. U.S. prices are relatively high.
    D. U.S. inflation is relatively high.
    Answer: B. When U.S. prices are relatively low, U.S. goods become more competitive overseas.

14. The price feedback effect occurs because, when there is an increase in the prices of U.S. imported final goods and services, relative to domestic prices, households and firms will tend to substitute _____, shifting the U.S. aggregate demand curve to the _____
    A. domestically produced output for imports, right.
    B. domestically produced output for imports, left.
    C. imports for domestically produced output, right.
    D. imports for domestically produced output, left.
    Answer: A. Higher prices for foreign goods and services will encourage U.S. buyers to demand more domestically-made output, shifting the AD curve to the right (and increasing prices).

OBJECTIVE 4: Explain why the demand for foreign exchange has a negative slope and the supply of foreign exchange has a positive slope. Describe the determination of the exchange rate in the foreign exchange market and explain how each determinant plays a role in the process.

The demand for foreign exchange is negatively sloped because as the price of a unit of foreign currency rises (costs more dollars to buy), foreign goods become more expensive and less attractive. The supply of foreign exchange is positively sloped because as the price of a unit of foreign currency rises (can be exchanged for more dollars), U.S. goods become cheaper and more attractive.

In a flexible exchange-rate system, an increase in the supply of a foreign currency or a decrease in the demand for it will cause that currency to depreciate in value and the dollar to appreciate. Demanders and suppliers of foreign currency include those who need foreign funds to import goods and services, those who wish to invest in overseas assets, and speculators. Accordingly, the major determinants of the exchange rate are relative price levels and relative interest rates.   (page 517/943)

TIP: You might find the foreign exchange market easier to understand if you remember that, when foreign exchange is supplied (by foreigners), it is because dollars are demanded. When foreign exchange is demanded (by U.S. residents), dollars are being supplied.

Any transaction resulting in an outflow of goods and services from the U.S. (exports) shows up as an increase in the supply of foreign exchange. (An increase in supply forces down the "price" of foreign exchange and increases the value of the dollar.) Any transaction that results in an inflow of goods and services (imports) shows up as an increase in the demand for foreign exchange. Example: A Japanese purchase of U.S. government bonds will increase the demand for dollars (and increase the *supply* of yen), while a U.S. purchase of a Japanese car will increase the *demand* for yen.

Graphing Pointer: Remember DIM SEX. Pounds are demanded (D) when we want to buy British IMports and securities—DIM. Pounds are supplied (S) when the British want to buy our EXports and securities—SEX. An increase in imports (exports) is mirrored by an increase in the demand (supply) of foreign exchange. Add these subscripts to your demand and supply diagram for foreign exchange. An increase in imports from Britain raises the demand for pounds and raises the "price" of the pound, an appreciation. A decrease in the British interest rate reduces the demand for British securities—demand for pounds decreases—and we can "export" more U.S. securities—the supply of pounds rises.

TIP: It is confusing and imprecise to talk of the "exchange rate" rising or falling—far better to refer to "the value of the dollar," and better still to utilize the terms "appreciating" and "depreciating." The dollar is appreciating when its value is rising relative to another currency such as the pound (£). A pound appreciation is the same thing as a dollar depreciation.

Graphing Pointer: In terms of the foreign exchange market graph, a northward movement along the "price" axis is a pound appreciation *and* a dollar *depreciation.*

Comment: Is it better to have a "strong" dollar or a "weak" dollar? You might think that a strong dollar must be an "improvement," but it depends on your viewpoint.

Suppose that the dollar experiences a substantial appreciation in value. Who will gain? Consumers, because foreign goods will now be cheaper. But will anyone lose? Exporters will, because they will find it tougher to compete overseas; producers of domestic substitutes (Detroit car makers, for instance) for imported goods will also be hurt.

Moral: An appreciation (or depreciation) has different effects on different groups in the economy. It makes sense to inquire into the special interests of any individual who is calling for an exchange rate change "in the national interest."

PRACTICE

15. A nation whose price level is rising relatively fast will see its exports become _____ attractive. Its currency will _____

A. more, appreciate.

B. more, depreciate.

C. less, appreciate.

D. less, depreciate.

Answer: D. As our price level rises, our exports become more expensive (less attractive). As the demand for a nation's exports falls, so does the demand for its currency. See p. 520/946.

16. A nation whose interest rate is rising relatively fast will see its securities become _____ attractive. Its currency will _____

A. more, appreciate.

B. more, depreciate.

C. less, appreciate.

D. less, depreciate.

Answer: A. As our interest rate rises, our assets become more attractive. As the demand for U.S. securities increases, so does the demand for dollars.

17. More French companies begin to invest in the United States. This will

A. increase the demand for dollars and increase the supply of francs.

B. decrease the demand of dollars and increase the demand for francs.

C. increase the demand for dollars and decrease the supply of francs.

D. increase the supply of dollars and decrease the demand for francs.

Answer: A. Holders of francs will place this currency on the foreign exchange market (increasing the supply of francs) to demand more dollars.

18. The demand for dollars in the foreign exchange market is downward sloping because, when the price of a dollar (the exchange rate) decreases, _____ because they have become relatively _____

A. Americans demand more foreign goods, less expensive.

B. Americans demand fewer foreign goods, more expensive.

C. foreigners demand more American goods, less expensive.

D. foreigners demand fewer American goods, more expensive.

Answer: C. A good that previously cost $2.00 (£1.00) becomes less expensive to a British buyer if the dollar weakens (and the pound strengthens). Each pound can buy more dollars, so the demand for American goods (and American currency) increases.

OBJECTIVE 5: Explain the reasoning behind the purchasing-power-parity theory.

The law of one price (purchasing power parity) suggests that, with minimal transportation costs, similar goods in different countries should have similar prices, and that the exchange rate should reflect this. If U.S. prices rise, the exchange rate should compensate (the dollar would depreciate in value). Similarly, on assets with equally attractive features, if interest rates diverge, changes in the demand for and supply of foreign exchange should cause the exchange rate to adjust to make the assets equally attractive once more. (page 520/946)

> **TIP:** Just as competition in the goods market will tend to bring about purchasing power parity, competition in the financial markets will cause a similar phenomenon—interest rate parity—to arise.

19. A TV set costs 20,000 yen in Japan and a similar set costs $200 in the United States. The exchange rate is 140 yen per dollar. We would expect the demand for Japanese TV sets to _____ and the yen to _____

    A. increase, appreciate.
    B. increase, depreciate.
    C. decrease, appreciate.
    D. decrease, depreciate.

    Answer: A. In yen, the American TV costs 28,000 yen. It is more expensive than the Japanese set; therefore the demand for Japanese TV sets and Japanese currency will increase.

20. The foreign exchange market is in equilibrium, with each British pound trading for $1.50. Now the overall U.S. price level increases. We would expect an excess demand for

    A. pounds. The pound will appreciate.
    B. pounds. The pound will depreciate.
    C. dollars. The pound will appreciate.
    D. dollars. The pound will depreciate.

    Answer: A. The British will wish to buy fewer American goods; Americans will demand more pounds in order to buy the relatively cheaper British goods.

OBJECTIVE 6: Describe the effects of exchange rate movements on imports, exports, GDP, prices, and the balance of payments.

A depreciating dollar makes exports more competitive abroad (less expensive to foreigners) and imports less attractive domestically (more expensive to Americans). A depreciation should increase GDP. The balance of trade should improve but the *J-curve effect* indicates that the trade balance may worsen before it improves, if the short-term demand for imports is relatively inelastic. In the longer term a depreciation, which makes imports more expensive and increases the demand for exports, will boost production and income, but it will also cause the price level to increase.

(page 525/951)

PRACTICE

21. The J-curve effect suggests that a depreciation in the value of the dollar may

    A. lead to an appreciation in the value of the dollar.
    B. increase American imports and decrease American exports.
    C. decrease American imports and increase American exports.
    D. cause the balance of trade to worsen before it improves.

    Answer: D. See p. 527/953.

22. A depreciation tends to increase the price level because

    A. the depreciation makes imported inputs more expensive.
    B. domestic buyers tend to demand more imports instead of domestically produced goods.
    C. the depreciation makes imported consumer goods less expensive.
    D. exports become less competitive in world markets, making demand decrease.

    Answer: A. It takes more dollars to buy the same number of barrels of imported oil, causing production costs to increase. Note that exports will increase, increasing aggregate demand.

23. A depreciation in the value of the dollar is more likely to improve the U.S. balance of trade if the demand for U.S. exports is _____ and the U.S. demand for imports is _____
   A. elastic, elastic.
   B. elastic, inelastic.
   C. inelastic, elastic.
   D. inelastic, inelastic.
   Answer: A. If the United States reduces the price of its exports, the effect will be stronger if the demand for exports is elastic. A currency depreciation increases the price of U.S. imports—the effect will be stronger if the demand for imports is elastic.

24. If the dollar depreciates, we would expect all of the following except
   A. a rightward shift of the aggregate demand curve.
   B. a leftward shift of the aggregate supply curve.
   C. an increase in the price level.
   D. a decrease in economic activity in the United States.
   Answer: D. If aggregate demand increases and aggregate supply decreases, the price level will increase, but the effect on the output level is ambiguous. Generally, the demand shift is stronger, in fact.

OBJECTIVE 7: Outline the effects of the exchange rate on the effectiveness of monetary and fiscal policy.

Monetary and fiscal policy actions have more complex effects in the "open" economy model. An expansionary monetary policy, for example, will depress the interest rate relative to that of other countries, causing the U.S. financial market to be less attractive. The dollar will depreciate. Because a falling dollar encourages exports and discourages imports, the effect of the monetary policy is stronger than in a closed economy—the multiplier is bigger.

In an open economy, the effectiveness of a fiscal policy is reduced unless the Fed cooperates. An expansionary fiscal policy will increase the demand for money and the interest rate, and the dollar will appreciate. A stronger dollar will encourage imports and discourage exports. This leakage of spending power overseas offsets the increase in expenditures on domestic production—the multiplier is smaller.

(page 528/954)

TIP: The end-of-chapter problem set in the textbook is highly recommended.

PRACTICE

25. In an open economy, an increase in U.S. government spending will _____ the interest rate and cause the dollar to _____
   A. increase, appreciate.
   B. increase, depreciate.
   C. decrease, appreciate.
   D. decrease, depreciate.
   Answer: A. Higher government spending increases transactions, the demand for money, and the interest rate. A higher U.S. interest rate draws funds from abroad, increasing the demand for dollars and leading to an appreciation.

26. In an open economy, the effectiveness of an increase in U.S. government spending is reduced because the dollar
    A. appreciates, increasing net exports and increasing aggregate demand.
    B. appreciates, decreasing net exports and decreasing aggregate demand.
    C. depreciates, increasing net exports and increasing aggregate demand.
    D. depreciates, decreasing net exports and decreasing aggregate demand.

    Answer: B. An increase in government spending results in an appreciation in the value of the dollar. Exports are relatively more expensive and imports are less expensive in the United States.

27. In an open economy, an increase in the U.S. money supply will _____ the interest rate and cause the dollar to _____
    A. increase, appreciate.
    B. increase, depreciate.
    C. decrease, appreciate.
    D. decrease, depreciate.

    Answer: D. An increased money supply will decrease the interest rate and stimulate aggregate demand. A lower U.S. interest rate will cause U.S. investors to buy foreign securities, decreasing the demand for dollars and leading to a depreciation.

28. In an open economy, the effectiveness of an expansionary monetary policy by the Fed is intensified because the dollar will
    A. appreciate, increasing net exports and increasing aggregate demand.
    B. appreciate, decreasing net exports and decreasing aggregate demand.
    C. depreciate, increasing net exports and increasing aggregate demand.
    D. depreciate, decreasing net exports and decreasing aggregate demand.

    Answer: C. An increase in the money supply (which increases aggregate demand) results in a dollar depreciation. Exports are relatively less expensive and imports are more expensive in the United States. Aggregate demand rises even more and the effect of monetary policy is intensified.

 PRACTICE TEST

I. MULTIPLE CHOICE QUESTIONS.

Select the option that provides the single best answer.

Use the following information to answer the next two questions. Arboc and Arbez are economies of similar sizes. Arboc's growth rate is 3% while Arbez is growing at a rate of 7%. The marginal propensity to import is the same positive value for both economies.

_____ 1. It is likely that Arbocali exports will _____ and that Arbocali imports will _____
    A. increase, increase.
    B. increase, decrease.
    C. decrease, increase.
    D. decrease, decrease.

_____ 2. *Ceteris paribus*, we would expect to see the _____ currency depreciating. The new exchange rate will _____ Arbocali consumers.
    A. Arbocali, hurt.
    B. Arbocali, benefit.
    C. Arbezani, hurt.
    D. Arbezani, benefit.

3. We have a flexible exchange rate system. It is in equilibrium and exports equal imports. Relative to Japan, the U.S. price level rises. The United States can expect to see a _____ on its balance of trade and a(n) _____ in the value of the dollar.
   A. surplus, depreciation.
   B. surplus, appreciation.
   C. deficit, appreciation.
   D. deficit, depreciation.

4. The current account includes all of the following except
   A. merchandise exports.
   B. capital investment.
   C. tourism overseas by U.S. citizens.
   D. shipping.

5. The balance on current account
   A. will be zero when merchandise exports equal merchandise imports.
   B. shows the direction and amount of gold flows between the nation and its trading partners.
   C. includes capital inflows but not capital outflows.
   D. shows the relationship between U.S. sales of goods and services abroad and U.S. purchases of goods and services from abroad.

6. Three of the following statements can be true at the same time. Which statement is the odd one out?
   A. Arbez has neither capital inflows nor outflows.
   B. The Arbezani capital account is equal to zero.
   C. The Arbezani current account is equal to zero.
   D. The current account and capital account sum to one.

7. The multiplier in an open economy is _____ than in a closed economy because, as income level increases, _____
   A. greater, there is a wider market available.
   B. smaller, some of the increase will be used to buy imports.
   C. greater, exports become more attractive to foreigners.
   D. smaller, consumers buy goods that had previously been sent abroad.

8. The U.S. has a trade deficit of $5 billion with Japan. To settle the debt, the U.S. can
   A. buy $5 billion worth of Japanese government securities.
   B. sell $5 billion worth of previously purchased private Japanese securities—e.g., those issued by Sony or Honda.
   C. lend $5 billion to the Japanese government.
   D. buy $5 billion worth of Japanese goods on credit next month.

9. The marginal propensity to consume is .75 and the marginal propensity to import is .15. *Ceteris paribus*, the value of the multiplier is
   A. 10.
   B. 2.5.
   C. 5.
   D. .9.

10. The British pound depreciates relative to the dollar. We should expect
    A. an increase in the number of British tourists visiting the United States.
    B. an increase in the U.S. demand for British goods.
    C. an increase in the British demand for U.S. goods.
    D. a decrease in the number of U.S. tourists visiting Britain.

_____ 11. The trade feedback effect shows that an increase in U.S. _____ will result in a subsequent _____
A. exports, depreciation in exchange rates.
B. imports, appreciation in the exchange rate.
C. income, increase in imports and increase in exports.
D. trade, reduction in income in the United States.

_____ 12. A one dollar increase in export income will _____ imports by _____ than one dollar.
A. increase, more.
B. increase, less.
C. decrease, more.
D. decrease, less.

_____ 13. The U.S. interest rate rises relative to that of the United Kingdom. We would expect to see the demand for
A. U.S. securities rising, and the dollar appreciating in value.
B. U.S. securities falling, and the dollar appreciating in value.
C. British securities rising, and the dollar depreciating in value.
D. British securities falling, and the dollar depreciating in value.

_____ 14. There is an increase in "foreign private assets in the United States." This would show up as a
A. credit on the current account.
B. debit on the current account.
C. credit on the capital account.
D. debit on the capital account.

_____ 15. A transaction brings foreign exchange into the United States. This will be recorded as a
A. debit on the balance of trade.
B. debit on the balance of payments.
C. credit on the balance of trade.
D. credit on the balance of payments.

_____ 16. The nations of the former Soviet Union have increased their purchases of U.S. machine tools by $200 million. As a result the U.S. economy has _____ and its net exports have _____
A. expanded, grown by $200 million.
B. expanded, grown by less than $200 million.
C. contracted, grown by $200 million.
D. contracted, grown by less than $200 million.

_____ 17. The _____ the marginal propensity to consume and the _____ the marginal propensity to import, the larger the multiplier.
A. larger, larger.
B. larger, smaller.
C. smaller, larger.
D. smaller, smaller.

Use the following information to answer the next four questions. The exchange rate is flexible. Assume that the two economies are similar in size. The marginal propensity to import is the same in both economies. The current equilibrium exchange rate is $1.00 = 1.60 marks (1 mark = $.625).

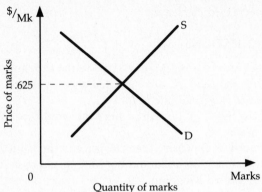

_____ 18. If the United States grows at a rate of 2% per year and Germany grows at 5% per year, we would expect the demand curve for marks to shift to the _____ and the supply curve for marks to shift to the _____
A. right, right.
B. right, left.
C. left, right.
D. left, left.

_____ 19. If the United States grows at a rate of 2% per year and Germany grows at 5% per year, we would expect the mark to _____. The exchange rate would be _____
A. appreciate, $1.00 exceeds 1.60 marks.
B. appreciate, $1.00 is less than 1.60 marks.
C. depreciate, $1.00 exceeds 1.60 marks.
D. depreciate, $1.00 is less than 1.60 marks.

_____ 20. The current equilibrium exchange rate is $1.00 = 1.60 marks. If there is an increase in the interest rate on U.S. government bonds, we would expect the demand curve for marks to shift to the _____ and the supply curve for marks to shift to the _____
A. right, right.
B. right, left.
C. left, right.
D. left, left.

_____ 21. The current equilibrium exchange rate is $1.00 = 1.60 marks. If there is an increase in the interest rate on U.S. government bonds, we would expect the mark to _____. The exchange rate would be _____
A. appreciate, $1.00 exceeds 1.60 marks.
B. appreciate, $1.00 is less than 1.60 marks.
C. depreciate, $1.00 exceeds 1.60 marks.
D. depreciate, $1.00 is less than 1.60 marks.

_____ 22. The supply of dollars in the foreign exchange market is upward sloping because, when the price of a dollar (the exchange rate) decreases, _____ because they have become relatively _____
A. Americans demand more foreign goods, less expensive.
B. Americans demand fewer foreign goods, more expensive.
C. foreigners demand more American goods, less expensive.
D. foreigners demand fewer American goods, more expensive.

_____ 23. In an open economy, the effectiveness of fiscal policy is _____
and the effectiveness of monetary policy is _____
A. increased, increased.
B. increased, decreased.
C. decreased, increased.
D. decreased, decreased.

II. APPLICATION QUESTIONS.

1. Suppose that the price of a Big Mac is $1.50 in the U.S. and £1.00 in the U.K. (and that the U.S. and the U.K. are close neighbors with minimal transportation costs). The $/£ exchange rate is $1 = £1.
   a. Calculate how much (in pounds) a Big Mac would cost a British tourist in the United States.
   b. Is this more or less expensive than the price in the United Kingdom?
   c. Calculate how much (in dollars) a Big Mac would cost an American tourist in the United Kingdom.
   d. Is this more or less expensive than the price in the United States?
   e. Because British Big Macs are cheaper than American Big Macs, what will happen to the demand for pounds (to buy British Big Macs)? What will happen to the demand for dollars to buy American Big Macs? When the demand for a commodity increases, what happens to its price?
   f. Which currency will appreciate in value?

   Suppose the $/£ exchange rate moves to $2 = £1. (Confirm that this is a dollar depreciation!)

   g. Calculate how much (in dollars) a Big Mac would cost an American tourist in the United Kingdom.
   h. Is this more or less expensive than the price in the United States?
   i. Calculate how much (in pounds) a Big Mac would cost a British tourist in the United States.
   j. Is this more or less expensive than the price in the United Kingdom?
   k. Because British Big Macs are more expensive than American Big Macs, what should happen to the demand for pounds (to buy British Big Macs)? What should happen to the demand for dollars to buy American Big Macs?
   l. Which currency will appreciate in value?
   m. Somewhere between $1 = £1 and $2 = £1 an equilibrium exchange rate will occur. Where does purchasing power parity suggests that it will be?

2. a. "An expansionary monetary policy by the Fed will cause the dollar to appreciate against other currencies." Is this true or false? Explain.
   b. "Short-term interest rates fall in Germany. The dollar should appreciate against the mark." Is this true or false? Explain.

3. The domestic price of Arbocali cloth is 4 opeks a yard. The domestic price of Arbezani leather is 12 bonga per hide. Arboc sells cloth to Arbez; Arbez sells hides to Arboc. The exchange rate is 2 opeks per bonga. The exchange rate is flexible.
   a. Ignoring transportation and other such costs, calculate the price in Arbez of a yard of imported Arbocali cloth.
   b. Calculate the price in Arboc of an imported Arbez hide.
   c. Calculate the number of units of the domestic currency per unit of foreign currency from the Arbocali perspective.
   d. Now the exchange rate changes to 4 opeks per bonga. For Arboc, does the exchange rate change represent an appreciation or a depreciation?

4. The exchange rate between Regit and Noil is 4 Regitani sponduliks per Noilian bonga.
   a. A bottle of Regitani sherry sells at home for 50 sponduliks. Calculate its price in Noil.
   b. A bottle of Noilian honey wine sells at home for 20 bonga. Calculate its price in Regit.
   c. Find the price of a bottle of wine relative to a bottle of sherry in Regit.

   Suppose that costs rise in the Noilian honey wine industry. The domestic price of honey wine rises from 20 bonga to 25 bonga. The exchange rate remains at 4 Regitani sponduliks per Noilian bonga.
   d. Calculate the Regitani price of imported honey wine.
   e. Find the relative price of wine to sherry in Regit.
   f. Is wine now relatively more or less expensive in Regit?
   g. Predict what will happen to Regitani imports and exports.
   h. What will happen to the trade balance for Noil?
   i. What will happen to Regit's aggregate demand curve?

5. In each of the following cases, should the Arbezanis expect an appreciation or a depreciation in the value of their currency?
   a. Because of financial uncertainty at home, Arbezani citizens find it more attractive to buy stock in the neighboring economy of Arboc.
   b. Arbezani income levels increase.
   c. The central bank, ArbeFed, increases the money supply.

6. Suppose the economy is described by the following model.

$$
\begin{array}{lll}
(1) & C & = 30 + .8Yd \\
(2) & I & = 50 \\
(3) & G & = 100 \\
(4) & EX & = 60 \\
(5) & IM & = .3Yd \\
(6) & T & = 80 \\
(5) & Yd & = Y - T
\end{array}
$$

   a. Calculate the equilibrium level of income (where $Y = C + I + G + EX - IM$).
   b. Calculate the value of expenditure multiplier.
   c. Calculate the value of imports.
   d. The current account balance is a _____ (surplus / deficit) of _____.
   e. The government has a _____ (surplus / deficit) of _____.

   Suppose that government spending is increased by 25.
   f. What will happen to the equilibrium income level?
   g. What will happen to imports?
   h. *Ceteris paribus*, what effect will this import change have on (1) the current account and (2) the capital account?

   Suppose imports are fixed at their new level (through the use of quotas). Now the government increases spending again, by 25.
   i. What will happen to the equilibrium income level?

   Go back to the original economy (no quotas, G is at 100).
   j. If exports were to increase by 36, indicate the effect this will have on:
      i. income level _____
      ii. imports _____
      iii. the current account deficit _____
   k. Given the original current account deficit, how much would exports have to rise to achieve balance on the current account? _____

     l.   Suppose a tariff is placed on imports, causing them to fall from their original level to 60. Indicate effect this will have on:
         i.   income level _____
        ii.   imports _____
       iii.   the current account deficit _____
    m. To remove the original current account deficit, by how much would imports have to be reduced initially? _____
     n. Explain this result.

7. Suppose that two goods, U.S. blue jeans and French wine, are traded between the U.S. and France: the exchange rate is 20¢ = 1 FrFr (exchange rate 1).
    a. If the exchange rate moves to $1.00 = 10 FrFr (10¢ = 1 FrFr) (exchange rate 2), with which rate is the dollar stronger?
    b. In their home countries, blue jeans sell at $10.00 a pair and wine sells at 40 FrFr a bottle. Calculate the price of wine, in dollars, at the two exchange rates.

      Exchange rate 1 _____   Exchange rate 2 _____
    c. At which exchange rate will French wine be more attractive to U.S. consumers?
    d. As the exchange rate moves from $1.00 = 5 FrFr (20¢ = 1 FrFr) to $1.00 = 10 FrFr (10¢ = 1 FrFr), what will happen to the quantity demanded of francs?
    e. Show this demand curve on a graph, with vertical axis as "dollars/franc" and horizontal axis as "quantity of francs."

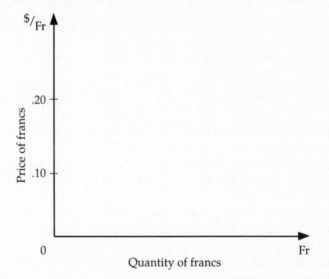

    f. Calculate the price of blue jeans, in francs, at the two exchange rates.
      Exchange rate 1 _____   Exchange rate 2 _____
    g. At which exchange rate will U.S. blue jeans be more attractive to French consumers?
    h. As the exchange rate moves from $1.00 = 5 FrFr (20¢ = 1 FrFr) to $1.00 = 10 FrFr (10¢ = 1 FrFr), what will happen to the quantity supplied of francs?
    i. Show this supply curve on the graph.
    j. Assume that the diagram is a fair representation of the demand and supply of francs for purchases of exports and imports. If the exchange rate were fixed at $1.00 = 5 FrFr (20¢ = 1 FrFr), would France have a current account surplus or deficit?
    k. What can you say about the balance on capital account?
    l. *Ceteris paribus*, will the French have net capital inflows or capital outflows?

8. Indicate whether each of the following transactions should be included in the current account or the capital account. Indicate whether it is a credit (+) or a debit (−).

	Account	±	Transaction
a.	_____	_____	U.S. citizens buy stock in Sony Corporation.
b.	_____	_____	Sony Corporation sells a Discman to a U.S. audiophile.
c.	_____	_____	Joe, who works in Japan, sends some money home to his mother in Tennessee.
d.	_____	_____	A U.S. insurance company sells a policy to a Japanese resident.
e.	_____	_____	Joe's mother goes to visit him in Japan for six months.
f.	_____	_____	A drug dealer smuggles some cocaine into Florida.
g.	_____	_____	A Japanese purchases some U.S. Treasury bills.
h.	_____	_____	A Saudi oil sheik buys a chunk of California real estate.
i.	_____	_____	Ford sells a consignment of cars to the Japanese.

9. Use the following table to answer the questions below. Government spending, investment, and exports do not change as output level changes.

GDP (Y)	Domestic Aggregate Expenditure (C + I + G)	Exports (EX)	Imports (IM)	Total Aggregate Expenditure
5,000	5,500	400	300	_____
6,000	6,400	400	400	_____
7,000	7,300	400	500	_____
8,000	8,200	400	600	_____
9,000	9,100	400	700	_____
10,000	10,000	400	800	_____

a. Calculate the marginal propensity to consume _____ and the marginal propensity to import _____.
b. Calculate the expenditure multiplier.
c. Complete the table.
d. The equilibrium income level is _____.

PRACTICE TEST

I.   SOLUTIONS TO MULTIPLE CHOICE QUESTIONS

1.   A. Because Arbez is growing, it will increase its imports from Arboc. Similarly, because Arboc is growing, it will import more.

2.   D. Because Arboc and Arbez are about the same size, Arbezani imports are growing more quickly than its exports. This imbalance will make the Arbezani currency depreciate or, at least, not appreciate as rapidly. As the Arbezani currency loses its value, the Arbocali currency increases in value. Arbocali consumers will benefit from the greater purchasing power of their currency overseas.

3.   D. If U.S. prices increase, exports will decrease and imports will increase because foreign goods are relatively cheaper. The balance of trade will slip into a deficit, and the dollar will decrease in value.

4.   B. Capital investment is included in the capital account. See p. 509/935.

5.   D. See p. 509/935. The balance on current account looks at merchandise exports and imports (Option A) but other items too. Capital inflows and outflows are reflected in the capital account (Option C).

6.   D. The current account and the capital account must sum to zero.

7.   B. The multiplier is smaller. See p. 513/939.

8.   B. If an economy spends more than it takes in, it must sell off some assets to make up the difference.

9.   B. Multiplier = 1 / [1 − (MPC − MPM)] = 1 / [1 − (.75 − .15)] = 2.5. See p. 513/939 for a discussion of the formula.

10.   B. A depreciation of the pound is the equivalent of an appreciation of the dollar. Because the dollar can now buy more pounds, British goods become cheaper to U.S. buyers.

11.   C. As U.S. economic activity increases, the positive marginal propensity to import will cause greater U.S. imports. The economic activity of exporting countries will be stimulated and, as a consequence, their imports of U.S. goods will increase.

12.   B. An increase in exports will cause an increase in economic activity. Given a positive marginal propensity to import, imports will increase. See p. 512/938.

13.   A. U.S. securities are offering a higher reward, relative to British securities. The demand for U.S securities, and the dollars to buy them, will increase. As the demand for pounds decreases and the supply of pounds (to buy dollars) increases, the pound will depreciate and the dollar will appreciate.

14.   C. An increase in "foreign private assets in the United States" means that foreigners have purchased U.S. assets. This requires that foreign exchange flow into the United States.

15.   D. If foreign currency flows in, the transaction is a credit. If the transaction involved is an export, it is recorded on the balance of trade. However, the transaction could be the sale of a government security, which would be recorded on the capital account. In either case, however, the credit would show up on the balance of payments.

16.   B. The increase in exports increases net exports by $200 million, and increases U.S. output. As output increases, imports increase and net exports are reduced.

17.   B. The multiplier formula is 1 / [1 − (MPC − MPM)]. The greater the proportion of income being consumed rather than saved or lost overseas, the larger the multiplier.

18.   A. Both economies are growing, so the imports of both economies will increase.

19.   C. In question 18, the demand curve and the supply curve both shifted right. Assuming that the economies are similar in size, the increase in German exports (demand for marks) will be less than the increase in German imports (supply of marks). A depreciating mark will now be worth less than $.625.

20.   C. More German investors will wish to buy U.S. securities and will supply more marks to buy dollars. Fewer U.S. investors will wish to buy German securities and will demand fewer marks.

21.   C. As demand decreases and supply increases for the German currency, its "price" will decrease—a depreciation. A depreciating mark will now be worth less than $.625.

22.   B. A British good that previously cost £1.00 ($2.00) becomes less expensive to an American buyer if the dollar strengthens (and the pound weakens). Each dollar can buy more pounds, so the demand for British goods and currency increases, as does the supply of American currency.

23.   C. An increase in government spending increases the demand for money and the interest rate, and the exchange rate will appreciate, encouraging imports and discouraging exports. Spending power leaks abroad, offsetting the increase in expenditures on domestic production. An increase in money supply decreases the interest rate. The exchange rate will depreciate, discouraging imports and encouraging exports. This adds to the increase in expenditures on domestic production.

II. SOLUTIONS TO APPLICATION QUESTIONS

1.   a. $1.50 × £1 = £1.50.
     b.   It is more expensive. A Big Mac in Britain costs £1.00.
     c.   £1.00 × $1 = $1.00.
     d.   It is less expensive.
     e.   The demand for pounds will increase. The demand for dollars will decrease. When the demand for a commodity increases, its price increases.
     f.   The pound will appreciate.
     g.   £1.00 × $2 = $2.00.
     h.   more. A Big Mac in the United States costs $1.50.
     i. $1.50 × £0.50 = £0.75.
     j.   This is less expensive than in the United States.
     k.   The demand for pounds will decrease. The demand for dollars will increase.
     l.   The dollar will appreciate.
     m. $1.50 = £1.

2.   a.   False. You can use a number of methods to prove the statement false. The purchasing-power-parity theory would explain the depreciation by noting that more units of U.S. currency have been printed. Similarly, a monetarist would note that an increased money supply increases U.S. prices, making each dollar worth less. Alternatively, an increased money supply will decrease the domestic interest rate, making foreign currency (needed to buy foreign securities) more demanded. An explanation is provided on p. 528/954.
     b.   True. If interest rates fall in Germany, investment in Germany will be less attractive. The demand for marks will decrease and, as Germans seek to invest in other economies, the supply of marks will increase. These changes will cause the mark to decrease in value (depreciate) and the value of the dollar to increase in value (appreciate).

3.   a.   A yard of imported Arbocali cloth will cost 2 bonga in Arbez.
     b.   An imported Arbezani hide will cost 24 opeks in Arboc.
     c.   In Arboc, the number of units of the domestic currency per unit of foreign currency is 2 opeks per bonga.
     d.   Arboc has experienced a depreciation and Arbez has experienced an appreciation.

4.   a.   Regitani sherry sells for 12.5 (50 / 4) bonga in Noil.
     b.   Noilian honey wine sells for 80 (20 × 4) sponduliks in Regit.
     c.   The price of a bottle of wine relative to a bottle of sherry in Regit is 1.6 (80 / 50).
     d.   With the new costs in Noil, honey wine will cost 100 sponduliks in Noil.
     e.   The price of a bottle of wine relative to a bottle of sherry in Regit is 2.0 (100 / 50).
     f.   Noilian wine is now relatively more expensive.
     g.   Regitani imports of wine will decrease since they are relatively more expensive while sherry exports to Noil will increase.
     h.   The Noilian trade balance will worsen: Noil will see its exports become less competitive while (relatively) cheaper imports will enter the country in greater numbers.
     i.   Regit's aggregate demand curve will shift to the right as its exports increase and its imports decrease.

5.   a.   The bandu will depreciate as the demand for foreign currency increases and the supply of bandu increases.
     b.   The bandu will depreciate. Arbezanis, wishing to buy more imports, will increase the supply of bandu.
     c.   The bandu will depreciate. An increase in the money supply will depress domestic interest rates. Lower interest rates will lead to a lower demand for bandu by foreign investors and an increased supply of bandu by domestic investors who wish to seek higher interest rates abroad.

6. a. $Y = C + I + G + EX - IM$
   $= 30 + .8Yd + 50 + 100 + 60 - .3Yd$
   $= 240 + .8(Y - T) - .3(Y - T)$
   $= 200 + .5Y$
   $Y = 400.$

   b. Multiplier $= 1 / [1 - (MPC - MPM)] = 1 / [1 - (.8 - .3)] = 2.00.$

   c. $IM = 60 - .3(Y - T) = .3(400 - 80) = 96.$

   d. $EX - IM = 60 - 96 =$ deficit of 36.

   e. $G - T = 100 - 80 =$ deficit of 20.

   f. Income will increase by 50 because the multiplier is 2.00.

   g. Imports will increase by 15. $IM = .3(450 - 80) = 111.$

   h. The current account $(EX - IM)$ deficit will increase by 15. The capital account surplus will decrease by 15. Recall that the two accounts must balance.

   i. The marginal propensity to import is zero (because of the quotas). The multiplier will be 5.00. Income will increase by 125.

   j. i. income will increase by $36 \times 2 = 72.$
      ii. imports will increase by $.3 \times 72 = 21.6.$
      iii. the current account $(EX - IM)$ deficit will fall by 14.4 to 21.6.

   k. Exports would have to rise by 90.

   l. i. income would rise by 72 to 472.
      ii. imports would fall by 14.4 $(-36 + 21.6)$ to 81.6.
      iii. the current account would have a deficit of 21.6 $(60 - 81.6).$

   m. 90.

   n. An initial fall in imports of 90 will make aggregate expenditure rise by an initial 90. The multiplier effect will cause income to expand by 180. As a result, imports will increase by 54. Net effect on imports: they fall by 36.

7. a. Exchange rate 2. $1.00 = 10 FrFr (10¢ = 1 FrFr)$ shows a dollar appreciation.

   b. Exchange rate 1: $8, i.e., $40 \times .20¢.$
      Exchange rate 2: $4, i.e., $40 \times .10¢.$

   c. Exchange rate 2 $(10¢ = 1 FrFr).$

   d. Quantity demanded will increase because Americans will wish to buy more of the (cheaper) French wine.

   e. See the diagram below.

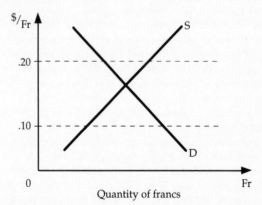

   f. Exchange rate 1: 50 francs, i.e., 10×5 FrFr. If $20¢ = 1$ FrFr, 5 FrFr = $1.
      Exchange rate 2: 100 francs, i.e., 10×10 FrFr. If $10¢ = 1$ FrFr, 10 FrFr = $1.

   g. Exchange rate 1 $(20¢ = 1 FrFr).$

   h. Quantity supplied will decrease because the French will be less keen on U.S. purchases. (It's assumed that demand for blue jeans is fairly elastic.)

   i. See the diagram above.

   j. It depends on how you have drawn the diagram—i.e., where the curves intersect. As shown above, France would have a deficit on its current account because French exports are less than French imports—the franc is overvalued.

   k. The balance on capital account will be showing a surplus equal in size to the current account deficit.

   l. The French will have a net capital outflow.

8. See the table below.

	Account	±	Transaction
a.	capital	debit	U.S. purchase of foreign assets
b.	current	debit	import of merchandise
c.	current	credit	private transfer
d.	current	credit	export of a service
e.	current	debit	tourism
f.	capital	debit	statistical discrepancy
g.	capital	credit	foreign purchase of U.S. assets
h.	capital	credit	foreign purchase of U.S. assets
i.	current	credit	export of merchandise

9. a. MPC = $\Delta C / \Delta Y$ = 900 / 1,000 = .9. MPM = $\Delta IM / \Delta Y$ = 100 / 1,000 = .1.
   b. Multiplier = 1 / [1 – (MPC – MPM)] = 1 / [1 – (.9 – .1)] = 5.00.
   c.

GDP (Y)	Domestic Aggregate Expenditure (C + I + G)	Exports (EX)	Imports (IM)	Total Aggregate Expenditure
5,000	5,500	400	300	5,600
6,000	6,400	400	400	6,400
7,000	7,300	400	500	7,200
8,000	8,200	400	600	8,000
9,000	9,100	400	700	8,800
10,000	10,000	400	800	9,600

   d. 8,000. Equilibrium occurs where Y = C + I + G + EX – IM.

ECONOMIC GROWTH IN DEVELOPING NATIONS

23

COMBINED TEXT

38

OBJECTIVES: POINT BY POINT

After completing this chapter, you should be able to accomplish the objectives listed below.

GENERAL COMMENT

The focus of this chapter is the ways in which developing countries might become developed and the problems that they might encounter along the way. If you study by making lists, be careful in this chapter because three separate topics are covered—a description of the Third World, how development might be promoted, and some Third World problems. Make up lists using each of these headings.

OBJECTIVE 1: Describe the relationship between economic development and economic growth. Distinguish among conditions in the so-called First, Second, Third, and Fourth World countries.

In the past, the nations of the world have been roughly divided into three groups: the First World (western, industrialized), the Second World (ex-Socialist, whose future is now uncertain), and the Third World (poor, largely agricultural). There is some mobility—Taiwan, Korea, and Brazil, for instance, are breaking away from others in the Third World category, while a number of nations are lagging so far behind that they have been called the "Fourth World" group. The main characteristic of a Third World country is that the great majority of its inhabitants are poor. Other dimensions that distinguish the "haves" from the "have nots" are: health care, educational facilities, and the percentage of the population engaged in agriculture.   (page 539/965)

> **Comment:** There's no single unambiguous term that distinguishes the "developing nations" as the textbook deals with them. After all, in one sense, the United States is a developing economy too. "Third World" tends to have some political undertones. Remember that these nations are a pretty varied group, including South American, Asian, and African countries as diverse as Mexico and Mali, Taiwan and Togo. Don't allow yourself to overgeneralize!

PRACTICE

1. The poorest of the developing nations are sometimes known as the
    A. First World.
    B. Second World.
    C. Third World.
    D. Fourth World.
    Answer: D. See p. 539/965.

2. Most of the Fourth World nations are to be found in
   A. Latin America.
   B. sub-Saharan Africa.
   C. Southeast Asia.
   D. the former republics of the Soviet Union and its satellites.
   Answer: B. Most of the very poorest nations are found to the south of the Sahara desert in Africa.

3. The developing nations of the world contain 75% of the world's population. They are estimated to receive _____ of the world's income.
   A. 5%.
   B. 20%.
   C. 25%.
   D. 33%.
   Answer: C. See p. 541/967.

4. Per capita GDP is _____ in developed countries, and infant mortality is _____
   A. higher, higher.
   B. higher, lower.
   C. lower, higher.
   D. lower, lower.
   Answer: B. See the table on p. 540/966 of the textbook.

OBJECTIVE 2: List the factors that influence economic development. Explain why capital infrastructure is important for economic development.

No single theory has emerged to explain the development process, but various factors have been identified as potential constraints on development. These include a low rate of accumulation of physical capital, a lack of human capital, a lack of social overhead capital (infrastructure), a lack of entrepreneurial ability, and a dependency on developed nations. (page 541/967)

> **TIP:** Pay attention to what is happening in your own state and locality. Many of the sources and strategies discussed in this chapter are not limited to poor foreign regions. Debates on economic development are frequent at the state and local government level.

Comment: As the textbook notes, economic growth and economic development are not the same phenomenon. Simply because an object is expanding doesn't mean that it is also developing. However, you'll find it helpful to refer back to Chapter 20 (35) and locate the factors that promote growth.

PRACTICE

5. The dependency theory argues that development is stunted by the dependence of
   A. a potentially fast-growing industrial sector on a slow-growing agricultural sector.
   B. a rapidly increasing labor pool on a more slowly accumulating stock of capital.
   C. a developing nation on developed countries as markets for its output.
   D. a fast-growing agricultural sector on an undermechanized manufacturing sector.
   Answer: C. This theory suggests that ex-colonies become dependent on the parent country. This weakens their bargaining position and works to their disadvantage. See p. 545/971.

6. The brain drain refers to
   A. the movement of talented personnel from a developing country to a developed country.
   B. the absence of skilled entrepreneurs in the developing countries.
   C. declining literacy rates.
   D. the loss of human capital through the ravages of malnutrition.
   Answer: A. See p. 544/970.

7. Each of the following has been advanced as a plausible constraint on development except
   A. the quantity of available capital.
   B. the quantity of available labor.
   C. the quantity of infrastructure.
   D. the quantity of entrepreneurial ability.
   Answer: B. The typical developing country has adequate numbers of workers, although specific skills may be limited.

8. Capital shortages are a typical problem for developing countries. Each of the following is a plausible cause of capital shortages except
   A. lack of incentives leading to low saving rates.
   B. the inherent riskiness of investment in a developing nation.
   C. government policies, such as price ceilings and appropriation of private property.
   D. widespread poverty resulting in little surplus after consumption needs are met.
   Answer: D. The vicious-circle-of-poverty hypothesis fails to account for the success of previously poor nations like Japan. See p. 543/969.

OBJECTIVE 3: Name and describe four strategies for economic development.

Four development strategies have been attempted.
a. Development used to be equated with industrialization; many Third World nations sought to move away from agriculture and toward industrial production. However, merely trying to replicate the structure of the developed nations does not guarantee development. Opinion now favors a balanced growth in both agricultural and industrial sectors—"walking on two legs."
b. *Import substitution* calls for the encouragement of home-grown substitutes for imported goods. This strategy has failed in almost every case; it results in high-cost production protected by trade barriers.
c. *Export promotion* calls for producing goods for the export market and has seen some measure of success, although it depends on the willingness of the developed nations to import Third World production.
d. Finally, the economy must choose the appropriate balance between free enterprise and central planning. Planning permits coordination of economic activities and the channeling of funds into efficient projects, but may be difficult for a Third World nation to administer. (page 546/972)

Following the Second World War, the initial emphasis was largely on rapid growth. The 1970s, however, saw increasing concern about how the benefits of growth were (or were not) being distributed. Despite growth, poverty persisted for a large percentage of those living in the developing countries, and aid was often tied to programs to satisfy basic needs. More recently, income redistribution has lost its prominence to market efficiency.

9. Experience suggests that, of the following, the development approach most likely to succeed is
   A. rapid industrial mechanization coupled with labor migration to the industrial centers.
   B. intensive training of human capital to occupy technologically advanced positions in import-substitution industries.
   C. a balanced promotion of both the agricultural sector and the manufacturing sector.
   D. slow, careful industrial growth combined with rapid expansion in food provision to improve human capital.
   Answer: C. This is the "walking on two legs" strategy. See p. 546/972.

10. Noil is a small sub-Saharan nation with few sophisticated resources. However, it constructs an airport and hotel with lavish Western facilities and offers safari trips into its beautiful mountain ranges to groups from the developed countries. Noil is best described as having opted for a(n) _____ development strategy.
    A. import substitution.
    B. export promotion.
    C. rural exploitation.
    D. balanced growth.
    Answer: B. Tourism is an export.

11. Generally, import substitution policies have
    A. failed in almost every case.
    B. succeeded, but only while the cost of imported oil was held down.
    C. not been an unqualified success but have had a better track record than export promotion policies.
    D. succeeded in Latin America but failed in Africa and had mixed results in Asia.
    Answer: A. Import substitution policies reduce exports and foster inefficient, inappropriate (i.e., capital-intensive) production methods.

12. The small Asian nation of Regit chooses to follow an import substitution strategy and builds a fertilizer plant to serve its rice farmers. Based on similar experiments elsewhere, we would expect to see all of the following except
    A. high fertilizer production costs.
    B. the imposition of tariffs to protect domestic fertilizer production.
    C. capital-intensive fertilizer production techniques.
    D. a rise in the international competitiveness of the nation's rice farmers.
    Answer: D. High-cost fertilizer will reduce the ability of the rice farmers to compete with foreign rice.

13. Each of the following is a tactic typical of the export promotion strategy except
    A. reducing the value of the domestic currency relative to other currencies.
    B. increasing the nation's ability to compete domestically with the exports of other nations.
    C. the provision of subsidies to exporters.
    D. the provision of preferential investment tax breaks to exporting firms.
    Answer: B. This is typical of import substitution. See p. 547/973.

OBJECTIVE 4: Outline the problems caused by rapid population growth and policies that have been instituted to deal with them.

The Third World death rate has tumbled sharply because of better medical treatment, but the birth rate has declined much more slowly. Although large families may provide a cheap labor pool today and support in old age tomorrow, rapid expansion in the population places burdens on public services and may be undesirable from the viewpoint of society. In some nations, economic incentives have been applied successfully to encourage smaller families. (page 550/976)

PRACTICE

14. Birth rate minus death rate equals the
    A. fertility rate.
    B. mortality rate.
    C. natural rate of population increase.
    D. development rate.
    Answer: C. See p. 553/979.

15. Malthus predicted that the world population would grow at a(n) _____ growth rate while the production of food would increase more _____
    A. increasing, rapidly.
    B. increasing, slowly.
    C. constant, rapidly.
    D. constant, slowly.
    Answer: D. See p. 551/977. Note that a constant rate of growth means rapid absolute growth in the population—10% of 100 is only 10; 10% of 10,000 is 1,000.

16. High fertility rates may cause all of the following except
    A. falling saving rates.
    B. reduced availability of social programs for each individual.
    C. labor shortages.
    D. food shortages.
    Answer: C. As the population expands, there should be no labor constraint.

OBJECTIVE 5: Outline Third World agricultural problems and the policies that have been used to deal with them.

Inadequate food supplies may be caused by policy actions. A nation that chooses to hold down prices for the benefit of consumers may see its farmers cutting back production. The so-called "Green Revolution"—the emergence of high-yield resilient plants—should increase productivity but it has been resisted, partly because it is new and risky, and partly because of the costs involved in change.   (page 555/981)

PRACTICE

17. Government establishment of low food prices is usually meant to
    A. discourage farming.
    B. make domestic farm production competitive with imports.
    C. please the small, but politically powerful, urban population.
    D. make domestic farm production more efficient.
    Answer: C. Urban dwellers may be more educated and organized—a bigger threat to the longevity of the government in power. See p. 556/982.

18. Third World food shortages are largely a consequence of
    A. the Green Revolution.
    B. natural limits on production.
    C. policy mistakes.
    D. exporting too much.
    Answer: C. See p. 556/982.

OBJECTIVE 6: Outline the evolution of the debt crisis and the problems confronting borrowers and lenders in resolving this crisis.

In the 1970s, banks, rich with the deposited "petrodollars" of the OPEC nations, reduced interest rates and embarked on a vigorous program of lending. Capital-starved developing countries chose to borrow—in some cases to pay for the trade deficits caused by high oil prices! In the late 1970s, the world economy faltered and Third World export revenues shrank. Interest on the loans became (and remains) hard to pay. Some nations threatened to default. Many sought to reschedule their debt repayment in exchange for promises of economic austerity designed to cut back on imports and to increase exports.   (page 557/983)

PRACTICE

19. Under a debt rescheduling agreement, the borrowing country is expected to increase incentives to _____ and to reduce _____
   A. consumers, export spending.
   B. consumers, imports.
   C. exporters, the federal government deficit.
   D. exporters, imports.
   Answer: D. A debt rescheduling agreement will require the country to increase exports and reduce imports. Only by increasing its foreign earnings can a nation hope to reduce its debt burden.

PRACTICE TEST

I. MULTIPLE CHOICE QUESTIONS.

Select the option that provides the single best answer.

_____ 1. Which of the following are characteristics of the average developing country?
   A. Large populations and high savings rates.
   B. Low levels of human capital and low per capita GDP.
   C. High infant mortality and high pollution indexes.
   D. Low health standards and high literacy rates.

_____ 2. Import substitution occurs when a country
   A. becomes developed.
   B. erects trade barriers.
   C. no longer has sufficient foreign exchange to buy imports.
   D. strives to produce goods that were previously imported.

_____ 3. Economic development occurs when there is an increase in the
   A. per capita nominal GDP.
   B. per capita real GDP.
   C. material well-being of the nation's citizens.
   D. labor force.

_____ 4. Lack of economic development might be caused by
   A. a low marginal propensity to consume.
   B. an excess supply of private overhead capital.
   C. a high literacy rate.
   D. inadequate amounts of social overhead capital.

_____ 5. Which of the following is an example of an improvement in social overhead capital?
   A. A multinational corporation opens a new plant.
   B. The workers at the local textile mill establish a credit union.
   C. There is an increase in the rate of growth of per capita real GDP.
   D. A national adult literacy program is established by the government.

_____ 6. Labor is relatively abundant in Arboc. Arboc might best be able to develop by
   A. using production techniques that are capital-intensive.
   B. using production techniques that employ labor and capital in fixed and equal proportions.
   C. specializing in the production of labor-intensive commodities which should therefore be relatively cheaper to produce.
   D. specializing in the production of capital-intensive commodities, which should therefore be marketable at relatively higher prices.

7. Local firms in Arboc are unlikely to undertake large investment projects such as highway construction because
   A. the government is unlikely to share the cost.
   B. interest rates are higher for the borrowed funds necessary for such projects.
   C. the "free-rider" problem will result in a low (or zero) rate of return.
   D. international agencies such as the World Bank and the IMF prefer short-term projects.

8. Adopting the strategy of "walking on two legs" means that
   A. men and women should be treated equally in the workplace.
   B. import substitution and export promotion should be attempted simultaneously.
   C. attention must be paid to developing both the industrial sector and the agricultural sector.
   D. the dependent links with old colonial nations should be severed.

9. Import substitution might fail to promote economic development if
   A. producers use domestic inputs that are lower in cost than imported inputs.
   B. firms make use of capital-intensive production methods that fail to reduce unemployment.
   C. such goods require labor-intensive methods of production.
   D. after establishment, these industries are subsidized by the state.

10. The "export promotion" strategy calls for
    A. the running of a balance of trade deficit.
    B. the production of goods that are demanded by consumers in the developed countries.
    C. the production of export goods for domestic consumers.
    D. the domestic production of goods that previously had been imported.

11. Sending savings from the Third World nation of Arboc to the United States _____ to growth in Arboc's physical capital. New Arbocali import controls will tend to _____ investment in Arboc.
    A. leads, increase
    B. leads, decrease
    C. does not lead, increase
    D. does not lead, decrease

12. Following the signing of NAFTA, capital flowed into Mexico. Initially this resulted in
    A. increasing external debt and an increase in the value of the peso.
    B. increasing internal debt and a decrease in the value of the peso.
    C. decreasing external debt and an decrease in the value of the peso.
    D. decreasing internal debt and a decrease in the value of the peso.

13. IMF stabilization policies might call for
    A. cutbacks in government spending and a currency devaluation.
    B. nationalization of foreign investment.
    C. higher subsidies to importers of capital goods.
    D. tax cuts and a currency devaluation.

14. The poorest 20% of the world's population is estimated to receive _____ of the world's income.
    A. .5%.
    B. 2.0%.
    C. 2.5%.
    D. 5.0%.

_____ 15. Which of the following variables tends to be high in the developing countries?
   A. Life expectancy.
   B. Literacy rates.
   C. Infant mortality.
   D. Proportion of the population in urban areas.

_____ 16. Under a debt rescheduling agreement, the borrowing country may be expected to _____ the value of its currency in order to _____ exports.
   A. increase, increase.
   B. increase, decrease.
   C. decrease, increase.
   D. decrease, decrease.

_____ 17. All of the following discourage Third World development except
   A. the lack of skilled entrepreneurs.
   B. insufficient social overhead capital.
   C. insufficient labor-saving technological innovation.
   D. inadequate amounts of human capital.

_____ 18. _____ is a development strategy that is designed to encourage sales abroad.
   A. Import substitution.
   B. Export promotion.
   C. "Walking on two legs".
   D. Dependency.

_____ 19. Rapid population growth rates may cause all of the following except
   A. an eventual increase in the proportion of working-age adults in the population.
   B. an increase in the number of dependents.
   C. decreases in the rate of capital formation.
   D. decreases in saving rates.

_____ 20. Governments may set food prices low in order to
   A. encourage greater food production.
   B. make domestic producers competitive with foreign producers.
   C. stimulate a willingness to adopt more efficient farming methods.
   D. maintain the political support of urban consumers.

II. APPLICATION QUESTIONS.

1. Compare and contrast the economic conditions in the "First World" and the Third World. Take a "typical" country from each group, for example, France and Peru. Examine such issues as life expectancy, number of doctors per thousand persons, educational level, rate of inflation, unemployment, and so forth. (A good source is the _World Development Report_, published annually by the World Bank—it will be in your library.) Compare the figures for an NIC (newly industrialized country), such as Taiwan or Korea with those of a sub-Saharan African nation. Is there really such a thing as a "typical" Third World nation?

2. Suppose that 10 units of food are required per person per year in the developing nation of Arboc. Due to improved crops and farming techniques, food production will increase by a fixed amount every 10 years—suppose this amount is 1000 units of food so that, in 1995, food production will be 11,000 units. Arboc currently exports its surplus food production. Imports run at a constant 2,000 units. Because of high birth rates and decreasing death rates, Arboc's population increases by 50% every 10 years.

a. Given the conditions specified, complete the table below.

Year	Food Production	Population	Food Requirements	Food Surplus/Deficit
1990	10,000	400	4,000	+6,000
2000	11,000			
2010				
2020				
2030				

b. What happens in or about the year 2020?
c. Other things unchanged, what will happen to Arboc's balance of trade?
d. Given the situation in 2030, what do you think will happen to Arboc?

3. Choose a typical developing country. Profile your country by doing research (by reading, for example, The World Bank's annual *World Development Report*) into the characteristics listed below.

The characteristics require numbers. The numbers in parentheses are the values for the United States from the 1994 Report.

a. Life expectancy   _____   (77)

b. Illiteracy rate   _____   (< 5%)

c. Population with access to safe water (%)   _____   (100)

d. GNP per capita   _____   ($23,240)

e. Agriculture as percentage of output   _____   (< 3%)

f. Birth rate (per 1,000)   _____   (16)

g. Death rate (per 1,000)   _____   (9)

h. Under 5 years mortality rate (male)   _____   (12)

ANSWERS AND SOLUTIONS

PRACTICE TEST

I. SOLUTIONS TO MULTIPLE CHOICE QUESTIONS

1. B. See p. 539/965 for a full discussion of the characteristics of developing nations.

2. D. Import substitution is a strategy that attempts to establish a domestic industry that can provide goods to replace imports. See p. 547/973.

3. C. Improvements in per capita GDP do not guarantee development. See p. 549/975.

4. D. To grow, an economy needs an adequate quantity and quality of resources, including socially provided resources.

5. D. Social overhead capital includes projects that cannot be undertaken privately.

6. C. This is an application of the Heckscher-Ohlin theorem from Chapter 21 (36).

7. C. Unless a toll is charged, use of this public good will be free.

8. C. The Chinese phrase "walking on two legs" describes the need to have both agricultural and industrial sectors developing together. See p. 547/973.

9. B. To be effective, the strategy must play to the strengths of its own economy—typically labor-intensive production. See p. 547/973.

10. B. See p. 548/974.
11. D. See p. 543/969.
12. A. See p. 558/984.
13. A. See p. 558/984.
14. A. See p. 541/967.
15. C. See the table on p. 540/966.
16. C. If the borrowing country reduces the value of its currency, its exports will be cheaper for foreigners to buy.
17. C. The quantity of labor is not a significant constraint in the Third World. Labor-saving technology, then, is not critical to successful development.
18. B. See p. 548/974.
19. A. As more children are born, even as the population ages, the proportion of adults will decrease.
20. D. See p. 556/982.

II. SOLUTIONS TO APPLICATION QUESTIONS

1. Although there is no single model for a developing nation, certain common characteristics emerge—high birth rates, improving life expectancy, improvements in literacy rates, better/more nutrition and shelter, and so on.

2. a. See the table below.

Year	Food Production	Population	Food Requirements	Food Surplus/Deficit
1990	10,000	400	4,000	+6,000
2000	11,000	600	6,000	+5,000
2010	12,000	900	9,000	+3,000
2020	13,000	1,350	13,500	−500
2030	14,000	2,025	20,250	−6,250

   b. Food requirements outstrip food production.
   c. As the food surplus decreases, less will be available for export and the balance of trade will become less favorable. Somewhere around 2015, the surplus will become a deficit.
   d. This is an open question. Arboc will be heavily in debt, and will need to import food to feed its population. Imports of industrial goods would slacken. Reduced health care (per person) might cause famine and disease, reducing the population. Arboc might borrow to finance its overseas spending and might have to receive ongoing foreign aid. Population control policies would have to be considered.

3. Answers will depend on the country chosen.

ECONOMIES IN TRANSITION AND ALTERNATIVE ECONOMIC SYSTEMS

24

COMBINED TEXT

39

OBJECTIVES: POINT BY POINT

After completing this chapter, you should be able to accomplish the objectives listed below.

General Comment

It is unlikely that you will have had much, if any, face-to-face exposure to other economic systems. The material that Case and Fair present will give you useful information and may clear up some misconceptions that you have built up over time. Be especially careful of value-laden labels when you encounter economic and political discussions in the media. Compare, for example, the sentence "The Arbezani Administration opened negotiations with the Arbocali regime" with "The Arbezani regime opened negotiations with the Arbocali Administration." Clearly, labels can reinforce or upset our perceptions.

OBJECTIVE 1: Distinguish between the capitalist and socialist economic systems and the democratic and communist political systems.

Capitalism and socialism are at the two ends of the economic spectrum; democracy and communism are at the two ends of the political spectrum. Economic systems are classified on the basis of where the ownership of productive resources resides—in capitalism, it's with the private individual; in socialism, it's with the government.

(page 565/991)

No economic system adheres to pure socialism or to pure capitalism—each economy is a blend of the two extremes. China is "socialist" but has (increasing) private owner-ship; the United States and Japan are "capitalist" but each contains a public sector.

PRACTICE

1. In a _____ economy, most capital is privately owned.
    A. democratic.
    B. communist.
    C. capitalist.
    D. socialist.
    Answer: C. Note that "democracy" refers to a political system, not an eco-nomic one.

2. In a _____ economy, the people own the means of production directly, without state intervention.
   A. feudal.
   B. communist.
   C. capitalist.
   D. socialist.
   Answer: B. In a communist economy, it was argued, the state would wither away. In fact, the communist economies of the world have really been socialist—e.g., the former Union of Soviet *Socialist* Republics.

3. The Austrian economist Hayek argued that
   A. political freedom is not necessary for economic freedom to exist.
   B. political freedom and economic freedom depend on each other.
   C. economic freedom is not necessary for political freedom to exist.
   D. political freedom and economic freedom, although desirable, are not linked.
   Answer: B. See p. 566/992.

4. In a socialist economy, economic decisions are made by _____; capital is owned by _____
   A. market, private citizens.
   B. market, the government.
   C. centralized planning, private citizens.
   D. centralized planning, the government.
   Answer: D. The Soviet Union, for example, made five- and one-year plans through the Gosplan agency. See p. 566/992.

OBJECTIVE 2: Explain the main aspects of the labor theory of value and why Marx believed that capitalism would perish.

There are two key elements to Marxian analysis: the labor theory of value and the exploitation of workers by capitalists.

The *labor theory of value* states that the relative value of each good and service depends on the quantity of labor used up in its production. Capital is used in production, of course; Marx explained that capital embodies past labor.   (page 567/993)

Marx considered capitalism to be unfair because profit derived from the ownership of capital is based on the exploitation of labor. The capitalist, who is in a strong bargaining position, expropriates the *surplus value* produced by labor, driving the workers' wage to subsistence level. Marx predicted that capitalism would collapse in the wake of falling profits, worker unrest, and increasingly violent business fluctuations. Capitalism would be replaced by socialism and, ultimately, communism.

> **TIP:** For Marx, production becomes less labor-intensive; with relatively less labor to exploit, the rate of profit will fall. To compensate, capitalists increase the rate of exploitation and wages are driven to the subsistence level. Eventually the system becomes unbearable, is overthrown, and is replaced by socialism and, ultimately, communism.

> **TIP:** You may have noted the adjective "Marxian." Marxian, rather than Marxist, is the correct term to use when referring to Marx's economic ideas.

> **TIP:** You'll probably find Marx's views pretty difficult to swallow, partly because of the new terminology but partly because the bulk of the textbook has been suggesting to you that the economy tends towards an equilibrium. Marx's extensive research made him see the industrialized world of the mid-nineteenth century quite differently.

> **TIP:** Think of the labor theory of value as explaining the long-run pattern of relative prices, although market imperfections and temporary fluctuations in demand and supply can cause actual price levels to deviate from this pattern.

Comment: Many students are surprised to learn that Marx undertook economic analysis; he is more often thought of as a political thinker.

Comment: Where neoclassical economists find harmony in production and distribution, Marx detected antagonism. In Marx's view, the vehicles for growth—the division of labor and new technology—became juggernauts that would crush and alienate the workers and move the economy toward greater concentration of power. Marx's account of capitalist accumulation predicted increasing instability rather than stability.

PRACTICE

5. For Marx, the "means of production" include
    A. only capital.
    B. only capital and labor.
    C. only capital and land.
    D. capital, land, and labor.
    Answer: C. The means of production are not equivalent to the "factors of production" you met in Chapter 3.

6. The Marxian term for profit is _____ and the Marxian term for the wage rate _____
    A. surplus value, rate of exploitation.
    B. surplus value, value of labor power.
    C. the value of labor power, surplus value.
    D. the value of labor power, rate of exploitation.
    Answer: B. See p. 568/994.

7. In Marxian analysis, which of the following statements is true?
    A. The rate of profit tends to fall over time.
    B. Additional capital accumulation increases the rate of profit.
    C. Additional capital accumulation increases surplus value.
    D. As wages fall, production will become more labor-intensive.
    Answer: A. Capital must be paid for but can't be exploited. Profits derive from the ability of the capitalist to exploit workers.

OBJECTIVE 3: Summarize the economic performance of the Soviet economy from 1945 until its collapse. Outline the steps necessary to make Russia economically viable as a market-based system.

The Soviet economy was centrally planned. Early Soviet growth rates were impressive, mainly due to remarkable rates of capital accumulation, but faltered in the 1980s. The Gorbachev proposal—economic *perestroika* (restructuring) coupled with political *glasnost* (openness)—called for decentralization, increased incentives, and the removal of price controls—in other words, a move toward a market system. It was a case of too little, too late. (page 569/995)

Russian progress towards a market-based economy was initially unsteady, with soaring inflation and plunging production. By 1995, privatization had taken root, but disagreement remains regarding how fast each new measure should be implemented.

> **TIP:** By the mid-90s, Cuba had begun shifting position on economic matters. The Vietnamese (and Vietnamese businesspersons in the United States) had argued successfully for the relaxation of U.S.-imposed commercial barriers. Both of these economies are well worth watching.

Comment: The economic reforms within the former Soviet republics and their allies in Eastern Europe are very much in the news. You should be able to flesh out the material in this chapter by keeping your ears and eyes open to the news reports. Are the economic reforms identical in each country? How much success/resistance are they experiencing?

Comment: Property owned communally, such as the bison, the dodo, or the grasslands of sub-Saharan Africa, is usually rapidly depleted. Taking the example of common grazing land, there is little incentive for the individual farmer to conserve pasture, and indeed the opposite may be true. Self-interest would dictate that one would make the most of the "free" resources, although such thinking by each farmer would lead to a depletion of resources. At this point you might note the old saying that "Good fences make good neighbors." Capitalism, then, relies on the emergence of self-interest and the rewards of private property because the former without the latter would result in the tragedy of commons.

PRACTICE

8. Each of the following is seen as a requirement for a successful transition from socialism to a market-based economy except
   A. price regulation.
   B. provision of a commercial infrastructure—i.e., market-supporting institutions.
   C. removal of trade barriers.
   D. a freely operating labor market.
   Answer: A. To ration scarce resources efficiently, prices should be free to adjust.

9. In the face of high inflation in August 1993, Boris Yeltsin announced that "old" (pre-1993) rubles would be worthless and, except for a limited amount, individuals could not convert "old" into "new." Yeltsin's main objective was
   A. to increase interest rates.
   B. to encourage workers to work longer hours.
   C. to stabilize prices.
   D. to attract the hard currency of tourists.
   Answer: C. The Russian economy was threatened by hyperinflation; Yeltsin was trying to drain away some of the money that was chasing too few goods.

10. Stalin's main economic objective was
    A. rapid industrialization.
    B. the establishment of a viable consumer goods sector.
    C. *perestroika.*
    D. a balanced budget.
    Answer: A. See p. 570/996.

11. Deregulating prices is likely to cause _____; removing subsidies will cause _____ in the short term.
    A. higher prices for staple items; unemployment.
    B. higher prices for staple items; increased employment.
    C. lower prices for staple items; unemployment.
    D. lower prices for staple items; increased employment.
    Answer: A. Staple items were underpriced; inefficient firms will be driven out of business without subsidies.

12. The notion that collective ownership of resources may be inefficient because individuals do not bear the full cost of their own decisions is called
    A. exploitation.
    B. the tragedy of commons.
    C. surplus value.
    D. the externality effect.
    Answer: B. See p. 574/1000.

13. Each of the following is an example of the tragedy of commons except
    A. pollution in the Great Lakes.
    B. overgrazing of shared tribal land.
    C. the decimation of the American bison by nineteenth-century settlers.
    D. the slaughtering of his entire herd by a Texan rancher.
    Answer: D. The herd is private property.

OBJECTIVE 4: Explain why the Chinese economy has grown so vigorously since 1978.

The Chinese economic system mirrored the Soviet system until 1958, when the Great Leap Forward signaled a move away from large-scale capital-intensive production toward smaller-scale localized production. Since 1978, ideological constraints have been loosened, personal incentives restored and, particularly in agriculture, dramatic improvements in performance achieved. There is private enterprise and foreign investment, and allocation through markets is increasing, but China is properly classified as a centrally planned economy because, in the main, resources are still owned by the government.   (page 577/1003)

PRACTICE

14. Which of the following statements about China is false?
    A. China has a stock market.
    B. Since 1990, China has actively discouraged investment by Western capitalist corporations.
    C. Since 1990, there have been reports of "capitalist mania" occurring.
    D. The Great Leap Forward featured a shift from large-scale capital-intensive production to small-scale labor-intensive production.
    Answer: B. China is a magnet for Western venture capital.

OBJECTIVE 5: Explain the economic performance of Japanese since 1945.

The Japanese "economic miracle" was based on high rates of saving and investment, the effective use of appropriate technology, an aggressive pro-growth economic stance by the government, and a flexible, well-trained labor force. In the 1990s, though, Japan's export-driven economy has faltered, partly because of the global economic slowdown and partly because of the rising value of the yen, both of which reduced the demand for Japanese goods.   (page 581/1007)

15. Which of the following statements about post-1945 Japan is false?
    A. Japan has used quotas, tariffs, and subsidies to protect key industries.
    B. Japanese households have a high rate of saving.
    C. Of the industrialized nations, Japan has the smallest public sector.
    D. Japan has always spent a larger portion of its GDP on research and development than the United States.
    Answer: D. Until the late 1980s, U.S. research and development spending was a higher proportion of GDP. See p. 581/1007.

16. The bases of Japan's "economic miracle" seem to have been all of the following except
    A. high rates of saving and investment.
    B. the development of a highly trained labor force.
    C. the adoption of appropriate technology.
    D. a government committed to a "hands off" position to industry.
    Answer: D. The Japanese government (which from 1955 until 1993 had seen power remain in the hands of one party, the LDP) consistently exercised significant control over the private sector, through MITI.

PRACTICE TEST

I. MULTIPLE CHOICE QUESTIONS.

Select the option that provides the single best answer.

_____ 1. According to Marx, the rate of profit has a tendency to
_____, causing capitalists to _____ the rate of exploitation.
    A. rise, increase.
    B. rise, decrease.
    C. fall, increase.
    D. fall, decrease.

_____ 2. For Marx, the conflicts in capitalism include all of the following except
    A. inflation and an increasing government deficit.
    B. alienation and increasing exploitation.
    C. progressively more violent business cycles.
    D. the emiserization of the workers.

_____ 3. Marx saw society evolving
    A. through imperialism, capitalism, and communism to socialism.
    B. through feudalism, capitalism, and socialism to communism.
    C. through imperialism, and capitalism, and feudalism to communism.
    D. through capitalism, feudalism, and socialism to communism.

_____ 4. Capitalism and socialism are distinguished primarily by
    A. the ownership of labor.
    B. the number of political parties.
    C. the ownership of capital.
    D. the distribution of income throughout society.

_____ 5. According to Marx, the wage is determined by
    A. the surplus value of labor.
    B. the cost of the bare essentials of subsistence.
    C. the marginal revenue product of labor.
    D. the marginal physical product.

6. In Marxian terms, the value of a machine must be dependent upon
   A. the amount of labor embodied within it.
   B. how productive the machine is.
   C. how productive the workers are who use the machine.
   D. the price of the final good produced by the machine.

7. Japan's economic success has been based on all of the following except
   A. very high rates of consumption.
   B. a highly trained labor force.
   C. rapid absorption of technology.
   D. a pro-growth government policy.

8. The "tragedy of commons" exemplifies the problem of _____ in the case of resources that are owned _____
   A. inefficiency, privately.
   B. inequity, privately.
   C. inefficiency, publicly.
   D. inequity, publicly.

9. Each of the following is seen as a requirement for a successful transition from socialism to a market-based economy except
   A. macroeconomic stabilization.
   B. privatization.
   C. price regulation.
   D. a freely operating labor market.

10. The surplus value of labor is
    A. equal to the wage rate paid to the worker.
    B. the difference between the subsistence wage and the actual wage received.
    C. the rate of exploitation.
    D. the difference between the value of production and the actual wage received.

11. In Arboc, the state provides goods such as education, national defense, universal health care, and roads. Other industries, which are privately owned, face government regulations on pollution and worker safety. Minimum wage legislation is present and wage earners are taxed on their income. Arboc is best described as
    A. socialist.
    B. communist.
    C. capitalist.
    D. totalitarian.

12. "Shock therapy" refers to
    A. the sudden change experienced by the Soviet Union following *perestroika* and *glasnost*.
    B. the overthrow of the Soviet Union's economic system.
    C. Stalin's goal of electrification of collective farms.
    D. rapid deregulation of prices, liberalization of trade, and privatization.

13. Each of the following is a major concern for China's future except
    A. food shortages.
    B. unemployment.
    C. bankruptcy and sale to foreigners of state-owned enterprises.
    D. inflation.

II. APPLICATION QUESTIONS.

1. In the Marxian economy of Arboc, 500 units of value are produced. Production requires current labor and machinery, which embodies 100 units of past labor.
   a. Calculate the value of current labor used in units of value.
   b. If workers are paid 300 units of value, how many units of profit will capitalists derive?
   c. Calculate the rate of exploitation (surplus value/value of labor power).
   d. Calculate the rate of profit (surplus value/value of production).

   Now suppose that output doubles.
   e. Output is _____ units of value.
   f. Calculate the value of current labor used in units of value.
   g. If the wage rate is unchanged, calculate the units of value that workers will receive.
   h. Surplus value is _____.
   i. Calculate the rate of exploitation (surplus value/value of labor power).
   j. Calculate the rate of profit (surplus value/value of production).

   Relative to the initial situation, output has doubled but, to achieve this, the production technique has become more capital-intensive. Machinery is worth 400 units of past labor.
   k. Calculate the value of current labor used in units of value.
   l. If the wage rate is unchanged, calculate the units of value that workers will receive.
   m. Surplus value is _____.
   n. Calculate the rate of exploitation (surplus value/value of labor power).
   o. Calculate the rate of profit (surplus value/value of production).

   Suppose that the subsistence wage is 200 units of value, given the current level of output. Machinery is worth 400 units of past labor.
   p. Calculate how many units of surplus value capitalists can expropriate.
   q. Calculate the rate of exploitation (surplus value/value of labor power).
   r. Calculate the rate of profit (surplus value/value of production).

2. List the following countries from most capitalist to most socialist:
   Russia; United States; France; Cuba; Japan; China.

3. The table gives the output of workers.

Workers	Output	Marginal Product	Subsistence Wage	Surplus Value
0	0	—		—
1	10			
2	19			
3	27			
4	34			
5	40			
6	45			
7	49			
8	52			

   a. Use the information in the table to calculate the marginal product.
   b. Suppose that the subsistence wage is 5 units of value. Fill in the fourth column.
   c. A profit-maximizing capitalist can hire as many workers as she wishes at the subsistence wage. How many workers would she hire?

d. Calculate the surplus value. Enter the values in the fifth column.

e. Calculate total production and the surplus value.

f. Calculate the rate of exploitation (surplus value/value of labor power).

4. Russia's economic reform package includes:

a. price controls: _____ (increased/decreased/removed)

b. market-supporting institutions: _____ (increased/decreased/removed)

c. ownership of resources: more _____ (centralized/privatized)

d. external aid: _____ (increased/decreased/removed)

e. job security: _____ (increased/decreased/removed)

f. trade: _____ (restricted/liberalized)

g. money supply growth: _____ (increased/curtailed)

ANSWERS AND SOLUTIONS

PRACTICE TEST

I. SOLUTIONS TO MULTIPLE CHOICE QUESTIONS

1. C. As additional capital is accumulated, the rate of profit falls. This decline prompts capitalists to increase exploitation of workers. See p. 568/994.

2. A. Marx did not consider inflation and the government deficit in his writings.

3. B. See p. 569/995.

4. C. In a capitalist system, ownership of the means of production (capital and land) is in the hands of capitalists and in the hands of the state under a communist system.

5. B. Capitalists, in search of profits, will drive down the wage to the minimum (subsistence) level. See p. 568/994.

6. A. The value of any type of production (including machines) is determined by the amount of labor involved in its production.

7. A. See p. 581/1007.

8. C. "Commons" are commonly-owned land. Typically, this resource is treated inefficiently.

9. C. To achieve efficiency, prices must be permitted to adjust to changes in demand and supply.

10. D. See p. 568/994.

11. C. With the exception of the health care, Arboc is quite like the United States.

12. D. See p. 576/1002.

13. B. Despite a burgeoning population, China is in need of skilled workers to meet the new demands of its economy. Indeed, many Chinese ex-patriates are going home.

II. SOLUTIONS TO APPLICATION QUESTIONS

1. a. 500 – 100 units of past labor value = 400 units of labor value.

b. 400 units of labor value – 300 = 100 units of profit.

c. Rate of exploitation = surplus value/value of labor power = 100 / 400 = .25.

d. The rate of profit = surplus value/value of production = 100 / 500 = .2.

e. $500 \times 2 = 1000$.

f. 1000 – 100 units of past labor value = 900 units of labor value.

g. 300.

h. Surplus value = 900 – 300 = 600.

i. Rate of exploitation = surplus value/value of labor power = 600/900 = .67.

j. Rate of profit = surplus value / value of production = 600/1000 = .6.

k. 1000 – 400 units of past labor value = 600 units of labor value.

l. 300.

m. Surplus value = 600 – 300 = 300.

n. Rate of exploitation = surplus value / value of labor power = 300/600 = .5.

o. Rate of profit = surplus value / value of production = 300 / 1000 = .3.

    p.   Surplus value = 600 − 200 = 400.

    q.   Rate of exploitation = surplus value/value of labor power = 400/600 = .67.

    r.   Rate of profit = surplus value/value of production = 400 / 1000 = .4.

2.   There can be some dispute here—systems evolve and emphases change—but a plausible ranking would be: Japan; United States; France; Russia; China; Cuba.

3.   a. See the following table.

Workers	Output	Marginal Product	Subsistence Wage	Surplus Value
0	0	—	5	—
1	10	10	5	5
2	19	9	5	4
3	27	8	5	3
4	34	7	5	2
5	40	6	5	1
6	45	5	5	0
7	49	4	5	−1
8	52	3	5	−2

    b. See the table above.

    c. 6.

    d. See the table above.

    e. 45; 15.

    f. $\frac{1}{3}$.

4.   removed; increased; privatized; increased; decreased; liberalized; curtailed.